Imagined Frontiers

Imagined Frontiers

Contemporary America and Beyond

Carl Abbott

University of Oklahoma : Norman

Library of Congress Cataloging-in-Publication Data

Abbott, Carl, 1944–
Imagined frontiers : contemporary America and beyond / Carl Abbott.
pages cm
Includes bibliographical references and index.
ISBN 978-0-8061-4836-6 (pbk. : alk. paper)
1. American literature—History and criticism. 2. West (U.S.)—In literature.
3. West (U.S.)—In mass media. 4. Western films—History and criticism.
5. West (U.S.)—In art. I. Title.
PS169.W4A23 2015
810.9'35873—dc23

2014045582

The paper in this book meets the guidelines for permanence and durability of the Committee on Production Guidelines for Book Longevity of the Council on Library Resources, Inc. ∞

Contents

Illustrations

Acknowledgments

The ideas and analysis in this book have developed over the course of the past fifteen years, with input from conference panel participants, anonymous journal referees, and editors. In particular, I appreciate that Melody Graulich, Rob Latham, and Carol McGuirk have being willing to open their pages to someone coming from outside the normal academic fields from which their journals draw. I also want to single out Michelle Nickerson, Darren Dochuk, and the contributors to *Sunbelt Rising*. With the support of the Huntington Library and the Clements Center for Southwest Studies, we were able to spend several days reading and critiquing each other's chapters, to the great benefit of "Real Estate and Race." "Jim Rockford or Tony Soprano" was first delivered as my presidential address to the Pacific Coast Branch of the American Historical Association, and I thank my colleagues who honored me with that opportunity.

The following chapters have previously appeared in somewhat different form as journal articles or book chapters and are used with permission. Several have been edited to eliminate repetition and identify points of continuity and comparison.

Chapter 7 appeared as "Rocky Mountain Refuge: Constructing "Colorado" in Science Fiction," *Science Fiction Studies* 39 (July 2012): 221–42.

Chapter 8 appeared as "The Light on the Horizon: Imagining the Death of American Cities," *Journal of Urban History* 32 (January 2006): 175–96.

Chapter 10 appeared as "Homesteading on the Extraterrestrial Frontier," *Science Fiction Studies* 32 (July 2005): 240–64.

Chapter 11 appeared as "Falling into History: The Imagined Wests of Kim Stanley Robinson in the Three Californias and Mars Trilogies," *Western Historical Quarterly* 34 (Spring 2003): 27–48.

Imagined Frontiers

Introduction

Places on the Edge

A frontier is an edge—a line on a map and the territories and communities that surround that line. Some frontiers are obvious from their geography, places defined by the edges of settlement like the core of the Colorado Rockies or a gated community tucked against the still-wild Santa Monica Mountains. Others are communities in development, places where new ways of life are struggling to emerge like the silicon suburbs of the West Coast or terraformed Mars. The following chapters consider the work of imaginative artists who have used novels, film, television, maps, and occasionally even performance art to examine and understand a variety of frontiers whose locations range from the neighborhoods of Los Angeles to the red deserts of Mars.

Any U.S. historian who uses "frontier" in a title has a lot of explaining to do. Didn't a generation of scholars try to banish it from Western history in favor of alternative organizing ideas ranging from region to race? Doesn't it ring with overtones of ethnocentrism and harmonics of imperialism? And isn't it really, really hard to pin down to any precise definition?

The answer to all of these questions is, "Sure, but. . . ." "Frontier" is useful for my project precisely because it has so many nested or overlapping meanings that artists can play with in different ways. Sometimes they are fixed, sometimes moving, sometimes limiting, sometimes liberating. Frontiers and their institutions may be designed to keep things apart or sometimes to bring them together, but they are always places and zones of convergence where people, products, and ideas can be exchanged and intermingled. Because they mark difference, they are also edgy places where change can happen—like the spark that rebalances electrical potential, like the chemical reaction that transfers electrons, or, maybe, like a dam bursting.

Some frontiers are discrete, identifiable boundaries defined by politics and military power. Walls, checkpoints, demilitarized zones, customs inspectors, and immigration officials all mark political frontiers. Change happens when you cross from one side to the other, exchanging the rules of one regime for another. The difference may be stark, as from the Republic of Korea to the Democratic People's Republic of Korea. Alternatively, a careful, knowledgeable eye may be needed to spy out a regulatory frontier like the Urban Growth Boundary around Portland, Oregon, or the Metropolitan Green Belt around London—the latter not quite as visible as Hadrian's Wall or Offa's Dike but still a politically defined frontier on the British landscape.

Political frontiers are often permeable, despite efforts at control and exclusion. The results are zones of trade and migration that constitute intermediate regions with their own blended character—the Rhine frontier of the later Roman Empire, the North-West Frontier Province of British India, the Mexico–United States border region. In places like these, the frontier stokes social and cultural change by allowing peoples and economies to intermingle. "Borderlands" as a plural noun has long been one of the key concepts through which historians of North America have thought about these interactive changes.

Frontiers are also zones of settlement and displacement where, historically, one numerous people or nation has assumed political and military control and occupied "empty" or "underutilized land" that had previously been the home of a less numerous people. Movement here is unidirectional, but always incomplete, starting as "middle grounds" of relatively equal interaction and moving toward displacement. "Settler colonialism" is now the common term to group the experiences of nineteenth-century Canada, the United States, Australia, New Zealand, South Africa, Argentina, and Chile, but it could apply as well to the southward movement of Han Chinese in the first millennium C.E. or the eastward movement of German peoples in the second millennium.

Frontiers, finally, are places of possibility for the invention of new institutions or the reinventions of self. Frederick Jackson Turner had his finger on something in his focus on the continental frontier as the central factor in American history, even if he got some of the specifics wrong in celebrating the westward movement as the wellspring of democracy and a safety valve for urban unrest—not to mention slighting the northward movement from Mexico and the eastward movement from Asia. There is a shadow of Turner's frontier in stories in which nuclear disaster or viral holocaust depopulate the landscape and force individuals and societies to re-create themselves with the tools of rugged individualism.

Popular culture shapes the ways we think about our surroundings and our lives (playing with Barbie, reports a recent study, does indeed limit the roles in which little girls can imagine themselves). Just as much, popular and literary culture reflects common understandings. Viewers love the Mos Eisley cantina scene in *Star Wars* and the opening scene in the first broadcast episode of the *Firefly* television series because they already "know" what western saloons were like from innumerable western movies and enjoy the idea that the future would be just like the past . . . plus maybe a bunch of aliens. Successful depictions resonate with what people think they already know about Tony Soprano's New Jersey or Jim Rockford's Los Angeles. Writers of postapocalyptic fiction have repeatedly sent survivors to find refuge in the Colorado Rockies because Colorado for the post–World War II generation epitomized the idea of the empty and isolated West. *Falling Down* worked with a Los Angeles setting because of that city's popular identification with freeways and Latino gangs, but moviegoers would have laughed if the story had been set in Akron.

The following chapters about ways in which Americans think about and imagine frontiers group these depictions at three different scales—the metropolitan frontier of suburban development, the classic continental frontier of American settlement, and yet unrealized frontiers beyond the bounds of a single planet. The groupings reflect my own scholarly interests in what I consider the overlapping fields of urban history and planning, western history, and science fiction. The focus is writers, artists, and scholars working during the second half of the twentieth century in an era of growing global economic and social reach.

My special interest is to set up a three-way conversation between popular ideas about cities, regions, and other places on the edge; the ways that historians and social scientists have tried to understand these places; and the ways in which artists reimagine them. The chapters thus juxtapose fiction, films, maps, and other images with urban theory and trends in historical interpretation. The cult-favorite television series *Firefly*, for example, relocates common myths of western America to a distant future, whereas Kim Stanley Robinson's novels about the settlement of Mars question and complicate these same ideas along the lines of the so-called new western history.

The materials for my analysis cut across multiple categories and genres. Peter Matthiessen's trilogy about E. J. Watson in South Florida reimagines a real person in the classic manner of historical fiction. Other novelists and screenwriters write mainstream fiction that places fully fictional individuals in real contemporary places that are altered just enough for the stories to work. Steps further away from the here and now (or then and now) are the imagined futures of real places, from metropolitan Portland and the Pacific Northwest a few years hence to a Colorado distant by decades or centuries. For these chapters, the materials range from "nonfiction" planning documents and business manifestoes to speculative fiction. At greatest remove are the frontiers beyond Earth that are the heart and soul of American science fiction.

There are parallels across the different scales. Subdivisions leapfrog across the Arizona desert, English-speaking settlers in North America leapfrog any coherent frontier line, and extraterrestrial homesteaders hop among moons and planets. Cascadia can be conceived as a refuge from crass and crowded California, the Rocky Mountains as a refuge from social collapse, and new planets as refuges from a failing Earth. The near-outlaws who operate a tramp space freighter for television science fiction are siblings of a South Florida planter and fisherman who operates beyond the reach of law. Science fiction writers raise the same questions as Peter Matthiessen about the validity and implications of recycling the narratives and tropes of western American history and fiction. The book starts with Sunbelt suburbia and the last chapter completes a circle, returning to the Sunbelt with imagined futures for Orange County as well as for Mars.

The topical span of this book is nicely summarized in the science fiction comic *Trekker*. Drawn by Ron Randall and first published by Dark Horse Comics in

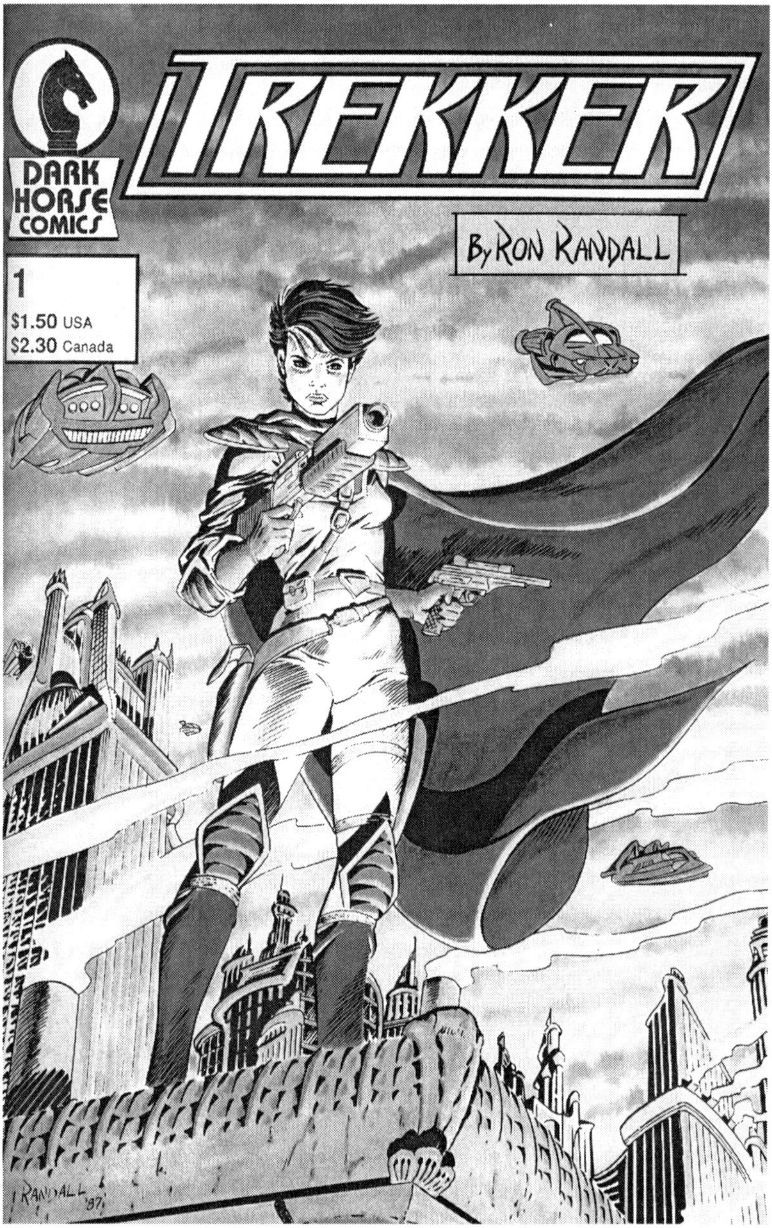

FIG. I.1. Trekker in New Gelaph. On the edge in the future city of New Gelaph, bounty hunter or "trekker" Mercy St. Clair stands atop a building in the urban jungle. "Smuggler's Blues" is the first story in the *Trekker* comic series. Her adventures cross and blend the metropolitan, western, and interplanetary frontiers. (Courtesy Trekker™ illustrations and story © 1987 by Ron Randall, originally published by Dark Horse Comics)

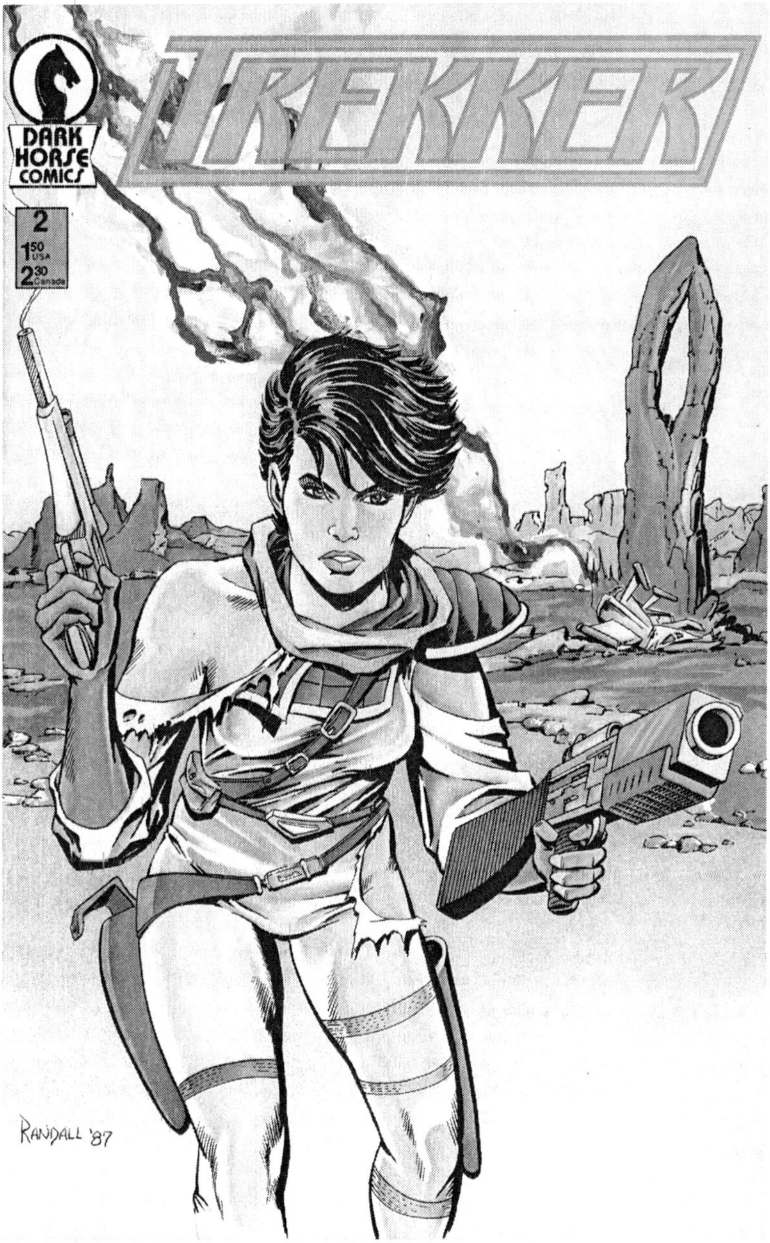

FIG I.2. Trekker in the wastelands. The second Mercy St. Clair comic, "The Trail to Scarmen's Burn," takes the bounty hunter outside her city into wastelands that look a bit like the Utah canyonlands. (Courtesy Trekker™ illustrations and story © 1987 by Ron Randall, originally published by Dark Horse Comics)

1987, *Trekker* focuses on the adventures of a bounty hunter—trekker—named Mercy St. Clair who operates out of the city of New Gelaph. The year is 2226 on an unspecified planet. The first issue follows Mercy through her city, whose sleazy noir slums and newer high rise, high tech districts make it look a lot like 1980s Los Angeles (fig. I.1). The second takes her out to the desert wastelands around New Gelaph, where bandits have robbed and murdered at an isolated trading post of the sort familiar from dozens of western movies (and *Terminator 2*) (fig. I.2). Because she's awfully good at what she does and can shoot amazingly straight with both hands at the same time, she clears the team of bad guys out of a landscape that looks a lot like Monument Valley or Arches National Park. So *Trekker* has it all: the metropolitan frontier and the old West frontier reimagined as parts of the same future.

PART I

Jack London Imagines the Suburban Frontier

Jack London, adventure novelist and political radical, was also a writer with a distinctly modern vision of the future American city. In *The Iron Heel* (1908) he described something that looks a lot like the sprawling, socially segregated American city of the twenty-first century—perhaps even the American city California style, appropriate for the imagination of a native Californian.

The Iron Heel drew upon Jack London's journalism as well as his imagination. Five years earlier, he had published *People of the Abyss*, an account of several months spent living in the vast teeming slums of East London. Exploring the same landscape that social scientist and reformer Charles Booth had delineated in seventeen massive volumes on *Life and Labour of the People in London* (1892–1903), he borrowed his title from H. G. Wells's own depiction of poverty in the British metropolis in *Anticipations* (1901). London turned his eye to the residents of workhouses, the people of the streets, children, the unemployed, and petty criminals and their victims.

> I went down into the under-world of London with an attitude of mind which I may best liken to that of the explorer. I was open to be convinced by the evidence of my eyes, rather than by the teachings of those who had not seen, or by the words of those who had seen and gone before. Further, I took with me certain simple criteria with which to measure the life of the under-world. That which made for more life, for physical and spiritual health, was good; that which made for less life, which hurt, and dwarfed, and distorted life, was bad. . . . The starvation and lack of shelter I encountered constituted a chronic condition of misery which is never wiped out, even in the periods of greatest prosperity.[1]

Having explored the world's largest city, what did London think that Chicago and other American cities will look like under a future of corporate capitalism? The answer: abject poverty in the core and happily isolated suburbanites on the fringe. The people of the American urban abyss are confined to miserable lives in the "great ghetto" of old neighborhoods that compound the worst of lower Manhattan, East London, and immigrant Chicago. The workers live "like beasts in great squalid labour-ghettos, festering in misery and degradation."[2] At the same time, corporate prosperity now satisfies and buys off the more skilled workers. The book describes their new suburban communities in language that anticipates the great labor-management bargain of post–World War II America: "The members of the great labour castes were contented and worked on merrily. For the first time in their life they knew industrial peace. . . . They lived in more comfortable homes and in delightful cities of their own—delightful compared to the slums and ghettos in which they had formerly dwelt."[3]

London was well aware of the suburban trend and its positive reception by urban experts such as Adna F. Weber. Author of the magisterial study *The Growth of Cities in the Nineteenth Century* (1899), Weber took comfort in the ability of suburbanization to ameliorate the ills of crowded cities. Writing in the *North American Review* in 1898, he argued that "the 'rise of the suburbs' is by far the most cheering movement of modern times. . . . The suburb unites the advantages of city and country both" to allow "the Anglo-Saxon race" to escape the "hot, dusty, smoky, germ-producing city tenements and streets." In the world of *The Iron Heel*, the worker slaves left behind were presumably not Anglo-Saxons.

There are suburban new towns as well—free-standing self-contained communities of the sort proposed by British critic Ebenezer Howard in *Garden Cities of Tomorrow* (1902). Unlike Howard's cooperative communities, however, London's version is the specialized homes of the mercenaries. These are the enforcers when force is needed (a cross between a Praetorian guard and company goons). They live privileged lives in self-governing cities of their own. Although there is luckily nothing quite like these towns today, there is an echo of both survivalist enclaves and politically independent suburbs that turn their cold shoulder to big city problems.

The elite has also suburbanized, to gated and protected communities. In the paroxysm of the Chicago Commune, the rebels can attack downtown office towers but "never once did they succeed in reaching the city of the oligarchs on the westside. The oligarchs had protected themselves well. No matter what destruction was wreaked in the heart of the city, they, and their womenkind and children, were to escape, unhurt. I am told [writes Avis Everhard] that their children played in the parks during those terrible days, and that their favorite game was an imitation of their elders stamping upon the proletariat."[4]

Here London took the model of early upscale suburbs like the communities of Philadelphia's Main Line or Chicago North Shore to a logical extreme. In 1908, such suburbs protected their status with purely symbolic entrance gates, restrictive real estate covenants, and the simple power of wealth. A century later, much of new residential development on the edges of American cities is built behind very real gates and walls—one of the issues that animates the novelists in the opening chapter in this book. "Real Estate and Race" explores ways in which four writers have depicted the land development industry and suburban real estate frontier in the Southwest. In each case, they see development as exacerbating racial inequalities and perpetuating the divided cities that Jack London had described and anticipated.

The second chapter, "Imagining Portland's Urban Growth Boundary," also deals with the future of raw land on the subdivision frontier—in this case as a target for protection and preservation rather than rampaging real estate development. It explores the way in which a line that demarcates one city's suburban frontier has become something more than a regulation. Spirited debate about its impacts on land uses and values has inspired vivid descriptions by both supporters and critics and spurred the imagination of artists and creative writers. The Urban Growth Boundary (UGB) has become a symbol, metaphor, and touchstone, as people read complex meanings into it that go beyond its simple legal function, addressing it through reflective essays, poetry, novels, photography, performance art, songs, and other exercises of the artistic imagination.

"Jim Rockford or Tony Soprano" explores differences in the American vision of East Coast and West Coast suburbs. In both television shows and the fiction of writers such as John Updike, Richard Ford, and Douglas Coupland, popular culture draws distinctions between the suburbs of the Atlantic Coast and the Pacific Coast. One difference revolves around the roles of place and space. The second is the varying weight of history, often as manifested through families and social ties. Eastern suburbs and suburbanites are commonly depicted as embedded in place, rooted in time, and entangled in social networks. Western suburbs and suburbanites are often imagined as the opposite—isolated in space, atemporal, and free (or bereft) of social bonds. The contrast might have appealed to Jack London, who added two entirely new "wonder cities" to the world of *The Iron Heel*—Ardis, finished twenty years after the failed revolution in 1942, and Asgard, completed in 1984. London didn't provide much detail, but with the timing, we might envision Irvine, California, for Ardis and Las Vegas for Asgard—both wonder cities in my book.

"On the Sidewalks of Los Angeles" concludes this section on suburban frontiers with the film *Falling Down*, whose central character William Foster is a Los Angeles aerospace worker who belongs to the modern equivalent of London's skilled labor caste. The promise of a comfortable home and labor peace collapses, however, when Foster loses his job and then finds himself stranded among the working-class communities to which his life has made him a stranger. The film traces his trek across the metropolis, from immigrant East L.A. (Jack London's "slums and ghettos") to the Pacific, as he tries and fails to reconnect with "the delightful city of his own." Together the film, television shows, and novels suggest alternative meanings for California freedom. What sort of reinvention is possible for the star of the Rockford Files in the 1970s compared to the character of William Foster in the much more troubled 1990s, and how does the openness of the younger West Coast contrast with the settled society of the Atlantic states?

Notes

1. Jack London, *Novels and Social Writings* (New York: Library of America, 1982), 5.
2. Jack London, *The Iron Heel* (1908; reprint, London: Journeyman Press, 1976), 192.
3. Ibid., 189.
4. Ibid., 213.

CHAPTER 1

Real Estate and Race

Imagining the Second Circuit of Capital in Sunbelt Cities

Kyra Menaker-Mossbacher is a whiz at selling real estate on the west side of Los Angeles. Working out of her Lexus and a Woodland Hills office, she's the "undisputed volume leader at Mike Bender Realty, Inc." Real estate is her life (apart from husband, son, cat, and Dandie Dinmont terriers). She knows how to put the best light on lowball offers, how to charm buyers out of sudden jitters, and how to "keep the avenues open" with former clients (31, 36).[1]

At the same moment in fictional time, Frank Dominic is cooking up plans to remake Albuquerque. Land developers have been buying up parcels in Old Town and low-lying barrio properties near the Rio Grande. Dominic is a banker and deal maker with mayoral ambitions who has a scheme to help these real estate speculations pay off by diverting the river through a set of newly dug canals in imitation of San Antonio. There will be tourists, casinos, and entertainment. Look out, Las Vegas!

Two decades earlier, Ladd Devine the Third had floated a similar plan to transform disused farmland in northern New Mexico into the Miracle Valley Recreation Area. After inheriting untilled grazing and farm land from his grandfather, who bought it from Hispano farmers at bargain-basement prices in the 1930s, he has been profiting from tourism with the Dancing Trout dude ranch. Now he hopes that a planned Indian Creek Dam will allow the "abandoned and apparently worthless land" to transmute into "a ritzy subdivision molded around an exotic and very green golf course" (23).

Most impressive of all is Leah Blue, wife of a mafia boss transplanted from Cherry Hill, New Jersey, to Tucson. Leah is into every dimension of real estate. Her starting capital is a reward for putting up with the cross-country move after Max Blue is nearly killed by an assassin and decides to downsize operations to a simple killer-for-hire business. Leah buys and sells and gets a rush that is almost like sex when she outsmarts a broker. She knows that "the real estate market in Tucson and southern Arizona was wide open, ripe for development" like San Diego and Palm Springs. She canvasses neighborhoods on the edge of town, "leaving her business cards in case large parcels of desert became available" (359, 361). She has a scheme for developing a desert Venice every bit as audacious as Frank Dominic's and as large in acreage as Ladd Devine's Miracle Valley.

Four Sunbelt Novels

Each of these characters—Kyra, Frank, Ladd, Leah—figures in a novel set in the contemporary Sunbelt Southwest. The books, in order of publication, are John Nichols, *The Milagro Beanfield War* (1974) for Ladd Devine; Leslie Marmon Silko, *Almanac of the Dead* (1991) for Leah Blue; Rudolfo Anaya, *Alburquerque* (1992) for Frank Dominic; and T. Coraghessan Boyle, *The Tortilla Curtain* (1995) for Kyra Mossbacher. The central role of real estate as both a background feature and plot element—its culturally embedded valuation, buying, selling, development, and protection—offers an entryway for understanding how important and influential writers have imagined and delineated one of North America's most rapidly changing regions.

The four books range from a near best seller (*Tortilla Curtain*) and a cult favorite (*Milagro Beanfield War*) to semipopular fiction (*Alburquerque*) with limited sales and self-consciously experimental fiction (*Almanac of the Dead*). *The Tortilla Curtain* and *Alburquerque* are tightly structured as traditional well-made novels, focusing on limited sets of protagonists who interact through rising action and find themselves in a conflict that resolves with a decisive ending. *The Milagro Beanfield War* is a community picaresque with adventures and misadventures observed over the shoulders of multiple characters, a few of whom may not actually exist.[2] The two New Mexico books are also comedies in the formal sense of stories that end with at least partial restoration of social balance and harmony (*The Milagro Beanfield War* is also uproariously funny). *The Tortilla Curtain*, in contrast, follows the classic trajectory of tragedy. Its characters act with good intentions but, flawed by stubbornness or moral blindness and buffeted by circumstance, move inexorably toward disaster. *Almanac of the Dead* is harder to categorize. It is a sprawling, multivocal amalgam with enough story lines for half a dozen more compact novels, causing reviewers for standard sources like *Publisher's Weekly* and *Library Journal* to throw up their hands in confusion.[3] Silko introduces and drops characters as her needs change, flips among half a dozen settings, and shifts tone from down-and-dirty realism to something akin to the semi-fantastic imagination of Latin American fiction. The modern West, she implies, is too complex and too unformed to sit still for a traditional novelistic portrait.[4]

Critics have most commonly approached these books with an eye to tensions and conflicts around race and ethnicity, for each author places Anglo-Americans in confrontation and conflict with people of color and their communities—Hispano farmers, Mexican Americans, Indians, Mexican immigrants. Anaya and Nichols depict long-rooted natives, whether urbanites or country people, who respond to the intrusive demands of Anglo-American society to remake specific places in the interests of monetary profit. Boyle sees two migratory peoples (educated Anglos and Mexican workers) colliding in Southern California. Both have claims to the same landscape that may be equal in right but are unequal in power. Silko casts the widest net as she depicts all of western America, from southern Mexico to Alaska, as a single Indian Country, whose future is weighed down by European Americans in both Mexico and the United States and where multiple Indian peoples, Mexican American proletarians, and African Americans are potential allies for a utopian apocalypse.

Within this broad framework, it is striking that each novelist places *land* at the center of the racial conflict. These are not stories that hinge on the problems of love across racial barriers. They are not about traditional class conflict and labor organizing. They do not try to explore the ways in which the natural resources of western North America have been developed and misused. They are not about heroic individuals seeking self-realization and redemption in the wild. In short, the authors are not rewriting *Ramona* or *The Grapes of Wrath*, nor are they crafting fictions in parallel to *Angle of Repose* or *Sometimes a Great Notion*. Race and ethnicity are certainly obvious and vital factors in the history and future of the Southwest, but the dimension of land and landscape suggests an additional way to read these fictions, viewing them not so much as "western" or "frontier" stories of conquest and resistance but as *Sunbelt stories*—stories in which the particular processes of late twentieth-century growth are central.

In this reading, a central goal of the books is to unmask the processes through which Anglo-Americans have asserted and established claims to the land. The attention to real estate makes visible what was previously concealed or invisible (the "invisible hand" of the market). The process of land conversion—the political deals and financial arrangements that underlie the development of the visible, physical metroscape—is front and center in the novels in the midsized cities of Tucson and Albuquerque and the ritzy side of megametropolis Los Angeles. The same factors are also at work in efforts to incorporate Milagro into the recreation hinterland of Denver, Dallas, and Albuquerque.[5]

In using narratives to describe, embody, and make visible the pathways through which capital accumulates in real estate, these novels offer insight into the social and political dynamics of the modern southwestern Sunbelt. In particular, they highlight ways in which Anglo-Americans continue to act as if western North America is *terra nullius*, land without prior ownership that is open for the taking. The action in all four stories is driven, at least in part, by the efforts of indigenous peoples to assert or reassert their own claims. The authors thus make visible the morally tottery foundation for the "white politics" that dominated the twentieth-century Southwest, whether as regional development policies of the New Deal regime or the laissez-faire policies of southwestern conservatism.

The Second Circuit of Capital

Spanning the different settings, plots, and styles of writing is a concern with the differences between land as *place* and *commodity*—another way to phrase the effects of running land through the real estate development machine. In each case, the complex trajectories of economic development, cultural adaptation, and demographic change are condensed and represented as land development. The wheeler-dealers in Alburquerque (using Anaya's spelling to differentiate the fictionalized city from the real place) want to evict residents in the long-established barrio to construct tourist attractions. Ladd Devine wants to see a golf course and condominiums on land that was once a part of the agricultural base of the Milagro villagers. Kyra Mossbacher sells houses in subdivisions that encroach farther and farther along chaparral-clad ridges, paving over the natural landscape that provides the raw material that her nature-writer husband mines for magazine columns. Leah Blue plans to use legal maneuvers to appropriate Indian water rights in order to adorn fantasy subdivisions. In every case, a landscape that might well be understood as an ecological whole is commoditized for nonproductive or marginally productive uses.

It is useful here to utilize the idea of a "second circuit of capital" as introduced by sociologist Henri Lefebvre in *La Révolution urbaine* (1970) and *La Production de l'espace* (1974).[6] When capitalist production matures, according to traditional Marxism, opportunities for profitable industrial production fall as a result of overproduction, increased competition, resource depletion, and workforce unionization. Owners of capital seek to restore profits by extracting additional surplus value from labor, leading to more and more intense conflict between workers and owners. Alternatively, however, capital can flow from industrial production (the first circuit of capital) into the built environment of housing, commercial space, and physical infrastructure (anything from freeways to golf courses). This creation of monetary value in real estate has its own dynamics of finance and its own logic of booms and busts and, therefore, constitutes a distinct, *second* circuit for capital circulation and accumulation. In addition, capital can also move into education, scientific research, and health care to constitute a third circuit that feeds back into the primary industrial sector through innovation, product development, and increases in the productivity of labor.[7]

The second circuit of capital depends on the availability of surplus capital whose owners are seeking profitable investments, but money does not "flow" of its own accord. The second circuit requires an elaborate system of financial institutions to assemble and redistribute investment funds. It also depends on government facilitation. The state works to stabilize the financial system, fund certain types of real estate investment such as transportation and utility infrastructure, and direct capital in particular directions (as through urban redevelopment programs). It may also be enlisted in corrupt alliances in which government authority favors particular interests (as Leah Blue well knows).[8] Finally, it depends on the real estate development and sales industries themselves to keep capital in motion by continually offering up new products and opportunities for investment.

In this analysis, the second circuit is the most sterile and least productive. Development of real estate does help to maintain the industrial sector by housing its activities and workers. It also provides the systems of physical circulation that make necessary connections between producers and consumers. However, projects in the second circuit do not put labor to work in the long haul, nor do they lead directly to technological change and industrial revitalization. Real estate capital can transform places like a New Mexico village or a California canyon rim into a marketable commodity, but it has little ability to add permanently to productive capacity.

Real estate development is also "faddish." Cities such as Houston or Las Vegas gain reputations as "hot" investment opportunities and attract real estate investment beyond the absorptive capacity of the local economy. As Joe Feagin argues, "Development and finance capitalists frequently make decisions about urban development which are irrational from a tough cost-accounting, profit-making approach. . . . There is a social psychological dimension to capital investments flowing into the secondary circuit."[9] Feagin's comments about Houston have fictional counterparts in Frank Dominic; in Charlie Crocker, the self-deluding Atlanta office tower entrepreneur who is center stage in Tom Wolfe's novel *A Man in Full*; or in the urban renewal schemers who hope to benefit from the abandonment of entire Saint Louis neighborhoods in Jonathan Franzen's *The Twenty-Seventh City*.[10]

All the writers under scrutiny tell stories that we can analyze in terms of the second circuit. They find it appropriate to contrast a natural, traditional, and sometimes spiritual connection to the landscape with artificial, profit-driven development. They also see the developments themselves as embodiments of fads and fashions—stoking a taste for conspicuous leisure, for conspicuous water consumption in the desert, for conspicuously gated enclave communities. Indeed, the real estate developers and sales people who populate these Southwest stories are themselves aware that they are dealers in fantasies and perhaps even scams. In contrast, the indigenous characters are more closely connected in community and more "in tune" with the land. Mysticism and mystery lie on one side of the economic and cultural divide. Markets lie on the other.

The idea of challenged authenticity places the Southwest in double juxtaposition to the rest of the United States. At the end of one axis are the gritty cities of the Rustbelt, which are "real" places that may be economically depressed and physically squalid but are no longer weighted down by myths of the future. Their residents know to cut through any illusions that may mask the exercise of power. In contrast, the Anglo-American cities of the Southwest are commonly regarded as rootless, shallow, superficial. After all, French philosopher Jean Baudrillard traveled to Los Angeles in search of stage-set society (simulacra and simulation in his jargon), not to Akron or Allentown.

At the end of another axis is the Sunbelt Southeast. Because black and white southerners arrived at the same time, neither group have prior rights to the land (neither is more authentic than the other). Members of each, nevertheless, have moral relationships to the land that are shaped and burdened by centuries of shared history (contrast the heritage of slavery and sharecropping with the dubious ideology of the Southern Fugitives and other romantic regionalists). In the Southwest, the indigenous folk are not only visibly present but also stand in obvious and troubling contrast to the waves of Anglo newcomers. In Tucson and Albuquerque and Los Angeles, indigenous people are "authentically" present to challenge superficiality by participating in the politics of development and shaping what our authors hope may be more equitable futures.

Capital and Community in Four Imagined Communities

Across variations in style and tone, we find some common elements among the four novels. Indigenous characters in various ways have rooted or "authentic" connections to the land. The forces of Sunbelt change, as represented by the real estate sector, are never the good guys. They are variously venal in *The Milagro Beanfield War*, vacuous in *The Tortilla Curtain*, mildly villainous in *Alburquerque*, and vulturine in *Almanac of the Dead*.[11]

John Nichols provided an early and straightforward version of this Sunbelt narrative with his fast-paced, often side-splitting portrait of Hispano and Anglo cultures in unanticipated collision. Two different views of the world are at play and in conflict. The people of Milagro do not see much reason to hurry into the modern world, and they find their strength in an intricate web of community connections. Ladd Devine, his local allies (notably a real estate dealer), and his more powerful friend in the state government see the benefits of greater participation in the national economy. The cultural difference is summed up with the saga of Milagro's single parking meter, a brainstorm of Mayor Sammy Cantu, Councilman Bud Gleason (the real estate man), and Sheriff Bernabé Montoya. Installed in front of the all-purpose General Store+Frontier Bar+Pilar Café, its purpose is to earn a few dollars for the financially strapped sheriff's office. But ancient and irascible Onofre Martinez regularly pulls his battered Chevy pickup into the metered space and tears up the parking tickets that appear like clockwork on his windshield. Installation, repairs, and the paper and ink required for the tickets have so far cost the city $553.13, while the meter has taken in exactly $1.91. As long as Onofre claims the space, no stray tourist can park there and naively feed the meter. Community values, in short, trump economic rationalization.[12]

The plot kicks off with Joe Mondragon, an otherwise ordinary and sometimes boneheaded member of the local community. Joe decides on impulse to chop a trench into the Miracle Valley's main irrigation canal, divert water onto an arid field, and plant beans. The first problem is that it may be his field but it is not his water. The second problem is that his action threatens Ladd Devine's plans for a dam in Milagro Canyon. Devine is the area's closest version of a land baron, which he owes to his grandfather buying large tracts of land in the 1930s and 1940s, when economic stress combined with new water laws to make subsistence farming problematic. But a planned conservancy district and new dam could restore actual water to Devine's holdings, providing the water to go with his water rights. The improvement district will spread the costs, in effect taxing away surplus value from local residents, but most of the water will flow to Ladd Devine's lands and benefit the Anglo investment community. Joe's action in illegally diverting a tiny fraction of water threatens the entire scheme from its foundation, like a gopher gnawing a hole in the side of a canal.

Over the course of the book, Joe's initial, individual action gathers force. Ladd Devine enlists the forces of the state, particularly in the form of state police detective Kyril Montana. Townspeople slowly overcome their reluctance to get involved and their fear of public officials. "Despite building tensions, hardly anybody had even admitted to Joe that they knew the beanfield existed. Most people still did not want to get involved. . . . They wanted to see if Joe could get away with it" (116). Nevertheless, folks in town begin to see the symbolic power of the single beanfield, gradually and sporadically rallying to the cause. There is a community meeting, a petition that few people want to sign, a bit of mild monkey-wrenching of signs announcing Ladd Devine's business interests. Tensions escalate, Joe is arrested, townspeople surround the jail in their dusty trucks, and the governor decides to put things on hold before outside agitators decide to show up from Denver.

Nichols wrote as a fierce 1960s liberationist and an adopted New Mexican. He had attended schools in half a dozen states, experienced the headlong gentrification that turned New York's South Village into trendy SoHo, had a transformative experience observing capitalism up close in Central America, and arrived in Taos in 1969 sensitized to look for the same patterns.[13] Three years later he penned *The Milagro Beanfield War* in a feverish eleven-week burst. He has made no secret of his political leanings, publishing an admiring essay on Reies Tijerina and writing that the world needs more examples like Che Guevara and Mother Jones. One of his models for novel writing is Emile Zola's *Germinal* (1885) with its politically passionate drama of labor conflict in French coal mines.

Nichols is clear that the underlying issue that he addresses in his entire New Mexico trilogy, which also includes *The Magic Journey* (1978) and *Nirvana Blues* (1981), is the outsiders, with an overabundance of money, seeking investment bargains. In a later essay, he wrote that "excessive capital, wielded by middle-class newcomers, has created harsh division between locals and immigrants. It has highlighted ethnic tensions, destabilizing ancient communities and their value systems."[14] Ladd Devine's desire to keep making money for its own sake drives the conflict in the novel, but he operates in a larger economic world. The politicians and string pullers in Santa Fe want to keep New Mexico open and inviting to outside investors. The vacationers and condo buyers will come from Boston and Dallas. From the governor's point of view, "Development swung votes . . .

and Ladd Devine's Miracle Valley project was the kind of thing people considered progress; it would bring outside money into the state" (433).

The novel follows a large cast of characters who weave in and out of the action and play outside stories. In action, the villagers are cantankerous and only occasionally cooperative. They are impulsive and unpredictable and largely contemptuous of bureaucratic society (like Onofre Martinez and the parking meter). Joe Mondragon decided to irrigate his beanfield on a whim, and he adamantly refuses to lead the growing resistance against Devine. Ladd Devine's side includes his various employees, state officials, Forest Service personnel, and a reluctant sheriff. Attorney Charlie Bloom, a newcomer who edits a radical regional newspaper, is a stand-in for Nichols himself (who contributed articles to a similar publication) and functions as an occasional commentator on the action. Herbie Goldfarb, a bumbling VISTA volunteer, is a comic mirror, whose misadventures simultaneously demonstrate the practical competence of Milagro's people and points up their hit-and-miss approach to the growing crisis.[15]

Embedded in the contrast between homeland and real estate are other differences. The story weighs the value of large-scale institutions (state government, Forest Service, conservation district) against the small-scale interests of the town. It pits progress, defined as economic growth, against tradition. The Anglo world embraces change, whereas the Hispano community is skeptical out of long experience. The Anglo world is rational, never more so than in the form of detective Kyril Montana, who as a sort of applied sociologist tries to figure out all the social gears and levers that make Milagro tick and fails completely. The residents, of course, have a deep affection for their home community. Even cynical Joe Mondragon holds on to memories of summer nights in the mountains with his father, helping to drive their sheep across the river, fishing in autumn, hunting through snowy hills, cleaning the ditches in the spring: "No getting around it, though: suddenly he held a profound tenderness for his people, that's what it was. His people. His gente. . . . Suddenly he loved the people he lived with, he cared about their lives. . . . His childhood, something he had all but forgotten, drifted out of a dim misty place" (116–17).[16]

In *The Tortilla Curtain*, T. C. Boyle offers a harder-edged narrative of the tension between land and real estate. Twenty years after Nichols wrote, it was difficult for Boyle or his readers to be quite so celebratory of traditional community. Los Angeles itself, of course, has long been a favored setting for cynical and satirical novels. Just compare the "noir" Los Angeles constructed in the work of James Cain, Nathaniel West, and Raymond Chandler and the alienating Los Angeles of Chester Himes, Budd Schulburg, and Joan Didion to the deeply rooted New Mexico pictured by Mary Austin, Oliver LaFarge, and Frank Waters. Boyle, writing as a relatively new Angeleno, grew up in suburban New York and came west in 1978 by way of Iowa City. He has a penchant for satire, and *The Tortilla Curtain* is filled with Los Angeles stereotypes deftly pinned to the specimen mat.

The novel opens with a literal competition for space. Nature writer Delaney Mossbacher in his freshly waxed Japanese sedan is speeding up Topanga Canyon. The illegal immigrant Candido is trying to sprint across the road when Delaney clips and injures him. Along with fright and worry about legal liability, Delaney is annoyed that those people are "camping out down there . . . crapping in the chaparral . . . thoughtless people, stupid people, people who wanted to turn the whole world into a garbage dump, a little Tijuana" (11). Soon thereafter, however, the tables are turned. Walking through his own upscale subdivision of Arroyo Blanco Estates after an evening property owners' meeting, Delaney finds himself shadowed by a big boat of a car with mag wheels, smoked glass, and ka-thumping stereo. The car paces him, then turns to freeze him in its headlights before driving off. "Who would be up here at this hour in a car like this? Was it burglars, then? Muggers? Gangbangers?" (64).

In fact, both of the men who collide on the Topanga highway are newcomers to Los Angeles, Delaney since two years and Candido for a matter of days. Each is looking for a way to stake a claim on the landscape. For Delaney, it is through his *Wide Open Spaces* magazine column "Pilgrim at Topanga Creek," where he records his observations of nature. Arroyo Blanco Estates is up the canyon, allowing Delaney to wander out his back door along the ridge lines of the Santa Monica Mountains. He found it hard to feel bad, "not up here where the night hung close around him and the crickets thundered and the air off the Pacific crept up the hills" (63). Candido's personal connection to the canyon and mountains is far more practical. On a side ravine, he has made a camp for himself and his wife América. It is far better than the streets of Los Angeles, for "the water was still flowing, the sand was clean, and the sky overhead was his, all his, and there was nobody to dispute him for it" (26). He finds a way to make the polluted stream, which first gives him terrible diarrhea, work for him. When their first campsite is discovered and trashed, he discovers an even more secluded place protected by an overhanging cliff and the pooled stream. Here he envisions a facsimile of a real home—a place where they can feel comfortable enough to express their mutual affection and physical love.

The conceptualization of land as refuge (spiritual or practical) runs up against the realities of land as real estate. The most effective claims are not those of hidden immigrant or sensitive writer. Instead, Arroyo Blanco claims the most power. The name itself appropriates Topanga Canyon for people on one side of the social divide, and its residents have the power to control uses of land inside and outside the community. They can build gates and then walls. They can decide to shut down a gathering place for day laborers to protect the value of their houses. In the form of college students with a chip on their shoulder, they can invade the little corner of the canyon where Candido and América are trying to turn a camping spot into a home. The superficial argument for these actions is to make residents feel that Arroyo Blanco Estates is a safe place (to enhance its "use value" in the jargon), but the underlying concern is also to maintain its exchange value as a real estate investment.[17]

In contrast, neither wife has a connection with landscape. América does not share Candido's feelings of pride in finding a secluded campsite, which is just another place of drudgery and danger. She wants a house with a roof, a refrigerator, a bathroom, beds. What she wants is what Kyra has for sale. Kyra defines herself in terms of real estate. She deals with jet-set money (one client has just moved back to Italy and left a multimillion-dollar house for sale) and she knows all the techniques for moving inventory. She knows how to display a house, psych out clients, and find exactly the right moment "to talk the place up, rhapsodize over the views, the privacy, the value and exclusivity" (107). She knows how to manipulate people with handwritten notes and housewarming gifts: "She knew that people in her area changed their place of residence once every 3.7 years, and that they had cousins, children, parents and old college roommates who needed housing too. And when the time came to list their property, they would go to Kyra Menaker-Mossbacher, the empress of goodwill" (156).

As a manipulator of symbols, Kyra is right at home in Arroyo Blanco. Her clients are musicians, television writers, investment company executives. Her neighbors range from lawyers to a corporate executive under house arrest for chicanery. One of the loudest voices for walling and protecting the community belongs to Jack Cherrystone, whose considerable wealth comes from doing the voice-overs for movie trailers. Just as trailers are manipulated and often misleading simulacra of cultural products that are themselves fictions, Jack is about as fake as a human can be yet becomes the "voice-over" for the community.

The Anglos have the literal high ground, the ridge tops and view lots as opposed to the canyon grotto. Hilltops are refuge against invaders, for many of Kyra's clients "wanted something out of the way, something rustic, rural, safe—something removed from people of whatever class or color, but particularly from the hordes of immigrants" (107). In spite of Delaney's liberal scruples, the Arroyo Blanco homeowners decide first to install gates to their private development, then to build a wall to keep out "coyotes," community shorthand for frightening humans as well as animals. Indeed, for Kyra, "the invasion from the South had been good for business to this point because it had driven the entire white middle class out of Los Angeles proper and into the areas she specialized in: Calabasas, Topanga, Arroyo Blanco. She still sold houses in Woodland Hills . . . but all the smart buyers had already retreated beyond the city limits. . . . There had to be a limit, a boundary, a cap, or they'd be in Calabasas next and then Thousand Oaks and on and on up the coast until there was no real estate left" (158–59).

Things go wrong when upcanyon and downcanyon interpenetrate. Delaney parks in the lower canyon for a hike only to have his car stolen and to encounter predatory criminals (who merely make him uneasy but who have raped América). The Da Ros house, with its magnificent view, is invaded by the same bad guys coming up the canyon. They do no direct harm when Kyra confronts them, but they return to deface the house with graffiti. Later, all Arroyo Blanco is threatened by a fire that sweeps up the canyon with a storm of rising heat, started when one of Candido's fires leaps out of control. It dies down only after consuming the Da Ros mansion, leaving Kyra fearing that "real estate had gone bad" and that the invaders are winning (310). Thereafter, things go from bad to very bad. Delaney becomes obsessed with immigrant refugees driven out of the canyon, seeking to find and root out shacks and shanties (real estate claims!) that have popped up in unburned scrub—nature writer turns vigilante. Fire season turns to rainy season. Flash floods rip the landscape. Delaney dies in the surging waters, closer to nature than he has ever been before. Candido and América survive, but América's child does not.

The novelist's satire throws off more barbs than an angry porcupine. As a morality play, the message is clear: nature dwarfs individual aspirations. Liberals are hypocrites. Environmentalists are romantic racists who prefer the idea of nature to its reality and choose nature in either form to other human beings. Delaney the nature writer becomes alienated from the land of benign flowers and birds. As if it has read Mike Davis's *Ecology of Fear* (1998), the commoditized landscape fights back with its natural systems. Fire and flood in succession undermine the hopes and plans of all four central figures.

As a real estate fable, the novel hammers home the shallowness of house buyers who see an investment rather than a home. Kyra knows that she is serving vanity rather than practical need when she peddles hilltop mansions. Delaney fights his neighbors' fetishizing of property values, then goes along with the gate and wall schemes, and finally falls for the rationalizations about property values even when he knows better. The novel implicitly attributes the contradiction between use and exchange values to the excess of available cash that is sucked into Los Angeles bank accounts through the entertainment industry and spurts out again in search of lucrative real estate deals by which individuals can try to skim some benefit as capital circulates through the built environment.

Like T. C. Boyle, Rudolfo Anaya is a seasoned writer who can craft a well-structured novel. He grew up in Santa Rosa (New Mexico) and Albuquerque and has spent much of his career at the University of New Mexico. He made his reputation with *Bless Me, Ultima* (1972), described by one commentator as a story of a young man's "bittersweet negotiations with family, church, peers, sexuality, and ethnic and cultural traditions as he stumbled toward adulthood."[18] Critics tend to dismiss *Alburquerque* as a lesser work, less steeped in regional culture and damaged by plot elements that aim at commercial success rather than authenticity.

Indeed, *Alburquerque* combines two very standard story lines. One centers on Abrán Gonzalez, a young man who has been raised as part of the working-class Chicano community but who discovers that he is the son of a well-known and wealthy artist who is an Anglo but who has developed a deep sensitivity to New Mexico. After meeting his mother for the first time at the end of her life, he seeks out the identity of his father, a quest that takes him to different neighborhoods and individuals representing different facets of the city. He becomes entangled in the second storyline, which involves a three-way contest for mayor between progressive Marissa Martinez, who has the support of barrio residents, along with up-to-date credentials as a battling district attorney; Walter Johnson, who represents the big money of the old Anglo business elite; and Frank Dominic, Hispanic entrepreneur and property developer who wants to bridge the difference as a modern patron, a new *alcalde mayor*. Abrán promises to return to the boxing ring (he was an amateur champion) under the sponsorship of Frank Dominic in exchange for being told his father's identity. Dominic, in turn, hopes his sponsorship will gain him points among Hispanic voters. At the end, all is made clear. Marissa wins the election, and Abrán learns that his father is the well-known Hispanic author Ben Chavez, whom he already knows and respects.

Embedded in the political campaign is Frank Dominic's proposal for a revolutionary land development that will "rebrand" the city as a leisure destination. He wants to promise jobs for the Hispanic barrio, cachet for the North Valley yuppies in their adobe-style houses, development opportunities for the real estate industry, and attractions for tourists. The solution: acquire rural water rights from nearby Indian pueblos and divert the Rio Grande through downtown in a series of canals and lagoons to create scores of waterside building lots for condos, office buildings, a casino, hotels, a performing arts center. "It was money *and* politics for Dominic. He was aiming to be governor, but he wanted to be mayor first. He wanted to bring in casino gambling and build a Venice on the Rio Grande. . . . Dominic had cooked up a big urban enhancement project. Canals full of Rio Grande water. Casinos. A Disneyland on the river" (58–59). With this scheme, Alburquerque can be Santa Fe and Las Vegas both.[19] At the meeting to roll out the scheme, the architect shows a model of "a desert Venice with beltways of green, ponds, and small lakes, all interconnected by the waterways that crisscrossed the downtown area" (115).

If it were reality rather than fiction, the "El Dorado" plan for Alburquerque would not stand alone. Tucson in the 1990s considered refilling the dry bed of the Santa Cruz River to revitalize downtown. Other Arizonans have successfully promoted development of the amazingly named Scottsdale Waterfront, where flats, shops, and the Fiesta Bowl Museum will hug the bank of the Arizona Canal as it channels irrigation water through the Valley of the Sun. Denver has turned a stretch of the unprepossessing South Platte River into a whitewater park. An investment of $54 million has remade a seven-mile stretch of the North Canadian River into the "Oklahoma River," where rowing and canoeing events attract Olympic athletes from around the globe.[20]

There is something Oklahoma City–like in the ambitions and financial connections of Alburquerque. Excited residents see the scheme as a chance finally to catch up with Dallas and Denver as well as to emulate Las Vegas. The scheme is intended to pull in mobile capital: "The businessmen are dreaming of rich Arabs, Hong Kong investors" (126). Money will flow in from New York and Tokyo with the help of local government in a nice example of the second circuit at work.

Anaya sets up the water scheme in ethnic terms, with the good of the people set against the good of property owners. The real estate juggernaut of which Frank's scheme is one component has two impacts on poor and indigenous communities. Hispanic residents are very much aware of the perils of neighborhood gentrification. The city's wealthy professionals have "discovered rural living and the Alburquerque abode style" and have overwhelmed older Hispanic communities on the north side as they carve out their enclaves. Frank Dominic himself tore down small businesses to make space for his Duke City Plaza office complex, causing one character to muse on the fate of a neighboring city: "Same thing happened in Santa Fe. People with money came to live the Santa Fe style, they bought the downtown barrios and built hotels, shops, condos. The old residents were swept aside, the people gone. . . . If Frank Dominic has his way, the barrio boys will be rowing boats up and down canals that cover the land where they used to live" (80). One of the last paintings by Cynthia Johnson, Abrán's mother, is commentary on gentrification. It shows "the Mexicanos as outcasts in their own land. People in one painting were walking away from the shining city" while "expensive cars, Hollywood faces, and women in the ostentatious Santa Fe style lined the streets. The painting depicted the end of an age" (154–55).

The scheme also impacts nearby Indian pueblos. Frank's scheme depends on buying the water rights that are "the blood of our valley" in the words of old *patron* Manuel Armijo (117). Skeptics doubt that he will ever secure the water, but Frank is confident in his access to Japanese money. "The pueblos are dying and the Hispanic villages up north are withering away," he tells the crowd at the unveiling. "We are promising each pueblo and each land-grant village a percentage of the casinos right off the top" (118). If the pueblos sell, says writer Ben Chavez, "the way of life they hold sacred will be sacrificed. Then they'll have to come into Dominic's city to work for minimum wages, make hotel beds, and hold Indian dances in the casinos for the tourists. The minute you become a tourist commodity, you die" (123).

Anaya hammers at the idea that there is an authentic world and an Anglo world, real world and unreal world, land users and real estate dealers. Hispanic and Indian characters have a deep spiritual connection with the land and the cycles of seasons. The land purifies and renews the spirit, giving extra strength to those who know how to make the connection. Most of the newcomers only see the surface. "There's religion in this earth," says one character, "but when you only come to rent the condo and you don't touch the mud, then you're not connected" (152–53). Looking over the sweeping mountains after riding from a Rio Arriba farm deep into the Sangre de Christo range, Abrán agrees with his newfound friend Lucinda that "this is real, and the world of Frank Dominic unreal" (171).

Almanac of the Dead has its own "El Dorado project," a scheme that sounds like a cross between Venice Beach and Palm Springs. Leah Blue, wife of a crime kingpin, wheels and deals in real estate. Her big development will be Venice, Arizona, where canals will link a chain of lakeside neighborhoods. The whole scheme will require an astounding amount of water. Leah plans to rely on wells run deep into an already depleted aquifer. All she needs is a compliant federal judge to dismiss an Indian water rights claim in Nevada, and she will have the legal precedent she needs. The judge is happy to offer a favor to his golf buddy Max Blue: "Arne believed in states' rights, absolutely. Indians could file lawsuits until hell and their reservation froze over, and Arne wasn't going to issue any restraining orders against Leah's deep wells either. Max could depend on that" (376). And yes, he could. The judge throws out the last motions for an injunction, and Blue Water Development Corporation is ready to start on hundreds of miles of canals. "Her dream city had been calculated with Arizona's financial collapse and Mexico's civil war in mind. Venice, Arizona, would rise out of the dull desert gravel, its blazing purity of marble set between canals the color of lapis, and lakes of turquoise. . . . Forget Tucson and start over" (662).[21]

In Silko's world, the second circuit of capital has an ugly face. A major purpose of Leah's real estate work is to launder cash from organized crime. Her father and brothers administer huge holdings in California, presumably acquired with dirty money, and the seed money for Leah's enterprise in Arizona comes via the New Jersey mob. Another character, Trigg, considers himself a legitimate businessman because he does not use guns to acquire assets, but he is also laundering money. He is buying downtown Tucson "block by shabby block" and knows how to manipulate zoning laws to turn cheap properties valuable. His real estate plans depend on money siphoned from his commercial blood banks, from detox centers, and then from a business in body parts for medical transplants harvested from murdered winos and cadavers imported from Mexico.

In the complex arc of the novel, the deepest story is that of indigenous peoples who rise against the inequities of five centuries of European conquest. Silko is mixed Indian, Mexican, and Anglo but is most often identified as an American Indian writer. She grew up with the Laguna Pueblo community while going to school in Albuquerque, graduated from the University of New Mexico, and relocated to Tucson in the 1980s. The novel includes a complex map that locates its characters in different places and parts of North America and traces their connections to Tucson (thus multiplying Silko's own life story). The map and novel chart out an east–west axis along which European Americans move and a north–south axis along which Indian peoples have moved for thousands of years, from the original journeys that peopled the continent to the recent northward migration of Mexican Indians. Individual characters reproduce the movements. Lecha, the Yaqui psychic who is the keeper of the ancient, prophetic almanac that gives the book its title, moves from her native Mexico to the southwestern United States, to Alaska, and back to Tucson via cities like Denver. Leah Blue moves from New Jersey to Tucson and has family connections in California. Because all indigenous America is a single land, revolution in southern Mexico is also revolution in Arizona, and the theme of resistance to conquest underlies the individual story strands that Silko weaves together in what amounts to a prophetic utopian manifesto.[22] It is here that the contrast of real estate and place is most clear: "El Feo [the revolutionary leader] had devised a simple and clear test to reveal whether so-called 'leaders of the people' were true or only impostors sent by the vampires and werewolves of greed. The test was easy: true leaders of the people made return of the land the first priority. No excuses, no postponements, not even for one day. . . . The land must be returned to the people whose ancestors had lived on the land for twenty thousand years continuously" (524).[23]

One-Dimensional Region

Silko's novel moves aquatic schemes and fantasies from the satirical to the sobering. Water in the Southwest is about progress as measured in terms of economic development and growth. Water is the determinant of the value of real estate and the future of industries—vital choices in a region where every city has been a land speculation.

As we have seen, water plays a key role in these fictionalized social and economic transitions, entering the plot as developers appropriate it for nonproductive uses (in *Tortilla Curtain* water appears suddenly as a flash flood to take the landscape's own revenge for misappropriation by real estate developers). "Properly," we suppose, water in the arid Southwest is supposed to be productive. It is supposed to nourish life—the natural life of native plants and animals or the ecologically rooted life of indigenous communities engaged in traditional agriculture. It is not supposed to be reduced to a decorative element and amenity. We are not supposed to abstract away its use values in favor of exchange values, to shift it from production to sterile consumption.[24]

But in the novels under discussion the "outsiders" try to do just that in the interest of real estate investment. Major characters in three of the books want both physically and legally to divert water that "should" nurture crops of beans or water stock on Indian reservations into an amenity and decorative element, while the householders in Arroyo Blanco Estates are presumably very high per capita water users in the midst of their often tinder-dry environment. This capture and abstraction of water are ways in which these authors depict the resource economy as inactive or in decline. The contrast is implicit in *The Tortilla Curtain*, where Los Angeles has no orange groves or celery fields left for Candido to pick and explicit in John Nichols's depiction of Milagro's failing farms that can no longer support its people. Sheriff Bernabé Montoya has six children, every one of whom has moved away to find work, and most other families are in the same situation, which is why Ladd Devine thinks that the lure of tourist industry jobs will win people over. It is explicit and symbolically freighted in *Almanac of the Dead*, where Leah plans to lease inactive Texas oil rigs to drill into deep aquifers. Because Arizona's copper industry has shut down, water is now plentiful; too bad if Leah's deep wells will drain the shallower wells of Indians and small owners. Water, essential for agriculture and for place-based communities, is thus captured by and for the second circuit of capital. Natural flows are tapped and diverted to assist the artificial flows of investment.[25]

These examples are reminders that the authors downplay or ignore the aspects of economic life that theorists like Lefebvre would call the first and third circuits of capital—aspects that are in fact very present in the real Sunbelt Southwest. The fictional residents of Tucson, Alburquerque, Milagro, and Topanga Canyon may all be captives of capital, but of a very limited sort.

The Sunbelt Southwest has been a manufacturing powerhouse with a prominent role in the first circuit of capital since the early decades of the twentieth century, but readers would not know it from these Sunbelt novels. One of Anaya's mayoral candidates does hope to lure a Japanese electronics plant, but the factory has still not been built by the final page. In *Tortilla Curtain* we read nothing of the vast Southern California industrial base with its assembly plants and aerospace giants, with the exception of a clothing sweatshop that América tries to find but cannot locate. Leah and Max's son, Bingo, runs the vending machines in El Paso and watches over gambling at the horse tracks, but the vast maquiladora industrial complex of El Paso/Juarez does not figure in his activities.

Where the industrial economy does appear in many novels of the Sunbelt Southwest, it comes as industry's end products of physical waste and trash. Garbage and toxic waste disposal is one of the areas for organized crime in Max Blue's Tucson. Don DeLillo similarly places garbage at the center of the Southwest economy in *Underworld*, where New Yorker Nick Shay finds himself in Arizona and Southern California working for Whiz Co., "a firm with an inside track on the future. The Future of Waste. This was the name we gave our conference in the desert. . . . We were the front-runners, the go-getters, the guys who were ready to understand the true dimensions of the subject."[26] The trope echoes *City of Quartz* (1990), where Mike Davis meditates on the ruins of Fontana, California, which encapsulated the rise and fall of the industrial economy in a mere half century. So does the scene when Nick visits a desert parking field for abandoned airplanes, where the products of the aviation industry, one of the giants of the actual Southwest, are being repainted as a huge art project that almost nobody will see—from economic bang to whimper.

Nor is much made of the universities and research laboratories that give the region a prominent role in the production of knowledge and economic innovation as recipients of third-circuit flows. Arroyo Blanco Estates is not far from UCLA, but presumably no history or literature professor can afford its houses.

The University of Arizona provides *Almanac of the Dead* with a student who triples as a federal law enforcement informer and lover of a drug dealer but is otherwise background noise. The University of New Mexico provides an office and back story for literature professor Ben Chavez, and two other characters are taking courses, but it is not an active presence. Kirtland Air Force Base and Sandia Labs rate a mention as the source of new residents who fueled a postwar demand for real estate but not as active generators of economic change. Dominic plans a performing arts center as part of his development to mollify upper-middle-class voters, but artists are bracketed with gambling as parts of a consumption economy.

As we have seen in the preceding discussion, other information workers are even less productive. They deal in information, but they do not create ideas that can expand productive capacities. They are lawyers, judges, politicians, undercover cops, entertainers, artists, gamblers, insurance brokers, and real estate dealers, and none of them appears in a sympathetic light. The "Hollywood nights" reputation of Los Angeles has been around so long that it is American folklore, but pity poor Tucson, which has long struggled to portray itself as more cosmopolitan than upstart Phoenix.[27] In Silko's version, it has "always depended on some sort of war to keep cash flowing" (598). It is a "city of thieves" (610) and "home to an assortment of speculators, confidence men, embezzlers, lawyers, judges, police and other criminals, as well as addicts and pushers, since the 1880s and the Apache Wars." A uranium mine on Laguna lands, a dubious enterprise but undeniably part of the industrial economy, becomes a setting for coke-snorting Hollywood types to shoot a movie and desecrate sacred relics.

So, our analysis leads back to real estate and the second circuit of capital. No one would deny that much of the Sunbelt's growth has involved vast amounts of real estate development out of the simple physical necessity to shelter millions of new residents and house their activities. However, in this imagined Southwest, the second circuit actively supplants the productive economy in the imagined Southwest. Profit comes by devaluing some land to shift value to other land (West Los Angeles suburbs rather than city neighborhoods, new subdivisions rather than old Tucson) or to allow its lucrative redevelopment (as in Alburquerque and Milagro). In the Southwest, the corrupt and corrupting aspects of land development are transparent because these are new cities—or at least places that are new for the dominant Anglo-Americans. The social framework of the region is still being *constructed* in a way that Georgia society or New Orleans culture is not. There are few institutional intermediaries to get in the way of deal making or to mask the identities and motives of developers. Government is a tool of capital rather than a broker among interest groups. Even in Alburquerque, the city depicted in the greatest practical detail, the narrative highlights power brokers and voters but not the possible intermediary institutions. Certainly, no one is capable or interested in interposing him- or herself between Arroyo Blanco and the homeless immigrants . . . nobody dares to get between Leah and Indian tribal rights . . . no one is capable of mediating between Milagro and Ladd Devine (the state police and Forest Service efforts are comic).

The real estate business in these fictions also plays a central role in the depiction of racial and ethnic divisions. Competition for land is what makes contemporary racial conflict go. Anglos continue their multicentury work of turning place into space, home into real estate. Money trumps tradition, and footloose capital displaces people.

This connection may seem obvious until we contrast the Sunbelt Southeast. This is a region where racial tensions are, if anything, more salient than in the Southwest. However, they are much more deeply tied to questions of family, sex, and miscegenation than they are to land and real estate. In Virginia-born Tom Wolfe's *A Man in Full*, the central character is a bombastic Atlanta real estate developer, and there is a conflict in which race is central, but the stories are perpendicular to each other. They overlap, but real estate development is not fundamental to racial relations. In Peter Matthiessen's trilogy about the settlement of the far Gulf Coast of Florida—*Killing Mister Watson* (1990), *Lost Man's River* (1997), and *Bone by Bone* (1999)—the tensions caused by real estate ambitions and racial relations are again independent. As explored in the next section of this book, racial tension is part of the background, but it is not central to the overweening ambitions of Ed Watson, who is driven fundamentally by "southern" pride rather than "western" ambition.

This difference among regions connects to the contrasting functions that the concept of a "Sunbelt" has served for different corners of the country.[28] The Southeast is imbued and burdened with its past. From William Faulkner, Robert Penn Warren, and William Styron to the present, writers dealing with the Southeast have struggled with the mythologies of Southern history. Echoing *Absalom, Absalom*, for example, Matthiessen's trilogy is about the way that history weighs on a descendent of Ed Watson, who discovers in turn how an earlier history shaped Watson himself. And the southeastern landscape frequently takes on the menace of history itself. Thick, knotted, dark, and dank, it is a place not merely of passive danger but of active menace. The tangled forest of William Faulkner's Mississippi (in "The Bear," for example) is a fictional counterpart to the Virginia wilderness than ensnared so many soldiers in blue and gray. The Everglades and its inhabitants both reach out to kill in Matthiessen's novels, and the jungle grows so rapidly over graves that it is virtually an accomplice in murder. Steamy southern Louisiana is just as menacing in James Lee Burke's novels of crime and moral decay: "The wake off the stern looked like a long V-shaped trench roiling with yellow mud, bobbing with dead logs. . . . I could see cottonmouths coiled on the lower limbs of willow trees, the gnarled brown-green head of a 'gator in a floating island of leaves and sticks, the stiffened, partly eaten body of a coon on a sandbar."[29]

In this context, the concept of a Sunbelt has been a tool for reversing or escaping history, a way for a "backward" region to reposition itself as up-to-date and cutting edge. Outside investment for the Southeast has been a tool of modernization, whether through northeastern industrial capital creating Birmingham and Miami, federal programs like TVA and NASA, headquarters relocating to Atlanta and Charlotte, northern retirees moving to Hilton Head and Fort Myers, or German branch plants in Spartanburg and Greenville. Investment through all three circuits of capital has driven the transformation from "the nation's number one economic problem" to the metropolitan Sunbelt South of the twenty-first century.

Yet history never goes away, even in the Sunbelt South—at least not in Walker Percy's novel *Love in the Ruins* (1971). Writing in the riot-ridden 1960s, Percy imagined a miniature apocalypse for suburban Louisiana at some time around the end of the twentieth century. Society continues to function, but things are falling apart and "the center did not hold." The Catholic Church has splintered. Southern states have established diplomatic ties with Rhodesia. Rusting Pontiacs dot the streets of half-abandoned Paradise Estates. Riots have left burned-out motels and shopping malls to be reclaimed by owls, alligators, and moccasins. "Beyond the cypresses, stretching away to the horizon, as misty as a southern sea, lies the vast Honey Island Swamp. . . . Yonder in the fastness of the swamp dwell the dropouts from and castoffs of and rebels against our society: ferocious black Bantus who use the wilderness both as a refuge and as a guerilla base from which to mount forays against outlying subdivisions and shopping malls." The protagonist's challenge is to come to terms with the limits of both individual and social action—with the burdens of sin and history.[30]

In the Southwest, "Sunbelt" has functioned differently, as an add-on and confirmation of an already powerful regional image that has emphasized the chance for Anglo-Americans to build communities from scratch. The fictions on which this essay has focused both confirm and contradict that image. They treat the landscape itself as entrancing but not actively menacing. It becomes dangerous only when people make foolish mistakes and get baked in the desert while trying to slip across the border or caught in floods exacerbated by the very real estate development from which they have been profiting. Even Topanga Canyon, for some of James Lee Burke's characters, is a refuge above the fray. It is a place where detective Dave Robicheaux can take his family after a particularly nasty case, in a landscape where "you could see almost every geological and floral characteristic of the American continent tumbling from the purple crest of the Santa Monica Mountains into the curling line of foam that slid up onto the beaches . . . and orange groves whose irrigation ditches looked like quicksilver in the sun's afterglow."[31] When you visit from south Louisiana, the landscape is as inspiring as it was once for Delaney Mossbacher.

As in Dave Robicheaux's view, southwestern landscapes and cityscapes are literally more visible than those of the Southeast. In the flatland forests and swamps of the Southeast, you are lucky to see fifty feet through the piney woods or around the next hummock. Atlanta suburbs nestle among forest remnants, shelter in convoluted terrain, and hide in the thick, humid air. In contrast, the Southwest is open, with its cities laid out for all to see from nearby mountains (think El Paso, Tucson, Phoenix, Albuquerque, Salt Lake City, Billings, San Jose, even smoggy Denver). Seeing the city from above is a common trope in writing about southwestern cities, with their open landscapes and (sometimes) clear air, used by writers as disparate as Ivor Winters and Simone de Beauvoir, Raymond Chandler and Cormac McCarthy.[32]

But the novels under consideration take their readers down from the mountains to the ravines, neighborhoods, and back alleys of the Sunbelt Southwest, where the seemingly empty landscapes are not empty at all. The novels remind us that contests over land and its uses remain central public issues in any region like the Southwest, where population is still growing and settlement is still in process. They were the meat of politics in the era of railroad land grants, mining booms, and court battles over Mexican land titles in the nineteenth century. They were the subtext for water allocation politics and conservation politics in the twentieth century. In the twenty-first century, they are the focus of growth management/property rights battles, environmental activism, and community development campaigns.

And in each century, the opportunities and rights of Indian and Hispanic residents have been at issue in the debates. No matter what nineteenth-century Americans imagined, the West was not vacant for the taking, and neither is the Southwest redefined as Sunbelt. What the novels show are the modern methods of dispossession. There is nothing as crude as the rampaging murderers of Cormac McCarthy's *Blood Meridian* (1985) when regional transformation is driven by real estate investors rather than scalp hunters. The novelists personalize that transformation in Kyra, Leah, and the other characters, but the ubiquity of real estate deals and dealing point up the power of the second circuit of capital as the modern Americanizing force. The town of Milagro wins a reprieve, not a permanent victory. In Albuquerque, even progressive mayor Marissa Martinez will end up pushing development plans—just not those of the old growth coalition. People will keep buying in the Los Angeles canyons despite fire and flood. Even Silko ends her novel with a vision of revolution but not its consummation. The battles are joined but not decided.

Notes

1. Page references to the four novels discussed in this essay are to the following editions: Rudolfo Anaya, *Albuquerque* (Albuquerque: University of New Mexico Press, 1992); T. Coraghessan Boyle, *The Tortilla Curtain* (New York: Viking, 1995); Leslie Marmon Silko, *Almanac of the Dead* (New York: Penguin, 1992); John Nichols, *The Milagro Beanfield War* (New York: Ballantine, 1996). I want to acknowledge the late Howard Rabinowitz, my predecessor as a history major at Swarthmore College and as a graduate

student of John Hope Franklin and Richard Wade at the University of Chicago. As a faculty member at the University of New Mexico, Howard delved deeply into the history of Albuquerque and taught us much of what we know about its recent development. He also introduced me to *The Milagro Beanfield War* sometime in the mid-1970s.

2. John E. Loftis, "Community as Protagonist in John Nichols' *The Milagro Beanfield War*," *Rocky Mountain Review of Language and Literature* 38, no. 4 (1984): 201–13.

3. One critic likens it to a spiderweb and another calls it a "web of quests." Caren Ire, "The Timeliness of *Almanac of the Dead*, or a Postmodern Rewriting of Radical Fiction" (239); Janet Powers, "Mapping the Prophetic Landscape in *Almanac of the Dead*" (263)—both in Louise K. Barnett and James L. Thorson, eds., *Leslie Marmon Silko: A Collection of Critical Essays* (Albuquerque: University of New Mexico Press, 1999).

4. These are not the only possibilities for this analytical approach. Real estate and its developers figure in novels of the Southwest that are as different as James Cain's noir melodrama *Mildred Pierce* (1941), Thomas Pynchon's extravagant fantasy *The Crying of Lot 49* (1966), and the Arizona-based mysteries of J. A. Jance. Real estate development also played a major role in novels from earlier eras as discussed in George Henderson, *California and the Fictions of Capital* (Philadelphia: Temple University Press, 1998).

5. For the claims that cities make on their environments, see Carl Abbott, "Land for Cities, Scenery for City People: Managing Urbanization in the American Grain," in James Foster and William Robbins, eds., *Land in the American West* (Seattle: University of Washington Press, 2001), 77–95.

6. Henri Lefebvre, *La Révolution urbaine* (1970), trans. *The Urban Revolution* (Minneapolis: University of Minnesota Press, 2003), and *La Production de l'espace* (1974), trans. *The Production of Space* (Cambridge: Blackwell, 1991). Lefebvre's ideas were adapted into English language theory by geographer David Harvey and have since been used and elaborated by many other critical sociologists. See Harvey, *The Urbanization of Capital: Studies in the History and Theory of Capitalist Urbanization* (Baltimore: Johns Hopkins University Press, 1985); Mark Gottdiener, "A Marx for Our Time: Henri Lefebvre and *The Production of Space*," *Sociological Theory* 11 (March 1993): 129–34, and *The Social Production of Urban Space* (Austin: University of Texas Press, 1985); Joe R. Feagin, "The Secondary Circuit of Capital," *International Journal of Urban and Regional Research* 11 (1987): 171–92, and *The New Urban Paradigm: Critical Perspectives on the City* (Lanham, Md.: Rowman and Littlefield, 1998).

7. The investments to enhance the productivity of human capital can be positive (education, social welfare programs, medical insurance) or negative (repression of labor organizations, inculcation of hegemonic value systems, imprisonment of criminals).

8. Lefebvre's work was part of an effort by European social theorists to update Marxist analysis to account for the revival of capitalist economies from the ruin of World War II. Jürgen Habermas, Manuel Castells, David Harvey, and others tried to formulate an intellectual foundation for progressive social action in the era of the German economic miracle, swinging England, and the general modernization of western Europe. In Lefebvre's case, his seminal *La Révolution urbaine* appeared two years after the political upheavals and failed rebellions of 1968. Even though the context for his work was far removed from the Sunbelt, his ideas have proved robust enough to be useful on both sides of the Atlantic.

9. Feagin, "Secondary Circuit of Capital," 186.

10. Tom Wolfe, *A Man in Full* (New York: Farrar Straus and Giroux, 1998); Jonathan Franzen, *The Twenty-Seventh City* (New York: Farrar Straus and Giroux, 1988).

11. "Vulturine" because corrupt Anglo and Mexican society thrives on death and its products both figuratively and literally—it is not a pleasant book.

12. "Ever since I learned how to drive the same year they invented cars," storms Onofre, "I been parking where I wanted to park and nobody ever made me pay money to do it . . . and I'll be goddamned if I'll start now" (59).

13. See Sharon Zukin, *Loft Living: Culture and Capital in Urban Change* (Baltimore: Johns Hopkins University Press, 1982); Neil Smith, *The New Urban Frontier: Gentrification and the Revanchist City* (New York: Routledge, 1996); Janet Abu-Lughod, ed., *From Urban Village to East Village: The Battle for New York's Lower East Side* (Cambridge: Blackwell, 1994).

14. John Nichols, "The Case for a Social Ecology," in *Dancing on the Stones: Selected Essays* (Albuquerque: University of New Mexico Press, 1993), 93.

15. Poor feckless Herbie is not really necessary to the novel, but he's lots of fun. In 1974, many of the novel's audience had just finished VISTA or Peace Corps stints or were considering them, and Herbie confirmed our worst nightmares about how we might appear in the communities we were sent to help.

16. The novel appeared at the same time as Robert Coles, *The Old Ones of New Mexico* (Albuquerque: University of New Mexico Press, 1973), which celebrated the cultural continuity and endurance of the rural people of Hispanic New Mexico.

17. One of the models for *The Tortilla Curtain* is Sinclair Lewis's 1922 novel *Babbitt*: Delaney Mossbacher and George F. Babbitt both deal in words as writer and real estate salesman; both are inordinately proud of their expensive automobiles; opening scenes take the reader through the wonders of the most up-to-date houses and neighborhood, with Arroyo Blanco Estates on its canyon rim as the latest version of Babbitt's Floral Heights on its rise overlooking Zenith; and each suffers a midlife crisis.

18. Richard Etulain, *Reimagining the Modern American West: A Century of Fiction, History, and Art* (Tucson: University of Arizona Press, 1996), 153.

19. "He was going to put Alburquerque on the map. . . . Create a city to rival Las Vegas" (59).

20. Katie Thomas, "Revival of a River Alters a City's Course in Sports," *New York Times*, April 22, 2008.

21. Silko wrote in the aftermath of the savings and loan crisis of the late 1980s, which hit Arizona particularly hard.

22. An insightful reading of the novel as prophetic manifesto is in William Katerberg, *Future West: Utopia and Apocalypse in Western Science Fiction* (Lawrence: University Press of Kansas, 2008). He places the book in the contexts of postfrontier fiction and utopian science fiction.

23. A multiracial group of veterans are also reclaiming the land by creating a camp on the outskirts of Tucson. El Feo believes that city people will easily identify true leaders because "true leaders would immediately seize all vacant apartments and houses to provide shelter for all the homeless" (524).

24. The standard narrative of the Los Angeles water system and its effects on the Owens Valley epitomizes this understanding. In the film *Chinatown*, even the orange groves are morally suspect because they are not planned to be permanent. I have not included the

film as a one of my texts because it is presented as historical fiction rather than a contemporary story.

25. We can also presume that the same pools of eastern and international capital that finance these fictional real estate developments (whether funneled through mafia rackets, the entertainment industry, or ordinary banks) also bought the state and corporate bonds that built real California prisons and Navajo reservation power plants.

26. Don DeLillo, *Underworld* (New York: Scribner's, 1997), 282.

27. Michael Logan, *Desert Cities: The Environmental History of Phoenix and Tucson* (Pittsburgh: University of Pittsburgh Press, 2006).

28. Carl Abbott, "New West, New South, New Region: The Discovery of the Sunbelt," in Raymond Mohl, ed., *Searching for the Sunbelt: Historical Perspectives on a Region* (Knoxville: University of Tennessee Press, 1990), 7–24.

29. James Lee Burke, *In the Electric Mist with Confederate Dead* (New York: Avon, 1994), 182–83.

30. Walker Percy, *Love in the Ruins: The Adventures of a Bad Catholic at a Time near the End of the World* (1971; reprint, New York: Picador, 1999), 15, 18. Percy presents his ideas about sin and history within a social satire, trying not to be self-righteous about his serious messages.

31. Burke, *In the Electric Mist*, 369.

32. Examples come from Ivor Winters, "A View of Pasadena from the Hills," Simone de Beauvoir, *America Day by Day*, Raymond Chandler, *The Little Sister*, and Cormac McCarthy, *Cities of the Plain*.

CHAPTER 2

Imagining Portland's Urban Growth Boundary

Planning Regulation as Cultural Icon

with Joy Margheim

In 1973, the Oregon legislature passed Senate Bill 100, enacting into law a comprehensive requirement and system for local land-use planning throughout the state. Six years later, the Council of the Metropolitan Service District, a recently established regional government, implemented one required element of the state planning system by adopting and enacting an Urban Growth Boundary that encircled substantial portions of three counties in the Portland metropolitan area, amounting to 229,000 acres in 1979 and since expanded to 259,000 acres. Friends and opponents soon familiarized the planning boundary as the UGB.

Fast-forward more than a quarter century to a scattering of days in 2005. Participants in the annual conference of the National Trust for Historic Preservation are finishing a tour of key points inside and outside the boundary with the guidance of metro public relations staff. Law professor Alafair Burke is depositing the first royalty check for her mystery novel *Missing Justice*, whose plot pivots on efforts to influence the location of UGB expansion. Nature writer David Oates is completing a circuit of the entire 260-mile boundary and thinking about the final sections of his book *City Limits: Walking Portland's Boundary*. San Francisco artist and planning activist Jeannene Przyblyski is re-enacting the Urban Growth Boundary through a combination of performance art and art installation that she calls "The Urban Growth Boundary Trail."[1]

What's going on here? What are *artists* doing with the UGB? Why should they care? What does it mean to them and to the audiences of their work? This chapter discusses a wide range of examples in which the UGB has been treated as something more than a regulation—as a symbol, metaphor, and touchstone. The following sections reintroduce the UGB as part of a statewide planning system and then explore the increasingly complex ways in which people have tried to describe, understand, and interpret the UGB as an element of everyday lives and landscapes. We explore the contrasts between official and unofficial descriptions, the utilization of positive and negative metaphors, the growing body of depictions of the UGB in poetry, photography, and painting, and finally the incorporation of the UGB into performance art. We conclude with some comparisons to the treatment of other planning icons and suggestions about implications for planning practice.

Portland and Its Urban Growth Boundary

Politicians and planners conceived and created the UGB as part of a comprehensive, government-mandated program for systematizing land-use planning for all 96,981 square miles of Oregon—rocky coastal headlands and lonely beaches, bountiful orchards and vineyards in the valleys between coastal mountains and Cascade volcanoes, long miles of central Oregon sagebrush and juniper flats, small cities like Pendleton and Klamath Falls, big cities like Portland and Eugene and their surrounding communities (fig. 2.1). In broad perspective, it is part of a modern effort to bring order and predictability to land-use changes by setting statewide priorities and charging experts and government officials with implementing these priorities.

Within the Oregon planning system, Urban Growth Boundaries are one of the tools for implementing Goal 14: Urbanization, whose purpose is formally defined

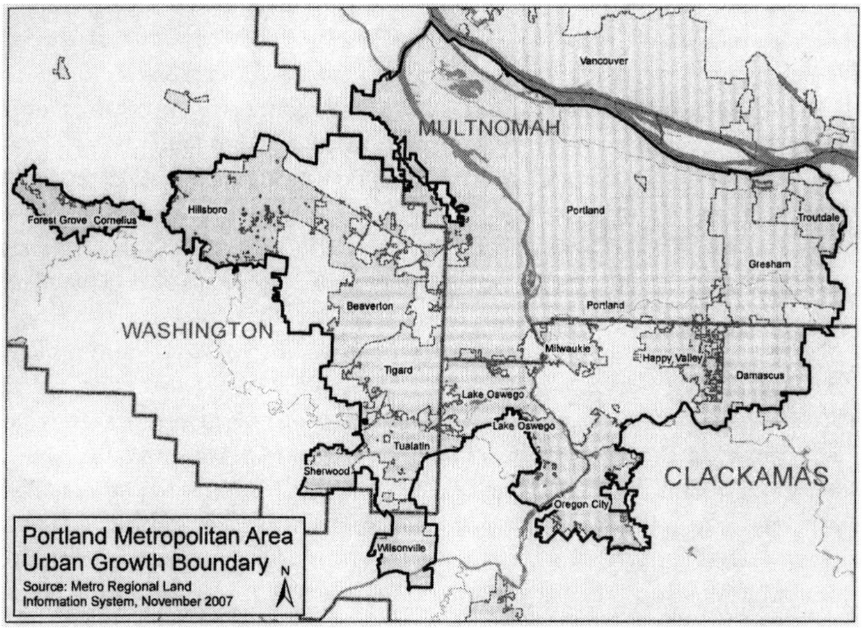

FIG 2.1. The Portland Urban Growth Boundary. First delineated in 1979, the Urban Growth Boundary for the Portland metropolitan area has been incrementally expanded in the following decades but still maintains its basic shape. (Courtesy of the Oregon Metro Data Center, www.oregonmetro.gov)

as follows: "To provide for an orderly and efficient transition from rural to urban land use." The goal continues with "urban growth boundaries shall be established to identify and separate urbanizable from rural land." Initial boundary decisions and changes, slightly paraphrasing from the official language, are to be based on (1) demonstrated need to accommodate long-term population growth; (2) needs for housing, employment, and livability; (3) orderly and efficient provision of public services; (4) maximum efficiency of land uses; (5) environmental, economic, and social consequences; (6) retention of high-value agricultural land; and (7) compatibility of urban uses with agricultural uses.

UGBs simplify land-use patterns by, fundamentally, dividing land into two rationally determined categories. The state requires a UGB around every freestanding municipality of any size and around every complex of contiguous cities, such as those of the Portland metropolitan area. Inside the boundary, the default assumption is that land that can be efficiently supplied with public services will be developed. Outside the boundary, hopefully, is environmentally sensitive land and productive farm and forest land. Here the baseline is to allow no further intensive development without very good reason. There is A land and B land, urban land and nonurban land, future metropolis and continuing countryside.

This is not to imply that UGBs are impermeable and static. Like many comprehensive schemes, the Oregon system of UGBs has its Ptolemaic epicycles, with variations such as "exception lands" and "urban reserves" to account for special situations. Development does occur outside the boundaries—in small amounts under the planning regime in place from 1978 to 2005 and potentially in larger amounts under the impacts of a series of property rights measures passed by Oregon voters. Metro is required to maintain a twenty-year inventory of developable land within the boundary. The result is periodic expansion after extensive study and political debate, such as the addition of 21,168 acres of residential and industrial land in three increments in 2002–2005 and 2,018 acres in 2011.

Many elements combine in making Portland a somewhat peculiar sort of city, including a regional sense of place and many other public decisions, but the UGB is a focal point of attention. By helping to keep the metropolitan region compact, it centers energy on downtown Portland and the inner neighborhoods that give Portland its unusual character.[2] The presence of farm and forest land relatively close to the city center enriches lives of city dwellers through opportunities for recreation, fresh food, and reminders of the importance of traditional economic activities. Along with housing demand generated by steady net in-migration since the late 1980s, the boundary supports the real estate market in early twentieth-century streetcar suburbs that have been recycled for new generations. As novelist Burke has one of her characters put it, "The city's strong neighborhood feel is what makes this place special, and those neighborhoods would be gone now if not for Metro."[3]

The UGB is also a target for critics who dislike its effect on land markets.[4] By artificially constraining the supply of buildable land, they argue, the UGB inflates land values and thereby raises the cost of both new and existing housing. In support, the critics cite data on rapid increases in land and housing prices. Supporters counter that housing price increases are demand driven and point to similar or higher rates of real estate inflation in cities without growth boundaries. Critics protest the unfairness of dividing metropolitan area landowners into speculative winners and losers, an argument that helped to persuade Oregon voters in 2004 to adopt Measure 37, a property rights measure that exempted a subset of property owners from UGB restriction by allowing them to claim the right to develop according to the regulations in effect at the time they acquired title or else to be compensated for lost value.[5]

Portland certainly is not the only city that has experienced neighborhood revitalization or that enjoys an increasingly lively downtown, and the UGB has obviously functioned within a set of national trends that have anticipated and reinforced its effects. Nevertheless, one reason it has received so much attention is because Portland is a city where discussion of planning issues in general is a busy industry that employs local journalists and university professors and brings in outside money through a continuous stream of visiting experts and junketeers. Portland has become an icon for a particular approach to urban and regional planning, walking (and biking and light-railing) the talk of compact growth. It is described as bikeable, clean, polite, sustainable, enlightened. For many observers it is an example of possibility, a demonstration that Americans can change the way that they build their cities. Other commentators are, quite frankly, fed up with hearing "Portland, Portland, Portland" held up as a challenge like a metropolitan Stakhanovite. They find its downtown too artificial, too precious, too cute to be true, too *Scandinavian*.[6] They find its planning regulations an example of excessive bureaucratization that ignores market realities and gives the cold shoulder to business.

In one interpretive framework that we find useful, Metro and the UGB display many of the characteristics of modern government that anthropologist James Scott has identified as "seeing like a state." One of the characteristics of the modern state is to impose cognitive order on its people and resources in order to better manage and direct them. Since the dawning years of the modern era, this has included the development of summary quantitative data through national censuses and statistical agencies. It has included systematic mapping of landscapes according to precise grids, whether in Britain, in British India, in Canada, or in the United States, through the national land survey and state and federal geological surveys. It has meant the development of comprehensive, top-down plans and development schemes: Brasilia and Cuidad Guyana, five-year plans, big dams for big rivers from the Columbia and Tennessee to the Nile and Yangtze. Metro is part of the state apparatus (both an agency of the state of Oregon and an embodiment of the "state" as abstract political force), and the UGB is clearly an example of the modernist impulse to govern through generalization.

But interestingly, this modernist land-use regulation has experienced a postmodern apotheosis: it has become a text! People read complex meanings into the UGB that go beyond its simple legal function. They try to capture and claim its essence through metaphors, depict it in paintings and photography, write poems about it (texts about a text), and interpret it through performance. This is curious. The world is full of land-use planning boundaries embedded in zoning codes and environmental regulations. As political boundaries go, land-use demarcations are mild or limited in their effects. They influence the value of land by constraining possible types of development and, indirectly, impact the social character of neighborhoods. Unlike state and national boundaries, however, they don't limit the flow of goods in interstate and global commerce, separate different regimes of taxation and representation, limit migration, or define citizenship with all its potential to control life and death. We are not surprised that the Berlin Wall is a fraught and powerful text or that the Ohio River plays a key role as Eliza flees from slavery to freedom in *Uncle Tom's Cabin*. At the other end of the scale, however, we are also not surprised that artists and novelists have found little occasion to place land-use boundaries at the center of their work. We live and work inside and across land use boundaries, but we seldom *see* them. This is not to say that we don't see the effects of land-use boundaries in dividing rich from poor or white from black. However, zoning lines, school boundaries, and the like are commonly unnoticed as things in themselves—only noticeable when they directly affect household choices. In contrast, people notice and talk about the UGB even when it is not impacting them directly and personally.

Adjectives, Synonyms, and Metaphors

One way we make sense of our surroundings is through comparison. New things become legible or comprehensible when we can define their similarities to older, familiar things. We live in a cloud of synonyms, similes, metaphors, and analogies. When we move to a new city, we look for features and places that evoke the place we left behind. When we think about foreign policy, we try to decide if the American involvement in Iraq is more like the war in Vietnam, the police action in Korea, or World War II. We are no different about the Urban Growth Boundary, stretching language to make the unfamiliar understandable.

As an official regulation the UGB is neutral, gray, unexciting. It is part of the background noise of modern life, blending with thousands of other rules and regulations that oil the machinery of society. Metro's website describes the UGB as "a legal boundary separating urban from rural land; one of the tools used to protect farms and forest from urban sprawl and to promote the efficient use of land, public facilities and services within the boundary." Given that it is legally framed, it is no surprise that the depiction of the UGB as a neutral instrument appears repeatedly in Metro documents and in descriptions by planning advocates and academics: it is variously a "management device," a "policy mechanism," and then again . . . and again . . . and again . . . a "tool." It is a "long-term management tool," "a flexible growth management tool," and "an important tool in managing urban growth."[7]

A tool is neutral in itself. A socket wrench incites little emotional response. A chainsaw acquires political and cultural meaning only as it is used to cut down forests or shape yard sculpture. "Management" is equally neutral, a term that highlights the tasks of keeping an institution or process heading in an established direction. It accords with the official nonpartisan character of the elected Metro Council. It also highlights the fact that professional planners at Metro and elsewhere put tens of thousands of person-hours into decisions about UGB enforcement and expansion. Presentation of the UGB as a management tool directs attention from content to process, to the little decisions and adjustments through which the uses of land are planned and controlled. No one gets upset about a vegetable strainer or empathizes with a toaster, and the same might hold of the growth boundary.

We suspect that the "management tool" description is frequently used because it seems a logical, accurate description to officials, planners, and commentators who are steeped in the incremental character of contemporary American land-use planning. There is no deliberate scheme to distract the public, simply the natural language choices of professionals who are trained and skilled in the interpretation and application of specific planning regulations. Metro is itself a somewhat gray and anonymous agency for which neutral language seems appropriate. It makes the news when it asks voters to fund regional open space purchases and when it debates UGB expansion but otherwise generates few headlines compared to feuding county commissioners, publicity-eager city council members, battling legislators, and embattled governors. Even its building, which occupies a relatively prominent location, bears little external identification and can be intimidating to first-time visitors. David Oates comments on the building as indicative of Metro's anonymity: "When approaching Metro headquarters from Grand Avenue (as most citizens do), one sees not a hint of what this thing is. . . . You can't find the entrance until you're directly in front of it." We can infer that the agency is happy to be seen as the keeper of a "growth management tool."[8]

A second common choice, especially in newspaper writing, is to describe the UGB as invisible. It is an "invisible line," an "invisible map," and an "imaginary line." To call the UGB imaginary and invisible is to make it simultaneously neutral *and* mysterious. The terms deserve some scrutiny, for many other political boundaries are equally "invisible" where they do not utilize natural seams in the landscape like rivers or mountain crests. Oregon's boundary with Washington for much of its distance is the mighty and very visible Columbia River, but the boundary with California is visible only along highways where the route markers change and "Welcome to . . ." signs promote tourism. Yet reporters don't write about state boundaries as imaginary and invisible, let alone the physically inconspicuous boundary between the western United States and western Canada. The UGB, in fact, is very clearly visible at some points on the landscape, although not others, as we explore in the following sections. What the trope of invisibility emphasizes is less the UGB's trace on the landscape than the technical planning processes and regulatory language through which it is defined and implemented.

One of the easiest ways to make the unostentatious UGB more understandable or "visible" is to use more vivid metaphors and analogies than "tool." Such linguistic tactics have been mobilized both by opponents and supporters but seldom by the bureaucrats and policy specialists who work directly with the UGB.

Skeptics have frequently turned the "invisible line" into a "wall" or even a "Great Wall of Portland."[9] It is "restrictive" to real estate development and an "obstacle" to expansion of the area's employment base.[10] Early opponents tried out "girdle" and "corset" to undercut growth boundaries with gender-loaded ridicule.[11] More recently the UGB has been called a "red line," a term that carries thick connotations of housing discrimination and racist inequality for specialists in urban planning and housing.[12] Even Anthony Flint, an advocate of Portland planning, recently called it "a line in the sand," a phrase with implications of belligerent confrontations and face-offs.[13]

Favorably disposed commentators, in contrast, sometimes reach across the Atlantic for comparisons (perhaps inspired by frequent remarks about the "European" feel of central Portland). The entire planning approach may be characterized as a "European-style mandate." The comparisons are to highly favored urban models. The UGB is thus said to create a "greenbelt" like the famous plan for London after World War II, even though it gets to the result by a very different regulatory route.[14] Coming upon points where urbanized land inside the UGB gives way abruptly to farms, others reach back to the tightly circumscribed and bounded cities of Renaissance Italy. The metropolitan edge is "as sharply delineated in many places as the edge of a fortified hill town in medieval Italy," writes design commentator Suzanne Lessard.[15] And in another way to score points in Portland, there is always the option to play the "not California" card, for the UGB stops sprawl "in its tracks" and prevents Oregon from repeating the experience of California suburbanization.[16]

Alternatively, there is the option, the one we prefer, of using an organic metaphor in which the UGB is a skin. An animal's skin beneficially contains and confines the vital functions of the organism but expands as the creature grows and matures. Similarly, the UGB is designed by statute to expand gradually as the metropolis grows. David Oates suggests that it is "a skin, a limit, a way to distinguish self from not-self . . . a way for a newish western town to assert that it indeed has an identity: that it knows where it ends and what it is."[17] Those with a literary bent might liken Portland to Italo Calvino's "invisible city" of Olinda, which grows like a tree in concentric circles.[18]

The Art of Contrast

When Metro employees or local planning experts take visitors to see the Portland UGB, the point of the tour is to counter the "invisibility" of the line by demonstrating its impacts on the ground. As a regulatory measure, the purpose of the UGB is to create a bifurcated real estate market in which "inside land" has higher value than "outside land," limiting both opportunities and pressures for the profitable sale and redevelopment of outside parcels. Its effectiveness has been well documented and was certainly one of the several factors behind the recent electoral and legislative battles over property rights versus planning.[19] Tours visit points where the contrast is most visible, with fields on one side and buildings on the other. There are some perennial favorites. One is a district in the northwestern suburbs where houses butt up on wheat fields, another is an area in the southwest side where suburbanization has been drawing a ring around a still rural valley, a third is a dead-ended suburban street where a traffic barricade fortifies the woods against further sprawl. Tours also spotlight protected open space and thriving farms outside the line. Such a choice to visit places where the UGB is least likely to expand emphasizes its firmness as a dividing line rather than its legally established flexibility—one of the tensions between the UGB as an icon and as a regulation. When urban policy author David Rusk visited Portland in 1996, for example, a pair of planning academics carefully took him to Sauvie Island, prime farmland along the Columbia River and just outside the growth boundary. Crossing the arching concrete bridge from mainland to island, writes Rusk, "We had a brief, panoramic view of what had become of Sauvie Island. It was still farmland stretching as far as we could see. . . . Gazing across fields and orchards we could see downtown Portland's tallest buildings to the south and Mount Hood etched sharply against the eastern horizon."[20]

The point is not that there is a divide, for every territorial entity has to end somewhere. It is more specific: Portland, without the physical constraints that have tended to keep a desert city like Las Vegas or an oasis community like Salt Lake City compact, has an urban form with *marked* edges. It does not feather out into its surroundings in the fractal pattern characteristic of Atlanta or Philadelphia. Instead, it grows incrementally from the center outward in a way that is easy to map and see.

Ann Altman's painting "Urban Growth Boundary" is a visual encapsulation of the typical tour. The viewer of the picture stands with boots planted in furrowed fields, looking across a foreground of plowed land and row crops. A road runs horizontally across the middle of the scene. Beyond the road, a line of houses sets the skyline. The artist is based in Silverton, Oregon, a small town closer to

Salem than to Portland, and the title does not explicitly identify the scene as Portland's UGB. The character of the landscape and the depiction of contrast however, make it applicable to any of the Willamette Valley cities.

The content of the scene itself does not necessarily suggest permanence or finality, and someone seeing the picture out of context might think the artist to be showing Indianapolis advancing across cornfields. Taken together, however, the title and the visual balance of the picture help viewers see the road as a dividing line rather than a connecting seam that stitches town and field together. Aspects of the composition give a sense of permanence and firmness. The colors are rich, heavy, autumnal reds, browns, blues, and greens—a bit like the palette of Georges Rouault. Oregon planners have taken to the picture as a representation of their work, displaying copies in a number of planning offices around Oregon and in one instance even adapting it as a screen saver.[21]

The same scene in Yalcin Erhan's photograph "Linda at Cedar Hills" (fig. 2.2) carries even stronger implications of permanence. Dancer and performance artist Linda K. Johnson in 1999 set up camp for thirty-six-hour stints at six different points on the growth boundary, living in a tent supplied with a TV set and Martha Stewart dishes and bedding. We say more about her experiences in the

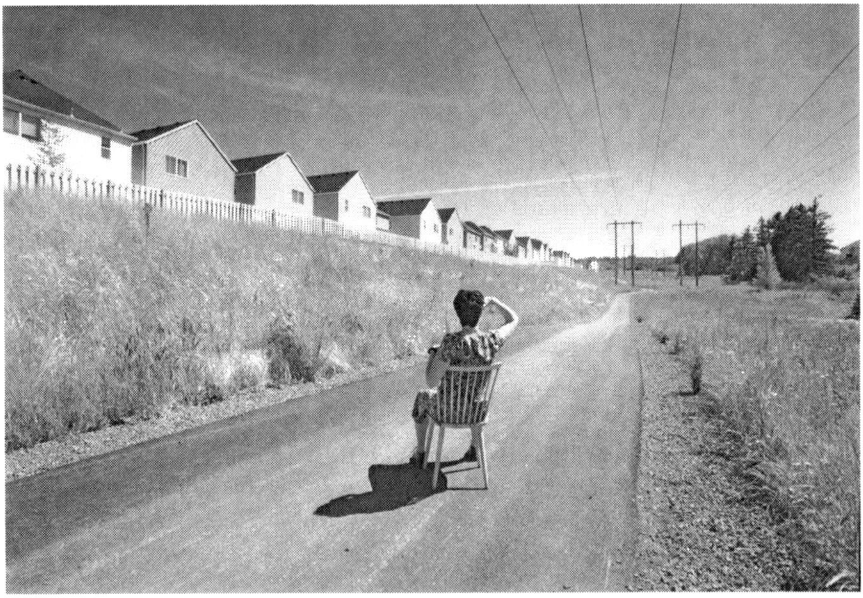

Fig. 2.2. Linda K. Johnson at Cedar Hills. This photograph by Yalcin Erhan shows dance artist Linda K. Johnson at the western edge of the Portland Urban Growth Boundary. Her visit there was part of a multiday performance art project to explore the role of the UGB in shaping residents' understandings of the metropolitan area. (Used by permission of Linda K. Johnson and Yalcin Erhan)

following section, but this and several other pictures of her "finding, marking and living on the line" quickly became icons that help give tangible form to the invisible line. Several of the photographs are now part of the Visual Chronicle of Portland, a program of the Regional Arts and Culture Council that each year acquires a number of paintings, woodcuts, drawings, and photographs that portray aspects of the metropolitan area.

"Linda at Cedar Hills" shows Johnson seated in a chair that is planted squarely in the middle of a road. She sits with her back to us, precisely at the divide between urban and rural, peering into the distance. To her right is farmland. Perhaps fifty feet to her left are the back fences and back elevations of a subdivision. Her eyes, and ours, follow the straight lines of field, road, overhead power lines, fencing, and houses as they all dwindle and converge in the distance like a textbook illustration of perspective. The fences are a signifier of permanence as well as difference, while the message of the whole composition is one of scale: the UGB goes on forever and lasts forever; it is a permanent and defining feature in a landscape of contrasts. The UGB is also quintessentially modern in this scene—totalizing, unsubtle, and expressed in a form that harkens back to the origins of modern Western art in the work of the Italian Renaissance.

Poet Judith Berck has also embedded the visual and conceptual contrasts of the UGB in "Driving Portland's Urban Growth Boundary."[22]

> Left side of the road stands a skeleton,
> steel beams in a big box, every second another bolt for strength, going up
> a building for minds that build machines for minds
> propped up by much yen and a thousand white-shirted hopes.
> Right side of the road a skeleton still stands, brown rotted beams at all angles,
> closer to earth after every storm, going down
> pressing against tall grasses,
> once a house for mares, black goats and a summer's worth of hay.
> You can see through the ribs to filbert trees and asparagus bolted wild,
> pushed into earth by hands and now skeletons.
> I drive between receding and arriving.

The poem offers a nested set of contrasts. The objects that the poem describes—old barn and new factory or office building—are caught in the same physical state, one because siding has peeled off to reveal beams and rafters, the other because walls have yet to be attached to a steel frame. The landscapes that face across the road are the familiar contrast of urban and rural, metal beams and bolts on one side, tall grass and bolted asparagus on the other. They also embody a dynamic, historical contrast between past and future as well as the spatial contrast of inside/outside. The poet sets the old farm economy against new electronics industry, entropy against construction, black goats in contrast to white shirts (reading black as a color of death or ending). She drives between "receding and arriving"—that is, in the midst of difference conceived in terms of temporal change. It is possible to embody this temporal contrast between life and death because the UGB is a physical marker of differences between the old farming economy and the new electronics industry.

Performing the Boundary

The art of contrast, by offering snapshots of particular places and points in time, overstates the permanence of the UGB, which is designed to expand over time. Even though tours of the UGB "perform" the boundary in a narrow sense, we included them in the previous section because a tour uses a set script or set of goals, conveys information in one direction, and shows the boundary at a single moment in time. Other ways to perform the boundary, however, have invited "audience" participation and dialogue around the balance between permanence and change.

One of the first instances of performing or enacting the boundary came with the "Spanning Boundaries" project of Orlo, a Portland-based environmental organization that has tried to use the arts to raise environmental issues and public awareness since the early 1990s. It publishes the nationally distributed magazine *Bear Deluxe* and has mounted a number of exhibits and public art installations, many of them easily described as irreverent or offbeat.[23] In 1999, Orlo sponsored "Spanning Boundaries," a project in which four different artists or artist teams created site-specific art at points along the UGB, followed by an exhibit at the Pacific Northwest College of Art. In its call to artists, Orlo stated, "The Urban Growth Boundary can be viewed, experienced, intellectualized, conceptualized, and perceived as a finite measurable line, a known quantity that is highly specific. Likewise, the urban growth boundary can be thought of as a less tangible, more abstract place that partially determines how we live and how closely we live together. . . . There are numerous ways to examine the UGB: analytically, metaphorically, abstractly, intellectually, politically."[24]

Two of the resulting projects were sculptural installations, one a rammed earth structure designed to melt over time in Oregon rains and the other a surveyor's grid laid over park land. A third was an imaginary subdivision intended to illustrate the choices and tensions involved in land development decisions (created by artists who were living adjacent to the boundary). The fourth artist was Linda Johnson, who described her proposal as an effort to make the abstract boundary meaningful by living overnight in a portable "home" at several different sites on the line. By making something of everyday life happen on the boundary, she wanted to create opportunities for citizens to "become reflective and form more experience-based opinions as the abstract has become real—the intended has materialized."[25]

Johnson soon discarded what might easily have become an ironic stance for interactive conversation. She replaced her specialized choreography with straightforward chats with visitors, pulling opinions from yuppies, school kids, construction workers, and architects. Out of the resulting "suburban still life" came new, complex understandings of the way that the UGB has affected "every single solitary aspect of the way we live . . . traffic, education, taxes, our desires about housing and architecture." For Johnson—and for many other Portlanders—the growth boundary has become "a different viewfinder to see the city through."[26]

A few years later, San Franciscan Jeannene Przyblyski offered a variation on performing the boundary. An art historian who specializes in the visual culture of nineteenth-century France, taught at the San Francisco Art Institute, and sat on the board of the San Francisco Planning and Urban Research Association, Przyblyski is also the guiding spirit behind the San Francisco Bureau of Urban Secrets. The bureau is a flexible, informal effort "to hook artists up with the city in direct and concrete ways" through installations and performance.[27] One example was a neighborhood-scale chess game performed by residents, another was a "Topographies" project about the San Francisco cityscape, a third is "urban essence," a perfume that tries to capture the smell of San Francisco.

In 2005, she came to Portland to create the "Urban Growth Boundary Trail" as part of an exhibit on "Monument Recall: Public Memory and Public Spaces" at Portland's Marylhurst University (fig. 2.3).[28] The brochure for the "Trail" highlights the differences between places inside and outside the boundary and the character of points on the line itself, thus mimicking the standard official tour. However, it democratized the tour by making it self-guiding and politicized it by referencing the potential effects of Measure 37 and the need to "landmark these urban wonders, thereby preserving them for future generations." A second change from the official tour is to illustrate the sites with photographs of "UGB trail trekkers," actual Portlanders caught by Przyblyski's camera while hiking, biking, waiting for a light rail train, and hanging out at the various sites—performing the UGB through their example. A third difference is to challenge trail trekkers to think of the UGB and the urban landscape as a "dreamscape" of multiple possibilities—and to help them along with ironic and sometimes fictional text (Multnomah County didn't really try to secede from Oregon).

Przyblyski approached the UGB with a simple question: "As an outsider, I just wondered if you could 'see' the UGB." And, she comments, "Turns out you can." One of her larger concerns was to understand how something that is not a building gets identified as a historic resource, thinking here about the nineteenth-century Oregon Trail, which she had recently retraced.[29] Noting the uncertain planning climate created by Measure 37, the UGB Trail brochure says that "the UGB Trail Conservancy (an agency of the San Francisco Bureau of Urban Secrets) has moved to landmark these wonders [planning accomplishments], thereby preserving them for future generations." It highlights a mix of sites. Some are locations are at the edge of the UGB where the boundary is physically visible. Others are close-in locations like Pioneer Courthouse Square and

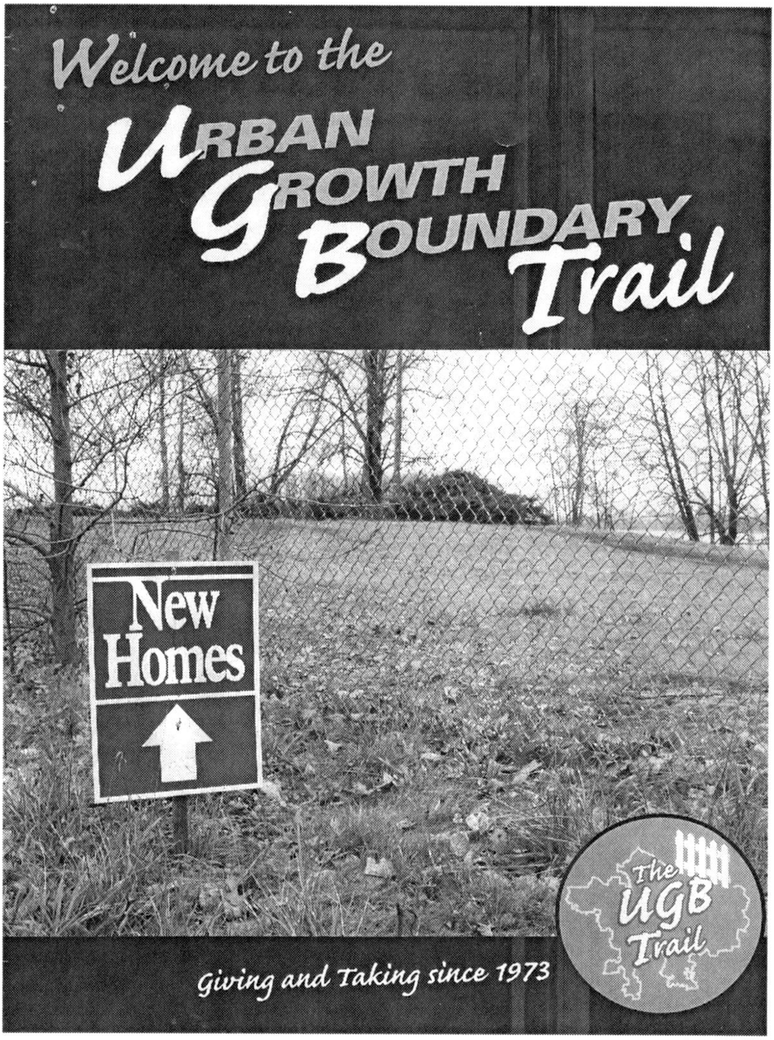

FIG. 2.3. Cover of "Urban Growth Boundary Trail" brochure. The brochure opens to a map that identifies fifteen points at which to view the UGB or contemplate its impact on the landscape. (Used by permission of Jeannene Prysklyski)

Tom McCall Waterfront Park that epitomize the vitality of the compact metropolis. Still others are sites where trails and boundaries have social and historic overtones—one that represents the history of racial segregation, another that marks the end of the historic Oregon Trail, a third that speaks to the dispossession of Native Americans, and a fourth that acknowledges the political nature of planning. The latter is the headquarters of the property rights group Oregonians in Action, identified also as "Future Site of the End of the UGB Trail Interpretive

Center," a tongue-in-cheek reference to the very real End of the Oregon Trail Interpretive Center in suburban Oregon City.

Our last example is writer David Oates, who performed and re-enacted the UGB at the onset of the twenty-first century by walking or kayaking the entire boundary over a span of twenty-six months, looking for contrasts of both place and people. He wrote up his observations and musings as *City Limits: Walking Portland's Boundary*. Much of the text is a physical description of the UGB landscape as it traces streams, cuts through blackberry brambles, follows roads, and divides busy from slow. The UGB for Oates is variously a mystery, a project, and a magic line. It is also a text for talking about the future, "our attempt to agree on how to live."[30]

Oates makes the conversation explicit in two ways. Like Linda Johnson, he talked with people he met along the boundary and reports on their reactions. He also invited a series of companions to share portions of his walk and to contribute short reflections. The companions included nature writers like William Ashworth, Ana Maria Spagna, and Kathleen Dean Moore, civic leaders like Metro executive David Bragdon and public relations specialist Gary Conkling, progressive business owners like builder David Hassim and winemaker Eric Lemelson. Out of the various conversations and comments, he sees residents trying to "see ourselves as a community, and to decide, collaboratively, what that meant."[31]

Regulation and Text

In 2007, Portlander-in-exile Ian Doescher produced an album of songs about contemporary Portland. Doescher grew up in Portland but found himself on the other side of the country pursuing a Ph.D. at Union Theological Seminary in New York. The songs are an exercise in upbeat and ironic homesickness that may, he hopes, help generate enough money to return to Portland.[32] They skewer several aspects of contemporary Portland, including transportation planning in "My Name Is MAX," the downtown housing boom in "Pearl Girl (She's Too Hip for Me)," and Portland's monster bookstore in "Lost in Powell's." The one that interests us most is "Urban Growth Boundaries Can't Stop My Love (I'll Go out to Gresham for You)." The song itself is about the divide between close-in Portland neighborhoods that are increasingly filled with cool young adults and the supposedly boring, middle-class suburbs to the east ("I tried not to cringe when you wrote: 'Let's meet today in Troutdale.'"). What is interesting for this discussion, however, is the way in which the UGB has become a familiar part of the metroscape that evokes both a sense of contrast and a sense of "Portlandness."[33]

To pursue the last point, Doescher's song is one of several examples of the way that artists have familiarized and humanized the UGB—and land-use planning more generally—by embedding it in the consciousness of everyday life.

Something of the same thing happened with Jeannene Przyblyski's part of the Monument Recall exhibit. Visitors especially liked the take-away buttons that showed a UGB outline with a section of picket fence superimposed.[34] The inclusion of a picket fence connected the abstract boundary to everyday landscapes, while the wearable button brought the abstraction down to human scale. The conversations that Linda Johnson and David Oates sparked with their visits to the boundary had the same effect of engaging individual discussion and showing the UGB as something that ordinary people talk about in interesting ways.

As Portland's Urban Growth Boundary has taken on an "imaginative identity" in addition to the legal identity codified in legislation, administrative rules, and court decisions, it has also become a part of the city's sense of itself. As the regulation has become a text, it has become part of the mental imagery by which observers and residents understand a regional sense of place. As outside observer Suzanne Lessard writes, "The city set in the countryside represents an idea, a choice, and a powerful, sustained political effort." Metro executive David Bragdon agrees that it is perhaps "better appreciated as a symbol than it is for its functional value—though the functional value of the UGB is very high indeed."[35] The UGB and the discussion that it generates help new arrivals in Portland learn something about the interconnected goals, policies, and processes that support the city's livability. It is regional and holistic, and, in that sense, it is visible as a symbol of much more complex and interconnected values.

A regulation has a single, formalized meaning that can only be negotiated through the formal processes of litigation and, in the specific case of the UGB, Metro's legislatively mandated procedures for boundary expansion. As a regulation, the UGB is technically and politically polarizing. Land is either inside or outside. Legislators tinker with it to please one set of constituents or another. Voters have repeatedly had to vote yes or no on measures to undercut the Oregon planning system, in effect giving the UGB and related regulations a vote of confidence or no-confidence. As a regulation, in short, the UGB is an expression of modernity. Clear, crisp, decisive, and comprehensive, it satisfies the taste for classification.

As a text, however, the UGB is an opportunity for conversation and interpretation from multiple perspectives. The multiple efforts to re-enact and interpret the boundary are postmodern in their indeterminacy and in their potential for bringing to the surface previously unheard voices and points of view. In other words, it is a "viewfinder" in Linda Johnson's terminology. A viewfinder is a device for zeroing in on an object or topic, but the word also suggests that the UGB is an opportunity to discover or find multiple views about the region's future. Metaphorically, the UGB as viewfinder is an opportunity for residents to discover and explore their own opinions—views—about the future of the metropolitan area.

Portland has been a relatively easy place for a regulation to turn into a text because residents talk and think about planning and land-use questions more than most American metropolites. Coverage is thick and detailed in the region's print media. Land-use questions are the most frequent issue for Portland's one-hundred-odd neighborhood associations and a common topic for civic organizations. Even the slick but interesting lifestyle magazine *Portland Monthly* has taken up the UGB conversation in a piece where one of the editors interviewed a variety of residents living near the boundary, including farmers—who do not want to be pressured one way or the other—and householders—who like the idea of a hard UGB that preserves *their* rural backyard just fine. "It is still at the edges where the debate over the urban growth boundary is being contested with the great sense of urgency," the editor wrote. "Because what happens at the edge remains at the center of the debate about the Portland area's future."[36] Novelist Alafair Burke comments that discussion of the UGB was in the air while she lived in Portland: "So when thinking about the kind of political/white collar plot I wanted for *Missing Justice*, the UGB sprang right to mind. It allowed me to be specific . . . much more interesting than some generic scheme cut from whole cloth. Even better, it was unique to Portland." So she is right on target when she has one character comment: "So you *must* know that Metro is talking about expanding the urban growth boundary," and her protagonist muse in response says, "Anywhere else in the country, that statement would sound a little like *You must know that Spock's Starfleet service number was S179-276*. But to people who live in my city, the urban growth boundary is the secret ingredient in Portland's warm gooey cinnamon bun."[37]

It is not often that a planning regulation takes on an intellectual life of its own. Many American planning icons are architectural renderings of possible cityscapes (such as the McMillan Committee plan for Washington, D.C.). Others are comprehensive, utopian maps for possible metropolitan forms, from Olmsted's park plans to the multitude of recent 2020, 2030, and 2040 schemes for various metropolitan regions.[38] These are the sorts of visuals, for example, that fill Peter Calthorpe and William Fulton's widely read book *The Regional Metropolis*.[39] The UGB is different because it crosses the boundaries of technical planning to enter different imaginative and symbolic realms.

This is not to say that it is unique. Daniel Burnham's 1909 plan for Chicago was a plan, a set of stunning visual renderings, and for many years a literal text, taught in Chicago schools in the form of *Wacker's Manual of the Plan of Chicago*.[40] Certainly "redlining" has evolved from a noun, used to describe a supposed method for racial and economic discrimination in mortgage lending, into a verb with wide use inside and outside planning (although many of the original Home Owners' Loan Corporation maps from the 1930s used color coding rather than literal red lines). The ideals of the Regional Planning Association of America took form not only in manifestos and specific community plans but also in the dramatic film *The City*, which utilized a documentary style for polemical purpose. One commentator on this essay has suggested that the towering, mysterious skyscraper cities of artist Hugh Ferris were a gloss on the New York zoning code of 1916; we find this intriguing but wonder how many people marveling over the pictures have made the connection. Perhaps a stronger analogy from a non-American setting might be the Green Heart of the Netherlands, an instance where a set of land-use regulations has created both a specific landscape and a deeply felt metaphor that carries its own power to influence public decisions.[41]

In the world of twenty-first-century planning theory, there is a strong assumption that many voices engaged in many overlapping conversations can help us to shape more equitable and sustainable cities. Portland, with its articulate citizenry, seems a good place to test this assumption. Will multiple conversations help the region's residents refine their shared vision? Or will plural voices simply mean a raft of Measure 37/49 land development claims that set neighbor against neighbor and effectively undermine the twentieth-century goal of compact urbanization? It is clear, however, that the Urban Growth Boundary gives residents of the Portland region a shared topic for these conversations, and one that inspires insightful—and sometimes funny—commentary. With this good start, we can assume that Portlanders are not likely to stop talking about the UGB anytime soon.

Notes

1. Alafair Burke, *Missing Justice* (New York: Henry Holt, 2004); David Oates, *City Limits: Walking Portland's Urban Growth Boundary* (Corvallis: Oregon State University Press, 2006); Jeannene Prsyblyski, "Welcome to the Urban Growth Boundary Trail" (2005), brochure in author's possession.

2. For discussion of Portland's strength at the center, see Carl Abbott, *Greater Portland: Urban Life and Landscape in the Pacific Northwest* (Philadelphia: University of Pennsylvania Press, 2001), and "Centers and Edges: Reshaping Downtown Portland," in Connie Ozawa, ed., *The Portland Edge: Challenges and Successes in Growing Communities* (Washington, D.C.: Island Press, 2004), 164–83.

3. Burke, *Missing Justice*, 189.

4. The negative arguments about the UGB are clearly summarized in Robert Bruegmann, *Sprawl: A Compact History* (Chicago: University of Chicago Press, 2005). A generally positive evaluation is Carl Abbott, "Planning a Sustainable City: The Promise and Performance of Portland's Urban Growth Boundary," in Greg Squires, ed., *Urban Sprawl: Causes, Consequences, and Policy Responses* (Washington, D.C.: Urban Institute Press, 2002), 207–236.

5. Measure 37 changed Oregon's statutory law. It substantially re-enacted Measure 7, a constitutional amendment passed in 2000 but nullified by the Oregon Supreme Court on technical grounds. In turn, passage of Measure 49 in November 2007 rolled back parts of Measure 37 to strike a politically acceptable balance between planning and property rights agendas. For Measure 7, see Carl Abbott, Sy Adler, and Deborah Howe, "A Quiet Counterrevolution in Land Use Regulation: The Origins and Impacts of Oregon's Measure 7," *Housing Policy Debate* 14: 3 (2003): 383–426.

6. Robert Kaplan, "Travels in America's Future," *Atlantic Monthly* 282: 3 (1998): 37–61.

7. Metro, http://www.oregonmetro.gov/urban-growth-boundary, last updated August 2014. Gerritt Knaap, "The Price Effects of an Urban Growth Boundary in Metropolitan Portland, Oregon," *Land Economics* 61:1 (1995): 26; J. W. Thompson, "Back from the Brink," *Landscape Architecture* 88 (July 1998): 56; F. K. Benfield, J. Terris, and N. Vorsanger, *Solving Sprawl: Models of Smart Growth in Communities across America* (Washington, D.C.: Natural Resources Defense Council, 2001), 193; William Ashworth, "Monopoly Money," in Oates, *City Limits*, 16.

8. Oates, *City Limits*, 118. The Metro headquarters occupies a prominent site on a major traffic street across from the Oregon Convention Center. Before Metro adapted the structure, it housed a very conspicuous Sears store.

9. W. Claiborne, "Cracks in Portland's 'Great Wall': A Strict Model of Controlled Growth Begins to Budge," *Washington Post*, September 29, 1997; Alan Ehrenhalt, "The Great Wall of Portland," *Governing*, May 1997, 20; Timothy Egan, "Seattle and Portland in Struggle to Avert Another Paradise Lost," *New York Times*, November 1, 1997.

10. David Bodamer, "Portland's Real Estate Market Is at Its Weakest Point in Two Decades (2003), www.cponline.com; B. Sperber, "How to Succeed in Boise," *Professional Builder*, October 1, 2004.

11. H. Jeffrey Leonard, *Managing Oregon's Growth: The Politics of Development Planning* (Washington, D.C.: Conservation Foundation, 1987).

12. M. Siakavellas, "Owners Feel Pressure of NOIs throughout the Pacific Northwest," *Multi-Housing News*, April 1, 2003.

13. Laura Oppenheimer, "Author Finds Sprawl Isn't the Be-all and End-all," *Oregonian*, July 2, 2006.

14. Randy Gragg, "The Road to Damascus," *Landscape Architecture* 92 (November 2002): 48–52; M. Lowe, "Alternatives to Sprawl: Shaping Tomorrow's Cities," *The Futurist* 26:2: 28–34; Jay Walljasper, "America's 10 Most Enlightened Towns," *Utne Reader* no. 81 (May–June 1997): 42–59.

15. Suzanne Lessard, "Clear in the Periphery: Discovering the Edge of Portland," *Architectural Record* 188 (November 2000): 53–54. Also see J. Echlin, "Reading Portland: The City as a Verb," *Places* 12 (3): 34–37.

16. M. Cooper, "Urban Sprawl in the West" *CQ Researcher* 7(37): 865–88. Retrieved September 25, 2014 from CQ Research Online, http://library.cqpress.com/cqresearcher/cqresrre1997100300.

17. Oates, *City Limits*, 8.

18. "Olinda is certainly not the only city that grows in concentric circles, like tree trunks which each year add one more ring. But in other cities there remains, in the center, the old narrow girdle of walls from which the withered spires rise, the towers, the tiled roofs, the domes, while the new quarters sprawl around them like a loosened belt. Not Olinda: the old walls expand bearing the old quarters with them, enlarged, but maintaining their proportions on a broad horizon at the edges of the city; they surround the slightly newer quarters, which also grew up on the margins and became thinner to make room for still more recent ones pressing from inside; and so, on and on."

Advocates of growth management argue that "Olinda" is far superior to the suburban sprawl of a city like Calvino's Penthesilea, where "you advance for hours and it is not clear to you whether you are already in the city's midst or still outside it. Like a lake with low shores lost in swamps, so Penthesilea spreads for miles around, a soupy city diluted on the plain; pale buildings back to back in mangy fields . . . a street of scrawny shops which fades amid patches of leprous countryside." See Italo Calvino, *Invisible Cities*, trans. William Weaver (San Diego: Harcourt, Brace, Jovanovich, 1994), 129, 156–57.

19. Arthur C. Nelson, "Using Land Markets to Evaluate Urban Containment Programs," *Journal of the American Planning Association* 52 (Spring 1986): 156–71; Knaap, "Price Effects."

20. David Rusk, *Inside Game/Outside Game: Winning Strategies for Saving Urban America* (Washington, D.C.: Brookings Institution Press, 1999), 154.

21. Ann Altman, personal communication, October 10, 2007. See the painting at www.annaltman.com/urban_growth.html.

22. Judith Berck, "Driving Portland's Urban Growth Boundary," *Oregon Humanities* (Spring 2000): 36.

23. The name Orlo comes from an Italian word meaning "edge" or "brink." For an analysis of Orlo within the context of Portland's public art organizations, see Svetlana Karasyova, *The Ends and Means of Public Art Making: A Case Study of "Public Art" and "Art in Public" in the Portland, Oregon Metropolitan Region*. Ph.D. dissertation, Portland State University, 2006.

24. Orlo, "Spanning Boundaries" [Call to artists, 1999], in author's possession.

25. Linda K. Johnson, "Orlo Proposal—Urban Growth Boundary Project Spanning Boundaries," in author's possession.

26. Randy Gragg, "Linda K. Johnson On Interpreting Urban Growth," *Oregonian*, October 15, 1999.

27. S. Whiting, "Essence of the City: Exploring San Francisco's Secrets, One Project at a Time," *San Francisco Chronicle*, March 14, 2004.

28. The Portland exhibit was a second stop for an exhibit originally mounted in San Francisco. The UGB Trail was one of several works added for Portland. Jeannine Przyblyski, personal communication, October 10, 2007.

29. It is a nice coincidence that the title of the first book about the Oregon planning system referenced the Oregon Trail to emphasize Oregon's pioneering role. Charles Little, *The New Oregon Trail* (Washington, D.C.: Conservation Foundation, 1974).

30. Oates, *City Limits*, 3.

31. Oates, *City Limits*, 2–3.

32. Margie Boule, "Puddle City Ditties Aim to Pave the Path Home," *Oregonian*, September 18, 2007.

33. Ian Doescher, *Portland: The Album*. Lyrics and a short audio sample are at www.creswelldoescher.com/portland/ (accessed September 25, 2014). The suburban locations mentioned in the song (Gresham, Troutdale, 197th Avenue) are all inside the actual UGB.

34. T. Hopkins, personal communication, October 15, 2007.

35. Lessard, "Clear in the Periphery," 54; David Bragdon, "Inside Out," in Oates, *City Limits*, 41.

36. Sylvan Goldberg, "Living on the Edge," *Portland Monthly*, June 2006, 78.

37. Alafair Burke, personal communication, October 13, 2007; Burke, *Missing Justice*, 189.

38. We are distinguishing plans and regulations from built projects that obviously have iconic functions—Central Park, Chicago's lakefront of parks and skyline, the Golden Gate Bridge. The pyramidal TransAmerica Building in San Francisco has iconic status as a physical object. The San Francisco Downtown Plan of 1985, however much it may be known and admired within the design professions, has not taken on an independent life with the general public.

39. Peter Calthorpe and William Fulton, *The Regional Metropolis* (Washington, D.C.: Island Press, 2001).

40. William Moody, *Wacker's Manual of the Plan of Chicago; Municipal Economy. Especially Prepared for Study in the Public Schools of Chicago, Auspices of the Chicago Plan Commission* (Chicago: H. C. Sherman and Company, 1911).

41. M. Van Eeten, "When Fiction Conveys Truth and Authority," *Journal of the American Planning Association* 66 (Winter 2000): 58–67.

CHAPTER 3

Jim Rockford or Tony Soprano

Coastal Contrasts in American Suburbia

"This is Jim Rockford. At the tone, leave your name and message. I'll get back to you." [*Beep*]

Each of the 122 episodes of the popular television series *The Rockford Files*, airing from 1974 to 1980, opened with Jim Rockford's answering machine, followed by a tongue-in-cheek message:

"It's Norma at the market. It bounced. You want me to tear it up, send it back, or put it with the others?" (Episode 101: September 13, 1974)

"It's Laurie at the trailer park. A space opened up. Do you want me to save it or are the cops going to let you stay where you are?" (Episode 105: October 11, 1974)

Jim Rockford is a suburbanite without roots, an intermittently employed private investigator who lives alone in a house trailer parked along the Pacific Coast Highway in Malibu.[1] He makes his own way with sporadic help from a handful of continuing characters. The opening credits emphasize his isolation, showing the inside of his trailer but no surroundings—a marked contrast with contemporaneous situation comedies and cop shows that used stock shots of landmarks and skylines to establish a sense of place.[2] In episode after episode, Rockford guns his 1970s muscle car along generic California streets and highways, far more concerned with executing dangerous maneuvers than with the passing scenery.

Tony Soprano is another suburbanite, but one who is deeply embedded in very specific networks and places. As a crime family boss, Tony can never truly be alone. He can scarcely act without juggling dozens of relationships from his stressful family life and even more stressful business world. He lives in a suburbscape that is assembled with careful detail from real places in northern New Jersey. Compulsive fans have tracked down scores of filming locations in a dozen cities and towns, including strip clubs doubling as strip clubs and markets doubling as markets. In eighty-six episodes of *The Sopranos*, which aired from 1999 to 2006, Tony Soprano lives, works, and kills in a thickly authenticized landscape.[3]

Jim Rockford and Tony Soprano are my launching pad for exploring differences in the ways that Americans have imagined East Coast suburbs and West Coast suburbs in multiple media, but particularly in literary fiction. The differences can be grouped around two themes. The first focuses on the roles of place and space. The second considers the varying weight of history, often as manifested through families and social ties. Eastern suburbs and suburbanites are commonly depicted as embedded in place, rooted in time, and entangled in social networks. Western suburbs and suburbanites are often imagined as the opposite—isolated in space, atemporal, and free (or bereft) of social bonds.

The analysis draws not only on these two iconic TV series but also on the work of three novelists who have set their stories and characters in suburbs of the later twentieth century. One of Tony Soprano's fictional neighbors is Frank Bascombe, the journalist turned realtor who is the central figure in the novels of Richard Ford's trilogy *The Sportswriter* (1986), *Independence Day* (1995), and *The Lay of the Land* (2006). He lives in Haddam and then Sea-Clift, New Jersey, the first a composite version of Princeton and nearby communities, the second of Seaside Heights and Seaside Park on the barrier island that forms Barnegat Bay.[4] Each book centers on a few days leading up to a holiday—Easter 1984 in the first, July 4, 1988, in the second, and Thanksgiving 2000 in the third. Frank is a moderately successful middle-aged man, coping with children, lovers, wives past and present, coworkers, friends, and casual acquaintances, as he attempts the errands and routines of everyday life. Ford has made it clear that one of his goals is to try to understand suburbia on its own terms: "The conventional wisdom is that suburban life is eventless and risk-free. When I started *The Sportswriter*, I thought to myself—how about if I wrote a redemptive novel about the suburbs, a paean to New Jersey and its suburban life?"[5]

Less than a hundred miles from Haddam is Brewer, Pennsylvania, the stand-in for novelist John Updike's home community of Reading. Here among three hundred thousand others in the metropolitan area lives Harry "Rabbit" Angstrom, the often befuddled protagonist of *Rabbit, Run* (1960), *Rabbit Redux* (1971), *Rabbit Is Rich* (1981), and *Rabbit at Rest* (1990).[6] Given American traditions, Updike may have had an easier task in convincing readers to appreciate a declining industrial city than Ford did in promoting an appreciation of the Garden State, but Rabbit spends much of his time in suburbs even less enticing than those of central Jersey. Chronicled in snapshot episodes from Rabbit's early twenties to his death at age fifty-six is a life of moderate upward mobility, marital screw-ups, and frustrating efforts to keep up with a changing world.

On the other side of the continent, metaphorically cruising some of the same western highways with Jim Rockford, although more likely in a beat-up Saab than in a Pontiac Firebird, are the nomadic "Gen-Xers" with whom Douglas Coupland populated *Generation X: Tales for an Accelerated Culture* (1991), *Shampoo Planet* (1992), *Microserfs* (1995), and *Girlfriend in a Coma* (1999). These are freestanding novels with a common sensibility. Their settings are the suburbs of North America's Pacific Rim, from Palm Springs and Palo Alto in California, to Redmond and Richland, Washington, and North Vancouver, British Columbia (Richland or "Lancaster" in *Shampoo Planet* is not technically a suburb, but it is suburban in all its characteristics). Coupland experiments with form and format, but each book offers incisive, satirical looks at footloose young people as they try to form adult lives in unformed suburban environments.[7]

Ford, Updike, and Coupland have all been astute observers of metropolitan life, offering nuanced descriptions of the neighborhoods, workplaces, social customs, consumer goods, and products of popular culture from which their characters construct their lives.[8] Their works fall in the tradition of writers who have tried to understand, document, and highlight the texture and pulse of middle-class Americans (and Canadians) in their most common environments. They work in the tradition of Anthony Trollope, Honoré de Balzac, and William Dean Howells. The latter is an author whom Updike explicitly admired and acknowledged, commenting that "it is, after all, the triumph of American life that so much of it should be middling. Howells's great agenda remains our agenda—for the American writer to live in America and to mirror it in writing."[9]

In theoretical terms developed by Michel de Certeau, these novelists are concerned with the tactics of everyday life—the specific decisions, behaviors, and routines by which individuals inhabit the economic, social, and physical settings in which they find themselves. My interest is in these details and in the social backstory and spatial "back-landscape" against which the characters live their moral lives. I set aside for others to analyze the moral progress of the individuals—Tony Soprano's adventures in therapy, Harry Angstrom's struggle to come to terms with failure, Frank Bascombe's efforts to deal with death, the ways that Coupland's people search for transcendence. Instead, I want to explore how they, and we, imagine the common places that undergird their individual labors and, in so doing, locate them within the flows and structures of space and of time.

Suburbs in Space: Transects and Fragments

The title sequence for *The Sopranos* is a good starting place. The ninety-six-second opening uses a collage of images that together represent the simultaneous connection and differentiation of New York and suburban New Jersey. Tony emerges from the Lincoln Tunnel, is fed onto the New Jersey Turnpike, passes an abandoned industrial building and Newark Airport, drives the streets of the town where he does business—constructed from fragments of North Arlington, Harrison, and Kearny—and pulls into a recently built suburban house in North Caldwell. From the mouth of the tunnel to the Bada Bing! club is ten miles or so, from there another dozen to "Sopranoville" in western Essex County.[10]

The sequence is what urban planners call a transect, a radial slice from city center to edge that reveals a range of social and physical habitats. The concept combines a standard research method from ecological and habitat science with the classic concentric zone model of urban neighborhoods developed by sociologist Ernest Burgess in the 1920s. In recent years, architect-planner Andres Duany has advocated the transect as a planning tool that can reveal the spatially layered development of U.S. cities. His prototypical American urban-to-rural transect is divided into six Transect Zones—urban core, urban center, general urban, sub-urban, rural, and natural—which develop and exist in organic relationship, each functioning as a specialized part of a larger whole.[11] Matching my own analysis, my colleague Ellen Shoskes has called the opening "a brilliant take on [a] transect through the New Jersey social-economic-cultural landscape."[12]

Richard Ford adopts the same trope. In *The Lay of the Land*, we get exactly what the title promises. A drive across the waist of the state, from Sea-Clift to Haddam and on nearly to the Delaware River, makes a lateral east–west transect of the Garden State. The trip is a litany of suburban landscapes observed astutely in detail but also in relationships. Subdivisions and neighborhoods connect together like ankle bones, leg bones, and knee bones. En route from the Jersey Shore, Frank passes white-and-pink bayside condos, clean cinderblock factories culturing human cells and turning out condoms, factory outlets and big boxes, "weathered pastel ranch-looking houses on curved streets," and then, closer to Haddam, "fat yellow Colonial two-of-a-kinds and austere gray saltboxes" (31). Beyond Haddam lies "old-style Jersey, with a tall white Presbyterian steeple beside a sovereign little fenced cemetery, just beyond that, a seventies-vintage strip development, with two pizza shops, a launderette, a closed Squire Tax and an H&R Block" (34–35), and then, finally, "the peaceable town 'n country housing pattern New Jersey is famous for: deep two-acre lots with curbless frontage, on which are sited large but not ominous builder-designer Capes, prairie contemporaries and Dutch-door ranches" (34–35).[13]

In another example, Frank Bascombe, on assignment for his magazine in *The Sportswriter*, visits another eastern city. He pilots his rental car from downtown Detroit to interview a retired football player in a distant suburb, noting the cityscape changes on the way.

> We get quickly out into the snowy traffic, weaving around dingy warehouse blocks and old hotels to Grand River, then head for the northwest suburbs. . . . Strathmore, Brightmore, Redford, Livonia, another Miracle Mile. We speed through the little connected burgs and townlets beyond the interior city, along white-frame dormered-Cape streets, into solider red-brick Jewish sections until we emerge onto a wide boulevard with shopping malls and thick clusters of traffic lights, the houses newer and settled in squared-off tracts. . . . . Ten minutes later we are into the rolling landscape of snowy farmettes and wide cottage-bound lakes beyond the perimeter of true suburbia, the white-flight areas stretching clear to Lansing. (149–51)

Back in New Jersey, all roads lead to (or from) Haddam. It is a place that is embedded in *places*. Locals can take Amtrak's "Merchants' Special" to Philadelphia (*Independence Day*, 1) or commute by rail to New York (*Sportswriter*, 347–51). A nighttime journey from central New Jersey to and through New York to suburban Connecticut takes a slice through the entire metropolis, with bleary-eyed Bascombe reeling off the freeways, bridges, and parkways with which he has to contend (*Independence Day*, 195–97). After hours on the road, Frank has driven a full transect from edge to center to edge, just as an ecological scientist might catalog the landscape from ridgeline to valley floor to opposite ridgeline.[14]

Frank connects to central New Jersey not only by his careful observations of landscape but also by current networks of reputation and affiliation that tie him laterally in place. He drinks and takes weekend excursions with a set of middle-aged men (not all of whom he necessarily likes). He interacts with coworkers, clients, and tenants for a handful of rentals. He serves on the board of Haddam's theological seminary. In *The Lay of the Land*, eight years after moving to Sea-Clift, he keeps his "Haddam affiliations alive and relatively thriving," maintains his Haddam Realty license current, and does "some referrals and appraisals for United Jersey, where I know most of the officers" (13). He also participates in an organization called Sponsors, a group of Jersey citizens who provide nonprofessional listening ears for people—strangers—who need to talk through a problem and get some friendly advice.

Reputation is equally important for Tony Soprano and Harry Angstrom. A crime boss rules by fear as much as by enforcement. Tony draws on local networks and depends on his reputation with other mob leaders and soldiers, with customers, with law enforcement people. In an early episode, older sister Meadow explains to her brother AJ why his experience at school is a little bit strained—nobody wants to cross or get too close to a *capo*'s kid. Rabbit carries a different reputation from his fame as a high school basketball star, although the reputation and its ability to bring in Toyota buyers fades as he ages. It is a premonition of his death when his son removes the display of yellowing old clippings from the automobile showroom in *Rabbit at Rest*.

Rabbit is also deeply embedded—mired—in his local environment. His bus ride from workplace in Brewer to home in the Penn Villas subdivision in *Rabbit Redux* is another radial slice through an urban region. In July 1969, at the end of a long working day, his bus takes him outward through rings of decay, starting in a declining business district with "its tired five and dimes . . . Kroll's Department Store . . . and its flowerpotted traffic circle where the trolley tracks used to make a clanging star of intersection." A few blocks farther out are "empty dusty windows where stores have been starved by the suburban shopping malls and the sad narrow places that come and go called Go-Go or Boutique . . . and the surplus outlets and a shoe parlor that sells hot roasted peanuts and Afro newspapers printed in Philly." Although Brewer's black residents number only a few thousand, they puzzle Rabbit and set the entire city on edge as Brewerites remember the explosive race riots of recent years in every major American city. Beyond the city limits, Rabbit's bus deposits its last black passengers. The landscape is now suburban, with "the twirlers of a car lot, the pumps and blazoned overhang of a gas station, the lakelike depth of a supermarket parking lot crammed with shimmering fins." Rabbit's destination is 26 Vista Crescent, a house faced with apple-green aluminum siding and "flagstone porchlet." He enters to news of a much longer commute that puts his own into perspective. "Hey Dad," his son calls as he steps into the living room to news about Apollo 11. "They've left earth's orbit! They're forty-three thousand miles away" (13–15).

Updike pairs his cityscapes. The highway strip with the in-laws' Toyota dealership where Rabbit finally makes some money is juxtaposed against downtown Brewer and Rabbit's vanished job as a linotype operator. The new development of Penn Villas where he buys his first house contrasts with the old suburb of Mount Judge where Rabbit grew up. His mother-in-law's fusty old house, to which Rabbit moves his family when arsonists torch his Penn Villas ranch house, is balanced by upscale Penn Park where Rabbit moves in late middle age. The new country club that Rabbit and his friends are able to join substitutes for the established club for Brewer's old-money families. The pairs are complementary and constitutive, each part offering meaning and identity to the other.

When Douglas Coupland juxtaposes suburb and city, in contrast, his purpose is to emphasize the difference and separation of Redmond from Seattle or Silicon Valley from San Francisco.[15] He narrates no connecting journeys and describes no transects. Instead, his Generation X and Generation Y protagonists inhabit freestanding islands of suburban culture. In *Generation X*, there's a sketchy bungalow court on the edge of a city that is simultaneously a Los Angeles satellite and an island in the desert. *Girlfriend in a Coma* takes place in a hillside suburb that backs up on the British Columbia wilderness. Seattle's self-contained and self-regarding eastside suburbs full of software specialists are themselves a mosaic of transient neighborhoods and office parks.[16] *Shampoo Planet*'s Lancaster, like the real Richland, is entirely a postwar city that is fully suburban in character and isolated "in the dry plains of southeastern Washington State, scientifically and strategically located so as to be as far away as possible from anywhere meaningful or fun" (9–10).

Coupland's young suburbanites are people who have stronger relationships with things than with people—and with ersatz at that. They peddle brand-name knock-off merchandise and pretend to live in a Dungeons and Dragons world in *Shampoo Planet*, create video games in *Microserfs*, and entertain each other in *Generation X* by making up stories like the young Florentines in *The Decameron*. One of the characters in *Microserfs* comments on the thinness of Silicon Valley as a society and the lack of any deeply articulated place with which to connect: "There is no center to the Valley in any real sense of the word. There is no one watching; it's pretty, but it's a vacuum" (136).

These free-floating suburban settings draw on a distinctive trope in western (meaning largely California) fiction in which residential subdivisions appear as worlds in themselves rather than parts of a larger whole. For examples, see the Pierce Homes subdivision that Herbert Pierce built on a three-hundred-acre ranch on the edge of Glendale in the backstory that James M. Cain devised for *Mildred Pierce* (1941). Readers can visualize its Spanish-style houses with their crimson drapes but not their specific placement in the metropolis. In Thomas

Pynchon's *The Crying of Lot 49* (1966), we first visit San Narciso when Oedipa Maas squints into the sunlight to see "less an identifiable city than a grouping of concepts—census tracts, special purpose bond districts, shopping nuclei, all overlaid with access roads to its own freeway."[17]

Coupland's coastal suburbia echoes the ideas of the "Los Angeles School" of urban studies, a cluster of geographers, sociologists, and urban planners who have argued that the classic model of a unicentric metropolis articulated by sociologists at the University of Chicago in the 1910s and 1920s no longer holds.[18] Instead, the new metropolis, as epitomized in Southern California, is multicentered, segmented, fragmented, and fluid—in a word, postmodern rather than modern. An example is geographer Edward Soja's feverish description of "exopolitan" Orange County, California, as scraps and shards in search of a city. "Perched beyond the vortex of the old agglomerative nodes, the exopolis spins new whorls of its own, turning the city inside-out and outside-in. . . . The metropolitan forms that have become so familiar to us . . . are now undergoing radical deconstruction and reconstruction, exploding and coalescing today in multitudes of experimental communities of tomorrow . . . [where] the solid familiarity of the urban melts into air."[19]

Soja's phrase riffs directly on Karl Marx, for the Los Angeles School emphasizes the dialectic of continually redefined conflict rather than the functional stability that the Chicagoans found. It also resonates with the judgments of Eurocritic Umberto Eco and literary scholar Fredric Jameson who see the American cultural landscape—epitomized in California—as detached and insulated from the real. Such observers uncover a variety of implications in the supposed lack of historical and societal depth. Jameson draws on neo-Marxist ideas to see the California landscape as an alienating product of a distinct stage of capitalism. In contrast, Jean Baudrillard found a certain amount of freedom, or at least an absence of constraint, in California's suburban superficiality.[20]

Suburbs in Time: Weighty and Weightless Pasts

As we shift attention from space to time, consider Jim Rockford, a man who has been cut loose from history. Five years in San Quentin Prison and a pardon for unjust incarceration have drawn a curtain across his earlier life, leaving him to build a new business from scratch. His father, Rocky, functions as a comic sidekick, not a link to family memory, and a second friend/sidekick is a con artist, whose connection dates back only to prison. His lawyer/love interest disappears after the fourth season (contract disputes). As was standard for 1970s television, the episodes feature continuing characters but self-contained plots that do not build a storyline from show to show—an obvious contrast with *The Sopranos*.

Coupland's characters are equally adrift from time, inhabitants of communities with shallow histories (table 3.1). Palm Springs was a winter resort from the

Table 3.1. Instant Communities of the Pacific Coast

	Population 1940	Population 2000
Richland, Wash.	500	39,000
Palm Springs, Calif.	3,000	43,000
Palo Alto, Calif.	17,000	59,000
Redmond, Wash.	500	45,000
Bellevue, Wash.	1,200	110,000

1920s and 1930s but evolved into a year-round city only since the 1960s, in the age of air-conditioning. Lancaster/Richland is entirely a creation of the atomic age, and Silicon Valley is an artifact of the even more recent electronic age. Richard Dorland and his friends in *Girlfriend in a Coma* live in a 1960s and 1970s suburb of the not-very-old city of Vancouver, where growth did not kick off until the 1880s, and the entire metropolis is "a city so new that it dreamed only of what the embryo knows" (7).

Given the age of these places, it is no surprise that Coupland's young adults are at home with the iconic structures of the last half century. They live among suburban apartment courts, convenience stores, and eight-screen theaters. Tyler and Anna-Louise in *Shampoo Planet* attend Lancaster Community College, which is "composed of brutal 1970s cement cubes and looks like dead air conditioners linked together by the little mesh catwalks of a hamster's fun run" (30). Six microserfs share a Redmond, Washington, split-level built in cedar-sided and moss-inviting Northwest style. They work in Microsoft's version of the generic office park, distinguishable from others by the most subtle details: Nintendoites work in "two-story industrial-plex buildings sheathed with Death Star-black windows," while Microsoft workers write code inside "sea foam-green glass" (*Microserfs*, 14). The corporate campuses of Palo Alto are futuretowns:

> Futuretowns are located on the outskirts of the city you live in, just far enough away to be out of reach of angry, torch-carrying mobs that might roam in from the downtown core. You're not supposed to notice futuretowns—they're technically invisible: low flat buildings that look like they've just popped out of the laser printer; . . . small backlit Plexiglass totems out front quietly brandishing the strangely anti-language names of the company housed inside: Cray. Hoechst. Diw. Unilever. Rand. Pfizer. Sandoz. Ciba-Geigy. NEC. . . . Futuretowns are like their own country superimposed onto other countries. (*Shampoo Planet*, 218)

As befits novels whose characters have grown up in the 1960s and 1970s, Lego toys provide Coupland a versatile metaphor for transitory environments and "anonymous landscapes."[21] The tidy mowed lawns at Microsoft are "green Lego pads," and the microserfs group house is just like the houses that Daniel Underwood built out of Legos as a kid. Later in that book, another character responds to the Northridge earthquake of 1994 by constructing a Lego freeway interchange to smash and rebuild. Meanwhile Daniel's father, cast off by IBM, has filled an entire room with a Lego city that seems to Daniel more real than the actual Palo Alto, even though it has taken weeks rather than decades to erect. If Redmond has Lego houses and Palo Alto is a Lego pad, Vancouver is like an entire Lego city that film crews can morph into "any North American city or green space with little effort and even less expense" (*Girlfriend in a Coma*, 88).[22] And Oop!, the software program/game that Daniel and coworkers develop during the Silicon Valley sojourn is a virtual Lego system.

Lego cities may be easy to smash, but interspersed with Coupland's suburban landscapes are actual *modern* ruins, further evidence of temporal shallowness. On the outskirts of Palm Springs sits West Palm Springs Village, "a bleached and defoliated Flintstones color cartoon of a failed housing development from the 1950s" (*Generation X*, 14–15). Lancaster has a failing shopping mall with half its stores plywooded or burned out, and even booming Palo Alto has an empty corporate research campus, unused after only two decades—"a 1970s utopian, *Andromeda Strain*ishly empty tech complex" (*Microserfs*, 211). In the background loom the ruins of atomic weaponry. A jar of Trinitite from the New Mexico test site makes an appearance in *Generation X*, and the vast atomic energy complex of Lancaster/Richland, being decommissioned and decontaminated in the 1990s, is one of the great ruins of the twentieth century.

Coupland's western suburbia thus echoes the early United States, when the country was growing and changing so rapidly that a building could experience the entire cycle of construction and abandonment in a decade or two. As Nick Yablon has explored in a fascinating book, such "untimely ruins" lacked the cultural resonance of deeply historical Europe.[23] Their peculiarity was a source of frustration for Nathaniel Hawthorne, but a source of celebration for Goethe in a sort of transatlantic signal crossing.[24] Most early Americans were on Goethe's side, with absent or untimely ruins taken as signs of vitality and opportunity. Coupland splits the difference, emphasizing the temporal shallowness of western suburbs but seeing that shallowness as fodder for art.

With the past figuring largely as untimely ruins, Coupland's suburbias are places outside of history, thin on the ground as physical places and only thinly represented in the fourth dimension. Lancaster has a "brief past" and a common "willful amnesia that propels the rest of the town's citizens into the sparkling and thrilling future" (*Shampoo Planet*, 10–11) At the Ridgecrest Mall, "people are interested only in staying as modern as possible, continually forgetting the past while envisioning a shinier more fabulous future" (*Shampoo Planet*, 141). Palm Springs is a town where one character comes "to erase all traces of history from my past" (*Generation X*, 36). In *Microserfs*, the most sympathetic character, Karla, comments that "we live in an era of no historical precedents—this is to say, history is no longer useful as a tool in helping us understand current change" (99). In *Shampoo Planet*, the very idea of history becomes absurd, reduced to Richard's satirical proposal to turn garbage dumps into theme parks (199–201).

In response to these observations, several critics interpret Coupland by invoking Francis Fukuyama's argument that the collapse of communism and the triumph of capitalism has meant the "end of history," at least as understood in Hegelian terms, that is, as the contest among competing political ideologies and, possibly, the descent into the shallow consumerism of an eternal present moment.[25] Coupland clearly takes on shallow consumerism as an intellectual challenge (what is the consciousness of consumerism?) but also tries to imagine avenues of escape and transcendence. In *Generation X*, he offers simple physical relocation to start over as petty capitalists in Mexico. In *Girlfriend in a Coma*, he explores the possibility of a modern-day atonement.

The apocalyptic break in *Girlfriend in a Coma* takes the absence of history to a logical extreme. Two-thirds of the way through the novel, a satirical comedy of manners morphs into magical realism. Society collapses when people all over the world fall asleep to be killed by their crashing cars, pulled off the beach by the rising tide, or simply never to awaken. The process takes days, not minutes, traced through chapters titled "The Past Is a Bad Idea," "2000 Is Silly," and "Progress Is Over." Only seven high school friends, now in their thirties, remain awake to watch the modern ruin from the North Vancouver hills: "The city lies before them, a glinting damaged sheet of pewter, with fires burning like acetylene pearls" (205). Karen, the girlfriend who fell into a seventeen-year coma because she could not bear her visions of apocalypse, has awakened as a witness. "The world's over now," she says, as her mind's eye sees the last person close her eyes and sleep. "Our time begins" (208).

These remnant crew members of spaceship Earth find themselves "at the end of the world and the end of time" (266). What they do with "their time" is not, initially, very edifying. They have booze to drink, marshmallows to toast, videos to watch, prescription medications to try before they go bad, and the Park Royal mall to plunder. In the first year as survivors, they parody suburban affluence. "They have money fights, lobbing and tossing Krugerrands, rubies and thousand-dollar bills at each other; at times they make paper airplanes from prints by Andy Warhol and Roy Lichtenstein and shoot them into the fireplace" (211–12). It takes prodding from a ghostly Jared, a high school classmate, who died from a football injury before the book starts and who returns as a blend of chorus and mentor for his surviving classmates, to get them thinking about next steps for the world for which they are now responsible.[26]

Douglas Coupland may propel suburban Vancouver completely out of history, but Richard Ford constructs central New Jersey firmly on its past.[27] Haddam and its environs are steeped in history. As a real estate agent in the second and third books, Frank has a keen eye for property development and community change. Ford periodically slows the action to reflect on Haddam's history since its founding in 1795 or describe the multiple layers of suburbia, as with the village of Penns Neck, now "become just one more aging bedroom community for other larger, newer bedroom communities" (*Independence Day*, 59). The landscape is a mosaic of development from different decades and for different ethnic groups; there is an old black district and new enclaves of Russians, Ethiopians, and Koreans. Social classes divide among a horsey district, older leafy streets, a new "wealth belt" for Philadelphia and New York commuters, starter condos for singles, starter ranches for young families, and retirement complexes. Taken as a whole, this complex environment of temporally and spatially layered communities is a microcosm of America, as Frank observes: "An American would be crazy to reject such a place, since it is the most diverting and readable of landscapes, and the language is always American" (*The Sportswriter*, 52). Historians should be reminded of the incisive book *A Consumer's Republic*, in which Paramus, New Jersey–born Lizabeth Cohen uses the postwar experience of her home state to explicate changes in American society and politics.[28]

As both a real estate salesman and a converted Jerseyite, Frank Bascombe consciously *learns* the history of his home territory and recounts it for the reader as he mentally comments on the roadside landscapes that fill the stories of comings and goings. Harry Angstrom grows up with local history as a constant context for his life, and he moves among the aspirations of multiple generations embodied in commercial and residential landscapes. We watch through his eyes as Brewer's economy declines and then revives with white-collar jobs that spill over from Philadelphia in *Rabbit at Rest*. We see new subdivisions appear and older subdivisions lose their cachet. We see the same restaurant through a new incarnation every decade, from Johnny Frye's Chophouse to Café Barcelona to the Crepe House and then Salad Binge.

Brewer is a metropolitan region where the landscape shows the results of a century-long process of industrial obsolescence—in contrast to the failed real estate speculations that create instant ruins in Coupland's world. The sidewalk cracks and heaves in front on Harry's childhood home, casued by trees having grown alongside multiple generations of residents. The abandoned factory that Harry often passes has stood empty for longer than he can remember. Even the "new" suburban house that he acquires at the end of *Rabbit Is Rich* is old, with the landscaping choices of previous residents having gone to seed in the natural processes of maturity and decay.

Harry's life is itself a transect through both the space and the history of metropolitan Brewer. Updike traces neighborhood change through Harry's own life history and uses neighborhoods to exemplify that history. Readers are never in doubt about how the different sections of Brewer and its environs fit together in both physical and social space. By moving Rabbit from one suburban neighborhood to another, Updike lets his very life trace transects—from pre–World War II Mt. Judge to postwar Penn Villas, from downmarket apartments to upscale Penn Park, whose mock Tudor houses are home to "the most successful dentists . . . the pushiest insurance salesmen, the slickest ophthalmologists" (*Rabbit Redux*, 12). For Rabbit himself: "Brewer, too, that torpid hive, speaks to him of himself, of his past grown awesomely deep, so that things he remembers personally, V-E day or the Sunday Truman declared war on North Korea, are history now" (*Rabbit at Rest*, 183).

For both Harry and Frank—and for Tony—the weight of external history is bound up with the weight of family. Popular culture commonly identifies suburbs as the proper setting for families and cities for singles, from *Leave It to Beaver* to *Home Improvement* on one side of the balance, and from *Mary Tyler Moore* to *Frasier* to *How I Met Your Mother* on the other. *The Sopranos* continues this tradition, for Tony Soprano is a family man by multiple definitions. He is embedded in the family crime business. He is also embroiled in the classic "suburban" story of raising a family with tensions among son, daughter, wife, and ferocious mother.

Like Tony Soprano, Harry Angstrom and Frank Bascombe are unable to escape their families. They feel the weight of history not only in their communities but in their personal lives, for each is haunted by the early death of a child—Harry a daughter by an accident when she was an infant, Frank a son from Reye's syndrome at age nine. Each has an alienated son with whom he tries but fails to connect. Harry and his wife, Janice, have alternating sexual affairs but keep returning to each other. Frank oscillates in the orbit of former and present wives and girlfriends. Family means a set of responsibilities that he may or may not fulfill, although his sense of "family" obligation is strong enough for him to take excursions with the crotchety father of a former girlfriend, a man who is as exasperating as any real in-law. For Harry, family is a web of burdens that he cannot escape: "The dead, Jesus. They were multiplying, and they look up begging you to join them, . . . Pop, Mom, old man Springer, Jill, the baby called Becky for her little time. . . . The obituary page every day shows another stalk of a harvest endlessly rich, the faces of old teachers, customers, local celebrities like himself flashing for a moment and then going down" (*Rabbit Is Rich*, 9–10).

Coupland—no surprise—inverts the expectations about suburbs and families. His stories bring together unrelated young adults in suburban landscapes where they work, hang out, take road trips, hook up, unhook, back each other up, get on each other's nerves, and occasionally break away. The groups in *Generation X* and *Microserfs* are random, the one assembled by casual acquaintance, the other thrown together by a corporate human resources department. The loose gang who hang out together in *Shampoo Planet* have community college in common but few real shared interests. The crew in *Girlfriend in a Coma* share the most as a high school clique from the same neighborhood who scatter to the winds in their twenties but come home to North Vancouver in their thirties. It is as if the cast of the megahit television series *Friends* were teleported from Manhattan to suburbia and turned dark, edgy, uncertain, and far too self-aware in the process.

These young western suburbanites have families as thin as their surroundings. Parents are ineffectual or left behind. The computer coders in *Microserfs* have long since rejected or ignored their parents, with the exception of Daniel, whose mom ends up as a den mother and dad as a mascot (after being laid off by IBM) when the group of Microsoft employees quit to try their own start-up in Silicon Valley. Back in the Northwest, in the midst of an offhand conversation at a Lancaster diner, Tyler realizes that "not one of my friends at the table has a biological father present and stable in our lives" (*Shampoo Planet*, 38). His own family includes a biological father who is a terminal hippie, a flaky mother, an ex-stepfather who is one step above a real estate scammer, and bankrupt grandparents with an Amway-like scheme to get rich again. It may seem a stretch across very different sensibilities, but Tyler and friends inhabit a social world not all that different from that of the film *E.T. the Extra-Terrestrial* (1982). Elliott and his siblings live in a new suburban house literally on the edge of development (the shooting location was Tujunga). Their father is absent and their mother well-meaning but clueless. Kids know how to navigate their environment in the final chase scene, but adults do not. It is a suburban world, in short, where neither generations nor history count for much.

Scattered, Centered, Thin, Thick

It's now time to pause from literary studies to kick back, slit open the cellophane around our complete DVD set for *The Sopranos*, and click the bookmark that takes us to *Rockford* episodes on Hulu.com. As we sit through some marathon viewing, we realize that each show had a rhetorical structure on which scriptwriters could hang their variations—a structure that reinforced its implied understanding of suburbia.[29]

The typical episode is off and running when Jim Rockford gets a call from a stranger or a plea to help a friend of a friend who finds herself in trouble. There are a few two-part shows, but every case and most episodes are distinct and self-contained. The investigation takes Jim to nondescript Los Angeles locations—motels, suburban commercial strips, gas stations, apartments, parking lots, restaurants. The scenes are connected by cars, stoplight conversations, and car chases, but only Jim Rockford behind the wheel knows how one setting connects to the others. Los Angeles is like the opening credits—a montage of distinct scenes with an occasional street sign to mark Ventura or Bel Air.[30]

Tony Soprano, in contrast, typically navigates two "family" stories in the course of his hour. There are problems in his nuclear family—his wife, Carmela, is restless, his daughter, Meadow, is alienated, and his son, A.J., is a screw-up. If that's not enough stress, there are problems with the extended crime family of blood relations and in-laws. The tension in both is the succession of generations as Tony displaces his uncle (who early on puts an unsuccessful hit on him), tries to groom his own lieutenants, and wonders whether his son will ever have what it takes. Like all stories of generations, the roots of the storylines are deep and their development sequential. The action is claustrophobic—the interiors of apartments, the back room at the club, dark streets, and nighttime meetings—all in the same heavily layered corner of New Jersey. These contrast starkly with *Rockford's* blue California skies and occasional investigations and chases that open into bright desert hinterlands.

The images of East Coast and West Coast suburbs are very different, whether in popular television or literary fiction, and resonate deeply in American culture. Take archetypal Los Angeles movies as an example. Quentin Tarantino's *Pulp Fiction* (1994) is a set of separate stories linked by the Venn-diagram overlap of a few characters but each with a distinct plot. The locations are Los Angeles fragments. There is a bit of Pasadena, some Hawthorne, a visit to West Hollywood, a stop in Canoga Park. The metropolitan background is like the *Rockford* metroscape drawn ninety-eight degrees darker. Another example is the *katabasis* of Michael Douglas in *Falling Down* (1993). His march to the sea at Venice Pier presumably traces an identifiable route through Los Angeles, but the screenplay offers a series of confrontations in visually unconnected locations.

Contrast these with Barry Levinson's Baltimore in *Diner* (1982), *Tin Men* (1987), and *Avalon* (1990). This is a richly imagined metropolis in which city and suburbs connect. The aluminum siding salesmen in *Tin Men* schmooze and swap leads in the city, but they flim-flam their customers in working-class suburban neighborhoods. *Avalon* follows three generations of a Jewish family from an older ethnic neighborhood to new suburban homes after World War II. A political take on the same theme of generational change and immigrant incorporation is Edwin O'Connor's *The Last Hurrah*, a 1956 novel and 1958 movie in which a traditional politico from the heart of Irish Boston runs for re-election as mayor, only to fall to a younger politician with all the postwar suburban accoutrements.

The point of additional examples is not to prove that eastern and western suburbia *are* different but that Americans *think* they are. Indeed, the popular imagery is often wrong. American metropolitan areas are rapidly converging on many dimensions, such as increasing ethnic variety in suburban Massachusetts, Georgia, Illinois, and California. When sociologists actually study California suburbanites, they find not the isolated, anomic individuals that Joan Didion depicts in *Play It As It Lays* (1970) but normal folks with as many social connections as everyone else.[31] Levittown and Lakewood are sister suburbs under the same sun (although they may be obscured by more clouds on one coast and more smog on the other).

When there are real differences, moreover, they often run contrary to the popular imagination. Western and southwestern cities are more compact than eastern cities, for one example. In 2000, the U.S. Census found forty-nine metropolitan areas with one million people or more. Ten of the twelve most densely populated lay in the West, not the East—Las Vegas, Los Angeles, San Diego, San Francisco, Phoenix, Sacramento, Seattle, Portland, San Antonio, and Salt Lake City. They do not look like high-rise Manhattan, but their growth has been compact and contiguous. The capitals of sprawl are places like Atlanta, Charlotte, and metro-Jersey, not Los Angeles or Seattle.[32] Despite complaints by New Yorkers who find western cities unfamiliar, they are also eminently legible, oriented into corridors by mountains and waterfronts, and often visible at a glance from encompassing hills.[33]

Pesky facts, however, miss the fun of working with popular culture and literary texts. Far more people enjoy television shows and read novels than labor over census data and federal research reports. When those shows and novels are well crafted and compelling, they serve to fix and reinforce a body of public knowledge, giving form and authority to our everyday impressions. Having perhaps grown up, like this author, with *77 Sunset Strip* (1958–64), viewers of *The Rockford Files* already knew that Los Angeles was about streets and fast cars. *The Sopranos* drew on what viewers thought they knew about North Jersey and reimagined that understanding in convincing fashion. Richard Ford utilized his own experience to describe a suburbanized state that seems right on target—at least to this occasional visitor. Coupland's acerbic depiction of the futuretowns in their shiny form (Bellevue, Palo Alto) and less shiny versions (Palm Springs, Richland) offers readers a shorthand vocabulary for understanding their surroundings.

As much as anything, this excursion beyond the "city limits" of social science and into the exurbs on the edge of historical scholarship confirms one important point about the American and Canadian imagination. Whether we are in Virginia Beach or Vancouver, Ottawa or Oakland, we *think* that the western states and provinces are different from the East, and we are ready to believe that this distinction has persisted over generations of development. The doings of Jim Rockford and Tony Soprano may look like riffs on current events, but they also reflect the power of imagination over history.

Notes

1. Malibu is suburban by standard definitions. It was an unincorporated section of Los Angeles County at the time of the show and has been an incorporated municipality since 1991. The location for Jim Rockford's trailer, the Paradise Cove Resort and Mobile Home Park, has also been the site for episodes of *Baywatch*, *Sea Hunt*, and *Charlie's Angels* as well as surfer movies.

2. Examples include the Milwaukee City Hall for *Laverne and Shirley* (1976–83), Michigan Avenue and the Chicago elevated train for *The Bob Newhart Show* (1972–78), Cincinnati landmarks for *WKRP in Cincinnati* (1978–82), and aerial views and landmarks for *The Streets of San Francisco* (1972–77).

3. For a description and analysis of Soprano country, see Dennis Gale, *Greater New Jersey: Living in the Shadow of Gotham* (Philadelphia: University of Pennsylvania Press, 2006), which emphasizes the close functional connections between New York and New Jersey and the role of organized crime families.

4. Charles McGrath, "A New Jersey State of Mind," *New York Times*, October 25, 2006, at www.nytimes.com/2006/10/25/books/25ford.html?pagewanted=all (accessed October 23,

2013). See Michael Ebner, "Experiencing Megalopolis in Princeton," *Journal of Urban History* 19 (1993): 11–55. In the interest of space, I give page numbers for the various novels of Richard Ford, John Updike, and Douglas Coupland in the text, rather than as notes. I used these editions of Ford's novels: *The Sportswriter* (New York: Vintage, 1986), *Independence Day* (New York: Knopf, 1995), and *The Lay of the Land* (New York: Knopf, 2006).

5. Phil Hogan, "To Be Frank," *The Guardian*, September 23, 2006, at www.guardian.co.uk/books/2006/sep/24/fiction.features (accessed October 23, 2013).

6. The page numbers from the John Updike novels come from these editions: *Rabbit Redux* (New York: Knopf, 1971), *Rabbit Is Rich* (New York: Knopf, 1981), and *Rabbit at Rest* (New York: Knopf, 1990).

7. The page numbers from the Douglas Coupland novels come from these editions: *Generation X* (New York: St. Martin's, 1991), *Shampoo Planet* (New York: Washington Square Press, 1992), *Microserfs* (New York: Harper Perennial, 1996), and *Girlfriend in a Coma* (New York: Harper Collins, 1998). For background on Douglas Coupland's settings, see Ryan Kray, "The Path to Paradise: Expropriation, Exodus, and Exclusion in the Making of Palm Springs," *Pacific Historical Review* 73 (2004): 85–126; John Findlay and Bruce Hevly, *Atomic Frontier Days: Hanford and the Atomic West* (Seattle: University of Washington Press, 2011); Carl Abbott, "Building the Atomic Cities: Richland, Los Alamos, and the American Planning Language," in Bruce Hevly and John Findlay, eds., *The Atomic West* (Seattle: University of Washington Press, 1998); Kate Brown, *Plutopia: Nuclear Families, Atomic Cities, and the Great Soviet and American Plutonium Disasters* (New York: Oxford University Press, 2013); Margaret O'Mara, *Cities of Knowledge: Cold War Science and the Search for the Next Silicon Valley* (Princeton, N.J.: Princeton University Press, 2004); and Glenna Matthews, *Silicon Valley, Women, and the California Dream: Gender, Class, and Opportunity in the Twentieth Century* (Stanford, Calif.: Stanford University Press, 2002).

8. Available online is the syllabus for a University of Texas English seminar that has used the John Updike and Richard Ford novels to explore "the customs and concerns, successes and failures, assumptions and ambitions of American life from the 1950's to the end of the century. Particular attention will be given to the intersection of private and public realms, as Rabbit Angstrom and Frank Bascombe contend with the challenges of everyday life (career and money, marriage and family, friendship and faith) against the background of political, economic, and social change." See www.utexas.edu/cola/files/369465 (accessed October 23, 2013).

9. John Updike, *Odd Jobs: Essays and Criticism* (New York: Knopf, 1991), 189. Also see ibid., 182–83: "Men and circumstances are mightily mixed, and crises are generally averted or deflected, and life does not fall into plots. Howells's novels press these truths upon us."

10. The shooting location for Bada Bing! is a club in Lodi, New Jersey, eighteen miles from New York, although not on the direct route from Newark to North Caldwell.

11. See Andres Duany, Jeff Speck, and Mike Lydon, *The Smart Growth Manual* (New York: McGraw-Hill, 2009); Center for Applied Transect Studies at www.transect.org/index.html; Gabriele Tagliaventi, "The European Transect: An Organic Way for Architecture to Develop Towns, Cities, and Metropolises," *Places* 18 (2006), at http://escholarship.org/uc/item/4xc2j7qw (accessed October 23, 2013).

12. Ellen Shoskes, personal communication to author, October 2, 2012.

13. Dennis Gale's term "crustal urbanization" applies here—continuous urban and suburban development that creates a "sprawling amoeba-like crust" of development over the landscape. Gale, *Greater New Jersey*, 64–65.

14. These journeys by Frank Bascombe and Tony Soprano have a distinguished literary ancestry. Sinclair Lewis set his novel *Babbitt* (New York: Harcourt Brace, 1922) in motion by sending businessman George F. Babbitt on his daily three-mile commute from his green-and-white Dutch Colonial house in the bright new subdivision of Floral Heights into the center of the thriving city of Zenith. Behind the wheel of his new motor car, Babbitt admires each part of the city in turn:

> The one-story shops on Smith Street, a glare of plate-glass and new yellow brick; groceries and laundries and drug-stores to supply the more immediate needs of East Side housewives. The market gardens in Dutch Hollow, their shanties patched with corrugated iron and stolen doors. Billboards with crimson goddesses nine feet tall advertising cinema films, pipe tobacco, and talcum powder. The old "mansions" along Ninth Street, S.E., like aged dandies in filthy linen; wooden castles turned into boarding-houses, with muddy walks and rusty hedges, jostled by fast-intruding garages, cheap apartment-houses, and fruit-stands. . . . Across the belt of railroad-tracks, factories with high-perched water-tanks and tall stacks—factories producing condensed milk, paper boxes, lighting fixtures, motorcars. Then the business center, the thickening darting traffic, the crammed trolleys unloading, and the high doorways of marble and polished granite. (31)

15. Tom Foster also notes that Coupland's Silicon Valley is an edge city/postsuburban environment that "no longer has a symbolic relationship with the urban core." However, I suggest that he may misread both the author and the social facts in arguing that Coupland presents Redmond and Palo Alto as different sorts of places. Tim Foster, "'A Kingdom of a Thousand Princes But No Kings': The Postsuburban Network in Douglas Coupland's *Microserfs*," *Western American Literature* 46 (2011): 302–24.

16. The Redmond-Bellevue that Coupland describes bears a striking resemblance to the Puget Sound metroscape analyzed in Anne Moudon and Paul Hess, "Suburban Clusters: The Nucleazation of Multifamily Housing in Suburban Areas," *Journal of the American Planning Association* 66 (2000): 243–64.

17. Thomas Pynchon, *The Crying of Lot 49* (New York: Harper Collins, 1999), 12, 13.

18. Michael Dear, "The Los Angeles School of Urbanism: An Intellectual History," *Urban Geography* 23 (2003): 493–509.

19. Edward Soja, "Inside Exopolis: Scenes from Orange County," in Michael Sorkin, ed., *Variations on a Theme Park: The New American City and the End of Public Space* (New York: Hill and Wang, 1992), 95. Also see Rob Kling, Spencer Olin, and Mark Poster, eds., *Postsuburban California: The Transformation of Orange County since World War II* (Berkeley: University of California Press, 1991). For Edward Soja as context for Coupland, see Andrew Tate, *Douglas Coupland* (Manchester, U.K.: Manchester University Press, 2007), 109.

20. Jean Baudrillard, *America*, trans. Chris Turner (New York: Verso, 1988). The Baudrillard reference is common in critical writing about Coupland: Robert McGill, "The Sublime Simulacrum: Vancouver in Douglas Coupland's Geography of Apocalypse," *Essays on Canadian Writing* no. 70 (Spring 2000): 252–76; Will Katerberg, *Future West:*

Utopia and Apocalypse in Frontier Science Fiction (Lawrence: University Press of Kansas, 2008), 40–41, 235n4, 236n25.

21. Tate, *Douglas Coupland*, 110.

22. *Girlfriend in a Coma* was written in the 1990s when Vancouver was indeed taking off as a center for television and cinema production.

23. Nick Yablon, *Untimely Ruins: An Archeology of American Urban Modernity, 1819–1919* (Chicago: University of Chicago Press, 2009).

24. Johann Wolfgang von Goethe noted the opportunity when he wrote: "America, you have it better than our old continent," being untroubled by Europe's useless memories and conflicts. It was not that better results were guaranteed, but there seemed fewer impediments to political progress. Goethe wrote *Den Vereinigten Staaten* in 1827 and published it in *Musen-Alamanach* issued by Amadeus Wendt in 1831.

25. Francis Fukuyama, "The End of History?" *National Interest* 16 (1989): 3–18; G. P. Lansbury, "Generation X and the End of History," *Essays on Canadian Writing* no. 58 (Spring 1996), 229–40; Katerberg, *Future West*; McGill, "The Sublime Simulacrum."

26. There could be long debates whether *Girlfriend in a Coma* is science fiction, magical realism, or some other genre and whether Jared's ghost actually is supposed to manifest outside the heads of the survivors.

27. Kathy Knapp offers interesting readings in "Richard Ford's Frank Bascombe Trilogy and the Post-9/11 Suburban Novel," *American Literary History* 23 (2011): 500–28. I disagree, however, with her assertion that "society" has ceased to exist in Bascombe's world (507), given that Frank is constantly navigating among professional, social, and business associates.

28. Lizabeth Cohen, *A Consumer's Republic: The Politics of Mass Consumption in Postwar America* (New York: Knopf, 2003).

29. Summaries of Rockford episodes can be found at www.tv.com/shows/the-rockford-files/episodes and Sopranos summaries at www.hbo.com/the-sopranos/episodes. Both accessed October 23, 2013.

30. Jim Rockford's Los Angeles is like that described by novelist Alison Lurie: "She gestured at Mar Vista laid out below the freeway: a random grid of service stations, two-story apartment buildings, drive-ins, palms, and factories; and block after block of stucco cottages." Alison Lurie, *The Nowhere City* (New York: Coward-McCann, 1965), 25.

31. Claude Fischer, *To Dwell among Friends: Personal Networks in Town and City* (Chicago: University of Chicago Press, 1982).

32. Between 1982 and 1997, Phoenix converted sixteen acres of land from rural to urban uses for every hundred new residents, Los Angeles converted fifteen acres, and Salt Lake City converted nine acres. In contrast, Nashville converted forty-two acres and Charlotte converted forty-nine acres.

33. Carl Abbott, "Southwestern Cityscapes: Approaches to an American Urban Environment," in Robert Fairbanks and Kathleen Underwood, eds., *Essays on Sunbelt Cities and Recent Urban America* (College Station: Texas A&M University Press, 1990), 59–86.

CHAPTER 4

On the Sidewalks of Los Angeles

Falling Down opened in American movie theaters on February 26, 1993. The film started well, with a gross box office take of $8,724,000 for its first weekend, but eventually dropped to thirty-seventh among 1993 releases with total domestic gross of $40,904,000 (that's just above *The Piano*, with its evocation of the New Zealand frontier, just below *Homeward Bound: The Incredible Journey* with its super appealing golden retriever, and way, way behind *Jurassic Park* and *Mrs. Doubtfire*).

Viewers saw two intercut stories. The central figure is William Foster (Michael Douglas), a redundant civilian defense worker who abandons his car with vanity D-FENS license plates when construction at a freeway access ramp jams up traffic (fig. 4.1). His air-conditioning stops working, the handle breaks when he tries to roll down his window, and he is simply fed up with petty annoyances. He starts walking toward the home of his estranged wife because it is his daughter's birthday. On the way he has increasingly violent encounters with a Korean convenience store owner, Latino gang members, a panhandler, a fast food manager, an obnoxious pedestrian at a phone booth, a neo-Nazi surplus shop owner (whom he kills), a rude construction worker (who inspires him to speed up work with a shoulder-held rocket launcher), and golfers at a private club. In the intertwined story, L.A. police detective Prendergast (Robert Duvall) spends his last day before retirement tracking a series of strange incident reports, identifying Foster, and pursuing him to his wife's home in Venice Beach. The film ends on Venice Pier with suicide by cop: Foster pulls what turns out to be his daughter's water pistol, forcing Duvall to shoot him.[1]

Critics either celebrated the film's ironic energy or hated what seemed, at first glance, to be its demonization of racial minorities and near-celebration of vigilante violence. The film drew protests from the Korean American Coalition and Latino spokespeople, not to mention the National Center for Career Change who thought it a bad model for surplused industrial workers. Some commentators worried that it would inspire copycat vigilantism. *Newsweek* called it a "deeply confused exploitation film." Ken Turan in the *Los Angeles Times* called it a "greedy picture" that wanted "to have things both ways, to spinelessly pander to a mass audience on the one hand while piously calling attention to pressing urban problems on the other." It struck him as "eager to get credit for the way it uses serious social problems as shallow window dressing in an urban fantasy" in which Everyman transforms into the Terminator.[2]

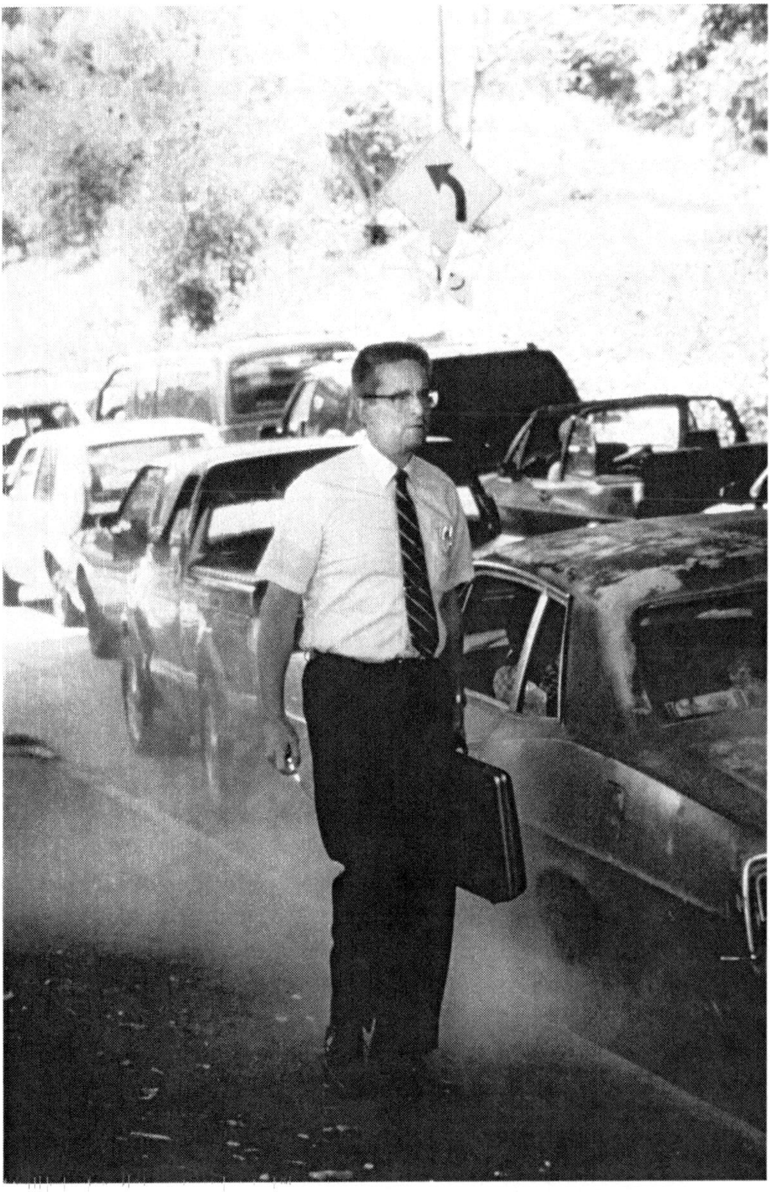

FIG. 4.1. William Foster abandons his automobile. Early in the film *Falling Down*, William Foster, as played by Michael Douglas, abandons his car in a traffic jam, to the disgust of other drivers. He grabs his briefcase with his lunch and starts a twenty-mile traverse of Los Angeles. (Courtesy Warner Bros./Photofest, Inc. © Warner Bros.)

Context is important. The last days of that February were not a good time for the United States. On the same day that the film opened, terrorists detonated 1,500 pounds of explosives concealed in a truck parked under the north tower of New York's World Trade Center, killing six people and injuring hundreds. Two days later, agents of the federal Bureau of Alcohol, Tobacco and Firearms raided the Branch Davidian compound in Waco, Texas, triggering a gun battle that killed four agents and six Branch Davidians and initiated a multiweek siege. Both events were precursors of worse to come—the fiery death of eighty cult members, when the government moved to end the Branch Davidian siege in mid-April of the same year, and the second devastating attack on the World Trade Center in 2001.

Things were no more comfortable in Los Angeles itself. Six days of riots had erupted on April 29, 1992, after the not-guilty verdict in the trial of police officers charged with excessive force in the arrest of motorist Rodney King. The riots interrupted the last days of filming for *Falling Down*. With a death toll of fifty-three, the L.A. riots were the nation's worst civil disturbance since the widespread disorder that had followed the assassination of Martin Luther King, Jr., in 1968. For a city where African American Tom Bradley was finishing his fifth four-year term as mayor, the riots were a painful reminder of the persistent racial tensions and class inequality that Mike Davis had recently described in his passionate polemic *City of Quartz* (1990).[3]

Falling Down is very much an urban film. Underlying all the action is the depiction of the ways in which the characters understand and navigate Los Angeles, and the ways in which they reveal themselves in their responses to the city and its neighborhoods. In the first of the following sections I look briefly at the standard critical response, which has expanded on the initial reviews by highlighting race and the crisis of masculinity. Race, gender, and economic status certainly bring out important aspects of *Falling Down*, but the film takes on additional character when approached in terms of both space and place. Space is the interpretive pivot for the second section, which explores what Los Angeles looks like from the sidewalk rather than the freeway. Place is lens for the third section, which considers William Foster's trek as an exploration of suburban frontiers.

Angry White Male

Given that the film was released when Los Angeles was still recovering from its civil upheaval and re-examining the relations among its mosaic of racial and ethnic groups, it was inevitable that critical analysis followed the media reviews by focusing on William Foster as a representative white male.

The character's whiteness caught people's attention and, indeed, director Joel Schumacher's attention. In a cover story in the July 1993 issue of film magazine *Empire*, he commented that African Americans were not the only angry people in the United States (the cover shouts "Mad As Hell: Has Michael Douglas Gone Too Far with *Falling Down*?"). Norman Klein has called *Falling Down* "the first remapping of the new Los Angeles myth—the city as Hispanic hell." Eric Avila frames Foster's journey through the "racialized milieu" of 1990s Los Angeles as an enactment of the nativist hostility to demographic change that would soon bring passage of Proposition 187 in 1994, denying social services to undocumented residents, Proposition 209 in 1996, curtailing affirmative action, and Proposition 227 in 1998, terminating bilingual education.[4] Vincent Brook similarly argues that Foster is "stuck in L.A.'s pre–Multicultural Era," remembering the city of the 1950s and early 1960s as a paradise. In the convenience store, he tells the Korean owner that he's "rolling prices back to 1965," which is of course the year of the landmark legislation that opened the United States to higher levels of Asian and Latin American immigration.[5]

Foster's first violent confrontation indeed crosses racial lines when he stops at a convenience store to ask for change for a phone call. Ticked off by the Korean American owner's insistence that he buy something and then outraged by the high prices typical of such stores in poor neighborhoods, he wrests a baseball bat from the owner, smashes the displays, and then carefully pays for his soda. Screenwriter Ebbe Roe Smith explicitly wrote the character as a Korean immigrant rather than generic Asian American.[6] The choice gave the scene authenticity, for convenience stores and small markets have frequently been entry points for entrepreneurial Korean immigrants. It also resonated painfully in 1993 because Korean businesses had been a major target for rioters the previous year—revealing a racial tension that had been obvious to poor Angelinos but perhaps a surprise to affluent whites in Brentwood and Pacific Palisades.

The second confrontation comes with stereotyped Latino gangbangers. Two tough guys hassle Foster as he takes a break on rubble-strewn land overlooking the core of the city, telling him that he is loitering and trespassing on their territory. He fights back with a baseball bat, driving the punks off with solid swats. Angry at their humiliation, they return to their car, unlimber firearms, and try to take out Foster in a drive-by shooting. They miss their target, hit innocent folks in front of a Latino storefront, and crash their car. Foster ends the confrontation by taking a whole bag of weapons and shooting one of the crash survivors in the leg—the next step in the growing escalation of his aggressive behavior (fig 4.2).

Hereafter, however, all of Foster's victims are white. His estranged wife (Barbara Hershey), who has taken out a restraining order and whose fear of his potential for violence hovers in the background, is white. He confronts a white fast food manager who refuses to serve breakfast after the breakfast hour (there's an echo of *Five Easy Pieces* in the scene). He has very testy encounters with a white panhandler in MacArthur Park (which actually has a heavily Hispanic clientele), a white pedestrian who wants him to get off a payphone he's using to call his wife, two different white construction workers, another rude white driver, the white

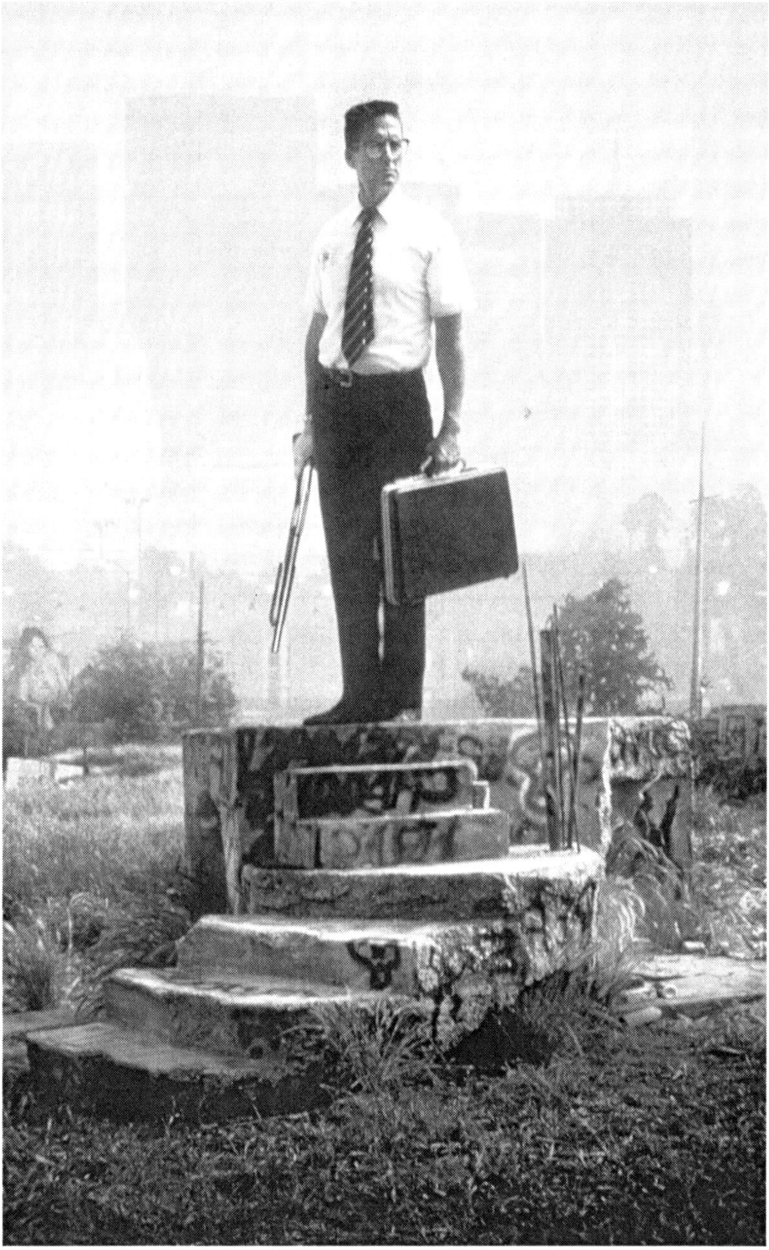

FIG. 4.2. William Foster takes on the world. Used in advertisements for *Falling Down*, this image shows Foster silhouetted against the downtown Los Angeles skyline. He carries a gun that he took from a gang member and uses on his angry trek through the city. (Courtesy Warner Bros./Photofest, Inc. © Warner Bros.)

gun shop owner whom he kills, and two elderly white golfers who object to his trespassing on their private course.[7]

In contrast, his first African American encounter is neutral in effect and underscores the stress of economic transition, while the second is perhaps the most relaxed encounter on his journey. In the first, a well-dressed black man is picketing a bank as Foster walks by. The man has banked there for seven years but has just been denied a loan because he is "not economically viable." Police arrive to take the picketer into custody. As they hustle him into their squad car, he locks eyes with Foster and says, "Don't forget me." Foster's response is a scarcely perceptible nod that acknowledges the sharing of economic status across racial lines, and he later applies the phrase "not economically viable" to himself. A few scenes later, Foster encounters a black middle-school-age boy, who casually instructs him on how to use a portable rocket launcher (the boy assumes that Foster is involved in making a movie).[8]

Foster's whiteness was so obvious, especially as Michael Douglas played him with quintessential nerdiness, that academics soon decided that gender was just as interesting as race. William Foster is said to represent not only racial tension but also a crisis of white *masculinity*. After two decades of women's studies, gender analysis was broadening in the 1990s to problematize male and masculine as social and cultural categories. Google's Ngram site, which searches for words and phrases in a huge database of English language books, indicates that "gender studies" first appeared in 1984. Usage grew rapidly to reach a plateau in 1993, still way behind "women's studies" but at least on the same page.[9] *Falling Down* was great material for the new specialists, a popular text with lots to say, apparently, about American men.

These analysts offer interesting perspectives. Nick Pfeil contrasts Foster's loss of masculine authority with the contrary trajectory of Detective Prendergast, who regains professional and personal authority as he tracks and kills Foster.[10] Jude Davies also contrasts Foster and Prendergast—one who fails as breadwinner and defender of his family, the other who re-establishes his position as the powerful male.[11] Common comparisons are drawn with action pictures from the same era such as *Die Hard*, *Unforgiven*, *Demolition Man*, and the various Rambo films.

In this social reading, however, what is central about Foster is not that he is white or male per se but that he is a downwardly mobile suburbanite who has lost the value of a sense of order. Lack of "economic viability" is as much Foster's problem as that of the African American picketer. As Ebbe Roe Smith points out, he is someone who has done his job too well.[12] The American defense establishment in the 1980s out-invented and out-produced the USSR, pushing the Gorbachev regime toward the *perestroika*, or economic and social restructuring that helped to undermine the Soviet system. The Cold War was over in 1993, defense spending had dropped, and California was experiencing a major downsizing of the aerospace industry. Service businesses are poor substitutes for real productive industry, at least in the mind of William Foster, who has little time for operators and patrons of shops, restaurants, and entertainment venues. The African American picketer's white shirt and tie don't protect his economic standing any more than they have protected Foster. The Whammy Burger manager wears the same middle-class uniform, suggesting that Foster reacts so strongly because he sees the manager as the embodiment of his own downsized future.

In a phrase, Foster has what I'll call the "Lakewood problem," named for the suburb of 17,500 houses built in the late 1940s and early 1950s on bean fields north of Long Beach. It was the California dream for the upwardly mobile middle class. The small 1,000 square foot houses were up to date (Lakewood was "garbage free" because each house had an in-sink disposal), and they did not all look alike. Dozens of parks and playgrounds helped to divide the development into distinct communities. Residents of each neighborhood staked a claim to "their" park, and kids only ventured into other parks at the invitation of a friend. Most of the residents would have agreed that it was "Tomorrow's City Today," with its very large shopping center and big new high school that was the "jewel of the town."

Lakewood in the 1950s, 1960s, and 1970s was an optimistic and very homogeneous community. Its dads, veterans of World War II and Korea, worked at the Douglas Aircraft plant or the Long Beach Naval Station. Moms stayed home with the kids. Boys growing up in Lakewood had a clear trajectory to success: high school sports, the military, and a job in the defense industry. It was also very, very white, completing a monoculture in terms of age, family patterns, economic class, and race. As one thoughtful native has commented, it was "the American Dream made affordable for a generation of industrial workers. . . . They were oriented to aerospace. . . . They worked at all the places that exemplified the bright future that California was supposed to be."[13]

The flip side of the successful 1950s and 1960s, however, was an inability to adapt to racial integration and the disappearance of industrial jobs in the 1980s and 1990s. Boys now graduated from high school with poorer prospects of defense jobs or military careers. With no layers of history, writes another of Lakewood's "original kids," the community "has the feeling of a club—the feeling that because everyone started out together, residents are entitled to lifetime 'charter membership.'"[14] Many Lakewooders did not like having darker skinned outsiders using "their" parks and using the real estate market to ask admission to the club, especially when they cast a wary eye on troubled multiracial communities like nearby Compton. By 2010, Lakewood itself would be split 50–50 between whites and people of color. No Lakewooders went on a D-FENS rampage, but they would have understood the economic and social pressures that made the fictional Foster snap.[15]

Foster's economic demotion challenges his sense of order. He carries an internal sense of what is right and proper (he is a tightly wound engineer type). He wants those standards recognized and gets increasingly frustrated when they are violated or ignored. That people of color sometimes perpetrate the violations is

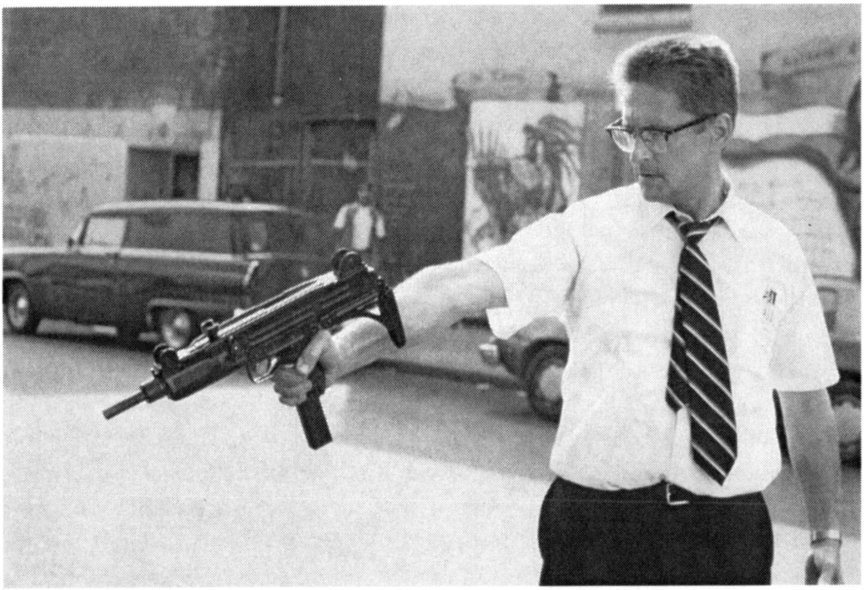

FIG. 4.3. Foster versus a pay phone. Well into the film, Foster is armed with an automatic weapon. Foster, hassled by a bystander who thinks he is taking too long at a pay phone, offers a lesson in good manners by blowing away the phone. (Courtesy Warner Bros./Photofest, Inc. © Warner Bros.)

important to him, but not central. The traffic jam itself is a color-neutral violation of order—a well-engineered transportation system will not clog up. Honking horns and yelling kids in a school bus add to the disorder. On his pilgrimage, Foster tries to enforce right order in the convenience store and polite behavior at a phone booth (fig 4.3). Later in the film, after committing murder, he still values civility and still dislikes people who yell and push out of line. Walking past another traffic jam, he punches a driver who is uselessly screaming at the lady in the next car. And he challenges what he sees as pernicious or false social order that is being promoted by white people: neo-Nazi values, Whammy Burger rules, golf club exclusion. For balance, Robert Duvall's detective represents the sort of calm rational order that Foster thinks he is upholding.

The Sidewalks of L.A.

A discussion of New York could easily start and end on its plazas and sidewalks, as with William H. Whyte's classic studies of *The Social Life of Small Urban Spaces* (1980). For Los Angeles it would more naturally start in an automobile on the Harbor Freeway or the 10 or the 101. L.A. is an automotive city whose postwar freeways developed a powerful imagery of freedom. To the literary imagination they offer the joy of the open road inside the metropolitan setting. The trope goes back at least to James Cain's *Mildred Pierce* (1941), whose title character gains freedom when she learns to drive and experiences a burst of joy when she cruises down Pasadena's Colorado Boulevard in the middle of the night with the traffic lights all in cycle. Reyner Banham was a British architectural critic who came to Los Angeles at the end of the 1960s and learned to drive so that he could experience the real city. He dubbed the city's new freeway system Autopia—one of the essential cityscapes that he explored in *Los Angeles: The Architecture of Four Ecologies* (1971). To learn L.A., he had to learn to drive, for he thought that the city will "never be fully understood by those who cannot move fluently through its urban texture" nor by those who cannot go with the flow of its unprecedented life." It was "a coherent state of mind, a complete way of life," and a "special way to be alive."[16] It is certainly a way to be alive for Jim Rockford, for whom liberation from prison means freedom to drive the streets and freeways of greater Los Angeles.

Los Angeles freeways supposedly offer peace and transcendence along with speed. They are elevated, sometimes on actual pillars and platforms, sometimes just metaphorically. California terminology contrasts freeways with "surface streets." The former are special (even when they are actually built on or below grade); the latter are mundane, ordinary, earth-bound. Freeway driving can be an escape, time to contemplate and consider apart from distractions. In typically oblique French fashion, Jean Baudrillard called driving "a spectacular form of amnesia," where things can be discovered as well as forgotten. Banham reported that the extreme concentration to drive L.A. motorways brought on "a state of heightened awareness that some locals find mystical." Joan Didion's character Maria Wyeth drives the freeways to deal with mental breakdown and social disconnection in her iconic novel *Play It As It Lays* (1970), and Didion later commented that freeway driving is "the only secular communion Los Angeles has," requiring "total surrender, a concentration so intense as to seem a kind of narcosis, a rapture-of-the-freeway."[17]

As Iain Borden points out in *Drive: Journeys through Film, Cities and Landscapes*, to transgress in the world of automobiles is to go too fast. Driving too fast is an explicit way to break rules—the rules of the road themselves and the larger rules of conformity. This can be simple illegal street racing—see *Rebel without a Cause* and *American Graffiti*—or as artsy as Claude Lelouch's eight-minute short *C'etait un rendezvous* (1976) in which he drove a Mercedes with a special bumper-mounted camera at breakneck and dangerous speeds through early morning Paris.[18] We get red light tickets and speeding tickets but not slowing tickets (even though freeways occasionally have minimum as well as maximum speeds).

William Foster's initial action is a curiously American twist on the tipping point story. Smith's inspiration for his screenplay was a news story about a big-rig trucker who went nuts on the highway, taking out his frustrations by ramming into cars from behind.[19] This episode was "road rage," a term that would take off in popular usage in 1994 and 1995. It was usually associated with drivers pulling guns on other drivers or ramming them or running them off the road—like Smith's idea-germ or the hyperbolic chase scene in *Terminator 3: Rise of the Machines* (2003). The rest of the film subjects Foster to the everyday annoyances that bother us all, but that build and build to the point of explosion.

Foster's transgression is the opposite of all expectations.[20] He can't feel meditative transcendence when he's trapped among other cars in the opening scene and bedeviled by a buzzing fly that is just as trapped and increasingly desperate as he. Nor can he take the opposite approach and use his car as a weapon of revenge when there's no place for it to go. His choice is to slow down, leaving the car as a traffic block rather than using it as a weapon. He becomes a pedestrian, a walker in the city, a status that unsettles his normal identity (middle-class engineers drive cars) and exposes him to the unexpected, the unfamiliar, and the unwanted.

The result is not what urban theorists have had in mind when celebrating the sidewalk as the site where city dwellers perform their identity through the rituals of strolling, shopping, sitting, and hanging out in "third places."[21] If we were in Vienna or Sevilla, it would be hard to knock his decision to get out and walk. Most famously, an idealized Paris stoked the imagination of Walter Benjamin and his celebration of the *flaneur*, the independent observer who helped to create the city by strolling, stopping, and discovering its multiple individualities. In larger framework, we can scale up the function of the Parisian flaneur to span streetcorner gangs and Jane Jacobs's idealized Greenwich Villagers who define their neighborhoods by both observing and acting in public space.

Michel de Certeau wrote in the same vein. He opened his chapter about "Walking in the City" in *The Practice of Everyday Life* (1980; translated 1984) by contrasting the view of Manhattan from the top of the World Trade Center with the everyday experience of the sidewalk. He argues that abstract plans do not create cities. Instead, "the ordinary practitioners of the city live 'down below.' . . . They are walkers, *Wandersmänner*, whose bodies follow the thicks and thins of an urban 'text' they write without being able to read it." Walking the city is both a literal activity and a synecdoche for the routines and actions of everyday life. Myriad individuals generate the meaning of urban space by moving through it, using it, and filtering it through their own perceptions and imaginations in ways that are beyond control and discipline. They intertwine to shape the places where they live without their being fully aware of the process. De Certeau offers a democratic—even utopian—vision in which the city emerges from the networks and interactions of individuals going about their lives.[22]

In *Falling Down*, unfortunately, Foster finds himself on the sidewalks of Los Angeles rather than the pavements of Paris. It is a city whose sidewalks have not inspired much poetry, where nobody sings:

> They'd part with all they've got, could they once more walk
> With their best girl and have a twirl on the sidewalks of Los Angeles.

Indeed, the best known depiction of Los Angeles on foot previous to *Falling Down* is Ray Bradbury's dystopian story "The Pedestrian," published in 1951 and set in the year 2053. Based on Bradbury's own experience of being questioned by police while walking in Pershing Square in 1940 and along Wilshire Boulevard in 1949, the story gives us Leonard Mead, who seems to be the last walker in his city, logging thousands of miles by day and night and never meeting another person on foot.[23] He takes the small pleasures of nighttime strolls along empty streets, but his muffled flaneurie ends as robotic police cart him off to a mental institution to be treated for his deviance from the norm. Walking in Los Angeles is a transgression.

William Foster is one of de Certeau's singular individuals, who not only performs his own identity but gives meaning to Los Angeles by his movement. Because he has opted off the freeway system, he cannot enter into a Didion/Banham bliss. Instead, there is an ever-changing spectacle for him to observe, but as an antiflaneur who finds the very opposite of delight in his random discoveries. He is not a detached observer but rather someone who interacts intimately with what he surveys. There is no place of restful observation. Phone booths are dangerous; Whammy Burger is not a Paris café. As he walks, he discovers a city he never knew. The transgressive action of being out of place (out of his car, out of his neighborhood) opens him to confrontations that inform him about the city and that also help to remold the experiences of everyone else: He can influence the city much more powerfully from the sidewalk than from his Chevrolet Chevette.

East Side, West Side

On and off the sidewalks, William Foster moves *through* his city on what could be an actual journey for which screenwriter Ebbe Smith tried to work out a plausible route. Foster's effort to reach his estranged wife and daughter starts in Pasadena, where he has been living in his mother's house, and takes its turn for the worse in East L.A., where he abandons his car for a journey that skirts downtown and aims west to Venice Beach.[24] It is a "suburban" or low-rise landscape of neighborhood commercial strips and single family houses, with the high-rise city seen only in the distance—visual settings that looked forward to *Pulp Fiction* (1994) rather than back to *L.A. Story* (1991). The total distance on foot would be somewhere around eighteen to twenty miles, a distance doable from morning rush hour to summer evening, especially if driven by adrenaline.

Maps twice appear in the film as police detective Prendergast plots a sequence of what he comes to understand as related incidents and sightings. The opening scene used a portion of the Pasadena Freeway, which borders the Lincoln Heights neighborhood northeast of downtown Los Angeles, and there is a later reference to the distance from Pasadena to Venice when a police officer is talking with Foster's wife. When Prendergast works with the first map (minute 40:50), his pointing finger suggests that Foster is moving south from Lincoln Heights through Boyle Heights. The map designates the site of the initial confrontation with the Latino gang members as the nonexistent "Angel Flight Hill" and also locates it southeast of downtown, although the shooting used the Temple-Beaudry neighborhood to the north of the city for its view of distant downtown towers.[25]

Foster's route then proceeds roughly westward: the construction site for the MacArthur Park subway station and then MacArthur Park itself in the Westlake district, westward through the Pico Union neighborhood, and then the more upscale Rancho Park neighborhood (which is adjacent to a couple of actual golf courses). On the second appearance of a map, Prendergast can now track a straight shot from Rancho Park through Mar Vista to Venice. The route is plausible but not perfect, at least if the maps are to be credited, since he would have to loop south around downtown and back north—out of his way—to MacArthur Park. Walking from Lincoln Heights to Temple-Beaudry to the park would be more direct.[26]

The route takes Foster across suburban frontiers. These are not the external suburban frontier of new housing pushing into vacant land—Lakewood obliterating bean and sugar beet fields, Leah Blue's Blue Water Development Company scheme for the Arizona desert in Leslie Marmon Silko's *Almanac of the Dead*, Arroyo Blanco Estates edging against the slopes of the Santa Monica Mountains in T. C. Boyle's *Tortilla Curtain*, or the urban growth boundary splitting the green landscape of Oregon. Instead, they are internal frontiers of ethnic difference and ethnic change within communities that date back to the first half of the twentieth century.[27] Foster goes from one territorial pocket to another. He restates the hassling by the gang members in white nerd language as "a territorial dispute" and the police later wonder what a white guy in a tie was doing in gangland. Homeless park dwellers make territorial claims, as do elderly white golfers.

In this sense, Foster is less a flaneur than an explorer who is testing boundaries—like Zebulon Pike trespassing into Mexico for a far-fetched analogy. He doesn't know these places he's traversing. He is a typical Angelino who has kept to the freeways rather than the surface streets, participating in the car culture that allows travelers to go from one place to another without the personal contact you have on New York or London subways. He has been able to get from one community to the other in a flash (or at least suspended animation), turning the city into the equivalent of flyover country—that freeway versus surface street distinction again. In contrast, by moving on foot, Foster has to perceive and deal with difference, and to treat L.A. itself as a frontier to be explored.[28] There is a savage tribe to be fought, and even familiar settings like fast food franchises and golf courses seem in his manic state to be the sites of exotic, inexplicable rituals.

These are internal frontiers that in actuality require repeated rediscovery by everyone in Los Angeles because they are in constant motion. The journey crosses the big boundary between the heavily Hispanic east side of Los Angeles and the whiter west side, but even that has never been a stable demarcation. At every scale, neighborhoods gentrify and decline. Ethnic groups move out of one area and into another. Planners and social scientists have a hard time keeping up, let alone someone like William Foster, whose life has been focused on work and family. By walking, he challenges the everyday assumption of the physical separation of class and race.[29] When screenwriter Ebbe Roe Smith commented in 1993 that "L.A. is the future of everywhere else. . . . Things that are happening here today will be happening everywhere else tomorrow," he may have been thinking of road rage and riots.[30] What the film shows in addition is the way in which all of the internal frontiers of U.S. cities are in constant change as metropolitan populations rearrange themselves. The moving frontier of the mythical American West is alive and well in metropolitan America.

The *Katabasis* of William Foster

In 401 B.C.E., Xenophon joined an army of Greek mercenaries hired by Cyrus the Younger to challenge his brother Artaxerxes II for the throne of Persia. When battle left Cyrus dead and his army stranded hundreds of miles deep into Persian territory, Xenophon helped to lead the surviving Greeks back to the safety of the Greek towns along the Black Sea. Xenophon's account is titled *Anabasis*, a term that references the march of the ten thousand into the interior of Asia in service of the Persian monarch. Most of the story, however, is the *katabasis* or return, a military retreat and a going down from high country to coast. "*Thalassa, thalassa!* The sea, the sea!" cry the remnant of the ten thousand when they reach the shelter of the coast.

Although born in Athens, Xenophon favored the oligarchic rule and military culture of Sparta—the state that pioneered an early version of the military-industrial complex. William Foster has spent his life devoted to building the national military and now, like Xenophon, finds himself a demobilized and redundant mercenary who has to make his way home. The old story and the new are about the adventures and battles met on the way to safety.[31] Foster's ends with the sea, where he finds not safety but at least a form of closure to what he knows is a ruined life. There is a double twist in the end of his journey. The sea that meant renewed hope and rescue for Xenophon represents the termination of the American continental frontier and the end of Foster's exploring expedition.[32] But the Pacific has also been the pathway for many of the newcomers who have transformed and revitalized the city during Foster's adulthood—including, no doubt, the Korean storeowner who so annoyed him early on.

Notes

1. The film won the 1994 Edgar Award for best motion picture, awarded by the Mystery Writers of America.

2. David Ansen, "Revenge of the Supernerd," *Newsweek* 121, no. 9 (1993): 80; Kenneth Turan, "Everyman Can't Keep from 'Falling Down,'" *Los Angeles Times*, February 26, 1993, at http://articles.LAtimes.com/1993-02-26/entertainment/ca-375_1_falling-everyman-fens (accessed September 25, 2014). Tim Appelo, "Up in Arms over 'Falling Down'—Laid-Off Workers Are Offended by the Michael Douglas Film," *Entertainment Weekly*, March 12, 1993, http://www.ew.com/ew/article/0,,305859,00.html (accessed September 25, 2014). Jude Davies, *Falling Down* (London: Palgrave, 2013), 1–2.

3. An additional context is the contrast between *Falling Down* and two other contemporary Los Angeles movies. *Grand Canyon* (1991) also initiated its plot with a car breaking down in a threatening minority neighborhood, but it proceeded with a complex narrative of lives that intertwined across racial and class divides and ended with at least a promise of hope and redemption. *L.A. Story*, from the same year, was a lovingly shot tribute to Los Angeles as a place of possibilities, helped along by a bewitched billboard that communicates personal messages to Harris Telemeter (like Telemachus a man in search of a true home). Its tone is not truly contradicted by the insertion of a freeway shooting episode that would have had far different narrative consequences if inserted into *Falling Down*.

4. Norman Klein, *The History of Forgetting: Los Angeles and the Erasure of Memory* (New York: Verso, 1997), 107; Eric Avila, *Popular Culture in the Age of White Flight: Fear and Fantasy in Suburban Los Angeles* (Berkeley: University of California press, 2006), 234.

5. Vincent Brook, *Land of Smoke and Mirrors: A Cultural History of Los Angeles* (New Brunswick, N.J.: Rutgers University Press, 2013), 212.

6. Author interview with Ebbe Roe Smith, January 10, 2014.

7. Smith inserted the golfers explicitly to add to the roster of white victims. The film also deleted an originally planned scene in which Foster was to frighten an African American family in their home. Ibid.

8. Vincent Brook suggests that Foster may feel a closer connection to African Americans than to Asians or Latinos because African Americans played a role as defense workers starting in World War II.

9. *Journal of Gender Studies* began in 1991; *Social Policies: International Studies in Gender, State, and Society* began in 1994; *Feminist Issues* changed to *Gender Issues* in 1998. And there are many more.

10. Fred Pfeil, *White Guys: Studies in Postmodern Domination and Difference* (New York: Verso, 1995), 238–43.

11. Jude Davies, "'I'm the Bad Guy? *Falling Down* and White Masculinity in 1990s Hollywood," *Journal of Gender Studies* 4 (1995): 145–51. In a recent book dedicated to the film, Davies devotes the central chapter to "The 'Crisis of White Masculinity'" and returns to "white male paranoia" as the focus in the last chapter.

12. Author interview with Smith, January 10, 2014.

13. Donald Waldie, quoted in Joan Didion, "Trouble in Lakewood," *New Yorker*, July 26, 1993, 47.

14. Alida Brill, "Lakewood, California: 'Tomorrowland' at Forty," in *Rethinking Los Angeles*, ed. Michael Dear, E. Eric Schockman, and Greg Hise (Thousand Oaks, Calif.: Sage, 1996), 107.

15. Liam Kennedy has commented on the "fear of falling" among the white middle class in the 1990s in "Alien Nation: White Male Paranoia and Imperial Culture in the United States," *Journal of American Studies* 30 (1996): 87–100. In his analysis, William Foster embodies the willingness of white men to claim victimhood in the midst of a changing racial and gender landscape.

16. Reyner Banham, *Los Angeles: The Architecture of Four Ecologies* (New York: Harper and Row, 1971), 23, 213–14.

17. Jean Baudrillard, *America* (New York: Verso, 1989), 9; Banham, *Los Angeles*, 215; Joan Didion, *The White Album* (New York: Simon and Schuster, 1979), 83.

18. Iain Borden, *Drive: Journeys through Film, Cities and Landscapes* (London: Reaktion Books, 2013), 180–86.

19. Ebbe Roe Smith, "When the Rooftops of Your Mind Come Falling Down," *Los Angeles Times*, February 21, 1993.

20. See the brief comments in Elaine Kuo, "California v. California: Law, Landscape, and the Foundational Fantasies of the Golden State," *California Legal History* 7 (2012): 445–68 at http://www.cschs.org/04_publications/images/CLH_2012-VOL-7-Web-Summary.pdf (accessed September 25, 2014).

21. For a book in which urban planners actually investigate different ways in which contemporary Americans use the sidewalks of Los Angeles and other cities, see Anastasia Loukaitou-Sideris and Renia Ehrenfuecht, *Sidewalks: Conflict and Negotiation over Public Space* (Cambridge, Mass.: MIT Press, 2011).

22. Michel de Certeau, *The Practice of Everyday Life*, translated by Steven Rendell (Berkeley: University of California Press, 1984), 93.

23. John Wilson, "Ray Bradbury, the Pedestrian," July 13, 2012, http://www.firstthings.com/blogs/firstthoughts/2012/07/on-the-square-today-268 (accessed September 25, 2014). Bradbury, who lived in Los Angeles from age fourteen, never held a driver's license.

24. Pasadena in Los Angeles imagery represents the old, comfortably white city of earlier decades, but in fact it is a multiethnic city. African Americans have been part of Pasadena since the early twentieth century, living in west and northwest Pasadena. In the late 1930s, housing specialists noted that this "old unrestricted area has long been inhabited by the servant class who were employed by wealthy families in the higher grade areas to the west and south." The city was 70 percent non-Hispanic white in 1970 but only 39 percent by 2010. For the quote from the U.S. Home Owners Loan Corporation, see Becky Nicolaides, "'Where the Working Man Is Welcomed': Working Class Suburbs in Los Angeles, 1900–1940," *Pacific Historical Review* 68 (November 1999): 546.

25. Of course there is the famous Angel's Flight funicular running up Bunker Hill in central Los Angeles, but the place in the film is nowhere near or like the real thing. Other made-up places in the film are the corner of "Quintero and Fourth" and the "Altimore Country Club."

26. Whether director Joel Schumacher shared an urban studies professor's concern about continuity between the narrative and the illustrative maps is unknown, of course.

27. Venice was laid out in 1905 and annexed to Los Angeles in 1926; Rancho Park was developed in the 1920s and 1930s.

28. Author interview with Smith, January 10, 2014.

29. Ebbe Roe Smith, commentary on DVD "Deluxe Edition" of *Falling Down*, at 32:30 minutes.

30. Ryan Murphy, "Falling Down Writer Has Seen the Future: It's L.A.," *Los Angeles Times*, February 21, 1993.

31. The 1979 film *The Warriors* retells the retells Xenophon's story in more literal transcription to Brooklyn youth gangs.

32. Kennedy, "Alien Nation," 98–99.

Part II

Continental Refuge

In 1981, the Indian spiritual teacher Bhagwan Shree Rajneesh relocated to the United States from Pune, India. While investigating possible sites for a religious community, he and his chief lieutenant Ma Anand Sheela had a Brigham Young–like experience when they visited the sixty-four-thousand-acre Big Muddy Ranch in central Oregon. They knew instantly that this was the place for their planned utopia and quickly purchased the ranch at top dollar.

Both natives of crowded India, the Rajneesh brain trust thought that they had found the back of the beyond, where they could create their own version of Mormon Deseret. Sixty miles south of the Columbia River on sagebrush hills that rolled down to the John Day River, the new settlement quickly attracted North American and European followers in the hundreds and then thousands. Transfers of capital from adherents financed the expansion. Within three years the community had roughly three thousand residents and the appurtenances of a regular town, including a water system and police force. Rajneeshees, a popular term that adherents disliked, were enacting the American myth of pioneer conquest and settlement (albeit with plenty of sex and dozens of Rolls Royce automobiles for the Bhagwan). Rajneeshees armed themselves and displaced the natives by moving in large numbers to the nearby town of Antelope, outvoting the town's rural residents, and renaming it Rajneesh in 1983.

It turned out, however, that central Oregon was not quite the lawless wilderness that Sheela imagined. Because the ranch was agricultural land in a rural part of Wasco County, creation of what was effectively a new city violated state land-use laws. Rajneesh leaders excluded Wasco County officials with physical intimidation and tried to incorporate as the city of Rajneeshpuram. If a separate city, then the community could legally control its own land uses and would no longer be constrained as rural land. Oregon attorney general David Frohnmayer argued vigorously that the incorporation was illegal because the community was closed to nonadherents, a position with which court decisions agreed. The Rajneeshees also ran afoul of Oregon election law when they tried to expand their political control by busing homeless people from around the country to register as voters in a failed effort to take over Jefferson and Wasco County governments.

On September 14, 1985, Ma Anand Sheela and several other leaders abruptly left Rajneeshpuram because evidence had mounted that top leaders had conspired in a series of crimes against the "natives." These included arson, wiretapping, attempted murder, and the planting of salmonella bacteria in the salad bars of several restaurants in the city of The Dalles, sickening 750 people. Bhagwan Shree Rajneesh denounced Sheela, then fled the community, perhaps attempting to flee from prosecution. He eventually made a plea bargain on immigration fraud charges and agreed to leave the United States. Ma Anand Sheela and several other leaders were convicted of an assortment of crimes. By 1986, Rajneeshpuram was another of the many western ghost towns—later to have its extensive infrastructure recycled for a church youth camp.

The rise and fall of Rajneeshpuram carries historical lessons about the North American continental frontier, which has been much more complicated than the Rajneeshees thought as they threw their weight around.

Peoples on the frontier get layered over, not obliterated. The few dozen residents of Antelope, down from 250 at the height of the region's sheep and cattle boom in the early twentieth century, were a stubborn obstacle to Rajneeshee plans. Only a couple dozen miles away was the reservation of the Confederated Tribes of Warm Springs, still present despite the best efforts of nineteenth-century Oregon pioneers to act as if they too had arrived in a lawless wilderness. These are some of the same issues that frame Peter Matthiessen's retelling of E. J. Watson on the South Florida frontier. Crackers and Yankees have to share the swamps and islands and Indians remain a presence. Watson's ambitions fall short, just like Sheela's, as slowly thickening social institutions limit the range of his towering ego.

Rajneeshpuram was a part—a peculiar part—of the coastal region that sometimes goes by "Cascadia" and lies at far remove from the South Florida of the E. J. Watson trilogy. Although the chapters "Cascadian Dreams" and "West by Southeast" address opposite ends of the contiguous United States a century apart, each corner of the continent has offered (at least in the imagination) empty land on which residents can try to implement their different social visions.

In many ways, South Florida was incorporated into the national economy through force of will. At the same time, European Americans projected their hopes and ambitions onto the northwestern coast of North America. The relatively undeveloped region has invited ambitions for economic development and counterambitions to make it a model of environmental stewardship. In the context of this many-faceted debate about the regional future that has included the best-selling utopian novel *Ecotopia*, the Rajneesh experiment in effect offered one more way to imagine the Pacific Northwest as an empty land to be transformed.

Rajneeshees, in their own minds, were also refugees from a crass and uncomprehending world—if not from nuclear disaster or plague—who sought safety in the unpopulated interior of North America. Almost all of the communards were big city people who were willing and eager to move to the outback in search of greater personal fulfillment. If their instant city looked to outsiders like a sort of big summer camp for yuppies (to borrow Frances Fitzgerald's metaphor), it was also a serious effort to escape soul-catching lives in soulless cities. What some may have thought they were building is something like the democratic free state of Boulder that refugees construct in Stephen King's novel *The Stand*, which figures in the final chapter in this section on continental frontiers. The narratives discussed in "Rocky Mountain Refuge" and "The Light on the Horizon" center on the establishment of refugee frontiers, one chapter about postdisaster survivors fleeing *to* Colorado and the other about flight *from* cities. The Colorado of "Rocky Mountain Refuge" is also a counterpoint to Cascadia—both western regions whose future is imagined as malleable and unconstrained—which is to say, like Americans have imagined frontiers.

CHAPTER 5

West by Southeast

Peter Matthiessen's Florida Trilogy as Western Fiction

> Early in 1894, the *Falcon* set me on the dock at Everglade, a trading post on a tidal creek called Shorter River. . . . That professor at the World's Fair in Chicago who claimed there was no more American frontier had never heard about the Everglades. No roads. Not even a rough track, in all this southern part of Florida, only faint Indian water trails across the sea of grass to the far hammocks. (Peter Matthiessen, *Bone by Bone*, 151)

The voice evoking the spirit of F. J. Turner is that of Edgar J. Watson, the pivotal figure in Peter Matthiessen's trilogy of novels set on the lower Gulf Coast of Florida. *Killing Mister Watson* (1990) re-creates the story of Watson as a planter/pioneer from the 1880s until his death at the hamlet of Chokoloskee on October 24, 1910, struck down by bullets and shotgun pellets fired by a crowd of townspeople. Did they shoot in self-defense, as a murderous mob, or in righteous vengeance for Watson's own multiple murders? The book backtracks from its violent opening to trace Watson's rise as a frontier entrepreneur through the eyes of ten individuals including his daughter, the local sheriff, associates, and business rivals. *Lost Man's River* (1997), which is set more than fifty years later, follows the efforts of Watson's son Lucius to reconstruct the truth about his father's life. *Bone by Bone* (1999) shifts to the first person to create Watson's narrative of his own life from his childhood in South Carolina to his violent end in Florida.

This chapter examines the ways in which Matthiessen imagines and depicts the development of the Everglades coast from Fort Myers south to Cape Sable as part of American frontier history—that is, as a suitable subject for Frederick Jackson Turner. He does so by moving his central character from the Southeast to Oklahoma and Oregon and then back to Florida; by emphasizing tropes characteristic of western myth and fiction; by highlighting similarities in economic choices on resource frontiers, including the rapacious destruction of natural fauna; and by weaving interpersonal violence and firearms into the fabric of the narrative.

In addition, the trilogy is an extended meditation on the meanings of history and memory. Eyewitnesses offer differing accounts of Watson's death. Historical documents both real and imagined, contradict themselves and the witnesses. Lucius Watson, seeking the truth about his father in *Lost Man's River*, constructs plausible narratives that collapse with the discovery of new evidence and need to be rethought and rebuilt. E. J. Watson himself shades the truth and sometimes finds it difficult to place the events of his life in a coherent pattern.

The Character, the Novelist, the Novels

Edgar J. Watson was a real figure in the development of southwestern Florida. He arrived sometime in the late nineteenth century, built a house and farm on Chatham Key, now part of Everglades National Park, and died at the hands of his neighbors—at least neighbors by the standards of frontier distances.

The outlines of Watson's life were documented in local newspaper stories and reminiscences and summarized more systematically by Charlton Tebeau, the distinguished Florida historian who taught many years at the University of Miami. Tebeau's books included *The Story of the Chokoloskee Bay Country: With the Reminiscences of Pioneer C. S. "Ted" Smallwood* (1955) and *Florida's Last Frontier: The History of Collier County* (1966).[1] Tebeau's books and the historian himself were sources and guides for Matthiessen's research, receiving direct acknowledgment in the dedication to the first volume. Moreover, Matthiessen adapted and fictionalized Tebeau's work as a *History of Southwest Florida*, which is anonymously excerpted in *Killing Mister Watson* and attributed to Edgar Watson's son Lucius in *Lost Man's River*, the book in which Lucius, a professionally trained historian, painfully tries to uncover the truth about his father.[2] Matthiessen also drew information about Watson's time in Oklahoma in 1888–89 from *Hell on the Border: He Hanged Eighty-Eight Men*, the well-known compendium of frontier crime and punishment on the Arkansas-Oklahoma frontier written and published by journalist S. W. Harmon in 1898.[3] In turn, *Hell on the Border* appears in *Killing Mister Watson* (118), where arrival of a copy in Florida triggers talk between Watson's daughter and wife, and in *Bone by Bone* (114), where Watson himself notes its impact on his reputation.[4]

Peter Matthiessen is one of the leading writers and public intellectuals of the last half century. He was a cofounder of the *Paris Review* in 1953, a political activist, a novelist, and an essayist whose scores of published articles have ranged across issues of social justice and the natural world. Six of his books gained wide audiences through prepublication serialization in the *New Yorker*. Matthiessen describes his own identity as someone who "writes nonfiction on behalf of social and environmental causes, or journals about expeditions to wild places."[5] His books on nature and natural systems appeal for the preservation of vanishing creatures and peoples, drawing stark contrasts between wild nature and the encroachments of American/global capitalism.[6] Some are relatively objective references such as the coauthored *The Shorebirds of North America* (1967). Others combine travel reporting, personal meditation, and spiritual musings, as in *The Cloud Forest* (1961), *Under the Mountain Wall* (1962), *The Tree Where Man Was Born* (1972), *The Snow Leopard* (1978), and *The Birds of Heaven: Travels with Cranes* (2001).[7]

Matthiessen is likely better known to historians of the American West for his engaged reporting on radical social movements of the 1960s and 1970s. *Sal Si*

Puedes: Cesar Chavez and the New American Revolution (1969) was one of the first books that presented and interpreted Cesar Chavez and the United Farm Workers for a national audience. *In the Spirit of Crazy Horse* (1983) took the side of Leonard Peltier in his legal battle with the federal government. Matthiessen followed with reporting on threats to Indian lands across the United States in *Indian Country* (1984).[8]

Matthiessen first learned about and became fascinated with E. J. Watson as a teenager on a vacation trip in Florida. Sailing north from Key West along the western coast, "my father showed me Chatham River on the chart. He said there was a house a few miles up that river . . . that had formerly belonged to a man named Watson, who had killed many people before he was finally shot to pieces by his own neighbors."[9] Over the next three decades Matthiessen worked to understand Watson and his milieu with repeated trips to northern and southwestern Florida. Some of the visits involved research on other Florida topics that he treated in essays and in chapters in *Wildlife in America* and *Indian Country*.[10] In pursuit of the Watson legend itself he interviewed surviving Watson descendants and plunged into archival research of the sort well-known to historians—reading old newspapers in county libraries, pulling vines off old grave markers, and poking through legal records in county courthouses. His research and painstaking writing are documented in a voluminous collection of scrapbooks, articles, correspondence, drafts, galleys, and page proofs now at the University of Texas at Austin.[11]

Texas archivist James G. Watson has examined Matthiessen's struggle to frame the Edgar Watson story within the freedoms *and* conventions of fiction. As author, he invented extra characters to go along with the real Watson, family, and neighbors, keeping some of his inventions and discarding others. He tried to imagine Watson as others saw him, resulting in the first volume. He fictionalized his own research in *Lost Man's River*, casting Lucius Watson as both family historian and professional historian.[12] In this second book, as historical novelists are wont, he incorporates references to real historical sources such as Ted Smallwood's memoir and *Hell on the Border*.[13] He tried to imagine Watson himself from the inside out for the Watson "autobiography" in the third volume.

There is a curious last step. In 2008, at age eighty-one, Matthiessen published a single volume that reworked and condensed the trilogy from more than 1,300 pages to 892 pages. He retained the basic three-part structure but made drastic changes to what was now the middle section, shortening it, deleting characters, and shifting the action from the 1960s to the 1920s. The resulting book, *Shadow Country: A New Rendering of the Watson Legend* won a National Book Award. We might consider this more in the nature of recognition of lifetime achievement than a judgment on the merits of *Shadow Country* itself, which is inferior in depth and complexity to the trilogy.[14] I base my analysis on the original books.

Southern Saga or Western Myth?

Edgar J. Watson was a southerner by definition. He was born in South Carolina, lived much of his life in Florida, and died there. As imagined by Matthiessen he is driven by a cultural heritage of southern violence and southern honor, topics for which Matthiessen consulted leading historical studies by scholars such as Richard Maxwell Brown, Joel Williamson, and Bertram Wyatt-Brown.[15] Murder and mayhem haunt Watson's family heritage. He is a self-made man who gains wealth by the sometimes violent exploitation of African American workers. He lives in an impressive white house among impenetrable swamps, ravenous reptiles, and unmarked graves. He dies at the hands of a mob. We have more than enough elements to classify the first and third installments as examples of the Southern Gothic.

There's more: A character at least half crazy with ambition and self-regard, E. J. Watson may quickly remind readers of Thomas Sutpen, the equally self-regarding center of William Faulkner's masterful novel *Absalom, Absalom* (1936). Sutpen, like Watson, comes from the older South to the newer South (Virginia to Mississippi). He constructs his life around the acquisition of land. He goes through a sequence of wives and mistresses in search of a suitable heir to continue a dynasty. He sets himself apart. In Faulkner's words, "He was amoral, he was ruthless, completely self-centered," a man who "did not believe that he was part of the human family."[16] After his death, his fine house burns spectacularly, taking son and dependents with it, just as Watson's abandoned house burns at the end of *Lost Man's River* with two of his sons inside.[17]

In both Faulkner and Matthiessen (and also in Robert Penn Warren's *All the King's Men*), the stories lead into discussion of the power of memory and the burdens of history. As southern narratives, they are about the inability of individuals to escape the deeds of the past—their own pasts, those of their families, and those of their communities. The novels are therefore constructed as historical investigations in which multiple accounts are discovered, weighed, and pieced together in an effort to cope with the power of myth and memory.

But Matthiessen also conceived the Watson story as a frontier/western narrative in which the driving force is the power of reinvention and escape from history. It is not news to Floridians that their southwestern coast was a late and thinly settled frontier. Previous critics and commentators on Matthiessen's work have noted that *Killing Mister Watson* is "a turn-of-the-century Everglades frontier western" and that the fictionalized protagonist exudes "rugged individualism and lawless frontier values" and illustrates "the frontier mentality at work."[18] Acknowledging that the trilogy can be read as a Southern Gothic, my goal is to unpack the concept of "frontier western" as Matthiessen has used it in the three books. He, or his characters, variously term late nineteenth-century Florida a wilderness, a virgin land (*Bone by Bone*, 65), and a frontier (*Bone by Bone*, 78), but exactly what sort of frontier does Matthiessen depict? How does it mirror or connect to the more commonly understood western frontier? Does Matthiessen really use the conventions of western genre fiction, and how does he do so?

Layers of Westernness

We find layers of westernness—at least westernness as embodied in myth and fiction—in the trilogy's plot, protagonist, and place.

Killing Mister Watson begins with a shoot-out, the most hackneyed trope in western fiction. There are variations, of course. Some are purely physical. On a Florida coast of islands, swamps, and inlets, "main street" is not a dusty road lined by false-front saloons and livery stables but the waterfront where fishing boats and schooners come and go. It is a horizontal standoff. Rather than the single axis that defines the western shoot-out—two men confined by buildings and wooden sidewalks within a narrow corridor—townspeople have lined up on the shore. Watson motors up the channel, kills the engine of his gasoline launch, drifts onto the beach because a recent hurricane has wiped out the dock, and steps from deck to shore to face a score of men who flank him as well as face him. The weapons on both sides are workaday shotguns and rifles, not six-shooters. With hurricane damage to be repaired, taking care of Ed Watson also may not be the biggest thing on the local folks' minds.

A second difference from the shoot-out cliché is moral. The killers openly share the responsibility for the homicide. The men of the community stand together to confront, warn off, and then shoot down Mr. Watson. For better or worse, whether they are executing a killer or assassinating an innocent man, they stand together rather than huddling in fear while a single brave lawman faces down the bad guy as in *High Noon* and numerous episodes of "Gunsmoke." Instead they are—potentially—a misguided lynching crew in the style of Walter Van Tilburg Clark's *The Ox-bow Incident* (1940).

Jane Tompkins in *West of Everything*, a literature professor's extended essay on classic western films and novels, highlights the centrality of *death*. And it is death depicted in a very specific way, with a focus on externalities rather than inward psychology. "The Western plot," she writes, depends "on external conflicts in which men prove their courage to themselves and the world by facing their own annihilation. . . . Events that would normally loom large—birth, marriage, embarking on a career—become peripheral" and attention centers on "a few extraordinary moments—the holdup, the jailbreak, the shoot-out."[19] How one *confronts* adversity is what counts, not what one thinks about it.

The men of Chokoloskee share the code. They will talk about what they believed about Ed Watson but not about inner struggles to reconcile and understand Watson's violent and courtly personas, for he could be as charming as he was ruthless. Nor do they reflect or regret in the following decades. For all that he tries, Lucius cannot get them to talk about their motivations. They did the deed, they thought they were defending themselves, and that's that. For a writer like Matthiessen, who developed his art during the psychoanalytically oriented 1950s, Watson and his killers are both tantalizing and frustrating subjects.

The tropes of shoot-out and firearms are the pivot for the plot of loner versus community. E. J. Watson arrives on the southwest Florida frontier and carves out a miniature empire that disrupts a rudimentary economy based on hunting and gathering, a modern entrepreneur in a struggling community on the margin between subsistence and the market. With his ability to grow and process sugarcane in bulk to produce high quality Island Pride syrup, he has entrepreneurial drive and business acumen like none of his neighbors. As he notes, "Although still short of capital, my syrup trade was growing fast and had great prospects, with buyers lined up for every drop I could produce" (*Bone by Bone*, 186). As a dynamic businessman, he establishes connections with Fort Myers bankers and Florida land investors, and shares brandy and cigars with the ambitious Napoleon Broward, a future governor and wheeler-dealer "in the mold of Gould and Astor, Carnegie and Frick" (*Bone by Bone*, 156). He even meets vacationing Thomas Edison and "enjoyed being included by our civic leaders in excited discussions taking place at the approach of the new century" (*Bone by Bone*, 179).

As Matthiessen constructs Watson, in short, he is both the western desperado with the hair-trigger temper and volatile sense of honor *and* the bad guy in a common western scenario. With his aggressive appropriation of other men's land (he runs off squatters) and ideas (he steals the idea of a clam dredge), he is the invasive, modernizing capitalist who squeezes out the homesteader families. He is like the big rancher who tries to appropriate water rights and displace a Hispanic landowner in *The Big Country* (1958), the mining company goons who shoot down McCabe in *McCabe and Mrs. Miller* (1971), and the railroad thugs who shot down homesteaders at Mussel Slough in fact and in Frank Norris's recreation in *The Octopus* (1901).

Edgar Watson as the protagonist is constructed as a *western character* and a *frontier character*—independent minded, a homesteader (despite his capitalist drive), a man driven by the pursuit of the main chance, knowledgeable about native peoples.

Watson and several other characters directly link the Southeast to the West. Watson himself tries his hand at pioneering in the Indian Nations of Oklahoma, where he kills the notorious Belle Starr and acquires a larger-than-life reputation. By rumor he takes refuge in Oregon before returning to Florida. The Indian Nations in 1888–89, of course, were a land of transplanted southerners—relocated southern Indians and white migrants from the older South to the New Southwest—there were "plenty of Southern cracker boys . . . most folks were Southern—Texas, Missouri, Mississippi" (*Bone by Bone*, 106). They were also a place of erratic and confused law enforcement that not only produced *Hell on the Border* but also gave a figure like Edgar Watson an opportunity to practice bloody-minded independence.

Watson's time in Oklahoma gives him a cachet that transcends simple southern violence.[20] He appears in northern Florida as a desperado from the West with an aura of dime-novel heroism and danger. He enjoys trying on "Wild West talk" to intimidate bystanders (*Bone by Bone*, 228), and he enhances his reputation by killing a thug with the western-movie-sounding name Quinn Bass. Watson was "this big strong well-dressed feller back from the Wild West, supposed to have been some kind of a gunman, supposed to killed some famous outlaws in the Injun Country," one distant acquaintance remembers (*Lost Man's River*, 127). Note the plural outlaws in his growing reputation. In *Bone by Bone* he appears to deny killing Belle Starr, but a close reading shows that he never speaks to the question directly but simply notes that there was not enough hard evidence for an indictment; his second wife, who was with him in Oklahoma, clearly thinks he did it (*Killing Mister Watson*, 119). Children make up stories, spy on him "hoping to see his guns, and listen to his tales of the Wild West" (*Lost Man's River*, 192). He makes up his own stories about himself as well, claiming an association with Jesse James and Frank James—it was the latter he could count on in "hard situations" (*Bone by Bone*, 230). After his death, he blends in local memory with Wyatt Earp and Wild Bill Hickok, other untamed men who killed now and then but probably in good cause (*Lost Man's River*, 384).

Another key figure with a western connection is Henry Short, the mulatto who may have been the first man to pull the trigger on Watson on the fateful October 24. Henry's father "had him a fine horse from his days out west as a buffalo soldier in the federal militia. Fought Comanches in Texas and the like" before returning to Florida. If Watson brings back a reputation as an outlaw that awed and titillated his neighbors, Henry's father brings back pride and bravery that gets him lynched: "He rode too hard and talked too much, he figure that was his bounden right as a cavalry soldier and a new citizen. Henry's daddy was just the kinds them redshirts and night riders would come after, and when he got mixed up with a white girl—well, that finished him" (*Lost Man's River*, 279).

Henry Short shares with Watson a traumatic childhood and extraordinary skills with boat and gun, but he is also a moral antithesis—racially mixed rather than arrogantly white, personally cautious rather than flamboyant, steady rather than mercurial, modest in ambition rather than overbearing and overweening.

A third east–west connection comes when Dab Rowland, a dark-skinned man from Grand Cayman, hooks up with Abbie Harden, the light-skinned daughter of a white/Indian family. When threatened by a lynch mob, they take off for Arizona: "Wrote back to inform us that out in the West where nigras ain't so plentiful, the Injuns and Mexicans are treated even worse," reports Abbie's nephew Whidden Harden. "Just ain't enough black people out there for good Christians to get worked up about, cause they already have their hands full, bein mean to Injuns" (*Lost Man's River*, 441).

Like generations of frontier heroes, Watson is prodigiously skilled. He knows his way in the woods and knows where game is found—alligators, plume birds, schools of fish. When he turns his hand to farming, his operation out-competes his rivals. He knows how to handle horses, but one of his defining skills is sailing. He is a master not of horses but of boats. He can follow the watery trails and pathways of the Everglades.

And he can shoot! Skill with firearms marks the frontier hero since Natty Bumpo, and Edgar Watson is no exception. He can handle shotguns, rifles, and handguns with skill that intimidates potential enemies. When he fires a warning shot to run you off his property, you know that his next shot will not miss—he can knock your hat out of your hand and even clip off half of your handlebar mustache. As one of his northern Florida relatives recalls, "E. J. Watson could beat you and your rifle with a damn revolver, which was why they claimed he made his money as a gunfighter out in the Nation" (*Lost Man's River*, 118). He dies with a gun in his hands, raising it ready to shoot.

The possession of land is equally central to Edgar Watson's character. Like other frontier entrepreneurs, he stakes legal and extralegal claims to land and defends them. His motivation in part comes from the loss of the family land in South Carolina, an eighteenth-century estate that has been divided and dissipated by previous generations. In Oklahoma the quarrel with Belle Starr begins over land that Watson wants to rent from her but that she leases to someone else, leaving him disgruntled with a less fertile parcel. In North Florida, where the Watson clan has relocated after South Carolina and whence Watson returns after Oklahoma, resentments over land ownership and tenantry set off multiple murders (Watson is charged but acquitted for one of them): "It's land that causes murder in this part of the country. . . . What caused the murders was Sam Tolen selling off what Watson thought was rightfully Watson land" (*Lost Man's River*, 121). It is a landed empire that Watson constructs at Chatham Bend, turning a wild island into a productive sugar plantation. It is jealously over another fragment of high land that drives him to murder a young couple, who have quarreled over back wages at Chatham Bend, discovered possible evidence that he killed his black farmhands rather than pay them, and taken refuge on Lost Man's Key where they begin to farm and fish. In response, Watson buys the quitclaim deed to the island, which he already had his eye on, and orders them off: "E. J. Watson bought that claim on Lost Man's Key," he snarls, "and he wants them people off of it by Monday next" (*Killing Mister Watson*, 160). Their defiance ignites implacable rage and premeditated murder in which he maniacally involves his oldest son as well as himself (*Bone by Bone*, 188–200).

Watson's fixation on land introduces the related set of ways in which Matthiessen constructs the place of Southwest Florida as frontier west. It is a land where pioneers arrive "creaking through the woods in covered wagons" (*Killing Mister Watson*, 110) and rapacious resource harvesting is the order of the day. Law is rough and only sometimes ready, and "taking the law into your own hands was worse in Florida . . . than out in the Far West (*Killing Mister Watson*, 88). As in the West, the arrival of the railroad marks the transition from then to now, leaving even Edgar Watson astonished by the change wrought at Fort Myers by "the new railroad with its bridge across the river, which now connected our frontier cattle town to the outside world" (*Bone by Bone*, 248).

Indeed, the books are filled with the presence of the cattle industry, surely a defining element of the fictionalized West. There are cows, cowboys, cattle drives, mavericks to be branded, rustlers, and open range in E. J. Watson's Florida. The Florida cattle industry had origins in Spanish colonial days, as it did also in Texas and California. In the time of Ed Watson, the Alachua Prairie in north central Florida was "still a trackless country of red wolves, bear, and panthers" with half-wild cattle surviving from the Spanish days (*Lost Man's River*, 167). DeSoto County is an "open range" (*Lost Man's River*, 84) cattle frontier where "range wars and cattle rustling and general mayhem were rife, . . . and gunmen and bushwhackers from the West found steady work," according to Lucius's history (*Lost Man's River*, 52). It was the same around Arcadia in central Florida in the words of Ed Watson himself: "For a few years in the early nineties, the range wars around Arcadia beat anything the Wild West had to offer. The ranchers were advertising for gunmen as far off as St. Louis, and every outfit had its own gang of hard riders" (*Bone by Bone*, 137).

Where there are cowboys, there are also Indians, although they play secondary roles in Matthiessen's trilogy. Indian resistance to white pioneers is noted as part of Florida's background history, but the books give only passing attention to Indians in turn of the century Florida and Indian communities within the Everglades. One Indian in *Lost Man's River* briefly acts as shaman/guide who prods Lucius into activity and launches the action. Mostly frequently, however, Indians enter the story through the complexities of racial mixing as their intermarriage with both whites and blacks complicates the racial binary by introducing varieties of physical appearance and cultural heritage. Although racial mixture is certainly an important element of western history, the three-way dynamic marks this as a particular "southern" part of the novels and their setting.

The towns matched the countryside. Fort White in northern Florida in the 1870s could have stepped out of a western movie. It had "dirt streets and a boardwalk, hitching posts and water troughs, kerosene lampposts and saloons—looked like the Wild West frontier we saw in pictures" as Watson remembers it (*Bone by Bone*, 78). In those days, Lucius discovers, the town's surroundings were "little more than frontier wilderness" and the "Suwanee country was still wild and life uncertain" (*Lost Man's River*, 53, 105, also 112 and 114). Nearby Arcadia is "a wild cattle town" in 1890 (*Killing Mister Watson*, 23) and the setting for a classic western confrontation between Watson and Quinn Bass, "the bad news in a big cattle clan around Kissimmee" who "liked to play with gun and knife" (*Bone by Bone*, 138). Watson is drinking in an Arcadia bar when Bass walks in and insults him—in a place "no different from Edgefield or Fort White or anywhere else on the

American frontiers. Not to defend your honor was your finish" (*Bone by Bone*, 139). The first meeting leads to a barroom fight but ends without mayhem, but Watson later hunts down Bass and kills him for bounty money.[21]

For the fishermen and plume hunters of the southwest coast, Key West is the Dodge City where these frontiersmen come to trade their hides, fish, and feathers. Key West is certainly the Wild South. The town was "a wilder kind of place, seamen and soldiers, ships from all over the world, DINING AND DANCING, NINE TO ELEVEN: FIGHTING FROM ELEVEN TO TWO—that was the sign in Eddie's Bar. There were so many fights that Mr. Watson could cut loose all he wanted, he just fit right in. For many years Ed Watson was the bad man in that town. . . . The men told strangers in the bar how their ol' pardner here, Ed Watson, had killed tough hombres out in Oklahoma. . . . There'd be a wild cheer for frontier justice" (*Lost Man's River*, 324).

There is also a south coast stand-in for the cattle industry. Here, where large tracts of dry land give way to swamps, islands, inlets, and tangled jungle, "Fish Wars" over fishing grounds were the "moral equivalent" of range wars like the famous conflict in Johnson County, Wyoming in 1892 (*Lost Man's River*, 353). Key West sponge fishers resent the arrival of Greek spongers out of Tarpon Springs, staging raids to burn boats and destroy diving equipment. Along the Thousand Islands coast there were fish wars in which fishermen, battling over fishing grounds and island bases, exchange shots and damage boats—the maritime equivalent of cutting fences. They sometimes kill each other.

One of the reasons for the climate of violence is the number of residents who are outside the law. The theme of the Confederate veteran who tries to start over on a frontier, where the law is weak, is a cliché of western stories—and no less of the trilogy—and one also found in science fiction in the television series *Firefly*. From the early nineteenth century, southern Florida was a land of Indians, outlaws, and fugitives—"runaways from the War Between the States, never got the word the war was finished" (*Lost Man's River*, 14). An important character is an admitted deserter from the Confederate army, unwilling to fight a rich man's war. Chokoloskee is settled by "outlaws and fugitives" (*Lost Man's River*, 259), "bitter and unregenerate men" driven southward by the war or its aftermath (*Lost Man's River*, 279). "This far south, there weren't no law cept what you made," comments Bill Smallwood (*Lost Man's River*, 368). Two generations after the action in *Killing Mister Watson* and *Bone by Bone*, the 1960s Everglades in *Lost Man's River* still shelter war-traumatized loners, criminals, self-obsessed self-made men, and crazy people.

Yet another parallel involves efforts to engineer the landscape into greater productivity. One of the central stories of the arid West is the coming of irrigated agriculture, first through community efforts in Utah and Colorado, then through private investment in the 1880s and 1890s, and finally with federal involvement in the twentieth century. In southern Florida the equivalent is the effort to dredge and drain, to get rid of too much water rather than compensate for too little. In both cases, the effort requires big money and ambitious engineering. The work begins with Philadelphia money in the 1880s, stalls, and resumes in the twentieth century with state sponsorship. Watson is full of ideas about the benefits of dredging and waits eagerly in 1906–1907: "The southwest coast would be next in line for the blessings of modern progress, and E. J. Watson was bound to be right up in front. My invitation to the statehouse in Tallahassee could show up in the mail almost any day" (*Bone by Bone*, 270).

Matthiessen develops the frontier theme by dwelling on the side effects of resource exploitation and exhaustion. Here his own voice comes through loud and clear, giving his own sentiments to members of the postfrontier generation. The natural ecologists of the southwest coast kill alligators for their stomach hide and let the rest of the carcass decay, rather like killing of buffalo for their hides and letting them rot down to bones. They take plume birds by the tens of thousands and systematically hunt rookeries into extinction, leaving devastation that even a hunter himself agrees "ain't a picture you want to think about too much" (*Killing Mister Watson*, 47). They overfish one species after the next. Meanwhile northern investors with deep pockets ditch and drain the edges of the Everglades for sugar cane plantations and sugar factories with "think high walls of oily smoke shrouding the flat horizons like dark fronts of oncoming evil weather." Not that E. J. would have minded, thinks Lucius: "The ruined land south of the dykes, the poor poisoned small towns of the migrant workers—the price of progress, Papa would have said" (*Lost Man's River*, 231).

Matthiessen's South Florida is a primal land, much like the "West" that Jane Tompkins analyzes: "In the Western, as in Genesis, the physical world comes first." Tompkins centers her attention on the reductive landscape of the desert, where space is defined by the absence of everything—trees, water, signs of civilization—and the land itself is a challenge to endure hardship. "The desert," she continues, "offers itself as the white sheet on which to trace a figure. It is a tabula rasa on which man can write, as if for the first time, the story he wants to live."[22] The Everglades are scarcely without water or trees, of course, but they are an equally challenging and unforgiving environment, where individuals live isolated lives and endure extraordinary hardships.

Like the West, Chatham Bend is a land of loneliness. E. J. Watson has wives and children but no sense of family, neighbors and associates but no friends, his own business but no social connections. Western riders often appear in the wide open spaces, silhouetted against the big sky. The reader first sees Watson as he appears out of the vast, featureless Gulf of Mexico, profiled against its own big sky: "Twilight gathers behind the coming boat. . . . The boat winds in among the oyster bars. The helmsman stands in silhouette, his broad hat forward on his head" (*Killing Mister Watson*, 6). The same image reappears at the end of the third volume, told now in Watson's own thoughts as he approaches Chokoloskee outlined against the western horizon, exposed to the men on shore. "As the boat moved closer to the island, the helmsman's outline would offer a bulky target. . . . Rounding the last bar and taking a new heading, the *Brave* slid remorselessly toward the shore. She was coming within rifle range, and my whole body longed to crouch down out of view. Instinct told me to stand straight and bold, but fear seeped in like a cold brine leaking through the seams of an old boat" (*Bone By Bone*, 406).

Novelist and Historians

The historian who probes and reconstructs the past is a well-tested character in fiction as a device to give first-person immediacy to third-person narratives—Jack Burden in *All the King's Men*, Lyman Ward in *Angle of Repose*. For Matthiessen, the device was blessing and curse. *Lost Man's River*, structured around the efforts of Lucius to conduct historical research into E. J. Watson's life and death, gave the author the greatest trouble in its composition but serves as the pivot of the trilogy. The first and third books give the reader historical sources through a set of oral testimonies. In the first volume, the testimonies are of the sort that historians would love to be able actually to obtain. In the third volume, the testimonies are a detailed but obviously suspect first-person account that reads as a sort of posthumous autobiography. In between, Lucius struggles like a good historian to uncover documentary evidence and reconcile it with the recollections of others and with his own memory.

As the fictionalized historian enacts much of Matthiessen's own research, he finds that memory is obdurate. Family members and the community have arrived at stories that reassure and make sense to themselves and justify their own actions. Lucius's evidence has no power to move them. One old Chokoloskee couple respond to his persistent questioning with stubborn denial: "That's what come down in our families," Penny Carr says looking at her husband. "That's right. It come down in our families," agreed Owen Carr (*Lost Man's River*, 316). Lucius too has a story of E. J. Watson as a virtuous man gunned down by jealous neighbors, a story based on his childhood memories, which are nearly impervious to evidence. "You going to tell me your dad's version of what took place here that afternoon?" he asks one of his contemporaries. "*Version?*" is the reply. "You talked all these years to all these people and *still* you ain't heard the story you want to hear?" (*Lost Man's River*, 380).[23]

Matthiessen's reconstruction of Southwest Florida amounts to a fictional endorsement of David Emmons's argument that we should conceptualize frontiers—particularly in the post–Civil War era—in terms of a set of social and economic conditions rather than in terms of an east/west dichotomy. In his definition, the iron, copper, and lumber regions of the Lake Superior region were as integral to the "frontier" as were Montana and Oregon. And as William Cronon noted in a comment on Emmons's proposal, the same criteria would add northern Maine and southern Florida to the functional "West."[24] The southern Florida that Matthiessen evokes and reconstructs certainly fits the Emmons-Cronon criteria for a frontier, including sparse population, resource economy, and rudimentary social and political institutions.

The trilogy also speaks to an analytical literature that links the South and the West as the American periphery in contrast to the national core that emerged first in the 1850s and 1860s with its anchoring corners at Boston, Baltimore, St. Louis, and Chicago. That was where economic and financial power resided, as Walter Prescott Webb complained in 1937 in a populist attack on the regionalization of capital. In *Divided We Fall* (1937) he argued that northern capitalists had used both direct economic power and control of the federal government to impoverish and subordinate the South and West. There was direct political ("imperial") control via southern Reconstruction and western territorial government followed by indirect control through tariffs, unequal return of tax dollars, favorable Supreme Court decisions, railroad rates, chain stores and banking consolidation. West and South shared a common dilemma—"the economic conquest of the South and West, carried out over a period of seventy-five years."[25]

Three generations later, Webb's populist passion gave way to the sober analytical maps of geographer D. W. Meinig and to a suggestive hypothesis from historian Elliott West, both of whom have explored the shared marginality of the South and West. The latter has recently posited that the period from the 1840s to the 1880s should be termed the Greater Reconstruction because it included not only the Civil War and Reconstruction of the South but also the acquisition of the Rocky Mountain and Pacific West and its incorporation within common national legal and bureaucratic systems.[26] Meinig has applied a model of core, domain, and sphere of influence to nineteenth-century North America, mapping the ways in which the spatial economy subordinated both the South and West to the industrial-financial power of the Northeast.[27]

Matthiessen makes Edgar Watson a figure who enacts both sides of frontier development and regional differentiation. In one persona he is an enterprising businessman who cultivates the state's power brokers, eagerly adopts new technologies, and hopes to be the local agent and conduit for outside capital. At the same time, he is an independent, bloody-minded egoist for whom violence is not only a tool but a source of satisfaction.[28] This Watson resists the very institutions of law, order, regulation, and financial control that he is otherwise laboring to bring to southern Florida. The men who kill Mr. Watson restore something of moral balance, but in so doing they mark the end of a frontier era.

Notes

1. Charlton Teabeau, *Florida's Last Frontier: The History of Collier County* (Coral Gables: Fla.: University of Miami Press, 1966), and *The Story of the Chokoloskee Bay Country: With the Reminiscences of Pioneer C. S. "Ted" Smallwood* (Coral Gables, Fla.: University of

Miami Press, 1955). Tebeau also wrote *A History of Florida* (Coral Gables, Fla.: University of Miami Press, 1971), the standard state history, through several editions.

2. There was a real Lucius Watson who worked most of his life as a fishing guide. In Matthiessen's telling, he works sometimes as a guide with the fictional role as historian added on.

3. S. W. Hartman, *Hell on the Border: He Hanged Eighty-Eight Men*, introduction by Larry D. Ball (Lincoln: University of Nebraska Press, 1992), 603–605 (facsimile reprint of 1898 book). Larry Ball notes that Harman's account of Watson as the murderer of Belle Starr came nearly verbatim from the anonymous *Belle Starr, The Bandit Queen, or Female Jesse James*, published by the *National Police Gazette* in 1889. Also see Glenn Shirley, *Belle Starr and Her Times: The Literature, the Facts, and the Legends* (Norman: University of Oklahoma Press, 1982), 230–45, 256–59, which carefully compiles and compares published accounts of Starr, the role of Edgar Watson in her death, and his subsequent death in Florida.

4. Parenthetical page references that appear in the text for quotations are to *Killing Mister Watson* (New York: Vintage, 1991), *Lost Man's River* (New York: Vintage, 1998), and *Bone by Bone* (New York: Random House, 1999).

5. Howard Norman, "Peter Matthiessen: The Art of Fiction, CLVII," *Paris Review* 150 (Spring 1999): 190.

6. Richard White, "The Natures of Nature Writing," *Raritan* 22 (September 2002): 145–61.

7. Peter Matthiessen, Gardner D. Stour, Robert Verity Clem, and Ralph S. Palmer, *The Shorebirds of North America* (New York: Viking, 1967); Peter Matthiessen, *The Cloud Forest* (New York; Viking, 1961), *Under the Mountain Wall* (New York: Viking, 1962), *The Tree Where Man Was Born* (New York: Dutton, 1972), *The Snow Leopard* (New York: Viking, 1978), and *The Birds of Heaven: Travels with Cranes* (New York: North Point Press, 2001).

8. Peter Matthiessen, *Sal Si Puedes: Cesar Chavez and the New American Revolution* (New York: Random House, 1969), *In the Spirit of Crazy Horse* (New York: Viking, 1983), and *Indian Country* (New York: Viking, 1984).

9. Norman, "Peter Matthiessen: The Art of Fiction," 206.

10. See Randy White, "The Travels of Peter Matthiessen," *Outside* 5 (April–May 1980): 18–20, 22, 67–71.

11. James G. Watson, "Man Writing: The Watson Trilogy: Peter Matthiessen in Archive," *Texas Studies in Literature and Language* 46 (Summer 2004): 245–70.

12. Lucius's imagined career includes studying history at the University of Florida before World War I and then implausibly returning to the university to teach [as a lecturer?] in 1957. See *Lost Man's River*, pp. 29, 35–36.

13. Matthiessen, incidentally, has denied that he wrote historical novels, presumably considering that a type of low-art genre fiction rather than high-art literary fiction. He also claims to scorn history as a limiting activity. In the preface to *Killing Mister Watson*, he say the book "is in no way 'historical,' since almost nothing here is history," by which he means that he has imagined context around his carefully assembled information. He has commented that "nonfiction at its best is like fashioning a cabinet. It can be elegant and very beautiful but it can never be sculpture. Captive to facts—or predetermined forms—it cannot fly. . . . A good essay or article can and should have . . . all the attributes

of fiction except the creative imagination, which can never be permitted to enliven fact. The writer of nonfiction is stuck with objective reality, or should be. . . . The best nonfiction has many, many virtues, among which simple truthfulness is perhaps foremost, yet its fidelity to the known facts is its fatal weakness." Here as elsewhere he confuses history with verifiable facts or with chronicle in the distinction of R. G. Collingwood and other philosophers of history. See Watson, "Man Writing," 246; Norman, "Peter Matthiessen: The Art of Fiction," 194–95.

Ironically Matthiessen then frames his three-decker novel as historical investigation and offers a sort of primer in historical sources and research methods. Volume 1 is constructed from oral testimony of the sort that historians would love to be able actually to obtain. Volume 2 puts a historian and his investigations at the center of the action. In Volume 3 we have a detailed but obviously suspect first-person account that reads as a sort of posthumous autobiography.

14. Matthiessen remarked in 1999 that *Lost Man's River* was "longer and more complex than the other two, but it is upsetting and sad and also funny." At the same time, it offered structural problems that led him to compare it to the torso of a dachshund suspended between two sets of legs, and he presumably trimmed and simplified it out of frustration. See Norman, "Peter Matthiessen: The Art of Fiction," 210.

15. Richard Maxwell Brown, *The South Carolina Regulators* (Cambridge, Mass.: Harvard University Press, 1963); Joel Williamson, *A Rage for Order: Black/White Relations in the American South since Emancipation* (New York: Oxford University Press, 1986); Bertram Wyatt-Brown, *Southern Honor: Ethics and Behavior in the Old South* (New York: Oxford University Press, 1982).

16. William Faulkner, "Remarks on *Absalom, Absalom*," in Fred Hobson, ed., *William Faulkner's Absalom, Absalom: A Casebook* (New York: Oxford University Press, 2003), 287.

17. Tom LeClair, "A History of Violence," *New York Times*, April 27, 2008, draws the Watson/Sutpen parallels.

18. John Cooley, "Matthiessen's Voyages on the River Styx: Deathly Waters, Endangered Peoples," in John Cooley, ed., *Earthly Words: Essays on Contemporary Nature and Environmental Writers* (Ann Arbor: University of Michigan Press, 1994), 183, 184, 187.

19. Jane Tompkins, *West of Everything: The Inner Life of Westerns* (New York: Oxford University Press, 1992), 30.

20. John Hope Franklin, *The Militant South* (Cambridge, Mass.: Belknap Press, 1956).

21. That is Watson's own version. In another telling, Watson kills Bass to prevent him from murdering another man whom he has down in a street fight. Peripheral to the Watson story but reinforcing the "western" tropes is a report on a shoot-out on the main street of Lemon City (*Killing Mister Watson*, 85).

22. Tompkins, *West of Everything*, 70, 74.

23. Sally Brown, Lucius's sometime companion and coresearcher and the estranged wife of Whidden Harden, serves as a counterpoint to Lucius and his fixation through her repeated effort to convince her husband's family and their neighbors to acknowledge what she sees as the Hardens' real racial identity. She takes that identity to be white and Indian while everyone else thinks the family are a mix of white, Indian, and African American, thus putting them on the wrong side of the color line. In this case hers is the story that does not jibe with the evidence. Indeed, "she had repudiated what she

perceived as the racism and redneck ignorance in her community which had made life so dangerous for her husband's family [several of whom were killed in fish wars]. But as she ruefully confessed, her fierce tirades in defense of the Hardens had reawakened a lot of the mean gossip that the family thought had been put to rest" (*Lost Man's River*, 36).

24. David Emmons, "Constructed Province: History and the Making of the Last American West," *Western Historical Quarterly* 25 (Winter 1994): 437–60; William Cronon, "The West: A Moving Target," *Western Historical Quarterly* 25 (Winter 1994): 478.

25. Walter Prescott Webb, *Divided We Stand: The Crisis of a Frontierless Democracy* (New York: Farrar and Rinehart, 1937), 24.

26. Elliott West, *The Last Indian War: The Nez Perce Story* (New York: Oxford University Press, 2009).

27. D. W. Meinig, *The Shaping of America: A Geographical Perspective on 500 Years of History*, Vol. 3: *Transcontinental America, 1850–1915* (New Haven, Conn.: Yale University Press, 1998). Meinig also maps for 1900 a southern "settlement frontier" in West Texas and South Florida (212).

28. In Watson's ability, or even need, to take personal pleasure from violence, he invites comparison with the figure of Judge Holden in Cormac McCarthy's *Blood Meridian; or, The Evening Redness in the West* (New York: Random House, 1985), although he differs fundamentally in retaining connections to social institutions.

CHAPTER 6

Cascadian Dreams

Imagining a Region over Four Decades

In 1997, the distinguished architect and urbanist Robert Geddes offered the suggestion that "Cascadia" would be the "shock city" of the twenty-first century, following in the pattern set in earlier eras by Manchester and Chicago, Los Angeles and Calcutta.[1] Come again? Cascadia? Where's that, and why might it be more interesting to twenty-first century scholars than Shanghai or Mumbai or Sao Paolo?

For Geddes, as for Ethan Seltzer, Anne Moudon, and Alan Artibise, the trio of urban scholars who contributed "Cascadia: An Emerging Regional Model" to Geddes's edited volume *Cities in Our Future*, Cascadia is a binational megaregion, which consists of the Portland, Seattle, and Vancouver metro areas and the farms and forests in between.

The Cascadia Megaregion is the newest in a series of recent efforts to reimagine a regional identity for the northwestern coast of North America. For a century and a half—beginning with the intrusion of Russian, British, and American fur traders, extending through imperial contests and boundary marking, through Anglophone settlement, and on through the dam-building and timber booms of the mid-twentieth century—the greater Northwest had a stable identity as a region rich in natural resources and driven by their exploitation and development. Whether as the prenational Oregon Country in the early nineteenth century or the U.S. Pacific Northwest and idiosyncratic British Columbia of the twentieth century, this was a remarkably constant region of the mind.

The vast territory has had subregions to be sure—an Empire of the Columbia, the inland sea from Olympia, Washington, north to Campbell River, British Columbia and an Inland Empire (that's the big one around Spokane, not the little one around Riverside). However, Wilbur Zelinsky's now classic study of vernacular regions found the Northwest firmly in place in the 1970s. His study compiled and tallied the regional adjectives that appeared in business and organizational names in the phone books of 276 of the largest U.S. and Canadian cities. "Northwest" was the dominant regional marker in Boise, Spokane, Eugene, Portland, Seattle and Tacoma, and made a strong second or third place showing in Missoula, Billings, Calgary, Edmonton, Vancouver, Victoria, and Anchorage (as Canada's windows to Asia, Victoria and Vancouver gave first place to "Pacific"). The regional core along Puget Sound and the lower Columbia River also joined the Canadian Maritime Provinces and the heart of Dixie in having the greatest regional self-consciousness as measured by the percentage of regional terms relative to all terms.[2]

Beginning in the same decade as Zelinsky's study, however, that identity began to come unstuck. For the last generation it has been up for grabs with competing metaphors and definitions that suggest very different planning and policy responses. Journalists, boosters, advocates, and scholars have tried out a series of ways to conceptualize and shape a regional identity for the northern Pacific Coast—as Ecotopia, as bioregional Cascadia, as boosterish Mainstreet Cascadia, and as the Cascadia Megaregion. Think of the change this way: the old identity was like a reliable older automobile with lots of miles but well maintained and still perking along. Suddenly, however, it is too boring, too unfashionable, inadequately trendy, causing us to shop for an alternative—perhaps a Prius? A Smart Car? A Ford F-350 pickup? A Lexus? All have their strong points, but none seems to satisfy every need and expectation. Stepping back from the simile, the goal of this paper is to interrogate these changing ways for thinking about the regional identity of the old Oregon Country.

Central to the discussion is an exploration of the ways in which the recent regional concepts have developed in a dialectic, each building on the previous but also reacting to it in substantive ways. I will note empirical criticisms, for these "regions" live far more in the imagination than on the ground in social, economic, and political interactions, but my central interest is the ideas themselves.

My analysis also reads the contemporary regional identities against the previous and long-standing identity of the Northwest as a land of individual prosperity fueled by abundant resources—the Eden at the end of the Oregon Trail, the promised land of the New Deal era.

In an even larger context, I argue that all of the recent regional imaginings share an assumption that northwestern North America is best understood as separate from the rest of the continent, not as a component of continental systems and nations. They thus work counter to a century of Canadian and American nation-building. They are international in crossing the political border. They are nonnational in dissolving continental connections and identifications in favor of Pacific connections.

The Promised Land

Fish, furs, Douglas firs, and falling water—according to historian William Lang, these are the iconic resources that have long shaped the economy and public identity of the northwest coast—to which list we might add fruit orchards and fields of wheat to keep the alliteration going.[3] In cumulating layers their abundance produced a region deeply embedded in and indebted to its natural setting. Lang's essay moves in sequence from the pre-European "people of the salmon" through the Hudson's Bay Company, the settlement of Oregon Trail pioneers in the Willamette Valley, the shift of the timber industry from the Great Lakes to the Northwest, and the engineering of the Columbia River, put to work as an "organic machine" in Richard White's felicitous phrase to float barges, pump irrigation water, power an aluminum industry, and light Cascadian cities.[4]

Historian John Findlay in a trenchant essay has labeled the idea of a Northwest regional identity a "fishy proposition," arguing that such an identity was more often imposed from outside boosters and promoters—from Hall J. Kelly pushing the virtues of the Oregon Country to railroad publicity departments marketing land. Nevertheless, the imagery of natural abundance still stands center stage.[5] Lang thinks that the imagery reflects the overlying realities of regional environment and economy, and Findlay thinks the reality is a bit shakier than the journalists and publicity departments might like to think, but nature—in the form of economically valuable resources—is still is the middle.

A third historian who has essayed a regional character portrait is Richard Maxwell Brown, who introduced the idea and imagery of the Great Raincoast of North America in several essays in the 1980s. Brown defined the Raincoast in direct contrast to Walter Prescott Webb's classic analysis of the Great Plains and his argument that aridity made the West a "perpetual mirage." Brown argues that the benign environment of the Northwest coast inverts all of Webb's conclusions. It has always been a place of easy subsistence, not struggle, dominated first by fishing and farming and then by the Lumber Kingdom and the Kilowatt Kingdom. Moderate climate and economic abundance led to "moderate conservatism" in public life and to "increasing cooperation and a rising sense of community." Although Brown draws conclusions about the region's political culture, his analysis remains grounded in the same layered resource economy that centers Lang's and Findlay's arguments.[6]

And all of these historians would likely agree that the first Cascadians were agents of European empires. Juan Francisco Bodega de Quadra sailed from California to the future Alaska panhandle in 1775. Alexander Mackenzie (1793), Meriwether Lewis and William Clark (1806), and David Thompson (1811) all explored routes from the Atlantic drainage to the Pacific. But I would nominate George Vancouver as the first Cascadian. Between 1791 and 1795 he traversed and explored the American Pacific Coast from California to Alaska, charting islands and fjords and leaving his name for two cities and a very large island.

From early on Europeans created institutions of governance that roughly matched the developing economic region. The North West Company after 1815 operated its fur trade through its Columbia District and New Caledonia (divided south and north by the Fraser and Thompson Rivers). The Hudson's Bay Company absorbed the North West Company in 1821 and consolidated Pacific Slope operations in a single Columbia District in 1827. They managed the vast territory from Fort Vancouver on the Columbia River after 1829 and networked with

California, Hawaii, and Alaska. Meanwhile, of course, geopolitics created the jointly occupied Oregon Country from 1818 to 1846 in the territory formally renounced by Russia and Spain.

The formal border divided the territory but not the growing resource economy.[7] In the late nineteenth and early twentieth centuries, the northwestern quadrant of North America was in many ways a single arena for resource production. The U.S.-Canada border was permeable to migratory workers, settlers, and investors. Gold rush prospectors from California treated British Columbia as an American annex. Immigrant merchants and workers crossed and recrossed the border as members of binational family networks. Aboriginal Canadians provided a migratory labor force for Puget Sound mills. Timber workers and timber land investors worked both sides of the border. Canadians took fish in American waters and vice-versa. All of these examples confirm the interpretive framework outlined more than half a century ago by Marcus Lee Hansen in *The Mingling of the Canadian and American Peoples*, a study that emphasized the openness of the transcontinental border through most of its history.[8]

The natural resource era climaxed in efforts to construct what Lang calls "the New Deal's quasi-utopian, new Pacific Northwest." The guiding assumption was that the greater Northwest remained a frontier still open for development of its underutilized resources. The National Resources Committee described the Pacific Northwest as a realm of "forest, fisheries, waterpower, recreational beauties, harbors" and the Columbia Basin as a region of "rolling wheat lands" with great potential for "hydroelectric manufactural industries."[9] The rhetoric and confidence are sometimes breathtaking. Washington senator Clarence Dill talked about "the future El Dorado."[10] Journalist Richard Neuberger, later to be elected to the U.S. Senate from Oregon, described the Northwest in 1939 as "the last frontier" and the "promised land," soon to be made fruitful and industrious by the "concrete Gargantuan" of Grand Coulee Dam.[11] Artists absorbed the same fascination with resource development. Dorothea Lange criss-crossed Oregon, Idaho, and Washington for the Farm Security Administration to photograph the successes (and failures) of the regional New Deal as manifest in structures as small as new houses and as large as irrigation projects, and WPA artists chronicled the progress of dam building.[12] On contract to the new Bonneville Power Administration in 1940, Woody Guthrie celebrated the Columbia River dams and the "Pastures of Plenty" that they would nourish . . . and also left behind "Roll On, Columbia" as the official Washington state folk song.

Take a look at *Life* magazine's June 5, 1939, issue on "America's Future." Here were articles on the New York World's Fair with the General Motors Futurama, items on the new consumer wonders of aluminum cookware and nylon stockings, a feature on John Steinbeck's blockbuster novel *The Grapes of Wrath*, an essay on "The American Destiny" by Walter Lippmann, a piece on the first sports television broadcast, and a column about scientific innovations by Buckminster

Fuller. Here also was a nine-page spread on the "Pacific Northwest: The Story of a Vision and a Promised Land." The land was "rich in nature's goods" and irrigation could make the Northwest bloom. The pictures were an Idaho ranch, the Anaconda smelter, a tower of boards in a Seattle lumberyard, Boise Valley irrigation, and at the end "Grand Coulee Dam: Power and Promise." Grand Coulee and Bonneville Dams together "will open up nearly the whole Columbia River to navigation, supply enough power to electrify an agricultural-industrial empire."[13]

These same worlds of production dominated the Northwest imagination through the twentieth century. H. L. Davis chronicled the regional resource economy in *Honey in the Horn* (1935), showing his protagonist Clay Calvert working at sheep herding, hop picking, hay making, and other agricultural variations. Norman Reilly Raine sent *Tugboat Annie* steaming in and out of Puget Sound's "Secoma" harbor in dozens of *Saturday Evening Post* stories from the 1930s to the 1950s. James Stevens claimed Paul Bunyan for the Northwest in 1925 and fictionalized the logging business in *Big Jim Stevens* (1948), to be followed by Ken Kesey's antisocial logging family in *Sometimes a Great Notion* (1964). Among the current generation, Craig Lesley's characters in *River Song* (1990) and *The Sky Fisherman* (1995) pick fruit, sell sporting goods to tourists, farm, and fish. Annie Dillard chronicled the evolution of a fictionalized Bellingham from farming settlement to mill town in *The Living* (1992). Molly Gloss writes about homesteading in *The Jump-Off Creek* (1989), logging in *Wild Life* (2000), and ranching in *The Hearts of Horses* (2007).

The liberal consensus that promoted federal policies and investments to support the private development of natural resources outlasted both World War II and Eisenhower era debates over public versus private power generation and survived into the 1960s. Columbia River dams lit booming cities and helped to produce aluminum porch furniture for California patios, Northwest forests supplied the 2 × 4s and plywood that built California suburbia, and the Alcan Highway linked the wilds of the Northwest to the even vaster frontier of Alaska. North of the U.S.-Canada border the provincial government of W. A. C. Bennett, in office from 1952 to 1972, vigorously pursued economic development and chamber of commerce capitalism ("The finest sound in the land is the ringing of cash registers" is a quote that captures the essential Bennett approach).

The era ended during the 1970s. In the United States the last dam on the Columbia rose in 1971 (John Day Dam) and the last on the Snake River in 1972 (Lower Granite Dam). Canadians continued to dam the upper reaches of the Columbia as late as 1973 with Mica Dam and 1984 with Revelstoke Dam. The 1970s were likewise the last flush years for the Oregon, Washington, Idaho, and British Columbia timber industries. Soon a combination of economic recession, overcutting, technological change, environmental regulations, and global competition from places as distant as New Zealand and Siberia put an end to what

Paul Hirt has called the "conspiracy of optimism" that supported a generation of unsustainable harvests.[14] The time *was* ripe for rethinking regional identity, or, to revisit my metaphor, to go shopping on automobile row.

Ecotopia: The Consumer's Utopia

The first alternative arrived not from the heart of the Northwest but from its fringe. Ernest Callenbach, Berkeleyite and editor at the University of California Press, coined the term ecotopia for his 1975 novel of the same name. Callenbach imagined an environmentally ethical, energy-conserving polity in a newly independent nation covering northern California, Oregon, and Washington, which he detailed in his utopian fiction. The term passed into larger circulation in Joel Garreau's *Nine Nations of North America* (1981). The central interest of the ecotopian vision was the shaping of alternative social and economic institutions around conscious individual choices and *thoughtful consumption*. The actual place—the north Pacific Coast—was a convenient and plausible locale for social and economic speculation.

Ecotopia is a classic utopia in form and content. Utilizing the trope of the reportorial visitor, it purports to be the "notebooks and reports" of William Weston, a skeptical visitor slowly converted to seeing things the ecotopian way. Ecotopia is idyllic and remarkably stable for a socioeconomic system quickly put in place only a few years before Weston's visit. Callenbach almost surely would have described ecotopia as "sustainable" had the terminology been readily at hand in the early 1970s. Ecotopia is woodsy, a place of careful consumption and pastoral indulgence. The book highlights the sensual interaction of people with nature and with each other (William Weston is converted in part through easy sex). Ecotopia is a sort of Bohemian Grove for the mass market.[15]

As a national manifesto, Callenbach wrote *Ecotopia* as an alternative to the post–World War II "consumer's republic," but consumption still remains central. In context of the first oil embargo and the Club of Rome's *Limits to Growth* report, Callenbach made the challenge of Ecotopia how to support continued consumption through more careful production. In the spirit of the *Whole Earth Catalog*, the ecotopian goal is to continue "getting" the good life (even if redefined) through more careful and conservative "spending" of energy and natural resources.[16]

Journalist Joel Garreau, at the time on the staff of the *Washington Post*, took up the term "Ecotopia" in 1981 in *The Nine Nations of North America*. The popular book, which divided the continent among nine economic/cultural regions, now reads as one-quarter D. W. Meinig and three-quarters dated John Gunther. His Ecotopia stretches along the U.S. and Canadian coasts from Monterey to the Kenai Peninsula, citing the biophysical commonalities but actually emphasizing the most consumerist aspects of Callenbach's utopia. The region is all about enjoying the outdoors, consuming nature through whitewater rafting, jogging, skiing, and other outdoors activity. As Garreau put it, "a thundering market" for natural amenities suddenly appeared in the 1960s and transformed the coastal strip into a region clearly separate from the "Empty Quarter," which is his name for the Rocky Mountains and dry plains.[17]

Nine Nations does not stand up very well after more than a quarter century. It draws expansive boundaries for Ecotopia but never addresses the potential contradictions of environmentalism as consumption choice. Nor does it acknowledge the problems of defining a cultural region that reaches from Big Sur and southern Alaska—what we might now call the long stretch from Nancy Pelosi country to Sarah Palin country. The paperback edition includes an image of Ecopotia that foregrounds a colorful pastoral landscape with a shining city in the background, which we assume to be full of urbanites ready for energetic outdoor recreation. We leave, even more starkly than in Callenbach's novel, with the vision that the identifying characteristic of the region is the consumption of landscape for personal pleasure.

Both books can be contrasted with the depth of Ursula Le Guin's imaginative ethnography of an alternative northern California in the curious and challenging novel *Always Coming Home* (1985).[18] The book tells about the Kesh, an agricultural people living in the Valley of the Na River in northern California. They are a people, she writes, "who might be going to have lived a long, long time from now." From maps that Le Guin carefully provides, we see that the Na is a version of the Napa Valley, lovingly depicted as "austere . . . generous but not lush," where long dry summers turn suddenly into wet, foggy winter, a land whose people intimately learn its meadows, rivers, roads, hills, and canyons.

Always Coming Home is not a traditional novel with a recognizable plot. Instead, Le Guin gives us a potpourri of anthropological data: poems, songs, legends, and fables told by the Kesh; maps; drawings of artifacts; descriptions of burial customs, musical instruments and food; charts showing the "lodges" and "societies" through which the Kesh organize and sort themselves; and other such chunks of data. We pick the book up to sample, as we might wander through the collections of a museum.

Unlike straightforwardly progressive ecotopians, the Kesh are deceptive. They seem to be—are—tribal and spiritual. They are literate, but they prefer to describe the world through recited poems and parables. They make no distinction between human and natural history. They seem in some aspects a sort of hippie feminist commune. Or, in another view, they follow a blend of European folk wisdom and Native American spirituality.[19] But the Kesh are *not* isolated and ignorant, nor are they always nice. Their young people sometimes wage unnecessary, deadly wars against their neighbors. Some Kesh are richer and some are poorer. They make careful and selective use of complex technologies to support their misleadingly simple lives. They use a wood-burning railroad and consult a master computer, but these complex technologies are tools like any other, to be used in the real work of inhabiting their place consciously and carefully—perhaps closer than ecotopians to the spirit of the "wise provincialism" advocated by the earlier Californian Josiah Royce.[20]

Cascadia: Bioregionalism As Alternative Production

Cascadia (fig. 6.1) emerged in the 1980s as a direct challenge to the tasteful but celebratory indulgence of journalistic ecotopia. This is a regional vision that takes ecology seriously, positing a "Great, Green Land" and giving natural systems first place. Articulated against both ecotopia and the consumer's republic, it argues for a revolution in production—or nonproduction—rather than changes in consumption. The message is that people need to live for the benefit of fish and trees just as much as fish live and trees grow for the benefit of people.

"Cascadia" is the brainchild of Seattle University professor David McCloskey, who began teaching a course on the "Sociology of Cascadia" in 1978 (squarely in the ecotopian moment). The terminology drew from the natural sciences, where it has been used to denote specific biotic and geological regions. In 1988, when McCloskey published stunning maps of Pacific Northwest river systems and ecosystems and an accompanying manifesto, the recession of the early 1980s and two terms of the Reagan administration had made a political ecotopia seem tenuous. Instead, his Cascadia is an effort to forge a new awareness of human relationships with the regional landscape, drawing on the bioregional connections that Garreau only hinted at (while it also harkens back to the earlier era when resources trumped political borders). His evocative map is a picture of water and its flows from northern California to Alaska. Provinces, states, and nations disappear under the imperative of the hydrologic cycle that endlessly links Pacific Slope and Pacific Ocean.[21] It is worth quoting McCloskey's eloquent language:

> Cascadia is a land rooted in the very bones of the earth, and animated by the turnings of sea and sky, the mid-latitude wash of winds and waters. As a distinct region, Cascadia arises from both a natural integrity (e.g. landforms and earth-plates, weather patterns and ocean currents, flora, fauna, watersheds, etc.) and a sociocultural unity (e.g. native cultures, a shared history and destiny).
>
> One of the newest and most diverse places on earth, Cascadia is a deep-furrowed, laminated and flowing land poured from the north Pacific Rim. The oldest myth of Cascadia suggests mountains rising from the sea. Rivers more ancient than today's Cascade or Rocky mountains continue to bind earth and sea and sky together in endless life-giving cycles.
>
> [There follows a roster of rivers like the naming of the Danaans in Book II of Homer's *Iliad*.] Columbia, Fraser, Skeena, Snake, Stikine [through] . . . Clearwater, Eel, Rogue, Deschutes, Bulkley, and Bella Coola.
>
> Cascadia is a land of falling waters.[22]

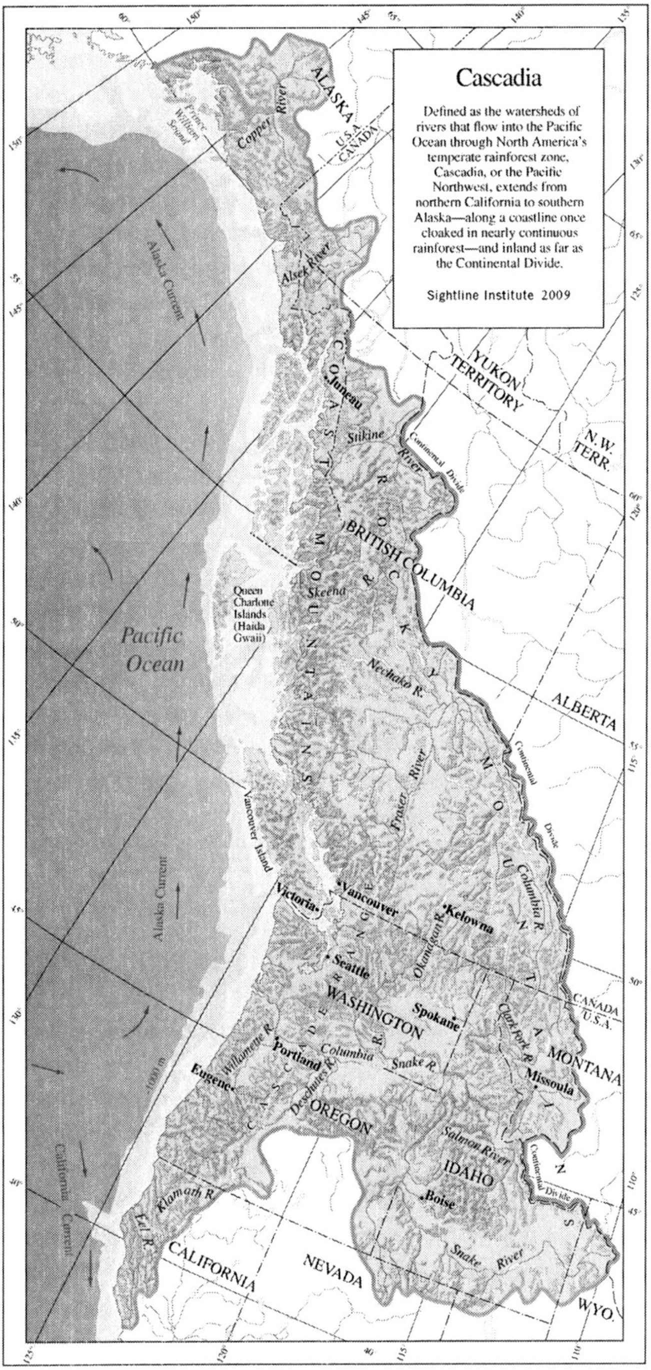

FIG. 6.1. Ecological Cascadia. The standard definition for Cascadia as an ecoregion includes the Pacific-flowing river valleys from northern California to Yakutat Bay, Alaska. This map is derived from David McCloskey's original maps of ecological Cascadia. (Used by permission of Sightline Institute)

McCloskey did not work in a vacuum. Bob Benson, an eccentric Portland socialist, vegetarian, and self-taught cartographer was there first. In the 1970s he drew a map of the maritime Northwest (fig. 6.2) that Portland historian and activist Steve Johnson has called "the first iconic map of our region." Composed by hand in a tiny cabin on the long high ridge that overlooks Portland and the Willamette River, the map views the Northwest coast from a stance above the Queen Charlotte Islands, looking south across Vancouver Island, Puget Sound, and the Columbia Valley. Benson mapped air and wind just as much as McCloskey mapped water.[23]

Ecological Cascadia also gains evocative power from the way in which water itself reverberates through regional literature. Rivers fill titles of books: *A River Runs Through It* (1976), *The River Why* (1983), *River Song* (1989), *Riverwalking* (1995). Daphne Marlatt's long poem *Steveston* (1988) depicts a Japanese Canadian fishing community on the Fraser River, where "this river is a riveting urgency." Rainstorms pounding off the Pacific structure Ivan Doig's *Winter Brothers: A Season at the Edge of America* (1980), introduce H. L. Davis's *Honey in the Horn* (1935), and drive the action in Don Berry's *Trask* (1960) and Ken Kesey's *Sometimes a Great Notion* (1964), The first paragraphs of the latter are virtually a prose reproduction of McCloskey's map:

> Along the western slopes of the Oregon Coastal Range . . . come look: the hysterical crashing of tributaries as they merge into the Wakonda Auga River. . . . The first little washes flashing like thick rushing winds through sheep sorrel and clover, ghost fern and nettle, sheering, cutting . . . forming branches. Then, through bearberry and salmonberry, blueberry and blackberry, the branches crashing into creeks, into streams. Finally, in the foothills, through tamarack and sugar pine . . . and silver spruce—and the green and blue mosaic of Douglas fir—the actual river falls five hundred feet . . . and look: opens out upon the fields.[24]

The evocation of water highlights an important geophysical connector but tends to conceal some of the physical differences that make an expansive Cascadia at least a bit problematic. The Salish Sea—a modern name that evokes native peoples to encompass the inland sea of the Strait of Georgia, Strait of Juan de Fuca, and Puget Sound—connects the Washington and British Columbia coasts and islands but not Oregon or California. The Cascade Mountains are a chain of volcanoes that march from northern California to northern Washington, but the convoluted granite ranges of British Columbia, Idaho, and Montana have a different origin and character. Moreover, the Fraser and Columbia drainage basins span two very different ecosystems, only one of which is great and green. The other is variously great and black where Columbia Plateau basalt shows through, great and brown much of the year, great and golden when wheat is ripe. Modern literary travelers have seldom spanned the entire territory. Sallie Tisdale's "cascadia" ran from Mount Shasta to the Olympic Peninsula, Jonathan Raban's coastwise from Seattle to Juneau.[25]

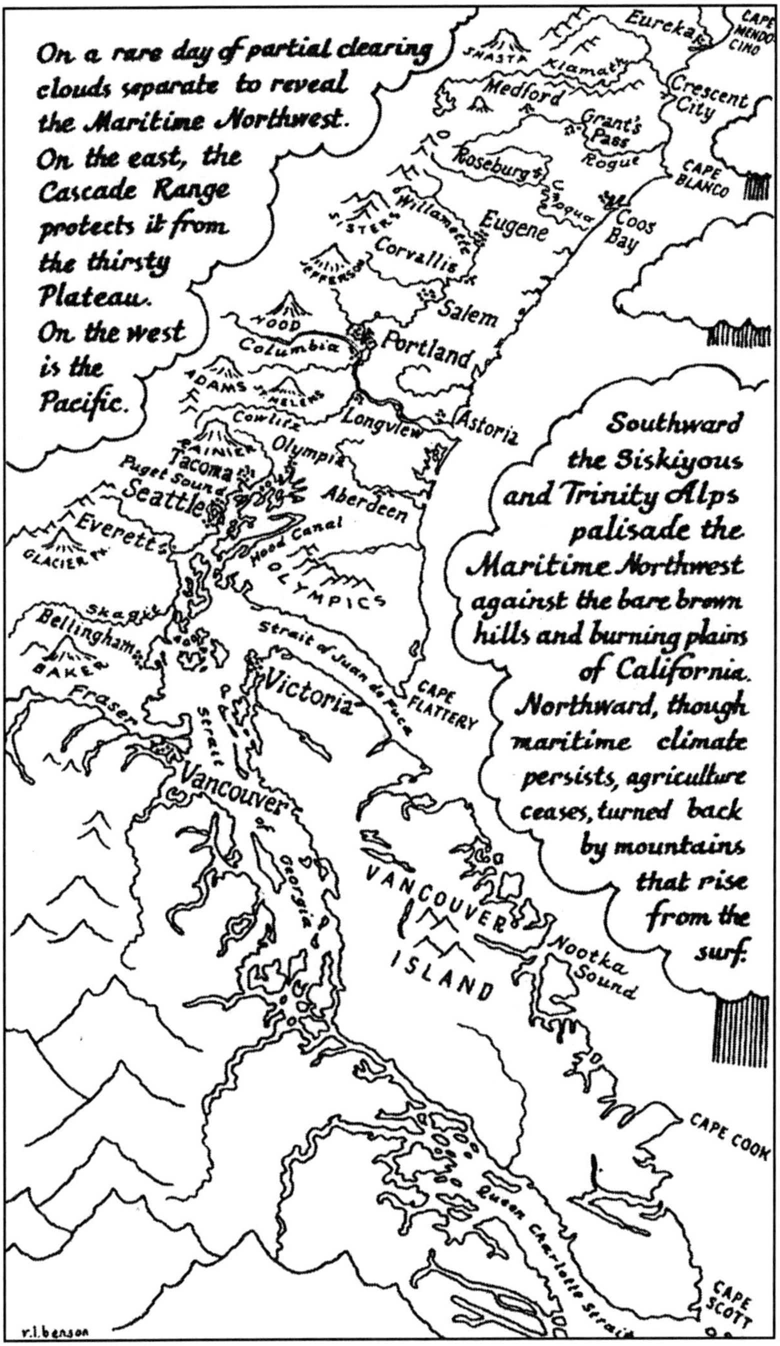

Fig. 6.2. Maritime Northwest. Bob Benson's perspective map, originally prepared for a book on maritime climate gardening in the Pacific Northwest, emphasized the central role of coastal waterways and rivers, highlighted by the north to south perspective. (Used by permission of Steven Reed Johnson)

Dissimilarities aside, Cascadia and Ecotopia both came out of a distinctive regional political culture. The San Francisco Bay Area, Portland, and Seattle were all centers of grassroots work on sustainable agriculture, communal living, alternative energy systems, and other re-evaluations of consumer society in the period roughly from the late 1960s to the early 1980s. In addition to *The Whole Earth Catalog*, as already mentioned, there were *Seriatim* and *Rain* magazines, edited out of El Cerito and Portland in the late 1970s and early 1980s. The Farallones Institute advocated new forms of architecture from northern California Writers such as Californian Gary Snyder and Oregonian Barry Lopez articulated deep environmental perspectives. Meanwhile, the tortuous ranges and hidden valleys of the coastal mountains were fertile territory for communes and marijuana farms.[26]

Environmental activists and organizations have since made bioregionalism a keystone of environmental work and environmental history at multiple scales in all corners of the world.[27] In the Northwest, "ecotopia" and "ecotopian" have dropped out of general use except for in ironic commentary, but Cascadia has continued to name a variety of causes. An International Cascadia Alliance of thirteen environmental groups lobbied, unsuccessfully, for a Cascades International Park in the early 1990s.[28] There is a Cascadia Region Green Building Council, a *Cascadia Weekly* (which is an arts and commentary newspaper from Bellingham), and a *Cascadia Times* (doing investigative reporting on regional environmental and natural resource issues). The good planning advocates at Seattle's Sightline Institute (previously Northwest Environment Watch) have adopted McCloskey's Cascadia as its territory of interest and publish a "Cascadia Scorecard" to rate the region's states and cities. There are websites: CascadiaPrime, Cascadia Rising, Cascadia Commons. As this chapter was written, a group of tree-sitters calling themselves Cascadia Rising Tide had just been arrested for blocking a southern Oregon timber sale.

Perhaps the most effective repackaging of McCloskey's Cascadia is the idea of Salmon Nation, developed and popularized by Ecotrust, a Portland-based nonprofit that works for sustainable economic development and microenterprise. The purpose of Salmon Nation is to enlist bioregional analysis on behalf of policy advocacy. The "Nation" is big: "Outlined both by its coastline and by the rivers that reach deep into its lands, Salmon Nation's geographical boundaries are simply defined: anywhere Pacific salmon have ever run." The map of Salmon Nation (subtitled "a region defined by natural boundaries") stretches the region from Arctic Yukon and Alaska to southern California. Salmon Nation is also "a community of caretakers and citizens that stretches across arbitrary boundaries."[29]

Mainstreet Cascadia: Efficient Production

"Mainstreet Cascadia" is a regional economic development vision that stands in clear contrast to bioregional Cascadia.[30] It draws on a long history of economic boosterism with its attention to Pacific markets, but it developed in the specific context of the U.S.-Canada Free Trade Agreement of 1989 and the North American Free Trade Agreement of 1994, with their promise of increased cross border trade. More broadly, it is an effort to envision the local consequences and opportunities that result from the global shift away from a production/manufacturing economy to an information/services economy. Its advocates are free-market cascadians in the terminology of political scientists Susan Clarke and neoliberals in the trenchant analysis of geographer Matthew Sparke. It is also the version that has most fully manifested in institutional arrangements, attracting the attention of social scientists who want to examine its practical effects.[31]

On one dimension, Mainstreet Cascadia has been an exercise in "rebranding" by figures such as Paul Schell, variously a Seattle real estate developer, University of Washington dean, and Seattle mayor (who had the misfortune to invite the World Trade Organization to convene in his city in December 1999). The promotional rhetoric was honed by the Discovery Institute in Seattle, the Cascadia Institute in Vancouver, and *New Pacific* magazine, devoted according to its masthead to the "dynamic megastate" that spans "geopolitical boundaries that have limited regional understanding [and] are rapidly becoming vestiges of the past" (although the magazine soon failed because it found neither audience nor advertisers). Robert Kaplan nicely captured the boosterish version for *The Atlantic Monthly* in 1998 writing that "what has emerged is nothing less than a strategic alliance of the business elite from Portland to Vancouver."[32] For committed bioregionalists, this rebranding is blatant hijacking. For other observers it is evidence that Cascadia is first and foremost a mental construct.[33]

In the twenty-first century, with key figures like Paul Schell out of office and entrepreneurial academic Alan Artibise relocated from Vancouver to the central United States, the promotional energy has lagged. Corporations briefly toyed with Cascadia as an advertising concept and travel agencies still offer Two Nation Vacation packages—although the term has also been appropriated for Maine/Maritimes, New Mexico/Mexico, and many other variations. "Cultural Cascades" is simply a listing of arts events in Vancouver, Seattle, Tacoma, Portland, and Eugene.[34]

The second dimension has been the construction of binational organizations and institutions that have emerged, in Susan Clarke's words, as "institutional fixes" in response to global competition. The most elaborate of these lobbying and coordinating organizations is the Pacific North West Economic Region (PNWER), begun in 1991 as a cooperative effort among the legislatures of British Columbia, Alberta, Washington, Oregon, Idaho, Montana, and Alaska. Already crossing the continental divide with Alberta and Montana, the PNWER came further unstuck from a bioregional Cascadia with the addition of Saskatchewan and the Yukon Territory. Essentially intended "to leverage regional influence in Ottawa and Washington," it has a substantial roster of conferences and working groups on agriculture, environmental technology, forest products, government procurement, telecommunications, tourism, trade and finance, and transportation. With sprawling territory and limited economic and cultural coherence, PNWER is essentially an alliance to work for federal investment and favorable national regulations—not much different from single nation organizations like the Western Council of State Legislatures.[35]

The Pacific Corridor Enterprise Council (PACE) is a British Columbia–Washington organization with membership drawn mainly from private businesses. It formed in 1989 "as a non-profit, business organization to promote cross-border transactions and advocate the removal of barriers that impede the legitimate flow of people, goods and services across the Canada/USA border." PACE "fosters and works toward the development of mutually beneficial trade and travel policies, and the elimination of unnecessary legal and political barriers between the two nations." In practical terms, this means mobility for knowledge workers and improvements to transportation.[36]

Also on the institutional list is the Cascadia Center for Regional Development, housed within Seattle's Discovery Institute (it was the Cascadia Project when founded in 1993). The motto is "Cascadia: Committed to Commerce, Community, and Conservation." But the focus—we might see this coming—narrows down to better intermodal freight systems, high volume surface transit, and improved metro transportation planning.[37]

In practical fact, the border has become tighter rather than looser in both the long run and short run. The porous boundary of the nineteenth century began to constrict in the mid-twentieth century. North of the international border, Canadian nationalism intensified after 1920, with results apparent in Canadian attitudes toward the Alaskan border and the Canadianization of European immigrants.[38] The United States added Canada to the system of national immigration quotas in 1931 (lumping it as a British nation). In 1996, Congress required everyone entering the United States to have a visa and leave on their departure date and exempted Canada only after several years of intense lobbying from both sides of the border. Then came the terrorist attacks of September 11, 2001, bringing emergency closures that backed traffic up for fifteen miles at some major crossings. The twentieth-century border was more tightly controlled than that of the nineteenth-century, and the twenty-first-century border is tighter yet, with armed soldiers at lonely crossing points and Americans required to show passports to re-enter the United States.[39]

The western border *is* permeable for personal consumption such as shopping and vacationing. Vancouver and Seattle news media depict the other city primarily as a scene for consumption. Shoppers and vacationers flood across the British Columbia–Washington border, with the direction of the flow depending on exchange rates and real estate markets.[40] Nevertheless, national pride and identity still override efforts to define common agendas for the organization of economic *production*. Immigration and capital investment still take place within national borders. It makes a difference whether a Korean electronics firm decides to invest its $2 billion in Oregon or British Columbia. It makes a difference whether someone from Hong Kong decides to move to Vancouver or Seattle. The government of British Columbia blocked the implementation of a Cascadia Corridor Commission (authorized by both national governments) because of fears of subordination to Seattle—a mirror of worries about the Alaska Highway fifty years earlier. Canadian concerns have been heightened by the effects of NAFTA on Canadian branch plant manufacturing. High-speed rail links to the southward meet similarly mixed reviews because of their possible erosion of Canadian distinctiveness and Canadian businesses.

Nor has binational trade quite lived up to expectations along the Pacific Coast. Transportation investments have not been made and leave both rail and road systems poorly articulated. In the post-NAFTA nineties, trade with British Columbia accounted for only 2.6 percent of Washington state's gross domestic product. Another econometric test suggests that British Columbia's degree of economic integration with the United States is less than that of Canada as a whole; that is, British Columbia does *less* of its trade with the United States than does the rest of Canada.[41]

Political scientists thus end up with skeptical conclusions. "Transborder regionalism in Cascadia is ad hoc and episodic," write Donald Alper. "It is not a movement for merging the laws and policy processes of Canadian and U.S. jurisdictions. It is neither the creation of supranational institutions, not does it signal an end to, or even severe erosion of, the border." Gerard Rutan similarly found little institutional connection or cooperation between Washington state and British Columbia. Instead, "what has emerged is the picture of two quite separate jurisdictions, each often pursuing its own ends on its own side of the border. . . . There is no consistent desire for a relationship beyond . . . the directly problem related, on the part of either jurisdiction."[42] Instead, we find lots of talk in working groups, conferences, roundtables, committees that seem, at best, to produce some policy parallelism and the agreement that *something* needs to be done to improve congested transportation.

Cascadia As City-State

The idea of a Cascadia Megaregion dates from the late 1990s, developed both to advance and to clarify the increasingly nebulous idea of a regional economic alliance. According to its proponents, a megaregion is a large connected network of metropolitan areas that share enough economic and cultural similarities to be useful units for policy decisions. A recent definition emphasizes the "economic functionality" of megaregions and the concurrent emergence of "cultural identity" emerging from this shared economy.[43]

Interest in megaregions in North America emerged from the New York–oriented Regional Plan Association (RPA), which convened an initial conference in the early 1990s. It took on new life when Robert Yaro of the RPA and Armando Carbonell of the Lincoln Institute of Land Policy taught a planning studio at the University of Pennsylvania and the Lincoln Institute and RPA convened roundtable meetings. In 2008 the RPA helped to form America 2050, a group of planners, business people, and policy makers. The evolving ideas—we might call them a moving target—have been repeatedly published in planning magazines, essay collections, a variety of web-based documents, and, in 2009, a book edited by Catherine Ross.[44]

The grand regional thinking embodied in the America 2050 project can be placed in several frameworks. It certainly updates the megalopolitan analysis that Jean Gottmann and Constantinos Doxiadis popularized in the 1960s.[45] More directly, it is also animated by a desire to emulate the urban-regional strategies that have developed in Europe under the aegis of the European Union, such as the European Spatial Development Perspective of 1999, and in East Asia in the wake of economic boom. Europeans since the 1980s have explored the ways in which sets of metropolitan areas string together in larger spatial units that sometimes get cute names like the Blue Banana, which curves from Manchester to Milan, and the Golden Banana, along the Mediterranean coast from Valencia to Genoa (the cosmological analogy is galaxies and galactic clusters). A European alternative is to describe a 20–40–50 pentagon, defined by London, Paris, Milan, Munich, and Hamburg and presumably containing 20 percent of the area of the European Union as of the early 1990s, 40 percent of its population, and 50 percent of its gross domestic product. In Asia the term of art is now "mega-urban region" or MUR.

Armando Carbonell, Mark Pisano, and Robert Yaro, in their 2005 document on "Global Gateway Regions," write: "As the number of economically competitive regions grows around the world, America's cities need to band together in order to strengthen their role in the global economy." It is important to "facilitate the emergence of nine new Mega-regions that can compete with similar emerging networks of cities in Europe and Asia." The same idea is front and center in the title of the new volume edited by Catherine Ross with contributions by a murderer's row of regional planning scholars: *Megaregions: Planning for Global Competitiveness*.[46]

A challenge for this grand spatial thinking is to identify a realistic scale for the expected robust economic interactions. Multicity regions can include long recognized conurbations like the English Midlands and the Dutch Randstadt, emerging conurbations like China Pearl River Delta and Shanghai-Nanjing, potential binational regions such as Copenhagen-Malmo, and what seem like rather imaginative constellations spanning hundreds of miles like Copenhagen-Stockholm-Helsinki-Saint Petersburg, Madrid-Seville-Lisbon, and (perhaps fetched furthest of all from the imagination) a Beijing-Seoul-Tokyo Corridor that loops blithely across both the Sea of Japan and some hundreds of miles of noncapitalist North Korea. Similarly the current North American analysis includes some regions with

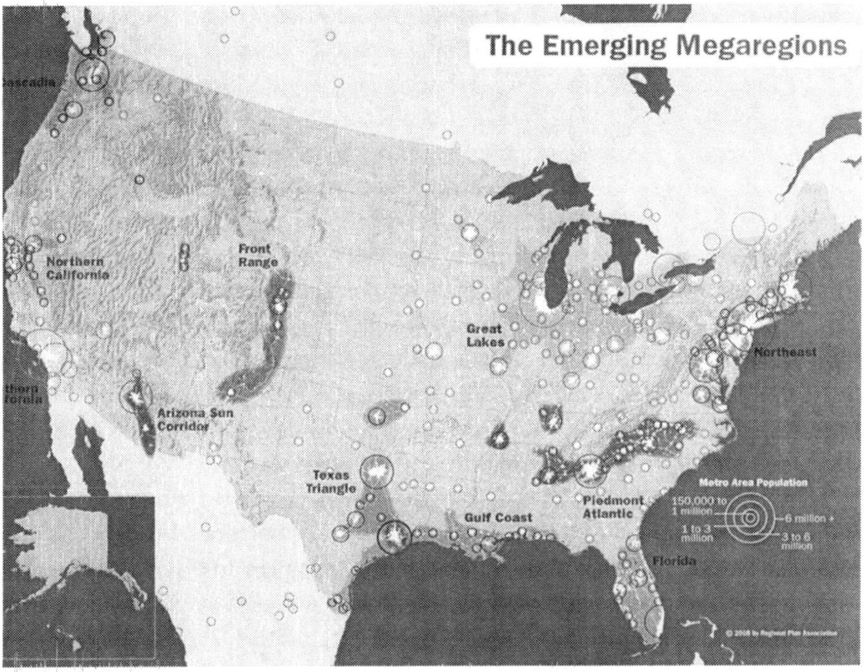

FIG. 6.3. Cascadia as emerging Megaregion. This map, one of multiple efforts to delineate urbanized megaregions, highlights the isolation of Cascadia compared to eastern or southwestern megaregions. (Courtesy Regional Plan Association, www.rpa.org)

a clear historic and current identity, such as the Boston–Washington, D.C., corridor, the Great Lakes industrial region, the San Francisco Bay area, and southern California. Others seem more dubious. Denver and Salt Lake City do not constitute a meaningful multicity region as listed by Jonathan Barnett, a point clear to anyone who has driven the long, dry road past Glenwood Springs, Rifle, Grand Junction, Fruita, Green River, Price, and Provo. Nor is it clear whether there is a functional Gulf Coast metro-region from Corpus Christi to Mobile or an I-35 region from San Antonio to Kansas City as posited by researchers at Virginia Tech.[47] Even America 2050 is a bit uncertain of the exact list, saying in 2005 that there were nine but only showing eight on a map, then upping the count to eleven on its current (as of July 2009) map (fig. 6.3).[48]

As suggested briefly above, advocates of the megaregion approach in northwestern America see themselves as offering a positive synthesis. In so doing, they lose some of their regional specificity, since all of the dozen or so North American megaregions must have something in common. The result is a tendency to generalize into standard triple-bottom-line sustainability rhetoric, as in the invocation of prosperity, equity, and environmental sustainability in "Global Gateway Regions."[49] If Ecotopia is the hook, Cascadia-1 is the real starting place, and Mainstreet Cascadia is the businesslike alternative, then Megaregion Cascadia tries to combine the best of all approaches. We can see the evolving imagery of the megaregion from an early schematic doodle through more detailed depictions.

The Cascadia Megaregion does seem to have some ground truth. Most broadly, the social and cultural values of western Canadians are closer to those of the adjacent United States than is the case in other parts of Canada.[50] There *is* a single string of large- and middle-sized cities along a highway/rail corridor (Eugene, Salem, Olympia, Tacoma, Bellingham, and Victoria in addition to Portland, Seattle, and Vancouver). The most recent map seems to add Yakima from east of the mountains but not Spokane, Richland-Pasco-Kennewick, or Bend. At least along the main corridor, the cities and region share some social and cultural commonalities, particularly in their orientation to the outdoors, as well as similar commitments to strong growth management systems.

Nevertheless, idea of a unified Cascadia Megaregion faces a number of questions, starting with all of the practical challenges of tightened borders listed for Mainstreet Cascadia. In addition, there is little complementarity among its three major cities. On the Pacific Coast, the often-cited model is the San Francisco Bay area where high-finance San Francisco, high-tech San Jose, thoughtful Berkeley, and brawny Oakland work as a metropolitan team.[51] When we turn back to Cascadia, however, we find a different situation. The three cities are too distant from each other for effective everyday interaction (the same distances as Prague-Vienna-Budapest, which proved an unstable combination in 1918 despite centuries of Hapsburg effort to the contrary). They are also too similar to form a complementary whole on the analogy of the Bay Area. Rather than meshing into a whole that is greater than the sum of its parts, they continue to compete for trade, transportation linkages, and foreign investment. The cities have grown and prospered as east–west gateways, competing with the others as a gateway to the Pacific and Asia for continental markets. For a specific example, Japanese trading companies tend to operate offices in all three of the major cities, replicating functions "rather than organizing their operations in a way that might attest to a singular pattern of Cascadian economic integration." They are competitive rather than complementary, especially Vancouver and Seattle, which would each see itself as the favored center, while Portland chafes at a supporting role.[52]

Moreover, each metropolis is large enough to support a full range of services ranging from research universities to advertising firms. A Portlander need not go to Vancouver to seek out a sophisticated architectural firm, and a Vancouverite need not go to Seattle for transpacific container service or air connections. In other words, it is not clear that the three cities working together are necessarily more than the sum of their parts. A realistic expectation for Main Street Cascadia may be less a merger of well-matched parts than a federation of otherwise similar city-states—a sort of Hanseatic League for the twenty-first century.

Anything more would require conscious decisions to generate economies of scale by systematically designating and developing agreed-on areas of economic specialization—a challenge in that Oregon and Washington have very different political cultures and styles of doing the public business, British Columbia politics look eccentric from south of the border, and Alaskans definitely march to their own drum and bugle corps. What remains, as for Mainstreet Cascadia, is the bedrock concern of transportation and energy infrastructure, topics that have long been central to cross border management.[53] Although locally claimed (as by several cohorts of Portland State University planning students who have produced increasingly elaborate reports on what they term "Ecopolis"), the Cascadia Megaregion looks like one more example to add to John Findlay's list of regional identities imposed from outside.

Its Own Separate World

These multiple imaginings of region may be in sometimes testy dialog with each other, but they also share an important element in common. Each is in some degree a secessionist imagining that reaches back in time, past the 150-year history of the promised land, to the geopolitical visions of the early nineteenth century.

Long before the era of railroads, continental visionaries like Thomas Jefferson and Thomas Hart Benton (speaking in 1825 on the Oregon question) anticipated sister republics on the Pacific Slope—independent but friendly nations settled and developed by free English-speaking Americans from the "original nest" along the Atlantic seaboard. Explorer Charles Wilkes, in the early 1840s, similarly anticipated that "the situation of Upper California will cause its separation from Mexico before many years. . . . It is very probable that this country will become united with Oregon, with which it will perhaps form a state that is destined to control the destinies of the Pacific."[54] The Mexican War and gold rush mooted the option for California, but it was achieved, for a few decades in the form of the American-dominated Kingdom of Hawaii and a few years as the Hawaiian Republic of 1894–98.

These early imagined and/or actual nations reflected the dominance of maritime connections. The British, Russian, and American fur trade was supplied and carried on along and across the Pacific, connecting Kodiak Island and New Archangel, Nootka Sound, Fort George/Astoria, Fort Vancouver, Spanish California, and the Hawaiian Islands to the Atlantic world.[55] The key towns of the first generation were sited for navigation and Pacific connections—Victoria on an island at the entrance to the inland sea, Port Townsend on a peninsula that jutted into the entrance to Puget Sound, Portland at the head of navigation on the Columbia/Willamette system.

In contrast to the Jeffersonian vision and to early commercial patterns, the great geopolitical projects of 1850–1950 were to connect western North America directly to the East and tie together two continental nations.

The process in the United States is embedded into the central national narrative. In the aftermath of territorial acquisitions in the 1840s, railroad building, capital flows, and trading partnerships that redirected historic and "natural" north–south flows of people and trade into east–west flows. This was accomplished first by attaching the Ohio Valley to the Northeast rather than the Gulf South in the 1850s, the fundamental prerequisite for Union victory in the Civil War. The project followed with the era of transcontinental connections to Puget Sound, Portland, San Francisco, and southern California and the national integration of the West as an economic colony of the industrial core along the northeastern seaboard and the Great Lakes.[56]

For U.S. audiences, the Canadian story merits a bit more detail. As the fur trade declined, Britain organized its chunk of Pacific North America as two separate crown colonies—Vancouver Island in 1851 and British Columbia in 1858, combined only in 1866, seven years after Oregon statehood. With the unpromising granite of the Laurentian Shield, vast prairies, and convoluted mountains separating British Columbia from the Saint Lawrence Valley, the colony certainly had the potential to evolve separately into an independent nation as a sort of North American New Zealand to the Australia of eastern Canada, with Victoria standing in for Wellington and Vancouver for Auckland. Out of this sense of isolation, a group of British Columbia residents in 1869 petitioned for annexation to the United States, and the province was essentially bribed into Canada in 1871.[57]

What followed was the creation of "Canada" as an economic as well as political union. Central here was the National Policy that Premier John A. Macdonald introduced in 1879, designed to develop an autonomous economy on an east–west axis as the United States erected post–Civil War tariff barriers. The Canadian Pacific Railroad was the centerpiece. The line reached Burrard Inlet in 1886, creating the city of Vancouver and supplementing British Columbia road systems that ran eastward from the coast while carefully avoiding connections to the United States.[58]

The new regional imaginary runs against that mission or cause and explicitly or implicitly argues for secession, for treating the region as something different from, apart from, detached from the rest of the nation(s): "The Far Corner" as journalist Stewart Holbrook called the region, or "upper left coast" in more recent political jargon to recognize the political tendencies of ecotopian territory.

Callenbach's Ecotopia, of course, depends on literal secession from the United States. Criticized for assuming a revolution rather than demonstrating how a "green" nation might emerge, he followed the 1975 book with *Ecotopia Emerging* in 1981. The revolution remains a thought experiment rather than an exploration of the real challenges of political action. As Callenbach describes it, a high school student invents an improved photovoltaic cell and decides to make it available to everyone; her mother organizes "cancer commandos" and the greens organize as a political party; an episode of rather nonecotopian nuclear blackmail forces the unenlightened parts of the United States to accede peacefully to independence and Ecotopia is born with a citizenry who want little to do with the old country.

In bioregional Cascadia, separation appears in the cartographic rhetoric. In McCloskey's key map, the rivers all run westward, while the rest of the continent is a blank, unknowable territory . . . or not worth bothering about. A second map that shows the rivers that drain eastward and northward from the Cascadian mountains offers far less detail about the Missouri, Saskatchewan, Mackenzie, and Yukon Rivers than it does about the Fraser and Columbia. It is the waters that tumble into the Pacific that really count.

Portland-based Ecotrust has picked up and developed the same theme in its own efforts to remap the Northwest. It identifies its home territory as the temperate rainforest that the Northwest shares with other western coasts. In effect, its map suggests that Cascadia should be understood as part of a discontinuous region that includes coastal Tasmania, New Zealand's South Island, southern Chile, Norway, and Caucasian Georgia rather than a part of continental North America.[59] The boundaries of a true "Salmon Nation" would encircle much of the Pacific, including Chile, New Zealand, Siberia, Kamchatka, Hokkaido, and even the very nonecotopian Democratic People's Republic of Korea.

Laurie Ricou has also pointed out that fiction and poetry from the Northwest is filled with characters who reach and balance on the continental edge, looking westward to Asia and thinking themselves on the very edge of things.[60] Annie Dillard's settlers of a fictionalized Bellingham in *The Living* (1992) arrive by sea and live by the sea. Clay Calvert in *Honey in the Horn* (1935) reaches the Oregon coast to stand at the very edge of North America, a place that Don Berry's mountain men previously reached in *To Build a Ship* (1963) and *Trask* (1960), where the protagonist's journey literally balances him on the knife edge of the continent over the surging ocean. Ivan Doig in *Winter Brothers* meditates on the life of Thomas Swan, "a westcomer, and a stayer," a being of "the continental edge that drew us both."[61]

Cascadia-2 is perhaps the version that holds most tightly to the continent by virtue of its emphasis on a north–south Anglophone community. Nevertheless, its promoters repeatedly cite data that purport to show that a separate Cascadia would be the world's tenth or eleventh or maybe twentieth largest economy. Moreover, Alan Artibise has argued that Cascadians on both sides of the border share a "bemused antipathy" toward their national capitals.[62] His suggestion resonates with the long British Columbian tendency to remain aloof from the rest of Canada. British Columbian intellectual leaders such as painter and writer Emily Carr came to value provincial isolation. We can note the adamant Britishness of Victoria, the distinctiveness of the British Columbia environment, and the simple distance from Toronto and Montreal.[63] Indeed, as the Canadian economy fell behind the United States in the 1980s and 1990s, British Columbians, as residents of the richest province, found a certain temptation toward casting their fate with the United States.[64]

Finally, the idea of emerging megaregions needs to be understood in the context of city-state theorizing. As discussed above, one of the basic arguments for thinking about North American megaregions is to compete effectively with Europe and Asia, a goal embodied in language about "global gateway regions." In turn, this thinking draws on the work of Kenishi Ohmae, who argued in the 1990s that the expanding global market is creating regional economic clusters with the potential to evolve into political communities rivaling and in some ways replacing nation states with "region states."[65] When wealth comes in bytes rather than carloads and information is instantly portable, say enthusiasts of electronic communication, national boundaries will erode under a hail of faxes, e-mail messages, and hits on websites. When the world is deconstructed to a network of direct connections of person to person, people to people, and corporation to subcontractor, it is likely to be reconstructed around quasi-independent city-regions such as Cascadia, with semi-independent, multilateral connections to the world economy.[66] Saskia Sassen, a leading theorist of global urbanization, suggests that the internal economic variety of megaregions enhances their self-sufficiency and supports the ability of megaregions to develop direct or "transverse" connections with the global economy independent of global cities like New York and Tokyo.[67]

Patrick Smith, a political scientist who has been studying "Cascadia" for many years, sees an emerging "globalist policy stance" with "institutionalization of global activity in the Cascadia city-region" in support of international linkages. He also argues that "territorial locations and inclinations have made the whole Cascadia region very much part of the Asia Pacific economy, even when much of its history links it to Europe.[68] This latter point is especially telling in British Columbia, given Canada's close historical association with the United Kingdom, and points up the province's long-standing ambivalence about the rest of Canada.

The Cascadian Moment

The Cascadian moment coincides with the end of the great North American boom of 1940–74. Both Americans and Canadians began to rethink their economic futures for an era of likely resource scarcity and shifting centers of economic power, calling into question two centuries in which regional identity revolved around resource exploitation. This necessity interacted with rising environmentalism in the 1970s and 1980s to frame Ecotopia and Cascadia. It interacted with the accelerating shift to global economic networks and institutions in the 1990s to frame thinking about Mainstreet Cascadia and Megaregion Cascadia.

As suggested previously, the different conceptualizations all respond to two centuries of imagining the Northwest as a resource frontier, but they have also interacted with each other in a semi-closed dialectic. Ecotopia served as the first, naive premise. Cascadia was a direct and antithetical response. Cascadia as a great, great land was in turn adapted (or "hijacked") by the Mainstreet Cascadia boosters and their reinvigoration of developmental rhetoric. And proponents of Megaregion Cascadia would argue that their synthesis accommodates the possibilities of growth that is both globally connected and environmentally sensitive.

In the wake of this decades-long dialectic, Cascadia in the second decade of the twenty-first century has become an increasingly permeable signifier easily available for appropriation. For many in the region, the term is familiar enough to be a simpler alternative for Northwest or Pacific Northwest—a bit like Dixie with environmental rather than racial overtones. Major League Soccer fans, for example, created an unofficial "Cascadia Cup" in 2004 that recognizes the Northwest team (Portland Timbers, Seattle Sounders, Vancouver Whitecaps) that has the best record against the other two. Bothell, Washington, a Seattle suburb, is home to Cascadia Community College. Rowing enthusiasts have held a Cascadia Regatta in Burnaby, British Columbia. As a marketing ploy, the term has appeared on labels slapped on beer bottles by microbrewers in Victoria, Olympia, and Portland. Many more examples are available to the energetic Googler.

Cascadia-2, or at least the verbal shadow of ecological Cascadia, seems to have had the greatest sticking power with a regional proliferation of environmental groups and initiatives. Someone seeking attorneys with environmental specialties with a March 2014 web search would find a Cascadia Law Group and a one-person Cascadia Law P.C. The Cascadia Green Building Council—Portland based with chapters from southern Oregon to British Columbia—promotes LEED construction (Leadership in Energy and Environmental Design) and broader sustainability goals. Portland's Cascadia Wild tries to connect people with their natural environment. Cascadia Wildlands supports grassroots environmental protection. The Cascadian Independence Project at www.cascadianow.org is about community activism and empowerment around governance, food systems, and sustainability—call it independence with a small "i." The "Mission" tab on its website references both the Cascadia bioregion and "the distinct social, geographic, and cultural aspects that make the Pacific Northwest unique."

The power of ecological Cascadia is also evident in the triumph of the McCloskey map as the standard image cited by "Cascadia groups" and the frequent appearance of a Cascadia flag with a Douglas fir tree against horizontal blue, white, and green stripes. Nevertheless, political boundaries remain inconveniently prominent. The Seattle-based Sightline Institute, which advocates for sustainable practices and policies, has published a Cascadia Scorecard since 2004, but the data available for its comparisons are almost always aggregated by city, metropolitan area, or states and provinces.

Northwesterners over the last four decades have been imagining difference from their larger nations rather than similarity. The emerging regional imaginary is both spatially and temporally separated. It emphasizes physical distance and difference from the Atlantic world while embracing the even vaster distances of the Pacific Rim. It also looks away from its past. Other American regionalisms have struck deep roots into their regional pasts—whether these involve efforts to understand and celebrate the distinctiveness of an American South and southern culture, to preserve the heritage of Francophone Canada, or to probe the long multiracial history of the Mexico-U.S. borderlands. Despite mutterings about nationhood, Cascadia is painfully thin as a political concept.[69] It takes its power, instead, from the continuing pull of the natural landscape and resources on the North American imagination.

Notes

1. Robert Geddes, ed., *Cities in Our Future: Growth and Form, Environmental Health and Social Equity* (Washington, D.C.: Island Press, 1997), 148; Alan Artibise, Anne Vernez Moudon, and Ethan Seltzer, "Cascadia: An Emerging Regional Model," in Geddes, *Cities in Our Future*, 149–74.

2. Wilbur Zelinsky, "North America's Vernacular Regions," *Annals of the Association of American Geographers* 70 (1980): 1–16.

3. William L. Lang, "Beavers, Firs, Salmon, and Falling Water: Pacific Northwest Regionalism and the Environment," *Oregon Historical Quarterly* 104 (Summer 2003); 151–65.

4. Richard White, *The Organic Machine: The Remaking of the Columbia River* (New York: Hill and Wang, 1995).

5. John M. Findlay, "A Fishy Proposition: Regional identity in the Pacific Northwest," in David Wrobel and Michael Steiner, eds. *Many Wests: Place, Culture, and Regional Identity* (Lawrence: University Press of Kansas, 1997), 37–70.

6. Richard Maxwell Brown, "The Great Raincoast of North America," in David Stratton and George A. Frykman, eds., *The Changing Pacific Northwest: Interpreting Its Past* (Pullman: Washington State University Press, 1988). Also Richard Maxwell Brown, "Rainfall and History: Perspectives on the Pacific Northwest," in Thomas Edwards and Carlos Schwantes, eds., *Experiences in a Promised Land: Essays in Pacific Northwest History* (Seattle: University of Washington Press, 1986).

7. The core of regional historiography centers on the processes and problems of resources development and the conflicts that have exploded out of competing demands: from the current generation are Andrew Fisher, David Arnold, Joseph Taylor, Chris Friday, and Lissa Wadewitz on fish and fisheries; Peter Boag, Robert Bunting, and Gail Nomura on farming; William Robbins, Paul Hirt, Norman Clark, and Nancy Langston on forests and wood products; Richard White, Daniel Pope, Karl Brooks, and Paul Pitzer on energy systems.

8. Marcus Lee Hansen, *The Mingling of the Canadian and American Peoples*, Vol. 1: *Historical*, completed by John Bartlett Brebner (New Haven, Conn.: Yale University Press, 1940). To the mingling of human workers we might also add Buck, introduced as fol-

lows by Jack London: "Buck did not read the newspapers, or he would have known that trouble was brewing, not alone for himself, but for every tide-water dog, strong of muscle and with warm, long hair, from Puget Sound to San Diego." As we remember from *The Call of the Wild*, Buck is snatched from his rural home in the Santa Clara Valley of California and transported to the Klondike supply center of Seattle, where he is brutalized and tamed. He is then shipped north to add his canine muscle power to the opening of the far Northwest frontier.

9. National Resources Committee, *Regional Factors in National Planning* (Washington, D.C.: Government Printing Office, 1935), 166.

10. Clarence Dill, *Where Water Falls* (Spokane, Wash.: C. W. Hill, 1970), 246–58, cited in Lang, "Beavers, Firs, Salmon, and Falling Water."

11. Richard Neuberger, *Our Promised Land* (New York: Macmillan, 1939).

12. Anne Whiston Spirn, *Daring to Look: Dorothea Lange's Photographs and Reports from the Field* (Chicago: University of Chicago Press, 2008).

13. *Life* 6 (June 5 1939): 15–23.

14. Paul Hirt, *A Conspiracy of Optimism: Management of the National Forests since World War Two* (Lincoln: University of Nebraska Press, 1994).

15. Ernest Callenbach, *Ecotopia: The Notebooks and Reports of William Weston* (Berkeley, Calif.: Banyan Tree Books, 1981) and *Ecotopia Emerging* (Berkeley, Calif.: Banyan Tree Books, 1981); Heinz Tschachler, "Despotic Reason in Arcadia? Ernest Callenbach's Ecological Utopias," *Science-Fiction Studies* 11 (1984): 304–16. My somewhat skeptical reading of Ecotopia is not shared by Will Katerberg in *Future West: Utopia and Apocalypse in Frontier Science Fiction* (Lawrence: University Press of Kansas, 2008).

16. Lizabeth Cohen, *A Consumer's Republic: The Politics of Mass Consumption in Postwar America* (New York: Knopf, 2003); Donella Meadows, Dennis L. Meadows, Jørgen Randers, and William W. Behrens III, *The Limits to Growth* (New York: Universe Books, 1972); *Whole Earth Catalog* (Menlo Park, Calif.: Portola Institute, 1968–71).

17. Joel Garreau, *The Nine Nations of North America* (Boston: Little, Brown, 1981), 261.

18. Ursula K. Le Guin, *Always Coming Home* (New York: Harper and Row, 1985). The book has attracted much critical commentary. See *Donna R. White, Dancing with Dragons: Ursula K. Le Guin and the Critics* (Columbia, S.C.: Camden House, 1999) for a summary.

19. Coyote figures on one of the Kesh origin stories, and Le Guin has commented that "Native American literary texts . . . served me as an unfailing inspiration for an ethic and aesthetic native to the western American earth." Ursula Le Guin interview, in Larry McCaffery, *Across the Wounded Galaxies: Interviews with American Science Fiction Writers* (Urbana: University of Illinois Press, 1990), 172.

20. Josiah Royce, *California from the Conquest of 1846 to the Second Vigilance Committee in San Francisco: A Study of American Character* (Boston: Houghton Mifflin, 1886); Robert V. Hine, *Josiah Royce: From Grass Valley to Harvard* (Norman: University of Oklahoma Press, 1992); Earl Pomeroy, "Josiah Royce: Historian in Search of Community," *Pacific Historical Review* 40 (February 1970): 1–24.

21. David McCloskey, "Cascadia," in *Futures by Design: The Practice of Ecological Planning* (Philadelphia: New Society Publishers, 1994), 98–105.

22. McCloskey, "Cascadia: A Great Green Land on the Northeast Pacific Rim," map with text, 1968. Text at http://www.washington.edu/uwired/outreach/cspn/Website/

Classroom%20Materials/Reading%20the%20Region/Aggressive%20Regionalism/Texts/18.html (accessed September 25, 2014).

23. *Knowing Home: Studies for a Possible Portland* (Portland: Rain Magazine, 1981).

24. Ken Kesey, *Sometimes a Great Notion* (New York: Viking Press, 1964), 1.

25. Sallie Tisdale, *Stepping Westward: The Long Search for Home in the Pacific Northwest* (New York: Henry Holt, 1991); Jonathan Raban, *Passage to Juneau: A Sea and Its Meaning* (New York: Pantheon, 1999).

26. Andrew G. Kirk, *Counterculture Green: The Whole Earth Catalog and American Environmentalism* (Lawrence: University Press of Kansas, 2007); Charles LeWarne, *Utopias on Puget Sound* (Seattle: University of Washington Press, 1975); Jeffrey Sanders, *Seattle and the Roots of Urban Sustainability: Inventing Ecotopia* (Pittsburgh: University of Pittsburgh Press, 2010); Steven Reed Johnson, "The Transformation of Civic Institutions and Practices in Portland, Oregon, 1960–1999" (Ph.D. dissertation, Portland State University, 2002). For different fictionalized versions of the north coast subculture, see Thomas Pynchon, *Vineland* (Boston: Little, Brown, 1990), Octavia Butler, *Parable of the Sower* (New York: Four Walls Eight Windows, 1993), and T. C. Boyle, *Drop City* (New York: Viking, 2003).

27. Dan Flores, "Place: An Argument for Bioregionalism," *Environmental History Review* 18 (Winter 1994): 1–18.

28. Sterling Evans, ed., *The Borderlands of the American and Canadian Wests: Essays on Regional History of the Forty-ninth Parallel* (Lincoln: University of Nebraska Press, 2006), 356.

29. Edward C. Wolf and Seth Zuckerman, eds., *Salmon Nation: People, Place, and Our Common Home* (Portland: Ecotrust, 2003), at http://www.salmonnation.com/index.php (accessed September 25, 2014).

30. *Opportunities for Achieving Sustainability in Cascadia* (Vancouver: International Centre for Sustainable Cities,1994); Paul Schell and J. Hamer, "Cascadia: The New Binationalism of Western Canada and the U.S. Pacific Northwest," in E. Earle and J. Wirth, eds., *Identities in North America: The Search for Community* (Stanford, Calif.: Stanford University Press, 1995).140–56; Alan F. J. Artibise, "Achieving Sustainability in Cascadia: An Emerging Model of Urban Growth Management in the Vancouver-Seattle-Portland Corridor," in Peter Karl Kresl and Gary Gappert, eds., *North American Cities and the Global Economy* (Thousand Oaks, Calif.: Sage Publications, 1995), 221–25; Theodore H. Cohn and Patrick J. Smith, "Developing Global Cities in the Pacific Northwest: The Cases of Vancouver and Seattle," in Kresl and Gappert, *North American Cities*, 251–85; John Hamer and Bruce Chapman, *International Seattle: Creating a Globally Competitive Community* (Seattle: Discovery Institute, 1992).

31. Emmanuel Brunet-Jailly, "Cascadia in Comparative Perspectives: Canada-U.S. Relations and the Emergence of Cross-Border Regions," *Canadian Political Science Review* 2 (June 2008): 112; Donald K. Alper, "The Idea of Cascadia: Emergent Transborder Regionalisms in the Pacific Northwest-Western Canada," *Journal of Borderlands Studies* 11 (Fall 1996): 1–23; Susan Clarke, "Regional and Transnational Discourse: The Politics of Ideas and Economic Cascadia," *International Journal of Economic Development* (July 2000); Patrick Smith, "Branding Cascadia: Considering Cascadia's Conflicting Conceptualizations—Who Gets to Decide," *Canadian Political Science Review* 2 (June 2008): 57–83.

32. Robert Kaplan, "Travels into America's Future," *Atlantic Monthly*, August 1998, 58.

33. William B. Henkel, "Cascadia: A State of (Various) Mind(s)," *Chicago Review* 39 (Autumn 1993): 110–18; Janet Johnson, "Cascadia: It's As Much a State of Mind as a Geographic Place," *Seattle University News* (Spring 1994): 21–23.

34. Cultural Cascades.com, http://www.cultutralcascades.com (accessed June 5, 2012).

35. Pacific NorthWest Economic Region, http://www.pnwer.org (accessed September 25, 2014).

36. Pacific Corridor Enterprise Council, http://www.pacebordertrade.org (accessed September 25, 2014).

37. Cascadia, http://www.cascadiaproject.org (accessed September 25, 2014).

38. Galen Roger Perras, "Who Will Defend British Columbia: Unity of Command on the West Coast, 1934–42," in John M. Findlay and Ken Coates, eds., *Parallel Destinies: Canadian-American Relations West of the Rockies* (Seattle: University of Washington Press, 2002), 181–202.

39. Reginald Stuart, *Dispersed Relations: Americans and Canadians in Upper North America* (Baltimore: Johns Hopkins University Press, 2007), 245–50.

40. Susan Holmberg, "Imagining a Cross-National Community: Mass Media in the Puget Sound," paper presented at conference "On Brotherly Terms: Canadian-American Relations West of the Rockies," University of Washington, September 13, 1996; Daniel E. Turbeville III and Susan L. Bradbury, "From Fur Trade to Free Trade: Rethinking the Inland Empire," *American Review of Canadian Studies* 29, no. 3 (1999): 447–71.

41. Howard Wall, "How Important Is the US-Canada Border?" *International Economic Trends* (August 1999); Brunet-Jailly, "Cascadia in Comparative Perspective," 109–10. The study applied a test originally developed by Jeffrey Frankel to examine economic integration in the European Union.

42. Alper, "Idea of Cascadia," 18–19; Gerard Rutan, "Micro-Diplomatic Relations in the Pacific Northwest: Washington State–British Columbia Interactions," in Ivo D. Duchacek, Daniel Latouche, and Garth Stevenson, eds., *Perforated Sovereignties and International Relations: Trans-Sovereign Contacts of Subnational Governments* (Westport, Conn.: Greenwood Press, 1988), 163–88; Brunet-Jailly, "Cascadia in Comparative Perspective"; Clarke, "Regional and Transnational Discourse."

43. Cheryl Contant and Karen Leone de Nie, "Scale Matters: Rethinking Planning Approaches across Jurisdictional and Sectoral Boundaries," in Catherine Ross, ed., *Megaregions: Planning for Global Competitiveness* (Washington, D.C.: Island Press, 2009), 11–17.

44. This institutional development, along with the interest of a number of universities, is compactly summarized in Margaret Dewar and David Epstein, "Planning for 'Megaregions' in the United States," *Journal of Planning Literature* 22 (November 2007): 108–24. For descriptions of the megaregion idea see Robert Lang and Arthur C. Nelson, "The Rise of the Megapolitans," *Planning* 73 (January 2007): 7–12; Robert Lang and Dawn Dhavale, America's Megapolitan Areas," *Land Lines* 17 (2005); America 2050, "About America 2050," at http://www.america2050.org/about.html (accessed September 25, 2014).

45. Jean Gottmann, *Megalopolis: The Urbanized Northeastern Seaboard of the United States* (New York: Twentieth Century Fund, 1961); Constantinos Doxiadis, *Ekistics: An Introduction to the Science of Human Elements* (New York: Oxford University Press, 1968).

46. Armando Carbonell, Mark Pisano, and Robert Yaro, *2050 Global Gateway Regions. The United States of America's 3rd Century Strategy: Preserving the American Dream* (New York: Regional Plan Association, 2005), 21, 24; Catherine Ross, ed., *Megaregions: Planning for Global Competitiveness* (Washington, D.C.: Island Press, 2009).

47. Jonathan Barnett, "What Are the Nation's Future Growth Trends," in Jonathan Barnett, ed., *Smart Growth in a Changing World* (Chicago: American Planning Association, 2007), 7–16; Robert Lang and Dawn Dhavale, "Beyond Megalopolis: Exploring America's New 'Megapolitan' Geography," in Metropolitan Institute Census Report Series (Alexandria, Va.: Metropolitan Institute, Virginia Tech University, 2005).

48. Most recently there are eight listed in Robert Lang and A. C. Nelson, "Megapolitan America: Defining and Applying a New Geography," in Ross, *Megaregions*, 107–26. Definitional criteria are still under debate, See Catherine Ross and Myungje Woo, "Identifying Megaregions in the United States: Implications for Infrastructure Development," in Ross, *Megaregions*, 53–80.

49. Carbonell, Pisano, and Yaro, *2050 Global Gateway Regions.*

50. Survey by Canada's Policy Research Institute, cited in Brunet-Jailly, "Cascadia in Comparative Perspectives,"112.

51. Manuel Castells and Peter Hall, *Technopoles of the World: The Making of 21st Century Industrial Complexes* (New York: Routledge, 1994); Annalee Saxenian, *Regional Networks: Industrial Adaptation in Silicon Valley and Route 128* (Cambridge, Mass.: Harvard University Press, 1993); Ann Markusen, Peter Hall, and Amy Glasmeier, *High Tech America: The What, Where, Why and How of the Sunrise Industries* (Boston: George Allen and Unwin, 1986).

52. Matthew Sparke, "Excavating the Future in Cascadia: Geoeconomics and the Imagined Geographies of a Cross-Border Region," *B.C. Studies* 127 (August 2000): 27–28; Carl Abbott, "That Long Western Border: Canada, the United States, and a Century of Economic Change," in Findlay and Coates, *Parallel Destinies*, 203–17, and "Crossing the Long Northern Border: Rhetoric and Reality in the Cascadian Region of Western North America," in Pierre Lagayette, ed., *L'Echange: Modalities et representations* (Paris: Presses de L'Universite Paris-Sorbonne, 2005).

53. For balance, it should be noted that Richard Maxwell Brown argues for similarities in political culture in "The Other Northwest: The Regional Identity of a Canadian Province," in Wrobel and Steiner, *Many Wests*, 285–90.

54. Henry Nash Smith, *Virgin Land: The American West as Symbol and Myth* (1950: Vintage 1957), 12, 28; Charles Wilkes, *The Autobiography of Rear Admiral Charles Wilkes, U.S. Navy, 1798–1877* (Washington, D.C.: Naval History Division, 1978), 171–72.

55. David Igler, "Diseased Goods: Global Exchange in the Eastern Pacific Basin, 1770–1850," *American Historical Review* 109 (June 2004): 693–719.

56. For the details of this process, the necessary starting point is D. W. Meinig's magisterial four volumes on *The Shaping of America: A Geographical Perspective on Five Hundred Years of History* (New Haven, Conn.: Yale University Press, 1986–2004), particularly volume 3: *Transcontinental America, 1850–1915*. The interpretation also draws on William Robbins, *Colony and Empire: The Capitalist Transformation of the American West* (Lawrence: University Press of Kansas, 1994).

57. Jean Barman, *The West Beyond the West: A History of British Columbia*, 3rd ed. (Toronto: University of Toronto Press, 2007), 407–408.

58. Stephen Clarkson, "The View from the Attic: Toward a Grand Continental Community?" in Peter Andreas and Thomas J. Biersteker, eds, *The Rebordering of North America: Integration and Exclusion in a New Security Context* (New York: Routledge, 2003), 68–89.

59. Peter Schoonmaker, Bettina von Hagen, and E. C. Wolf., *The Rain Forests of Home: Profile of a North American Bioregion*, (Washington, D.C.: Island Press., 1997).

60. Laurie Ricou, "Crossing Borders in the Literature of the Pacific Northwest," in Robert Lecker, ed., *Borderlands: Essays in Canadian-American Relations* (Toronto: ECW Press, 1991), 286–308.

61. Ivan Doig, *Winter Brothers: A Season at the Edge of America* (New York: Harcourt, Brace, Jovanovich, 1980), 5.

62. Quoted in Matthew Sparke, "Cascadia and the End of the Nation-State: Interrogating the bases of Transborder Boosterism," retrieved from http://www.goeg.ubc.ca/iiccg/papers/sparke_m.html (accessed January 15, 2010).

63. Barman, *West beyond the West*, 401; Richard Maxwell Brown, "The Other Northwest: The Regional Identity of a Canadian Province," in Wrobel and Steiner, *Many Wests: Place, Culture, and Regional Identity*, 279–314.

64. "Even before September 11, 2001, it was clear that the generation of 1967 had failed to build and maintain a country as prosperous as the United States. The general standard of living in Canada was lower, productivity increases had not kept pace, and the quality of many public services, health, and social security systems had obviously declined over a twenty year period." In 2001, Canadian GDP per worker was 81 percent of U.S. GDP, and after tax income was 69 percent. Louis Pauly, "Canada in a New North America," in Andreas and Biersteker, *Rebordering of North America*, 97.

65. Kenishi Ohmae, *The Borderless World* (New York: Harper Business Books, 1990), and *The End of the Nation State* (New York: Free Press, 1995).

66. Jane Jacobs, *Cities and the Wealth of Nations* (New York: Random House, 1984); Neal R. Peirce, Curtis W. Johnson, and John Stuart Hall, *Citistates: How Urban America Can Prosper in a Competitive World* (Washington, D.C.: Seven Locks Press, 1993); Allen J. Scott, ed., *Global City: Regions, Trends, Theory, Policy* (New York: Oxford University Press, 2001).

67. Saskia Sassan, "Novel Spatial Formats: Megaregions and the Global Intercity Geographies," in Ross, *Megaregions*, 219–49.

68. Smith, "Branding Cascadia," 70, 72.

69. *Time* magazine for January 10, 2011, ran a feature on "Top Ten Aspiring Nations" that included Cascadia and the Second Vermont Republic among serious contenders—Scotland, Quebec, Western Sahara, South Ossetia, and the Basque country. The contrast with regions that have had serious and sometimes violent ethnically based independence efforts points up the weakness of Cascadia as a purely political concept. See http://content.time.com/time/specials/packages/article/0,28804,2041365_2041364_2041373,00.html (accessed September 25, 2014).

CHAPTER 7

Rocky Mountain Refuge

Constructing "Colorado" in Science Fiction

On the publicity circuit for his blockbuster apocalypse-vampire-quest novel *The Passage* (2010), Justin Cronin made a telling point to a *Denver Post* interviewer: "When you're in Colorado you feel sheltered and hidden away. The mountains of Colorado are very good for that. It seemed like the perfect place for a top-secret installation." Cronin is not a Coloradoan. Nevertheless, he had preexisting ideas about the state that he drew on for *The Passage*—ideas that he then made concrete by repeated visits to his setting to absorb the details of topography and light. More recently he elaborated that he "wanted someplace in the middle of the country, remote and mountainous, off any major highways. . . . Telluride worked for me because of its particular ruggedness, the placement of the river, the architecture of its canyons."[1]

For Cronin as for many Americans, Colorado carries implied—and widely shared—meanings. We know enough about Colorado that it seems an apt and appropriate setting for some things and not for others. The place is distant from coastal population centers. It has high, steep mountains. It is good for hiding away, whether for hippie dropouts, secret scientists, or refugees from continental disaster. In the discussion that follows, I try to probe such meanings of place by examining the ways in which Cronin and other American science fiction writers have deployed, employed, reinforced, or altered the common meanings of Colorado. The analysis begins with the character and image of Colorado and uses this analysis as a springboard for thinking about how science fiction utilizes place as a substrate for narrative.

My examples span several periods in the development of speculative fiction, from the *Astounding* era to last year's best sellers. Philip K. Dick's *The Man in the High Castle* (1962) is a monument of science fiction that has received extensive critical analysis. Walter Miller, Jr.'s, *Saint Leibowitz and the Wild Horse Woman* (1997) is a posthumously published sequel to his famous *Canticle for Leibowitz* (1959). Several are less frequently read works or secondary works by important science fiction writers: Robert Heinlein, *Sixth Column* (1949) and *The Door into Summer* (1956), Ursula Le Guin, *City of Illusions* (1967), and Leigh Brackett, *The Long Tomorrow* (1955). Two are mainstream best sellers: Ayn Rand, *Atlas Shrugged* (1957), and Justin Cronin, *The Passage*. The purpose of this eclectic selection is to show how thoroughly a distinct and narrow conceptualization of a particular place can run through very disparate works that differ in time of writing, subgenre, and authorial ambition.[2]

Regional identities emerge from the interaction of imaginative representations and social and economic conditions, and every writer of fiction who chooses a particular setting enters into a distinct stream of imagery and description, simultaneously drawing on popular understanding and helping to reconfirm or reshape that understanding.[3]

The more fully developed the popular regional identity, of course, the harder it may be to redirect or reimagine—Boston comes with more baggage than Boise. This challenge and opportunity is particularly interesting for science fiction writers. They have, in the abstract, wide freedom to take regional settings in new directions. At the same time, they are constrained by their own internalization of regional identities and by reader expectations.[4]

For a century and a half, Colorado has stood for the larger Mountain West region in popular culture. It has simultaneously been the nation's most accessible western tourist attractor and adventureland, a place that invites self-discovery, and a refuge from the threats of the future. Science fiction writers have drawn on its constructed identities as tabula rasa and as fortress to imagine the state, and the central Rocky Mountain region more generally, as a place of isolation. Like Justin Cronin, they have found Colorado a good place for characters not only to hide, take refuge, or simply survive, but also to find or invent new selves.

Heart of the West

To elaborate briefly on Colorado's common or popular identity, it has functioned for many Americans as the epitome of the Mountain West. Apart from California, which has been a world of its own, Colorado has been the most extensively publicized of the western territories and states from the time of the Pike's Peak gold rush of 1858–59. For writers from elsewhere, "Colorado" has been an easy stand-in for the vast mountainous interior of North America.

Western railroads and eastern writers made Colorado a prominent tourist destination as early as the 1870s, when the blood was scarcely dry from the wars that drove the Cheyennes and Arapahos from the plains. Front and center was the instant city of Colorado Springs, conceived and created from the ground up by the Denver and Rio Grande Railroad and its founder William Jackson Palmer.[5] First laid out in 1871, it was entertaining twenty-five thousand visitors a year before the decade was over. It was the Saratoga of the West and "Little London" because of the numbers of English visitors—a place splendidly separated from its region's Spanish and Indian histories.

Building on the success of Colorado Springs, tourism spread through the Colorado mountains with the West's most extensive travel promotion literature. Coastal people might know specific sites in Wyoming (Old Faithful) or Montana (Glacier National Park) or New Mexico (Santa Fe), but they were not likely to have strong conceptions of "Wyoming" or "New Mexico" as larger regions and communities. They did have an image of Colorado built from travel books, promotional brochures, and the actual experience of the Denver and Rio Grande Railroad's "Around the Circle Tour" that put a four-day, one-thousand-mile loop through Rocky Mountain scenery within reach of middle-class families.[6]

Colorado was tabula rasa in these tourism depictions, as historian Thomas Andrews compellingly argues. The tourist landscape ignored the state's vast industrial apparatus of mines, company towns, smelters, and slag heaps. The bloody and troubled history of labor-management violence at Leadville and Cripple Creek and Ludlow disappeared, as did its communities of Greek, Italian, and Slavic mine and factory workers. The travel industry erased the industrial landscape to replace it with an imagery of unspoiled wilderness. As if they did not represent lives of toil, mining ghost towns became part of the "natural" picturesque landscape, returning literally to the land as their buildings decayed.[7]

Visitors could also start *themselves* anew, for Colorado was a health resort. The air, said physicians and land developers both, was pure, exhilarating, and stimulating—perfect for people with tuberculosis. The altitude itself was said to quicken the life processes. "Lungers" came to Colorado by the tens of thousands in the late nineteenth and early twentieth centuries, seeking it out as a "great and beneficial sanatorium," where one's body could be made anew. Governor Fred Pitkin's claim that Colorado could almost revive the dead was a little strong, but Dr. Samuel Fisk agreed that "there is a wealth of life stored up in the dry, sunny climate of this state."[8]

The reimagining of Colorado continued after World War II. The story of Aspen's transformation from a dying mining town into a cultural center and ski town and then into one of the most fashionable locations in the country is well-known. Squeezed by the rising prices of "Aspenization," ski bums repeated the process at Crested Butte, Telluride, and other re-created communities.[9] John Denver captured Colorado's connection to personal reinvention in his 1973 hit "Rocky Mountain High," whose first stanza is a statement of rebirth: "He was born in the summer of his twenty-seventh year," leaving yesterday behind to be "born again" in Colorado.

Paradoxically, Colorado in the ski bum and hippie eras of the 1950s and 1960s was also isolated from the more powerful flows of east–west commerce. Until the interstate highway builders shoved I-70 through the Eisenhower Tunnel in 1979. Colorado was easy to get *to*, but not so easy to get *through*. The first transcontinental railroad detoured north of the Colorado mountains. The Southern Pacific and Santa Fe Railroads detoured south, as did the famous Route 66 from Chicago to Los Angeles. That isolation interacted in the early years of the Cold War with a strong national interest in dispersing people and industry outside crowded city centers and off the coasts to minimize vulnerability to aerial bombardment.[10] Denver was already promoting itself as the "The Second Capital of the United States" because of the many federal branch offices that opened during the New Deal and World War II and put in a pitch in 1945 for the headquarters of the new United Nations, only to be aced out by New York.[11] Fully uprooting the federal government never got very far, but Colorado did get its special Cold War fortress in the form of the blast-hardened operations center for the North American Aerospace Defense Command, completed in 1966 beneath Cheyenne Mountain near Colorado Springs.

Remnant and Refuge, Redemption and Reconstruction

Few of the authors with whom I'm dealing had a close association with Colorado or deep experience of the central Rocky Mountain region. Robert Heinlein did live in Colorado from 1949 to 1965, but only after he had begun to use the state in his stories. Ursula Le Guin's mother grew up in Telluride, Colorado. Others have traveled or vacationed there, but that is about it. I therefore argue that their use of Colorado drew much less on direct experience and knowledge than on a widely shared popular sense of the area's physical isolation and social newness, constructing fictions that have reiterated and reinforced that very sense of isolation.

These novelists imagine Colorado in four overlapping and intersecting ways: as a remnant society or location, as an isolated refuge or hiding place, as a place to restart or reconstruct a better social system free from the encumbrances of the past, and as a place of self-discovery and redemption. As a remnant location, Colorado is a place where elements of an earlier America persist or survive under varying degrees of threat from foreign invaders or the chaos of social dissolution. Colorado as refuge can be the hiding place for secret laboratories or the place where survivors of disaster deliberately gather for the protection that isolation can provide. In some instances, the refuge offers not only an opportunity for survival but a place where society can be actively rebuilt rather than simply maintained. As these definitions suggest, most of the examples in this chapter deal with social systems and social change. In addition, however, the discussion includes novels that also utilize Colorado isolation as the occasion for individual change—redemption—rather than social reconstruction. For clarity, the following discussion groups these books in pairs around particularly prominent themes, while noting also how they deal with other aspects of "Coloradoness" as well. The grouping is not to suggest mutual influences among the writers but rather to emphasize parallels and commonalities in the use of Colorado settings.

The common use or understanding of Colorado that I explore does not embrace the classic American frontier as theorized and described by Frederick Jackson Turner. The frontier for Turner and his followers is a process rather than a place. It is a zone of active development and sequential transformation by explorers, traders, farmers, miners, boosters, engineers, railroad builders, and many others. Turner's successive frontiers all grow up to be incorporated into a modern urban-industrial nation. Such a process is central to the actual history of Colorado—how else do you get a metropolitan Denver of three million people—but not to the science fiction Colorado, which is so often pictured in terms of static isolation.[12]

After Conquest: Remnant America

Robert A. Heinlein, pioneer of so many science fiction ideas, provides an entry point into Colorado as refuge and remnant. *Sixth Column*, written in 1941 for *Astounding Science Fiction*, published in book form in 1949 and republished as *The Day After Tomorrow* in 1951, is a late example of the Yellow Peril fiction that flourished in the early twentieth century. In Heinlein's story, Pan-Asian imperialists have just conquered the United States using superior weapons and are cowing the American people into submission. Heinlein identifies the victors as a blended people from several East Asian nations, but their practice of ritual suicide pinpoints the Japanese as the dominant element, especially since Japan in 1941 was absorbing much of China into a Great East Asia Co-Prosperity Sphere. Somewhere beneath the Colorado Rockies, however, is the Citadel, secret hideaway of ultramodern laboratories, whose existence is unsuspected by the enemy. The half-dozen mismatched survivors in this underground research facility quickly harness previously unknown sources of energy with which to fight the Pan-Asians and hatch a fake religion behind whose façade they assemble a resistance movement. They utilize super engineering to erect an instant temple on top of the Citadel, open a church in Denver, spread the word across the country in a matter of months, and bamboozle the Pan-Asians into surrender by humiliating the governors and military officer class. It is an early version of Heinlein's common theme of the achievement of large ends by the manipulation of public opinion.

Heinlein drew the outline for *Sixth Column* from "All," a then unpublished story by John W. Campbell, Jr., that the editor passed along to him. The skeleton of the plot is the same—Asian conquest, development of super weapons by a few American scientists deep in the mountains and promulgation of a new religion as a mask for a resistance movement. The Temple of All is located in the "Province of Colorado," in a "lone, lost canyon" that carves a great gash through the yellow sandstone. However, Campbell did not otherwise develop or use the setting, either for local color or as a plot element, leaving Heinlein all the room he might want for his own version.[13]

Colorado is not essential to the plot of subversive organizing—the first organized church of the God Mota could have been located in many other cities other than Denver—but the Rocky Mountains are necessary for the Citadel to have adequate concealment as the base of operations. Heinlein visited Denver for the 1941 Worldcon, where he was guest of honor at a meeting with ninety attendees, but his direct knowledge of the state was otherwise limited when he was writing the serial for *Astounding*. His Rocky Mountains are vaguely sketched. Little is said about how the entrance to the Citadel is concealed or what its physical surroundings are like. Nor is it precisely located, although it has to be somewhere in the Front Range. There are towns nearby and a medium-sized city within a three-day walk (presumably Pueblo or Colorado Springs). It is also close enough to Denver that people can go easily back and forth when they are spreading their fake religion. Denver itself is equally vague, a sort of cartoon or stage set city with generic elements like a police station and a warehouse district rather than the specifically named streets and neighborhoods that a local author might have used.

If Heinlein followed Campbell's outline, he also employed a script suggested by the prominence of Colorado in the twentieth-century American imagination. Where would you hide a research facility? Among and underneath big mountains. Which big mountains? The Rockies are the easiest ones to name. Where in the Rockies? Colorado is the best known Rocky Mountain state, the easiest for Heinlein to write about, and the easiest for readers to picture.

Fifteen years later, Heinlein revisited fictional Colorado in the time-travel novel *The Door into Summer*, this time as remnant rather than refuge. Heinlein was now a local, having moved in 1949 to Colorado Springs, a city he described as "remote."[14] When *The Door into Summer* begins, the Six Weeks War has left the United States victorious over the Russians at the cost of a devastated eastern seaboard, causing the federal government and capital to relocate to Denver. The novel begins and ends in southern California, but protagonist Dan Davis makes two visits to Denver, one in 1970 and another in 2001. Both descriptions are a bit more grounded than in *Sixth Column*, each with a reference to Colfax Avenue, the main east–west street that carried travelers on U.S. Route 40 through the heart of the city in the decades before Interstate Highways.

The Denver of *The Door into Summer* is a thriving survivor in which a victorious nation is adapting to a new political and economic geography. In 1970, soon after the war, it is "still getting used to being the national seat of government and was not quite happy in the role, like a boy in his first formal evening clothes. . . . The city was being jerry-built in all directions to house the bureaucrats and lobbyists and contact men and clerk-typists and flunkies; buildings were being thrown up so fast that with each one there was hazard of enclosing a cow inside the walls" (134). A generation later, Davis can no longer find Colfax Avenue and the city seems more crowded that Greater Los Angeles. Combined with the thriving metropolis is a version of refuge, "everything essential to the government was buried back under the Rockies" (116). As in *Sixth Column*, the plot does not depend on Colorado or Denver specifics, but the setting fits easily into the story because the state so easily represented the much larger midcontinent/mountain region.[15]

Unlike Robert Heinlein with his fifteen-year sojourn in Colorado, Philip K. Dick was a Californian start to finish. His only apparent connection to Colorado was to pass through the state as a babe in arms during a parental road trip in 1929.[16] Nevertheless, Colorado serves as the counterpoise to California in a novel that revisited some of Heinlein's subject matter with a vastly different sensibility. *The Man in the High Castle* depicts an alternative history in which the Axis powers win World War II. The Nazis occupy the eastern half of the former United States. Japan controls California, Oregon, Washington, and Nevada through the puppet Pacific States of America. In between are the Rocky Mountain States, nominally independent but "loosely banded to the PSA" (14). The "Colorado" action moves along the Front Range from the smaller town of Canon City to Denver to Cheyenne, Wyoming, less than ten miles north of the state line and essentially part of the Front Range metropolitan region.

The Rocky Mountain States are a buffer and backwater. They include Colorado, Utah, Wyoming, the eastern part of Nevada, the "open empty desert states," and the "pasture states" of the Great Plains (34), but the Colorado Front Range cities are their political and economic center. With the United States defeated rather than victorious in the global war, Canon City and Denver have none of the vitality shown in *The Door into Summer*. In Dick's version of Colorado there is nothing for the young and ambitious, unlike the "East Americans" who "like the big time." Juliana Frink, who is stuck in Canon City, comments to a visitor: "This is just the sticks to you, the Rockies. Nothing has happened here since before the war. Retired old people, farmers, the stupid, slow, poor . . . and all the smart boys have flocked east to New York, crossed the border legally or illegally" (36).

Colorado was the most convenient representative for remnant America because it could be viewed as generically western and historically unencumbered. It lacked the social complications that would have ensued had Dick picked Utah with its Mormon heritage or New Mexico with its Hispano population. Few Americans in the 1950s remembered the Colorado Indian wars and the Sand Creek Massacre (the state's past had no Indians as famous as Sitting Bull, Cochise, or Chief Joseph). The state's mining history with its complex ethnic labor force was easy to forget. This ordinariness of Colorado is a point that Dick makes with intended irony when the reclusive author Hawthorne Abendsen turns out to live not in the rumored fortress that has "guns all over the place . . . charged barbed wire around the place, and it's set in the mountains" (85). Instead, he lives on the outskirts of Cheyenne in "a single-story stucco house with many shrubs and a good deal of garden made up mostly of climbing roses" (231). The places among which Juliana travels, in short, are remnant America. They are physically marked with the sorts of suburban subdivisions that would stipple the entire continent in a world in which the Axis won and are thus a refuge for American values as they are under pressure from occupying powers east and west.

Dick's remnant America is thus very different from Heinlein's—no surprise here. Heinlein's Colorado retains the supposed American values of go-getting enterprise and adventure. Dick anticipates the quotidian America of subdivisions and truck stops, a society with more limitations than possibilities. Juliana

Frink is a judo instructor at Ray's Gym in Canon City, scraping by with a small apartment. She eats at Tasty Charley's Broiled Hamburgers where the jukebox plays hillbilly songs, and she saves a passing trucker from a bed at the Honey Bee Motel when she picks him up for a one-night stand. The trucker turns out to be a Nazi agent who is able to afford a snazzy Denver hotel, but after Juliana kills him, she returns to the working-class world of waitresses and fry cooks who drift from job to job. Like the United States that Philip Dick would have known during and after World War II, Colorado in *High Castle* is still getting over the effects of a war that has disrupted families, short-circuited careers, and turned many people into loners like Juliana, who is well at home grabbing a chicken salad sandwich and a Coke for dinner at an all-night drugstore.[17]

High Mountain Refuge

Ayn Rand was a radical free-market utopian with no sympathy for any of Philip Dick's marginal characters. Her drugs of choice were nicotine and alcohol, not LSD. With utmost seriousness and self-confidence, she promoted a philosophy that she called Objectivism, mixing Adam Smith with Social Darwinism to argue for the untrammeled development of individual abilities with the fewest possible social strictures and legal limitations. In effect, she gave uncompromising allegiance to the sorts of libertarian ideas that Robert Heinlein sometimes ascribed to his characters and accepted personally only in part. At the same time, she elevated the trope of the hidden laboratory that Heinlein had played with and made it pivotal in a massive fictional manifesto for her philosophy. In *Atlas Shrugged* Colorado plays multiple roles overtly and in sequence, first as the last remnant of the dying capitalist economy and then explicitly as refuge from which society can be rebuilt around the social ideals that have been systematically destroyed outside.

In the early sections of the sprawling novel, the American economy is imploding under the pressures of labor unions, socialism, and bureaucratic parasitism. The collapsing United States refers back to Rand's own experience of Russia in the early 1920s under the stress of transition to communism. In her imagined America, incompetent worker committees and inept government officials try to supplant the captains of industry.[18] Colorado is the potential saving remnant, the last place where vigorous capitalism survives, perhaps because of its distance from coastal corruption—a vestige of heroic entrepreneurial America rather than everyday America as in *High Castle*. The heroine Dagny Taggart strives to keep alive her family's vast transcontinental railroad empire by building a new spur line into Colorado, while industry collapses in other parts of the nation. The line is a success but the national government passes a draconian version of antitrust legislation that crushes the railroad. Even the Colorado economy begins to wither—what Rand in her notes for the novel and in the book itself called "the destruction of Colorado."[19]

Seven hundred pages in, Colorado shifts suddenly from remnant to refuge. Dagny Taggart stumbles onto—drops into—the secret retreat of great men who have been abandoning the nation. She finds the refuge only by accident when her small plane crashes through thick clouds into a Colorado mountain valley that is protected by "refractor rays" (704) that project a concealing mirage. "Galt's Gulch," a spectacularly scenic basin deep in the Colorado Rockies, takes its nickname from the heroic genius-inventor John Galt. With Galt's instigation, the nation's most brilliant inventors, scientists, artists, and entrepreneurs have gathered as an idyllic, market-based "community" in isolation from the larger society that hobbled and disrespected them. Under the refractor screen, amid towering cliffs, crashing waterfalls, and soaring trees, titans of mind and mammon live in comfort as self-satisfied refugees, who have gone on strike from the ignorance, greed, and stupidity of the "looters," the ordinary people (like Juliana Frink?) whom they, and Rand, despise.

The valley itself has undergone a quick transformation from playground to fortress. Banker Midas Mulligan acquired the valley originally as a private retreat. He bought it piecemeal "from ranchers and cattlemen who didn't know what they owned," thus enacting the erasure of the resource production landscape in favor of a leisure landscape that Thomas Andrews has analyzed. Mulligan continues that "the valley is not listed on any map." This improbability would have been laughable to actual Coloradoans who know how many fur trappers, miners, geologists, sheep herders, and tourists had combed the state, but it highlights its aura of isolation as seen from Los Angeles or New York. Mulligan "cut off all possible avenues of approach, except one road—and it's camouflaged beyond anyone's power to discover . . . so that I could live here for the rest of my life and never have to see the face of a looter" (747).

Rand modeled Galt's Gulch on Ouray, Colorado, an old mining town at the head of the Uncompahgre River. She picked it from a map (as she did many of her settings for the novel) and visited it in 1949. She raved that she had fallen in love with Colorado as "the most beautiful part of the country" and told a correspondent that she could not wait "to tell you about the valley we discovered." A decade later she called Ouray "the most beautifully dramatic spot in the whole state, and it's surrounded by a ring of mountains (though Galt's Valley would be somewhat larger)."[20] There is no evidence, of course, that Rand ever did a systematic comparison with other claimants to Colorado's scenic crown, but Ouray is indeed spectacular and was extremely isolated in 1951.

The hidden valley is a familiar trope. Everyone on the 1940s knew about Shangri-La through James Hilton's novel *Lost Horizon* (1933) and the movie version with Ronald Colman and Jane Wyatt (1937), especially everyone who, like Rand, had connections with the film industry. One of her favorite books as a child was Maurice Champagne's *The Mysterious Valley* (1915), a French-language adventure-fantasy for children set deep in the Himalayas. Written in the well-developed mode of imperial fantasies by H. Rider Haggard and many others,

Rand's childhood favorite matched the hidden valley with manly, thinking heroes like the rational capitalists of *Atlas Shrugged*.[21]

Rand also imagined a special sort of hidden valley—an American West sort of place. As Jennifer Burns notes, the powerful individuals who gather there practice western informality and represent the producer ideology against the corrupt eastern establishment.[22] They thus reflect a long line of western protest against the parasitism of eastern corporations, although Rand presumably abhorred the cooperative or collectivism forms that such protest had historically taken in the Granger movement, Populism, and the radical labor organizing done through the Western Federation of Miners and the Industrial Workers of the World. It is the West of mythical individualism rather than the frontier of worker organization that makes Colorado the suitable place for tycoons to take refuge and plot the retaking of America. Indeed, at the novel's end the secret sanctuary has become the base from which to build society anew according to Galtian principles. As the lights go off in New York, Dagny Taggart recognizes the futility of trying to salvage the family railroad corporation and throws in with the elite. The hidden Colorado valley will be the nucleus from which a new, more vigorous United States can be reborn. The nation will not be restored but reborn as a supercapitalist utopia, although its tycoons will change not a wit.

Leigh Brackett, a novelist and Hollywood screenwriter like Rand, anticipated Galt's Gulch by two years in *The Long Tomorrow*. Her postapocalypse novel similarly sends its protagonist to discover another hidden Colorado valley full of scientific experts and ends with the promise of social reconstruction. Brackett's story takes place eighty years after "the War." The United States has adopted a new constitutional amendment: "No city, no town, no community of more than one thousand people or two hundred buildings to the square mile shall be built or permitted to exist anywhere in the United States of America" (14). With results that mirror the ultimate decline of Rand's imagined collectivized America, technology has reverted to level of the early 1800s. The surviving nation is a set of small farming settlements and trading towns linked by annual trading fairs and steamboats.

The action revolves around young Len Colter, a name that echoes early explorer and mountain man John Colter. Len flees the enforced limits of the formally conservative society. In a bit of Mark Twain homage, he takes a steam-powered barge down the Ohio and then up the wide Missouri. At the mouth of the Platte River the group switches to mule-drawn wagons for a trek southwestward across the "large and lonely prairie" (139). At a rendezvous along the South Platte (where small fur-trading posts could have been found in the 1830s and 1840s), they meet other wagons that have come up the Arkansas Valley or eastward over South Pass following other historic trading routes. Finally their route penetrates through red rock canyons deep into the heart of the Colorado Rockies.

Deep behind the wall of the Front Range is a forward-looking community built on the past. The ordinary silver-mining town of Fall Creek is cover for

Bartorstown, a refuge where science is kept alive, concealed from nomads and farmers by indirection rather than gizmo technology like refractor screens. Occasional visitors see only an ordinary mountain settlement. As one of the residents comments, "Main thing is to look like everybody else, and then they don't notice you" (152). In case indirection fails, the town and facility are also guarded by the equivalent of closed-circuit television and hemmed in by the mountains: "The cliffs were too steep to climb, the narrow gorge of the stream bed was too broken and treacherous with falls and rockslides. . . . The site had been carefully picked, and it had not changed in a century. The eyes of Bartorstown watched, the ears listened, and the hidden death was always ready in the winding lower pass" (196).

Outsiders do not know that behind a steel blast door deep in the old mine shafts the pre-Destruction government had built a secret research facility, whose original staff of forty swelled into the hundreds with postcollapse refugees, a somewhat more realistic idea than Heinlein's "secret six" in *Sixth Column*. For the past decades technicians and scientists have been tending a 1950s-style supercomputer and trying to find a way to tame atomic energy and reintroduce advanced technology that will not lead to war. In the 2030s, Len Colter thus finds a self-conscious refuge for scientists and engineers of the sort Rand admired, although the community's goal is not ego-stoking entrepreneurship but the technical and social control of new technology.[23]

Where Rand's philosophy demands disjuncture, Brackett emphasizes continuity and restoration. Galt's Gulchers are secessionists, but Bartorstown was seeded by the government. Its scientists are survivors and conservators of past knowledge, who have the conviction that the purpose of a Colorado refuge is to provide time to figure out how to do it better next time, a point the author makes clear in a sequence between Colter and the Bartorstowners (177):

> "Someday atomic power will come back no matter what anybody does to stop it."
>
> "A thing once known always comes back."
>
> "And the cities will come back too."
>
> "In time, inevitably."
>
> "And it will happen all over again, the cities and the bomb, unless you find a way to stop it."
>
> "Unless men have changed a lot by tomorrow, yes."
>
> "Then," said Len, still frowning, still somber, "then I guess you're trying to do what ought to be done."

Journeys to Self-Discovery and Redemption

Mysterious mountain hideaways are fun for authors to imagine, and so are transcontinental treks. The former make for great set-piece descriptions, while the latter can nearly write themselves with blizzards, sandstorms, equipment failures, or attacks by nomads always available to keep things moving. Leigh Brackett enjoyed writing Len Colter's journey, and Ursula Le Guin took equal or greater satisfaction in taking her protagonist across the continent in her early novel *City of Illusions*. She commented in the introduction to the 1978 reissue that one of the pleasures of the book was "the chance to imagine my country, America, without cities, almost without towns, as sparsely populated by our species as it was five hundred years ago . . . the sense of time, but more than that the sense of space, extent, the wideness of the continent. The wideness. The wilderness."[24] The novel gets its evocative power from the contrast between that empty land and a fantastic alien city perched on the very top of Colorado.

Far into the future, North America has been nearly abandoned by humans and there remain scattered, quiet settlements and ruins of older times. The hero Falk, suffering loss of memory, awakens in the eastern forest and heads westward in search of the great city of the Shing, the people who have made themselves the masters and tyrants of Earth. His journey retraces the route of nineteenth-century pioneers—and of Len Colter—across great rivers and vast prairies and finally reaches the alien city of Es Toch that soars into the sky on both sides of the Black Canyon of the Gunnison River—a location that is only forty miles from Ouray by Shing aircar.

Es Toch is isolated in both site and function. To reach it on foot is "to clamber over the roof-tree of a continent. Range after range of mountains rose; day after day the two crept upward into the world of the heights, and still their goal lay farther up and farther on. . . . One great mountain bulwark remained to cross, and for four days they climbed it, till the air grew thin and icy, the sky dark blue, and the sun of April shone dazzling on the fleecy backs of clouds that grazed the meadows far beneath their way" (108–110). Falk finally surmounts the last mountain bulwark to glimpse the spectacular city:

> The City of the Lords of Earth was built on the two rims of a canyon, a tremendous cleft through the mountains, narrow, fantastic, its black walls striped with green plunging terrifically down half a mile to the silver tinsel strip of a river in the shadowy depths. On the very edges of the facing cliffs the towers of the city jutted up, hardly based on earth at all, linked across the chasm by delicate bridge-spans. Towers, roadways and bridges ceased and the wall closed the city off again just before a vertiginous bend of the canyon. (113)

Es Toch is one of a kind, a center of high culture and technology on a continent that the Shing deliberately keep primitive. There are no other cities in North America, just roaming tribes and rudimentary settlements on the plains and eastern forests in one direction and vast open, unpeopled territory westward to the Pacific in the other. It is simultaneously a command post, a mountain-moated fortress, and a place of safety for the Shing. "Es Toch gave no sense of history, of reaching back in time and out in space, though it had ruled the world for a millennium. . . . Though there were said to be so many of the Lords, yet on

Earth they kept only this one city, held apart. . . . Es Toch was self-contained, self-nourished, rootless. . . . Yet it was wonderful, like a carved jewel fallen in the vast wilderness of the Earth: wonderful, timeless, alien" (159).

Why the Black Canyon? Le Guin stopped there in the 1950s on a vacation trip and had a fright when her two very young children disappeared over the edge of the lookout (they had jumped down safely to a second ledge). As she has told me, the incident inscribed the canyon in her memory: "It gave me, you could say, an uneasy feeling about the canyon. But it was beautiful and strange, and I began imagining what if you built a city in it."[25] For Le Guin and her character Falk, the canyon in the heart of the Colorado mountains was fascinating and awe inspiring. For Le Guin and her characters the Shing, it was a place with few past occupants to deal with or wipe away, where a city could be imagined or built ab ovo. Colorado for the Shing is the empty planet where they "were still alien, then, after twelve hundred years" (195).

Colorado may be tabula rasa for the Shing, but it is a place of self-discovery for Falk. He discovers that he is "actually" Ramarren, one of the survivors of an interstellar expedition from the planet Werel that the Shing intercepted and destroyed, and that his present identity is only six years old. He agrees to the revival of his earlier identity, a process that is supposed to erase "Falk." Through power of will, however, he preserves the more recent personality while regaining his older self: "He was Falk, and he was Ramarren. He was the fool and the wise man: one man twice born" (188). Dagny learns new things about the world in Galt's Gulch; Falk learns new things about himself in Es Toch.[26]

Treks toward self-discovery and transformation are also central to Justin Cronin's *The Passage*—along with a secret Defense Department laboratory that is described as a guarded and isolated compound high on a ridge or plateau in the San Juan Mountains of southwestern Colorado. Cronin depicts the compound in more careful and realistic detail than Heinlein or Brackett provide for their fortresses of science, but Colorado is more than anything else a place for individual transformation, first by external force for evil ends and then possibly by volition for personal redemption. In a complex echo of John Denver's lyrics about rebirth, the isolated mountain location is thus a place of new beginnings at the most basic level of human personalities.

Central to the journeys that structure the action is Amy Bellefonte, the young girl whose fate is central to the plot. Amy takes two journeys to the Colorado installation. In the first visit, federal agents kidnap and spirit her to the laboratory, where she is to be the final test recipient of a slowly perfected virus that has turned its twelve previous recipients into telepathic vampires. For Amy the virus brings near immortality but not the ravening hunger of the twelve. At the end of the first section of the novel, the vampires break loose to spread the virus to the entire continent. Amy escapes to reappear ninety-two years later at First Colony, a fortified community of survivor-descendents located in the San Jacinto Mountains of southern California. Her profoundly disturbing presence catalyzes a small group of the colony's younger generation to flee its impending collapse in order to return her to the laboratory that turned her into a near immortal.

Whereas Le Guin began to write with the destination for Falk's trek in mind, Cronin began with starting point for an expedition, choosing California as the setting for the colony of survivors and extrapolating to Colorado because he wanted an end point for a journey that would involve changes of topography and weather.[27] The route from California to Colorado passes the very bad city of Las Vegas on its way to the defunct laboratory. Like Le Guin, he enjoyed the chance to contribute to the tradition of epic storytelling around the classic American theme of "the individual's confrontation with the vast open spaces of the continent."[28]

As previously noted, Cronin chose Colorado because of its distance and isolation and also as the geographic pivot for his balanced plot as roughly equally distant from Memphis, the start of the first journey, and Riverside County, California, the start of the second. Within Colorado he picked the old mining and modern resort town of Telluride, which is only ten miles on a map from Ouray/Galt's Gulch (although fifty miles by passable highways). "Telluride worked for me because of its particular ruggedness, the placement of the river, the architecture of its canyons. I had not been there before but had several friends with houses there, and canvassed them a bit for information."[29]

Cronin heightens the sense of isolation by revealing the location of the compound by hints in the first section and directly only in the course of the second trek. We first see it through the eyes of FBI agent Brad Wolgast, who knows only that it is six hours west of Denver. Then we see it through the eyes of Grey, one of the support staff who is hired in Dallas, flown to Cheyenne, and driven in a blacked-out van with occasional views outside that indicate they are going to Colorado. This is indirection, since Cheyenne to Telluride is the long way to get there. Is it to keep the reader guessing? Is it to indicate how careful the managers of the project are? We next see it through the eyes of Carter, the last of the death row subjects, who is flown from Houston to "someplace cold" (105) and again past small towns with McDonald's and into the mountains. Descriptions emphasize the isolation of the compound as an island floating in the clouds (119) where the view is "empty pine forest" (173).

Ninety-two years later, as the double refugees take a carefully plotted route across Nevada and central Utah, the location of the compound is slowly identified as Telluride. Cronin twice drove the route to get accurate details and did much the same for Telluride itself: "Once I made this choice, I visited Telluride several times, once in the early winter (I actually got snowed in during the first major snowfall of the season), when my characters make their ascent."[30] For Amy's return, he describes the approaches in detail, both in terms of the sorts of things that a group on foot would notice (how to cross rivers, where the climbs are, where to find shelter) and in terms of the beauty of the scenery and the effects of shifting sunlight in narrow mountain valleys.

The return to Colorado provides catharsis without final resolution. Amy regains her ability to speak during the journey and begins to come to terms with her memories: "She often spoke like this, in vague riddles. Yet something felt different this time. It was as if the past were rising up before her eyes, stepping into view like a deer from the brush" (627). Some circles are closed and others left open. Amy reunites briefly with a supportive figure from her traumatic childhood. The most feral and fearsome of the twelve master vampires perishes along with the remnants of the laboratory. But Alicia, the fiercest warrior among the Californians, is transformed by a version of the virus into a sort of superwoman with implications unknown. From this place of multiple rebirths, where the human psyche is tabula rasa, the Californians divide and continue their journey with more suffering and more questions in the offing.

For the people of *The Passage*, the Rocky Mountains are a place of self-discovery and change but not a refuge. In contrast, Walter Miller, Jr., located multiple remnants and refuges on the Colorado Piedmont, within the valleys of the Rockies, and in the intermountain desert on the western slope. The abbey in *A Canticle for Leibowitz* is located west of the mountain rampart formed by the Sangre de Christo Range and north of Santa Fe. Perhaps the most precise location is found in the sequel *Saint Leibowitz and the Wild Horse Woman*. The map, which posthumous collaborator Terry Bisson took great pains to develop, places it at Abiquiu, New Mexico, where there is indeed a present-day Benedictine monastery.[31] Although the monastery is the primary remnant and refuge, Colorado settings also play a prominent role in *Wild Horse Woman*. The Papacy, expelled from New Rome at the site of the earlier city of Saint Louis, has relocated to Valana, part of the Denver Free State. This is a new city located, according to Bisson, at the site of Colorado Springs. "Valana had grown up rapidly around an ancient hilltop fortress which had in earlier centuries been a bastion of defense by the mountain people against the more savage Nomads of an earlier age. . . . Before the exiled papacy had moved here, the city had become a sort of middle kingdom among the contiguous communities of the populated region, where merchants traded with miners for silver and pelts, with Nomads for hides and meat, and with farmers for meat and corn" (83–84). The advantage here is the isolation of distance, putting the reviving religious center at far remove from the continued savagery of the Mississippi Valley and the growing Texark Empire.

Also in *Saint Leibowitz* is New Jerusalem, a haven for genetically handicapped refugees from Texark tyranny. The "isolation of New Jerusalem . . . its resources and natural defenses, made it the largest congregation of genetically dubious persons outside the Valley [of the Misborn, in the Watchit-Ol'zarkia region] and most appealing as a sanctuary for permanent fugitives" (169). To get to New Jerusalem from Valana requires winding across the first ranges of the Rockies to the western side, placing it somewhere around the margins of Colorado's San Luis Valley or South Park valley.

In the second book, Miller was thus building a more complex region than in *Canticle*. The southern Rocky Mountains of Colorado and New Mexico now host a more elaborate social ecology of multiple communities that interact through trade, politics, and religious hierarchy and are struggling to build, in effect, an independent state that is protected by physical separation from other emerging centers of power. In Miller's chronology, *Wild Horse Woman* is roughly contemporaneous with "Fiat Lux," the second of *Canticle*'s three free-standing sections. That section centers on the initiation of a new scientific revolution in which both the abbey's monks and its carefully preserved archives play an important role in such fields as the rediscovery and restart of techno-scientific culture and society. This is the aim of the residents of Bartorstown, of course, but without Miller's Christian pessimism about the economic dependence of science, the temptations of power, and the cyclical nature of history. Given that the central issue of *Wild Horse Woman* is the challenge of reviving political structures in ways that are not inherently flawed, Miller in effect examines two complementary facets of social reconstruction from what geographer D. W. Meinig (1972) might term a Rocky Mountain "core region."[32]

The Power of Place

This discussion of Colorado as refuge in stories of near and far futures is a reminder of the importance of place as well as politics and culture as a positive element in the imaginative process of science fiction. Science fiction writers work within a continuum of place freedom. The further their setting is from now and here, the fewer constraints it offers. Trantor, Coruscant, Athshe, and Pandora can be anything their creator wishes, with whatever degree of internal world-building consistency she or he deems important. Stories set on Mars or Ganymede should adhere to known planetology, but the sense of place is still up for grabs.[33] When the setting is Earth itself, landscapes and cities come with established identities that can take active roles in the construction of the future by fixing expectations and bringing popular understandings into play.

This chapter explores what we might gain if we pay close attention to place by using the case of "Colorado" and examining how it has functioned both as background and as actor. Its image and identity in popular culture has enabled authors to use the Colorado setting to evoke shared responses that circle around the ideas of isolation, safety, and opportunity for rebirth. Although many of the stories could have been set somewhere else in the Rockies, it is telling that they were not. The popularly constructed image of Colorado, its accessibility as a tourist destination, and its function as a shorthand for "mountain West" has made it a setting of choice.

At the same time, that common understanding makes the setting itself an active element that shapes the responses of the human characters to each other and to their situation. Protagonists in *The Man in the High Castle* can take risks because Colorado's isolated location allows the political independence that protects them from the daily influence of Japanese and German authority. The industrialists in Galt's Gulch and the technocrats in Bartorstown have chosen to hide in the Colorado mountains because they *represent* isolation, even though there are parts of the American West that were and are more remote and unreachable in fact. The fictional bureaucrats who have sited Heinlein's Citadel and Cronin's U.S. Army Medical Research Institute for Infectious Diseases before the stories begin "know" that the Colorado Rockies *mean* isolation.

The powerful and persistent Colorado imaginary comes in two complementary versions, as a place of isolation and refuge and also as a place whose sparse settlement and thin (or even erased) history make it an appropriate setting for social reinvention. The two roles operate together in all of the novels under discussion. In Heinlein, Brackett, and Rand they appear in an imagined historical sequence in which a remnant or refugees first shelter in Colorado and then, in the last chapter, commence to rebuild something of the society they have lost—although each anticipated future is different from the others. Philip Dick and Ursula Le Guin juxtapose the two versions ironically. Dick's remnant Rocky Mountain States have at least marginal freedom for social reconstruction but no obvious interest in the opportunity, while the Shing have used their isolation not for social liberation but to construct and maintain tyranny. Cronin puts the roles directly in conflict. *The Passage* reverses the common polarity; human beings are created anew in Colorado but to bad consequences, and a semblance of safety is elsewhere. His characters are a long moral stretch from the successful scam artists of *Sixth Column*, but they inhabit what is recognizably the same Rocky Mountain region.

An illuminating juxtaposition to this relatively straightforward conceptualization of Colorado is more complexly imagined California. California is a land of aspiration, technology, and extracontinental connections—a place that we imagine will cast off both past and present in search of its future.[34] In that state's northern reaches, Lauren Olamina in Octavia Butler's *Parable of the Sower* (1994) can find the room to invent a new religion and society. The same jumbled valleys hide a post-hippie culture in Thomas Pynchon's semi-science-fictional *Vineland* (1990). In more populated parts of the state, future San Francisco and future Los Angeles take on active identities that draw on popular images of the two places. San Francisco is a city of creativity in the work of Pat Murphy and William Gibson and a city with a soul—quite literally in Fritz Leiber's *Our Lady of Darkness* (1977). In works too numerous to catalog, Los Angeles is the city of the next thing. Whatever is coming, it's coming first to southern California—social breakdown or technological transformation, besieged neighborhoods or arcologies, Asian invasion or android infiltration, blade runners or terminators, or even the utopian possibilities of Kim Stanley Robinson's *Pacific Edge* (1990).

One common theme that runs through many of the Colorado stories is the minimization of work. The Citadel and the Temple of All, Bartorstown, Galt's Gulch, and the compound all appear ready-made in their stories. We take it on faith that someone has previously done the strenuous engineering, earth moving, and construction to create these isolated and self-contained places. Fictional Bartorstown and real Telluride are old mining towns that are now facades for scientific research. Galt's Gulch is the epitome of Thomas Andrews's tourist landscape, its mining and ranching economy eradicated for the convenience of billionaires.

Because work can imply change, especially in the history of the American West, its limited presence connects to the second commonality that science-fictional Colorado is a very static place—or static idea about place. In that sense it is a less rich setting than California or, for a more distant example, Mars. As Robert Crossley has recently shown, Mars is a dynamic imaginary. Depictions of the planet have evolved in response to changes in earthly society and politics and to expanding knowledge about the planet itself. In contrast, the Colorado imaginary has changed very little, even though the state itself has grown from a little over one million people when Campbell and Heinlein wrote to five million today, with concomitant changes in economic and social patterns. Some of the more recent writers like King, Bishop, and Cronin provide more accurate descriptions and details about their settings but with variations on the old themes rather than new ways to imagine Colorado.

Notes

1. Richard Vidimos, "Author Justin Cronin Recounts His Own Literary Passage," *Denver Post*, July 18, 2010, www.denverpost.com/entertainment/entertainmentlastold/ci_15526538 (accessed September 22, 2014); Justin Cronin, personal communication, February 28 2011.

2. Page references are to the following editions and will be cited parenthetically in the text: Leigh Brackett, *The Long Tomorrow* (Garden City, N.Y.: Doubleday, 1955); Justin Cronin, *The Passage* (New York: Ballantine Books, 2010); Philip K. Dick, *The Man in the High Castle* (New York: Putnam, 1962); Robert A. Heinlein, *The Door into Summer* (1956; reprint, New York: Signet, 1959) and *Sixth Column: A Science Fiction Novel of a Strange Intrigue* (New York: Gnome Press, 1949; republished as *The Day After Tomorrow*, New York, Signet, 1951); Ursula Le Guin, *City of Illusions* (New York: Ace Books, 1967); Walter Miller, Jr., *A Canticle for Leibowitz* (Philadelphia: Lippincott, 1959) and *Saint Leibowitz and the Wild Horse Woman* (New York: Bantam, 1997); Ayn Rand, *Atlas Shrugged* (1957; reprint, New York: Dutton, 1992).

3. For standard sources on American regions, see Raymond Gastil, *Cultural Regions of the United States* (Seattle: University of Washington Press, 1975); Wilbur Zelinsky, *The Cultural Geography of the United States* (Englewood Cliffs, N.J.: Prentice-Hall, 1973); Joel

Garreau, *The Nine Nations of North America* (Boston: Houghton Mifflin, 1981); Edward L. Ayers, Patricia Nelson Limerick, Stephen Nissenbaum, and Peter S. Onuf, *All Over the Map: Rethinking American Regions* (Baltimore: Johns Hopkins University Press, 1996); and geographer D. W. Meinig's magisterial four-volume study *The Shaping of America* (New Haven, Conn.: Yale University Press, 1986–2004).

4. A story set in Cincinnati or Saint Louis has carte blanche with most readers but not so for San Francisco or Tokyo. The more often disaster novels and movies represent national or global devastation with images of New York in ruins (Page, Yablon) or Los Angeles laid low (Davis), the more these cities seem like the most proper embodiments of catastrophe. See Max Page, *The City's End: Two Centuries of Fantasies, Fears and Premonitions of New York's Destruction* (New Haven, Conn.: Yale University Press, 2008); Nick Yablon, *Untimely Ruins: An Archeology of American Urban Modernity, 1819–1919* (Chicago: University of Chicago Press, 2009); and Mike Davis, *The Ecology of Fear: Los Angeles and the Imagination of Disaster* (New York: Metropolitan Books, 1998).

5. Kathleen Brosnan, *Uniting Mountain and Plain: Cities, Law, and Environmental Change along the Front Range* (Albuquerque: University of New Mexico Press, 2002), 91–117; Carl Abbott, Stephen J. Leonard, and Thomas J. Noel, *Colorado: A History of the Centennial State*, 4th ed. (Boulder: University Press of Colorado, 2005), 220–39.

6. Richard Harding Davis, *The West from a Car Window* (New York: Harper and Bros., 1892), 270; David Wrobel, *Promised Lands: Promotion, Memory and the Creation of the Modern American West* (Lawrence: University Press of Kansas, 2002), 21–23; Abbott, Leonard, and Noel, *Colorado*, 227–28.

7. Thomas G. Andrews, "'Made by Toile'? Tourism, Labor, and the Construction of the Colorado Landscape, 1858–1917, *Journal of American History* 92, no. 3 (December 2005): 837; Samuel A. Fisk, "Colorado for Invalids," *Popular Science Monthly* 25 (July 1884): 313.

8. Samuel A. Fisk, "Colorado for Invalids," *Popular Science Monthly* 25 (July 1884): 313–19.

9. Alpine skiing is a Germanic activity brought to the United States by German, Austrian, and Swiss instructors, and thus one more erasure of the state's multiracial past, as Annie Gilbert Coleman has explored. See Annie Gilbert Coleman, "The Unbearable Whiteness of Skiing," *Pacific Historical Review* 65 (November 1996): 583–614; E. Duke Richey, "The Aspenization of Telluride: Coming of Age and Mythologizing Change in Ski Country, 1945–1985," *Pacific Historical Review* 79 (May 2010): 231–64.

10. Margaret Pugh O'Mara, *Cities of Knowledge: Cold War Science and the Search for the Next Silicon Valley* (Princeton, N.J.: Princeton University Press, 2005; Michael Dudley, "Sprawl as Strategy: City Planners Face the Bomb," *Journal of Planning Education and Research* 21 (2001): 52–63.

11. President Dwight Eisenhower's choice of Colorado for summer vacations added to the aura, recapitulating the efforts of a local promoter in 1911 to build a Summer White House in the foothills west of Denver.

12. The characterization of Colorado as a place of isolation and refuge distances my examples from science fiction that emphasizes the plot tropes of the western themes (see chapter 9 on the television series *Firefly*) or develops analogies to resource and settlement frontiers. See Carl Abbott, *Frontiers Past and Future: Science Fiction and the American West* (Lawrence: University Press of Kansas, 2006). However, it does resonate with

analyses that emphasize the juxtaposition of lone individuals with wilderness as a central theme of both western fiction—see Jane Tompkins, *West of Everything: The Inner Life of Westerns* (New York: Oxford University Press, 1991)—and "frontier" science fiction—see David Mogen, *Wilderness Visions: The Western Theme in Science Fiction Literature* (San Bernardino, Calif.: Borgo Press, 1993); David Mogen, Scott P. Sanders, and Joanne Karpinski, eds. *Frontier Gothic: Terror and Wonder at the Frontier in American Literature* (Rutherford, N.J.: Fairleigh Dickinson University Press, 1993); and Gary K. Wolfe, "Frontiers in Space," in David Mogen, Mark Busby, and Paul Bryant, eds., *The Frontier Experience and the American Dream: Essays on American Literature* (College Station: Texas A&M University Press, 1989).

13. "All" was later published along with two other previously unpublished Campbell stories in Roger Elwood, ed., *The Space Beyond* (New York: Pyramid Books, 1976). The quote is on p. 77.

14. Robert A. Heinlein, *Grumbles from the Grave*, ed. Virginia Heinlein (New York: Ballantine, 1989), 139.

15. Heinlein's 1959 story "'All You Zombies—'" places scenes in a "Sub Rockies base" and a "Sub Rockies Annex—HQ Temporal DOL," but these are throw-in locations whose specific spatial coordinates are not essential. The story is reprinted in Arthur Evans, Istvan Csicsary-Ronay, Jr., Joan Gordon, Veronica Hollinger, Rob Lathem, and Carol McGuirk, eds., *The Wesleyan Anthology of Science Fiction* (Middletown, Conn.: Wesleyan University Press, 2010), 324–36.

16. Greg Rickman, *To the High Castle: Philip K. Dick: A Life 1928–1962* (Long Beach, Calif.: Fragments West/Vallentine Press, 1989), 367.

17. Pueblo, Colorado, is the location for a sort of surviving government in John Barnes's recent *Directive 51* (New York: Ace, 2010) and *Daybreak Zero* (New York: Ace, 2011). After a series of nanoplagues have destroyed most rubber, plastic, and electrical conductors and pushed industrial and communication technologies back a century, rival remnant regimes claiming constitutional legitimacy arise in Athens, Georgia, and Olympia, Washington. In between is the Reconstruction Research Center that coordinates efforts to understand the rapidly changing new world and serves as a third power center and neutral broker.

18. Jennifer Burns, *Goddess of the Market: Ayn Rand and the American Right* (New York: Oxford University Press, 2009), 135; Anne C. Heller, *Ayn Rand and the World She Made* (New York: Doubleday, 2009), 193–94.

19. David Harriman, ed., *Journals of Ayn Rand* (New York: Dutton, 1992), 704.

20. Ayn Rand to Pincus Berman, Sept. 10, 1949, and Rand to John Hospers, August 29, 1960, in Michael S. Berliner, ed., *Letters of Ayn Rand* (New York: Dutton, 1995), 456, 509.

21. Heller, *Ayn Rand*, 12–14.

22. Burns, *Goddess of the Market*, 169–70.

23. For additional interpretations of *The Long Tomorrow*, see Diana Parkin-Speer, "Leigh Brackett's *The Long Tomorrow*: A Quest for the Future America," *Extrapolation*, 26 (Summer 1985): 190–200, and Donna M. DeBlasio, "Future Imperfect: Leigh Brackett's *The Long Tomorrow*," in Carl Yoke, ed., *Phoenix from the Ashes: The Literature of the Remade World* (New York: Greenwood, 1987), 97–103.

24. Ursula Le Guin, *The Language of the Night: Essays on Fantasy and Science Fiction* (New York: Putnam, 1979), 147.

25. Ursula Le Guin, personal communication, April 18, 2010.

26. The wildly popular young adult novel *The Hunger Games* by Suzanne Collins (New York: Scholastic Press, 2008), is set in a postenvironmental disaster America ruled from Panem, a shining city "built in a place once called the Rockies" (41). It is a Shing-like place that is isolated from the thirteen surrounding, politically subordinate provinces. "The mountains form a natural barrier between the Capitol and the eastern districts. It is almost impossible to enter from the east except through the tunnels. This geographical advantage was a major factor in the districts losing the war. . . . Since they had to scale the mountains, they were easy targets for the Capitol's air force" (59). Like Es Toch, the city is grand: "The magnificence of the glistening buildings in a rainbow of hues that tower into the air" (59). Once the protagonists have arrived in Panem, however, its location ceases to play a role in the plot.

27. Vidimos, "Justin Cronin."

28. Justin Cronin, "Justin Cronin on Salon Reading Club" (2010), at www.salon.com/books/feature/2010/07/06/justin_cronin_interview (accessed September 22, 2014).

29. Justin Cronin, personal communication, February 28, 2011.

30. Ibid.

31. Terry Bisson, personal communication, April 23, 2010; and "A Canticle for Miller," at http://www.terrybisson.com/page4/page4.html (accessed September 22, 2014).

32. D. W. Meinig, "American Wests: Preface to a Geographical Interpretation," *Annals of the Association of American Geographers* 62, no. 2 (1972): 159–84.

33. Robert Crossley, *Imagining Mars: A Literary History* (Middletown, Conn.: Wesleyan University Press, 2011).

34. William H. Katerberg, *Future West: Utopia and Apocalypse in Frontier Science Fiction* (Lawrence: University Press of Kansas, 2008); Abbott, *Frontiers Past and Future.*

CHAPTER 8

The Light on the Horizon

Imagining the Death of American Cities

Americans have to *imagine* the devastation that modern warfare can wreak on cities. The British incendiary raid on Washington, D.C., in 1814—the closest that the independent United States has come to invasion, occupation, and destruction of a city by a foreign power—is scarcely noticeable in such company as the capture of Nanking or the siege of Leningrad. The experience of the Civil War is no more helpful. Although federal armies burned sections of Columbia, Richmond, and Atlanta, the scale of damage and terror were orders of magnitude less than in Hamburg or Tokyo. No battle has ever raged for months through the streets and factories of Pittsburgh as it did through Stalingrad. No army of millions has ever rolled through Chicago like the Soviets into Berlin. Nuclear weapons detonated directly over Hiroshima and Nagasaki, but the closest that nuclear explosions have come to an American city were carefully monitored tests seventy-five miles from Las Vegas.

With this thankfully thin history to describe and analyze, Americans have only been able to *imagine* their cities as battlegrounds and killing fields. This essay therefore turns to fiction, both in literature and in film, where Americans have tried to think about the consequences of war on their nation and cities. For its preparation, I owe a debt to several scholars who have done much of the hard work of describing and categorizing the fictions of future war and apocalypse, particularly I. E. Clarke, Bruce Franklin, Warren Wagar, David Seed, Mick Broderick, Paul Boyer, and Paul Brians.[1]

What I hope to add is attention to place as well as time. The literature of disaster and apocalypse is inherently structured by the arrow of time—the contrasts of before and after, cataclysm and rebirth. Within this inclusive framework, my particular concern is the role that cities play in American depictions of apocalyptic warfare. How have we imagined cities as the great war looms? Where are cities in the struggle for survival? Do cities help or hinder as remnant communities claw back to civilization? The essay makes no claims to completeness, for there are hundreds and hundreds of post-holocaust stories, novels, and movies, but it does claim to examine influential examples and to identify dominant themes and approaches.

In these imagined futures, cities are most conspicuous by their absence. American writers are much more interested in envisioning the impacts of total war on small towns and rural enclaves than on cities. They prefer to extrapolate a postwar world of empty spaces and tribal communities to a future of reconstructed cities. When cities do appear in postapocalyptic fictions, they are dangerous and deadly far more often than desirable, bearing the burden of old times rather than the hopes of the future.

One reason for this treatment is a basic problem of narrative structure. If nuclear war is likely to destroy cities, it will also destroy any characters living in those cities and thus short-circuit the story. After the bomb, there will not be any city people to write about, only the refugees and the country people beyond the circles of death. Since Virgil wrote the story of Aeneas, fictions about the effects of total war have often been tales of survivors—their ways of coping, their wanderings, their efforts to start anew.

The second reason for writing *around* cities rather than about them is the deeply embedded American preference for the middle landscape.[2] For more than two centuries, American culture has emphasized the value of nonurban people and places, of yeoman farmers, frontiersmen, and country towns. Even today, when 80 percent of Americans dwell in metropolitan regions, opinion polls show that we picture the small town as the most attractive place to live. American thinkers from Ralph Waldo Emerson to the present have recognized the economic and intellectual benefits of cities, but most of their fellow citizens would prefer to enjoy those benefits while living on a rural farmette or along a small town's leafy Elm Street. Novelists and film makers can tap these feelings (which, of course, may be their own) by setting postwar stories outside the city: in suburbs beyond the blast zone, in rural enclaves, in desert hideaways, in the sheltering forest or across the broad prairies.

Ancestral Voices

We can cover the late nineteenth and early twentieth centuries quickly. From the 1870s through the 1920s, Americans followed the transatlantic lead when they considered the death of cities. The establishment of the German Empire through an unsettling succession of quick wars between 1864 and 1871 triggered a spate of imaginary war stories in which Europeans tried to rethink the dynamics of the Great Power system. The great popularity of *The Battle of Dorking* (1871), describing a German assault on England, introduced dozens of imagined war scenarios. Germany, France, Britain, and the other nations of the unstable alliance system attacked each other's fleets, marched on each other's cities, and defended themselves in short, heroic contests—all between the covers of books and magazines.

Americans in these years were imitators who produced relatively few books about future wars, in part because they had trouble figuring out plausible enemies. Park Benjamin's story "The End of New York" (1881), which pictured a Spanish bombardment of New York and American rescue by the Chilean navy, was scarcely credible, but Spain was back again in 1897 in J. H. Palmer's *The Invasion of New York: Or, How Hawaii Was Annexed*. Here Japan attacks San Francisco while a Spanish armada assaults New York, but the tide turns when shore defenses destroy the Spaniards and the American Pacific fleet crushes the Japanese, takes the battle to the Home Islands, and assures American annexation of Hawaii. Given a history of warfare and a century of diplomatic tension, a threatening and jealous Britain was a bit more likely. In Samuel R. Reed, *The War of 1886, between the United States and Britain* (1882) and Henry Grattan Donnelly, *The Stricken Nation* (1890), the British fleet wallops New York and other eastern cities. Samuel Barton's *The Battle of the Swash and the Capture of Canada* (1888) looks back from the supposed vantage of 1930. The perfidious British assail New York from the sea, reducing lower Manhattan to rubble and collapsing the proud new Brooklyn Bridge into the East River . . . but then a swarm of secret torpedo boats sink the British fleet, Britain cedes Canada and Jamaica to the United States, and Russia seizes India from the weakened empire. Germany, as the rising European power, might have been a logical choice for imagined enemy, but it was far removed from most Americans' concerns. It took outsider H. G. Wells in *The War in the Air* (1907) to posit a really nasty German air attack on New York, and Germany supplanted the UK as a favorite fictional foe only after the Rape of Belgium. Cleveland Moffat's *The Conquest of America: A Romance of Disaster and Victory* (1916) is a good wartime example with the standard elements: naval bombardment of coastal defenses, an airship that bombs the city of Baltimore, an invasion force that lands on Long Island, the hapless Brooklyn Bridge in ruins, and secret aerial torpedoes to crush the German fleet (invented with the help of Thomas Edison).[3]

The threat of Asian hordes, a secondary worry for members of European state system, seemed more likely from North American shores. Yellow peril futures drew on the American interest in dominating the Pacific basin and played off deeply embedded anti-Asian prejudice. The subgenre started with Pierton W. Dooner, *The Last Days of the Republic* (1880), in which the enemy is hordes of Chinese laborers who have infiltrated the nation in order to rise up and wrest control from the white race. By the time Japan won stunning victories over China (1894–95) and Russia (1904–1905), that other island empire seemed more dangerous even than Britain. Homer Lea in *The Valor of Ignorance* (1909) offered a detailed scenario for Japanese conquest of Hawaii, Seattle, Santa Monica, and other West Coast cities, even suggesting where the invaders would place their guns in San Francisco Bay to command the Golden Gate and level San Francisco.[4] John Ulrich Giesy in *All for His Country* (1915) has Mexico distracting the U.S. army, Japan bombing New York, and Japanese domestic servants rising up in California . . . but wait! a *double* superweapon consisting of aero-destroyers carrying magnetic bombs obliterates the Japanese fleet in Chesapeake Bay (Chesapeake Bay?!?) and forces surrender. By 1921, when Peter Kyne published *Pride of Palomar*, Mexicans were in good graces again; Bolsheviks in Siberia were now the distraction from the Japanese threat to California. A few years later, Buck Rogers started his adventures on the comic pages by fighting twenty-third-century Asian overlords.[5]

Eighty-two years after Dooner's book, science fiction writer Philip K. Dick managed to invert the whole yellow peril myth (and *Battle of Dorking* genre) in one of the best of all alternative reality novels. In *The Man in the High Castle* (1962) he imagined a world after German and Japanese victory. World War II finally ended in 1947, its results inevitable after the British defeat at Cairo and the German capture of the Middle East. Now, in 1962, Germans control the eastern United States and Japan directs a puppet government for the Pacific Coast, with the Rocky Mountains states as a small, independent enclave. We see no ruined cities. The Germans apparently inflicted significant conventional damage on Atlantic Coast cities, but they have been energetically rebuilding New York and Baltimore and reconstructing the economy in a sort of Speer Plan as the defeated people and ambitious young Americans flock to New York. San Francisco apparently fell without becoming a battlefield. It remains undamaged, while the culturally sensitive Japanese try to mitigate the worst impacts of German racism. They cherish the peacefulness that they have brought to the Pacific Coast ("completely different from—back there"). They treasure artifacts from prewar America like Colt revolvers and see a Mickey Mouse watch as "most authentic of dying old U.S. culture, a rare retained artifact carrying flavor of bygone halcyon day."[6]

After the Bomb

With the coming of atomic weapons, the situation changed. After all, it was *our* bomb, at least for the first few years. Americans were not only inventors who brought atomic weapons to the world but also literary innovators who developed many of the tropes of postatomic fiction. And after Nagasaki, war itself obviously had to be rethought. It had to be reconceptualized by the professionals in war colleges and general staff offices. It also had to be reimagined for popular consumption.

Editors of mass circulation magazines made sure to cover each round of atomic tests in Nevada and the Pacific, and they introduced their readers to "nonfiction" scenarios of nuclear war. The specifics were new, but the genre was familiar from the imagined invasions and fleet engagements of earlier decades. In November 19, 1945, *Life* magazine ran a nine-page spread on "The 36-Hour War." Illustrations and text summarized the latest future-war thinking from the Pentagon, including intercontinental ballistic missiles and antimissile defenses that hold U.S. losses to only thirteen cities and forty million people. *Colliers*, one of *Life*'s major competitors, published its summary of "The War We Do Not Want: Principal Events of World War III" on October 27, 1951. The war begins with Russian intervention in Yugoslavia, proceeds with atomic bombing of Detroit, New York, and Washington, D.C., and ends as U.N. tank armies push eastward through Poland and Ukraine to achieve the success that eluded Hitler.[7] The continuing effort to develop realistic projections of nuclear wars and terrorism by military planners, civil defense authorities, and think tanks have provided background for fictional portrayals. At the same time, however, the literary genre of post-disaster fiction has taken on a life of its own with later novelists and screenwriters framing their stories as extensions and reactions to earlier fiction.

Writers of fiction rather than forecasts have faced a greater problem, however. The atomic age presents a huge challenge when writing stories and novels about war and cities. If nuclear weapons can destroy an entire metropolis in an instant, there is no *story*. When everyone perishes in a flash of nuclear energy, their deaths abruptly cancel opportunities for plot complications, character development, and sympathetic identification of readers with hero and heroine. Nor can the outcome of the story emerge, in proper Aristotlean fashion, from the strengths and weaknesses of the protagonists themselves. A novelist or scriptwriter can lead up to the crack of doom with the interlocking stories of ordinary citizens, but if she is writing about ground zero, she cannot finish off the story with the standard adventure fiction technique of watching the same people cope with the aftermath. For example, the film *Miracle Mile* (1988) asks what an ordinary resident of Los Angeles might do if he gets a tip, via an intercepted phone call, that nuclear war is scheduled to break out in seventy minutes. Well, he would try to find the girl of his dreams whom he met only that day, struggle to survive rising lawlessness and panic, hope that the phone call was a hoax, and sink into the La Brea tar pits in his lover's arms as the bomb explodes.

It is no surprise that few novelists and screen writers have taken up the challenge of actually writing about "The Day" itself from the perspective of ground zero. By and large, depiction of the immediate effects of atomic attack was left to civil defense pamphlets and news reports about weapons tests. In addition to the problem of sustaining a storyline in which the characters must, realistically, be eliminated suddenly and simultaneously, it also was difficult for any fiction writer to match John Hersey's harrowing factual reporting in *Hiroshima* (1946).[8] One partial exception was Philip Wylie's *Tomorrow* (1954), a thinly plotted but quick-moving novel that described the impact of a one-hundred-kiloton fission bomb on the twin middle western cities of River City and Green Prairie. The book is 268 pages of lead-up to the moment of detonation, 20 pages vividly detailing the effects of heat and blast, 60 pages describing the secondary firestorm, radiation, mob panic, rescue operations, and the slow or faster deaths of the seriously injured, and finally 25 pages showing survivors picking up the pieces two years later. Like most disaster fictions, it introduces a dozen or so characters, follows their quotidian lives up to the moment that the "plutonium fist" strikes the city, and then describes their death or traces their survival. Another partial exception is Whitley Strieber and James Kunetka's *Warday, and the Journey Onwards* (1984), which posits a United States five years after a limited nuclear exchange. The book takes the form of a documentary report of a journey across North America that inventories the destruction as well as recovery efforts.[9]

Most of the options for fictionalizing nuclear conflict move away from the actual face of war. One possibility is to write about political intrigue, concentrating on the tensions and decisions leading up to war, as in the novels *Fail Safe* (1962) and *Seven Days in May* (1962).[10] The reader is placed in presidential offices, command posts, air force ready rooms, and underground bunkers, not down in the streets with ordinary citizens. For Americans, the fiction became almost too real with the Cuban Missile Crisis of 1962 and then nearly unsupportable after the bitter satire of *Dr. Strangelove* (1963).

A second option draws on the conventions of suspense fiction. Cities can be background actors in find-the-bomb-before-it-is-too-late stories. The film *Port of Hell* (1955) focused on intrepid security staff, who have only twelve hours to prevent a smuggled Chinese bomb from exploding on a freighter in the Los Angeles harbor. Sean Connery and Roger Moore have saved the world from nuclear blackmail quite a few times. The tall and lovely Nicole Kidman spends some frantic moments in midtown Manhattan in *The Peacemaker* (1997), playing a physicist who helps track down a suicide bomber who plans to destroy the United Nations with a nuclear warhead stolen from Russia. New York traffic and sidewalk crowds add to the tension. However, the fact that the bomb is atomic rather than conventional does not change the dramatic structure of the story itself. The contests of wit, courage, and quick action that drive suspense fiction are the same whether the threat to be averted is blackmail with a stolen nuclear weapon, the planned assassination of Charles De Gaulle, a bomb planted in a city bus, bioterrorism, or any other source of danger.[11]

A third and most popular approach to fictionalizing nuclear war is to write postwar stories about survivors. These stories can begin with the run-up to war, but the characters have to be physically distant from ground zero to outlast the seconds of destruction and come through into a postwar world where they can *do* things—interesting, challenging, heroic, painful, and sometimes clever things. They can be craven or brave, self-serving or self-sacrificing; they can reveal the nature of human beings through their inherent goodness. These are, in broad terms, apocalyptic stories of ends and beginnings. Like the last book of the Bible, they contain both the destruction of an old order and the creation of new things.[12]

The following sections look at these postwar stories in more detail. Some are stories of the immediate days and months after the blowup, others talk about atomic war by substituting "natural" disasters, and still others take a longer view that looks generations and centuries into the future.[13] In each case, I am keeping watch for the depiction and role of cities in the aftertime.

The Days After

Even in stories set in the immediate aftermath of nuclear exchange, the targeted cities are off stage. They appear not as complex interweavings of people, institutions, and physical structures, but as heart-stopping bursts of light on the horizon. Folks in an outlying community or district see the flash and hear their radios go dead, but they are too far away to be immediately impacted. As survivors, they have to pick up the pieces, often in the knowledge that their coping may prove to be in vain. Cities are, in effect, the villains. They share partial blame for the nuclear war itself by their very existence as tempting targets. In the days and weeks after the attack, they continue to be the source of danger from dispersing radiation, creeping epidemics, and hungry, half-mad refugees.[14]

In 1950, when nuclear weapons were still fission bombs that devastated only a few dozen square miles, Judith Merril's *Shadow on the Hearth* focused on a suburban Westchester County housewife and her daughters as they try to deal with the aftermath of an attack on New York City. As the mother waits for her husband to make it home, she is sometimes timid and irrational, but she slowly gains confidence and recognizes the strength of her older teenage daughter. The novel deals realistically with issues of food, water, and fallout. It also makes the neighborhood a political battleground between authoritarian civil defense workers and postwar progressives represented by the high school science teacher and local doctor. The ending is reasonably upbeat.[15]

Ray Bradbury's short story "There Will Come Soft Rains," also appearing in 1950, was an elegy rather than a survival story. The time is 2026, the setting an automated house in suburban California, the only one left (inexplicably) standing after the nuclear war. Off in the distance are the glowing ruins of the city. Here, however, the house still functions. The household robots and automated systems cook breakfast, wash the dishes, dispose of uneaten food, sweep the carpets, water the garden, set out cocktails, and control the lights. The residents of the house are remembered by their menu preferences, their taste in poetry, and the west facade of the house, which was "black, save for five places. Here the silhouette in paint of a man mowing a lawn. Here, as in a photograph, a woman bent to pick flowers. Still further over, their images burned on wood in one titanic instant, a small boy, hands flung into the air higher up, the image of a thrown ball, and opposite him a girl, hand raised to catch a ball which never came down. The five spots of paint—the man, the woman, the children, the ball—remained. The rest was a thin charcoaled layer." The end comes when a crashing tree branch sparks a kitchen fire that consumes the house down to a single wall, from which the last automated voice repeats: "Today is August 5, 2026, today is August 5, 2026, today is. . . ."[16]

The development of fusion weapons in the mid-1950s, with hundreds of times the power of the first atomic bombs, along with increasing awareness of the dangers of radioactive fallout, forced the stories further away from cities. By 1959, Helen Clarkson (Helen McCloy) set *The Last Day: A Novel of the Day after Tomorrow* on the coast of Maine. Some of the survivors initially welcome a return to a simpler existence, but the author will have none of that. Children begin to succumb to radiation poisoning, then the rest of the townspeople. Vacationer

Bill Corbett dies in the arms of his wife, Lois, who a few days later lies down to die on the shore. With its careful attention to the details of death at a distance, the novel is a sort of Physicians for Social Responsibility information tract in fictional form. With its tone of regret and resignation, it echoes the elegy of "Soft Rains."[17]

In the same year, 1959, Pat Frank's best-selling *Alas, Babylon* focused on a small town beyond the circle of blast and fire. In Fort Repose, deep in the Florida countryside, residents can see the flash from the nuclear bombing of Miami, Tampa, and Jacksonville but are saved from radioactive fallout by favorable winds. The bomb that obliterates Orlando also takes out the electric power supply: "Thus the lights went out, and in that moment civilization in Fort Repose retreated a hundred years."[18] This is a Florida of four million people rather than today's nineteen million, with Walt Disney World yet unbuilt, leaving elbow room to regain some of the survival skills of nineteenth-century farmers. Because they are still close to the land—fishermen, recreational hunters, farmers—the people of Fort Repose do a pretty good job of imitating their great-grandparents. With strong leadership from former military officers, they organize a barter economy and fight off a relatively tame set of highwaymen, who are actually crooks from Las Vegas (!!) stranded in Florida. Civil society frays around the edges but holds. After a year the survivors are reconnected with a fiercely damaged but victorious United States.

Meanwhile, cities have been the victims of their own excesses. The people of Fort Repose hear the list of destroyed cities: "The voice went on, ticking off Mobile and Birmingham, New Orleans and Lake Charles. It moved into Texas, obliterating Fort Worth and Dallas . . . and Abilene, Houston, and Corpus Christi. . . . The voice moved up to Oak Ridge, in Tennessee, and then spoke of Chicago, and everything around Chicago in northern Indiana, and crept up the western shore of Lake Michigan to Milwaukee, and Milwaukee's suburbs. Inexorably, it uttered the names of Kansas City, Wichita, and Topeka."[19] They are sorry about the deaths of tens of millions, often bitterly sorry, but they are also pleased that they have themselves remained true to rural America. They realize that the nation should never have become so centralized and dependent on cities and the economic efficiencies that they offer and that the postwar world may actually be a healthier place.

Fifty years after Pat Frank's best seller, James Howard Kunstler recycled the same proposition about the resiliency of small towns in the face of comprehensive disaster in *World Made by Hand* (2008). A novelist turned social critic in the 1990s, Kunstler made his reputation in urban planning circles with *The Geography of Nowhere* (1994), an acerbic attack on soulless suburbia that held up his home town of Saratoga Springs, New York, as a model of social and physical community. He followed with *Home from Nowhere* (1998), advocating the design principles of "New Urbanism," and then with *The Long Emergency* (2005) about the devastating effects that will come with the exhaustion of petroleum supplies.

World Made by Hand blends the two jeremiads in a story about postpetroleum survival.

The backstory is an overdetermined catastrophe in a not-too-distant future: terrorists have nuked Washington, D.C., and Los Angeles, a mutated virus has been killing people by the millions, resource wars have broken out because fossil fuels are exhausted or unavailable, and climate change has disrupted agriculture. The story follows Robert Earle, a former computer executive from Boston who finds himself in Union Grove, New York, a small town that would once have been within commuting range of Albany—just like Saratoga Springs. He survives with old carpentry skills in a world where roads and bridges are crumbling, bartering has replaced money (worthless without a functioning government), electricity flickers on for half an hour each month, and animal power is a primary energy source.

The novel is basically a thought experiment that presents alternative approaches to maintaining order and argues for the virtues of the democratic, self-organizing society that is possible in a small town. A large landowner has managed to re-create a landed estate with dependent workers and develop "long distance" trade with Albany. Members of a tight-knit religious commune, who arrive from Virginia with scattered news of the outer world, are standoffish but willing to cooperate with the ordinary townspeople, who maintain a semblance of town government. Led by Robert Earle, they combine to rid the town of a gang of outlaws.

Kunstler's Union Grove is not a peaceful place, but it is a setting in which survival and perhaps even recovery is possible. Small towns offer the possibility of self-sufficiency at a manageable scale. Isolated families, who try to live without community support in the outback, fall to starvation or violence. At the opposite scale, those large cities than luckily avoided nuclear destruction have descended into racial violence. Union Grove, whose name recalls Grover's Corners, New Hampshire, the setting for Thornton Wilder's 1938 play *Our Town*, is just the right place for people to make do with what they have, help each other out in what Bill McKibbin calls the "economics of neighborliness," and slowly rebuild as alternatives to the cities that will never again rise to dominance.

The idea that a deurbanized postdisaster world might be a better place is picked up in the subgenre of "end time prophecy" and "rapture" novels that dramatize the beliefs of premillenialist Christian fundamentalism. A number of popular novels since the 1960s have fictionalized biblical Armageddon as it might arrive next week or next year. It turns out that cities, being particularly hospitable to the anti-Christ, are likely to collapse into chaos before the very final end, giving more virtuous country folk one more lesson about the consequences of right and wrong choices.[20]

Alas, Babylon has an upbeat ending (as do rapture novels from their own peculiar point of view) but not the films *The Day After* or *Testament*. Both movies appeared in 1983, at the height of tension in the Second Cold War. Made for television and heavily publicized, *The Day After* had one of the largest U.S. viewing audiences to date, estimated at one hundred million. It is set in Lawrence, Kansas, a pleasant university town that is literally at the center of the United States. The movie starts with the local reactions to rapidly escalating international tension, shows American missiles surging skyward into the blue Kansas sky, zeroes in on the panic that suddenly grips the community, graphically depicts the destructive impact of two warheads hitting Kansas City in a four-minute sequence (the equivalent of the twenty pages in *Tomorrow*), traces unavailing efforts to cope with the disaster, and follows its characters into death by starvation and sickness.[21]

Testament is set in a northern California suburb of the San Francisco Bay metropolis. The movie opens with an emergency newscast that East Coast cities have been hit with nuclear weapons, followed quickly by a great flash from another, closer bomb. The situation is similar to that of *Alas, Babylon*, centering on an isolated community that is thrown to its own devices. No one knows how the war came out. No one knows if basic services will ever be restored. Again like Pat Frank's novel, the story centers on a morally strong character who tries to maintain order amid the fear of chaos. Housewife Carol Wetherly struggles valiantly to keep her family together and to fight off the growing disorder. But systems begin to break down—children stop going to school, adults quit showing up for work, canned food runs short. There is no successful recapture of frontier skills, no rescue by the U.S. Air Force—only radiation working its inexorable death.

Substitute Bombs

A problem of fusion bombs and their modern delivery systems, from a writer's point of view, is that they compress space and time in a truly postmodern way. The enemy's targeting decisions are unknowable to the victims and therefore arbitrary. The nuclear warhead comes from nowhere we can see (from above via an ICBM) and arrives nearly instantly. When earlier writers imagined *pre*nuclear wars, they could realistically take time for anticipation and preparations, detail the advance of the Germans or Martians, describe defensive efforts, retreats, the rallying of the defenders, and finally produce the secret superweapon or lowly microbe to set things right again. All of this fascinating military point and counterpoint disappears in a nuclear exchange, where the war is over in minutes.

If the thermonuclear warhead is translated into a natural catastrophe, however, there *is* room for a plot. The problem may be triggered by human error or folly, or it may simply happen. Disaster can build as slowly or rapidly as the author wishes. We therefore have all manner of earthquakes, ice ages, tidal waves and rising oceans, mutated ants and ravenous plants, plagues, superstorms, meteors, an itinerant planet that eats the moon and perturbs the tides, and monsters awakened from the deep by nuclear explosions. Plus we've had more than a century to worry about extraterrestrial invaders, from the *War of the Worlds* (1898) to recent special-effects films like *Independence Day* (1996). In every case, the story can follow the classic suspense-adventure plot. The threat appears, expands, overcomes initial efforts to fight back, may be fended off, reappears, overwhelms, destroys everyone or leaves a remnant to rebuild. If the threat is Godzilla, King of Monsters, it can even reappear in sequels.[22]

Although some of these depictions of deadly futures have emerged directly from worries about human impacts on the natural environment, it is clear that most of them are indeed surrogate war stories.[23] The doomsday story appeared long before atomic warfare. Warren Wagar has accumulated many early twentieth-century examples of survivors clawing back toward civilization after earthquakes, encounters with watery nebulae, plagues, and the like. However, the possibility of atomic warfare gave new life to old tales about scarlet plagues and purple rain.[24] Simply compare a depiction of Manhattan as victim of a meteor, taken from Willy Ley's *The Conquest of Space* (1949), with visual renderings of the impact of atomic weapons—it is the same disaster, no matter its origins.[25]

If you hear that one of these disasters is coming, LEAVE TOWN! Cities are vulnerable. They are custom-made for spreading disease. Let the forces of social order and discipline weaken, and country folk will presumably go on behaving like solid citizens, but urbanites will turn into a mob. Ever since Thomas Jefferson was frightened by the Parisian turmoil of the French Revolution, Americans have seen an urban mob around every historical bend. With the New York draft riots and the Paris Commune looming just behind, social reformer Charles Loring Brace in the 1870s wrote about *The Dangerous Classes of New York* (1872). "Let but Law lift its hand from them for a season, . . . and if the opportunity offered, we should see an explosion from this class which might leave this city in ashes and blood." Ignatius Donnelly in *Caesar's Column* (1890) imagined internal civil war between a corrupt oligarchy and brutalized workers, who rise up as the Brotherhood of Destruction and institute a reign of terror in New York (Caesar's column is a pyramid of skulls built by the mad rebel leader). Nathaniel West imagined the consumption of Los Angeles by fire and riot in *The Day of the Locust* (1939).[26]

Survival from plague, storm, and meteor is to be found outside the city in distant refuges with a vague—or not so vague—Hitlerian tinge. British writers tend to send their survivors to northern Scotland (where it is hard enough for sheep to survive, let alone soft city refugees). Americans like the open spaces of the West. Larry Niven and Jerry Pournelle in *Lucifer's Hammer* (1977), for example, posit a straying asteroid. After blast, tsunami, and fire have done their work, the story dissolves into a confrontation between well-prepared, thoughtful (and white) survivors who barricade themselves in the California mountains and a crazed horde of cannibals who have coalesced from the dregs of Los Angeles and Oakland. Chelsea Quinn Yarbro, *False Dawn* (1978) follows two refugees from the disease-raddled towns of northern California to refuge in the Sierra Nevada south of Lake Tahoe.[27]

A more sophisticated treatment of city and refuge is found in *The Stand* (1978).[28] In this very hefty 823-page horror-suspense novel, refugees from cataclysmic plague trek from cities across the nation to reconstruct and reassemble only the best elements of the vanished world. Accidental release of mutating influenza from a biological warfare laboratory has killed the vast majority of Americans. A handful of survivors come together from scattered points in the South and the Northeast, responding to visions and dreams that call them to the middle landscape of Boulder, Colorado. Hundred-year-old Abagail Freemantle, who figures as a sage and prophet, sees herself going west, "at first with just a few people, then a few more, then a few more. West, always going west, until I could see the Rocky Mountains . . . and there would be signs. . . . No, not signs from God but regular road signs, and everyone one of them saying things like BOULDER, COLORADO, 609 MILES or THIS WAY TO BOULDER" (513).

In Boulder the refugees rebuild a Free Zone and a semblance of normal life. There are a few dozen at first, then a few hundred by the time their first Colorado winter closes in the town, then something like eleven thousand by the following April. Boulder, it turns out, is relatively a blank slate because most of its residents seem to have tidied up and left town before the plague hit; the corpses are few, the houses habitable, and the electricity is easy to restore. In the process of restoring physical systems, they also buckle down to the nitty-gritty of reconstituting civil society. The residents come together at the Chautauqua Auditorium—a real place located where the town gives way to mountain parks and one that harkens back to earlier American traditions of community. They restore symbols of community by reaffirming the Declaration of Independence and the Constitution. They create a steering committee, hold town meetings, reconstitute civil society, and get the electricity working. Like true pioneers, the people of the Free Zone have been tested and strengthened by their westward trek.

Why Boulder? Because it invented itself as the polar opposite to stressful cities and bland suburbia. Think Celestial Seasonings tea, a brand founded in Boulder in 1969. Think hippie environmentalists and the city's pioneering efforts to preserve its character by establishing a greenbelt. Author Stephen King lived in this self-satisfied and self-consciously progressive community in 1974–75, at the height of its hipness and attractiveness. That was just a few years before Boulder would seem a suitable setting for Robin Williams to play an extraterrestrial on *Mork and Mindy* (1978–82)—a show that used college-town jokes but would not have worked if set in Urbana-Champaign, Illinois.

King sets Boulder in contrast to Las Vegas. Other survivors, attracted by evil rather than good, pass directly through Colorado on their way to Vegas. Seemingly the most artificial of cities, it is the center for an alternative empire of darkness in the far western states (there is a shadow of Mordor in the geography, with Las Vegas situated with the rings of mountain ranges that create the Great

Basin of Nevada and adjacent states). In juxtaposing the two places, King directly inverts Ayn Rand's *Atlas Shrugged*. The bad guys, led by the fantastically powered Randall Flagg, create a place of rigorously enforced rules and order guided by objective thought. Flagg is, the Boulderites realize, "the last magician of rational thought, gathering the tools of technology" (919). Residents of the Free Zone, in contrast, practice deliberative democracy rather than untrammeled individualism, are open to the tides of emotion and spiritual leadings, and even value the Randian bête-noire of self-sacrifice and altruism.

Zoners triumph after the strongest of their number take the up the burden of traveling to Las Vegas to confront physical evil with spiritual strength. The showdown comes in the heart of Vegas in front of the MGM Grand Hotel. In the end, the snake of evil devours itself when the most crazed of Flagg's followers appears with a live atomic bomb that Flagg accidentally detonates. The handful of Boulderites who have confronted Flagg become a sacrifice as the entire city vanishes in blast and fire, leaving the people of Boulder free to set their own course—which involves hiving off new settlements before the town grows dangerously into a city again.

Meanwhile it is clear that Las Vegas as an exemplar of crime and excess is an easy symbol for the-city-to-be-avoided. In *Alas, Babylon* it supplies a few troublesome gangsters. It is the model and exemplar of evil in *The Stand* and a breeder of bad things in *The Passage*. Cronin employs the classic trope of the deserted city when his Colorado-bound expedition reaches Vegas. As in countless science fiction before, his small band explore abandoned buildings in the hope of finding treasures (fuel and supplies) but encounter traps and terror instead. Boulder's empty buildings are neutral containers that can be readapted by refugees, but the toppling towers of Las Vegas are nests of danger and disaster.

The Long Tomorrow

In the long tomorrow, decades and centuries after the Flame Deluge, the great central valley of North America will nourish a horse culture of nomads, raiders, and empire builders who blend the power of Genghis Khan with the fierce independence of plains Indians. Market agriculture has also revived in the river valleys, although not at a scale to support real cities. Guardians of knowledge live quietly in the hills and deserts. And in the far distance are the dangerous, haunted shells of ancient cities.

Walter Miller, Jr.'s, *A Canticle for Leibowitz* (1959), for example, extrapolates a future North America in which Benedictine monks of Leibowitz Abbey, following the example of the blessed martyr Isaac Leibowitz, hide away in the New Mexico desert and preserve learning from before the Flame Deluge by salvaging, memorizing, and copying any surviving fragment of twentieth-century writing. Many centuries into *that* future, the world that Saint Leibowitz tried to reconstitute through the preservation of learning has spawned nasty barbarian clans on the grassy plains, whose territory separates agricultural kingdoms such as the Empire of Denver, the Laredan Nation along the Rio Grande, and the Mississippi Republic. Along the Red River where Arkansas, Louisiana, Texas, and Oklahoma once met is the town of Texarkana. It supports an ambitious and wily ruler, but it is small and modest enough to be supplied by pack animals and built as a disorderly maze of streets from the rubble of a larger, ancient city.[29]

As discussed in the previous chapter, Leigh Brackett codifies the nonurban future in *The Long Tomorrow* (1955), when a future United States has adopted a constitutional amendment prohibiting towns of more than one thousand people. The surviving nation is a set of small farming settlements and trading towns linked by annual trading fairs and steamboats. It is a "wide and cityless land, the green, slow, comfortable agrarian land in which only a few old folk could remember the awesome cities that had dominated the world before the Destruction."[30] Counterpoised to farmers and nomads are islands of survivors who try to keep learning alive, with the people of Bartorstown tending a surviving research laboratory and supercomputer concealed deep in the Rocky Mountains.

The quest for surviving knowledge is a standard theme in postapocalypse fiction. Somewhere *out there* is often a wildcard—long-ruined cities that may be sources of danger, troves of knowledge, or—most likely—some of each. The young protagonists in the low-budget 1971 film *Glen and Randa* leave their rural enclave of survivors to search out "Metropolis," which Glen knows from comic books. Their journey takes them past relics of the former world—a motel that they ransack for canned goods, the carcass of an automobile strangely deposited in a tree. Randa dies in childbirth but Glen carries on the search.

Glen may be happy that he never reaches Metropolis, for American writers imagine the cities of the various long tomorrows in ways that reflect our persistent American ambiguity about the merits of cities and city life. We have long known that cities are engines of prosperity as efficient centers of exchange. We also know that the juxtaposition of different people and activities nurtures creative thought—that ideas come out of Athens and not Boeotia, from Florence and not an Apennine village, from New York and Chicago rather than Gopher Prairie. Nevertheless, we fear cities as settings that corrupt youth, cater to sin, give birth to the mob, and undermine a political system designed for independent farmers. Throughout post-holocaust stories, cities play these contradictory roles: They are mythical places of knowledge and repositories of learning and valuable artifacts, but they are also dangerous. They may still be radioactive. They may be filled with mutants and monsters. Even their knowledge itself may be dangerous, an idea which goes as far back as Nathaniel Hawthorne's story "The New Adam and Eve." Here God abruptly ends all human life and repopulates the world that is left with a new first couple, who wander through the empty streets of Boston. They marvel over a church, prison, a court of justice, a mansion house, a bank, and finally "the rich library of Harvard University." Eve this time persuades Adam to come away from this new Tree of Knowledge before he tastes of "perversions and sophistries, and false wisdom . . . the narrow truth . . . all the wrong principles and worse practice, the pernicious examples and mistaken rules of life . . . all the sad experience, which it took mankind so many ages to accumulate, and from which they never drew a moral for their future guidance."[31]

Andre Norton's *Star Man's Son: 2250 A.D.* (1952) brings together these themes.[32] North America after nuclear holocaust is inhabited by scattered tribes. There are the proud, horse-mounted, nomadic Plainsmen, dark-skinned farmers moving up from the south, and the Star Men whose mission is to explore abandoned places and add to knowledge. The latter are the descendants of technicians and scientists, who had been preparing a voyage to the stars. Now they seek out scraps of information: "Many times around the evening fires had the men of the Eyrie [the Star Men] discussed the plains below and the strange world which had felt the force of the Great Blow-up and been turned into an alien, poisonous trap for any human not knowing its ways. Why, in the past twenty years even the Star Men had mapped only four cities, and one of them was 'blue' and so forbidden."[33]

Fors is the son of a Star Man and a plainswoman. Born a mutant, with white hair and night-sight, he is frozen out of chance to become a Star Man himself. He therefore takes off on an adventure of exploration, with a semisentient wildcat as his companion. He meets one of the southerners and has various adventures before proving himself and being accepted back into the clan. In the course of the adventure, he finds a city: "In the morning sun far ahead he saw battered towers rising into the sky. This was one of the cities, the great cities of huge sky-reaching towers! . . . His city—all his . . . an untouched storehouse waiting to be looted for the benefit of the Eyrie. . . . Libraries—those were what one was to look for—and shops, especially those which had stores of hardware or paper. . . . Hospital supplies were best of all."[34]

The city seems largely intact, perhaps the victim of disease after the nuclear war. It holds ruined buildings and a museum that has not yet been ransacked. But lurking in the shadows and cellars are the subhuman and cruel Beast Things. In one explanation, they are offspring of city dwellers and invading soldiers caught in radiation, creating children so mutated as no longer to be human. In another, they are the result of failed experiments to combine human and rat genetic material. "Whichever theory was true, the Beast Things, though they aroused revulsion and instinctive hatred among the humans, were also victims of the Old Ones' tragic mistake, as shattered in their lives as the cities had been."[35] Conflict escalates when the Beast Things stir out of the cities where they have long lived and harry the people on the plains. The Plainsmen and southerners begin to war against each other, but Fors helps them unite against Beast Things, wins acceptance among his own people, and begins to plan his next exploring trip to urban outfitters.

Even when physically normal, humans who have reinhabited cities are likely to be impure of heart. They are susceptible to re-catching the urban disease of domination and empire building and doing the wrong things all over again. Kim Stanley Robinson in *The Wild Shore* (1984) extrapolates a future in the neutron bombing of the United States that has left a scattering of farming and fishing villages along the southern California coast, connected to near neighbors by occasional trading fairs. Trouble comes up the coast from San Diego, where a petty dictator has consolidated power in the ruins of Mission Valley. His agents offer a tempting deal—connection to a larger political unit by a railroad that is slowly pushing northward in return for a modicum of taxes. When the villagers of San Onofre travel south to see for themselves, they find a society that is already corrupted by power and embarked on the seductive path of industrialization. There are not yet dark, satanic mills on the San Diego mesas, but the villagers can see them coming and want nothing to do with the emerging empire.[36]

Aldous Huxley—perhaps an honorary American from his many sun-drenched decades in California—also sees the seeds of recorruption in the postwar city. The bitter satire of *Ape and Essence* (1948) is set in the year 2108, after bombs and plague have devastated the northern hemisphere. Explorers from New Zealand discover a remnant Los Angeles, whose inhabitants worship Belial, the Lord of the Flies. The degraded Angelenos worship their false gods in the great spaces of the Los Angeles Coliseum (built for the 1936 Olympic Games) and sacrifice mutant children. Huxley is engaged in a romantic philosophical critique of the idea of progress, not in careful extrapolation of a possible future, but it is telling that he imagines the *city* where he was living so comfortably as the rallying point of evil.

And then there is underground Topeka, Kansas, in Harlan Ellison's 1969 story "A Boy and His Dog." In 2034, after perhaps several wars, the surface of North America is the province of roverpacks, gangs of violent young men who live and loot among the ruins. Below the surface are "downunders," entire underground cities that have reproduced a nostalgic image of the early twentieth-century town as understood by "Southern Baptists, Fundamentalists, lawanorder goofs, real middle-class squares." Vic is a solo who roams the surface with his sentient dog, Blood. Quilla June Holmes is a luscious young woman from deep Topeka who has been sent to the surface to lure a potent male below to improve the gene pool. She succeeds, leading Vic to her city of 22,680 dull, middle-class Americans. Topeka is built in a buried tube twenty miles across, but it looks just like a small town with "neat little houses, and curvy little streets, and trimmed lawns, and a business section and everything else a Topeka would have. Except a sun, except birds, except clouds, except rain, except snow . . . except freedom." In quick sequence, Vic recognizes the iron hand of social regimentation, realizes his mistake, escapes from the ruthless city with Quilla June, and finds an injured and hungry Blood waiting for him at the top of the entrance shaft. When Quilla demands that Vic choose between caring for a woman and caring for Blood, he decides that what's needed is fresh meat: after all, "a boy loves his dog."[37]

Dying Offstage

"A boy loves his dog" is a great tag line for a sick story. It is also a good metaphor for the way that cities figure in American catastrophe fiction. Americans still believe that they are the young, self-reliant people of an adolescent nation. For young America, freedom to roam the wide continent, even with all its dangers, is preferable to anything associated with the constricted life of a carefully preserved Topeka. In the American calendar of horrors, getting stuck in New York City is especially fearsome—recall the scene in *The Stand* where survivors make their way through a Lincoln Tunnel clogged with cars and corpses when you screen videos of *Soylent Green* (1973), where forty million people crowd into Manhattan, or *Escape from New York* (1981), where the city is an anarchic prison colony. We love the wild and the half wild more than the settled community, the frontiersman more than the New England town builder, Blood more than Quilla June.

By and large, cities die off the stage, and news of their passing comes from afar. In near-future stories a terrible light in the sky announces the end of Boston or San Francisco or Tampa. When an author posits a limited nuclear war with survivors, little loving care is lavished on urban reconstruction. The most detailed examples, such as Philip Wylie's *Tomorrow*, describe old crowded cities rebuilt for the better in full suburban style as long low buildings in seas of roads, grass, and parking.[38] The new Green Prairie will not really be a nasty *city*, but something quieter, milder, and nicer.

These are not stories that revel in the aesthetics of destruction.[39] Instead, by worrying about the mechanics of survival, they offer a half-way escape from confronting the full horrors of mass death.

We can also read these fictions as part of a larger flight from modernity and its cultural pressures. Taking Lewis Mumford's indictment of necropolis and his prescription for population dispersal quite literally, most writers who imagine the world after the big blowup look to the small town and the open land for the promise of a different and better future. As Martha Bartter has pointed out, the destruction of cities in some cases is presented as an ultimate benefit that opens opportunities for renewal and improvement by returning society its rural roots.[40] Cities were the places that germinated the seeds of their own destruction. Their wealth made them targets that called down death on the whole world. Their alienated residents were unable to help themselves, falling quickly into senseless mobs. And cities may plant the same seeds again if they reappear in the distant future. Walter Miller, Jr., made this connection explicit in *A Canticle for Leibowitz*, where North America a millennium after the Fire Deluge regrows cities, re-creates weapons of mass destruction, and launches them again for the devastation of the world. If Aeneas had been an American, he would have stayed the hell out of Carthage, holed up in some mountain valley in the Alps, and kept his distance from Rome.[41]

So we're back to the middle landscape and the desire to protect knowledge without the apparatus of urban institutions. The Star Men plunder urban ruins for medicines and books, but they keep their settlement as a tribal refuge that reminds us of a summer resort colony in the mountains. The Bartorstown scientists know that they have to keep their town small, not only for secrecy but because it is the better thing to do. Of all the books that have been mentioned above, *Alas, Babylon* probably has had the largest readership. The most watched of the movies has been *The Day After*. Both place smaller towns front and center. If we perish in the aftermath, we believe that places like Lawrence, Kansas, will hold on to civilized values the longest. If we hope to survive, it had better be in places like reinhabited Boulder or Union Grove or Fort Repose, where the bonds of community can still function and one small public library contains all the practical knowledge that is needed.

Notes

1. I. E. Clarke, *Voices Prophesying War: Future Wars, 1763–3749* (New York: Oxford University Press, 1992); W. Warren Wagar, *Terminal Visions: The Literature of Last Things* (Bloomington: Indiana University Press, 1982); H. Bruce Franklin, *War Stars: The Superweapon and the American Imagination* (New York: Oxford University Press, 1988); Paul Brians, *Nuclear Holocaust: Atomic War in Fiction* (Kent, Ohio: Kent State University Press, 1987); Mick Broderick, *Nuclear Movies: A Critical Analysis and Filmography of International Feature Length Films Dealing with Experimentation, Aliens, Terrorism, Holocaust and Other Disaster Scenarios, 1914–1989* (Jefferson, N.C.: McFarland, 1991); David Ketterer, *New Worlds for Old: The Apocalyptic Imagination, Science Fiction, and American Literature* (Bloomington: Indiana University Press, 1974); Paul Boyer, *By the Bomb's Early Light* (New York: Pantheon, 1985); David Seed, *American Science Fiction and the Cold War: Literature and Film* (Chicago: Fitzroy Dearborn, 1999).

2. Leo Marx, *The Machine in the Garden: Technology and the Pastoral Ideal in America* (New York: Oxford University Press, 1964); Morton White and Lucia White, *The Intellectual Versus the City: From Thomas Jefferson to Frank Lloyd Wright* (Cambridge, Mass.: Harvard University Press, 1964); R. W. B. Lewis, *The American Adam* (Chicago: University of Chicago Press, 1955); Elizabeth Cummins Cogell, "The Middle Landscape Myth in Science Fiction," *Science Fiction Studies* 15 (July 1978): 134–42.

3. Clarke, *Voices*, 42, 88; Franklin, *War Stars*, 24, 46–47; Wagar, *Terminal Visions*, 121.

4. Homer Lea, *Valor of Ignorance, with Special Maps* (New York: Harper and Brothers, 1909). The most interesting feature is the detailed maps showing exactly where Lea thinks the Japanese might land, establish strong points, and make other military moves. Lea's book was an argument for a larger and stronger standing army and navy to support the new imperial and international role of the United States.

5. Jean Heffer, *United States and the Pacific: History of a Frontier* (Notre Dame, Ind.: University of Notre Dame Press, 2002), 184–89; Mike Davis, *The Ecology of Fear* (New York: Henry Holt, 1998) inventories many examples of yellow peril literature.

6. Philip K. Dick, *The Man in the High Castle* (New York: Vintage, 1992), 69, 44.

7. Boyer, *By the Bomb's Early Light*, is the best source on the range of American reactions to the early atomic age. Also see Franklin, *War Stars*, 157; Clarke, *Voices*, 167.

8. John Hersey, *Hiroshima* (New York: A. A. Knopf, 1946). Brians, *Nuclear Holocaust*, makes this point very well. Hersey's stylistic choices are analyzed in David Seed, "The Dawn of the Atomic Age," in David Seed, ed., *Imagining Apocalypse: Studies in Cultural Crisis* (New York: St. Martin's, 2000), 88–102. Science fiction writer C. L. Moore chose ironic detachment as the way to deal with the reality of nuclear war. Her 1946 story for *Astounding*, "The Vintage Season," imagines time travelers from the future visiting New York to watch its atomic destruction as a tourist attraction.

9. Wylie supposed that Los Angeles, San Francisco, Washington, Philadelphia, and New York were obliterated by H-bombs and that twenty-five smaller cities were hit with fission bombs. The book is dedicated to the Federal Civil Defense Administration and serves as a plea for strong civil defense preparations. Philip Wylie, *Tomorrow* (New York: Rinehart, 1954). Whitley Strieber and James Kunetka, *Warday, and the Journey Onwards* (New York: Holt, Rinehart and Winston, 1984).

10. Eugene Burdick and Harvey Wheeler, *Fail-safe* (New York: McGraw-Hill, 1962); Fletcher Knebel and Charles W. Bailey II, *Seven Days in May* (New York: Harper and Row, 1962). The movie versions had the misfortune of appearing in 1964, the year after *Dr. Strangelove*.

11. Madison Smartt Bell's *Waiting for the End of the World* (1985) is a more sophisticated variant that uses the atomic terrorism plot to explore the sociology and psychology of alienation.

12. Wagar, *Terminal Visions*, 11; Ketterer, *New Worlds for Old*.

13. My discussion deliberately excludes two types of postapocalypse stories in which cities scarcely figure at all, even offstage. One is the Adam and Eve story where a handful of survivors (maybe even just two!) have to decide whether to perpetuate the human race. This is the premise of *Five* (1951), a very early movie about life after the bomb, *The World, the Flesh, and the Devil* (1959), and *The Last Woman on Earth* (1960). In *End of August at the Ozone Hotel*, a 1966 film from Czechoslovakia, bands of women search for the last fertile male. Soldiers in *2019: After the Fall of New York* (1983) battle through the streets of the post-holocaust city to seize the last fertile woman. The Adam and Eve plot has been especially attractive to science fiction short story writers, who like the challenge of devising one more twist on the two-person plot.

The second story type is the "Mad Max" quest, in which one or a handful of survivors have to make their way through postnuclear dangers of nasty people and mutant beasts to find shelter, water, and other basics for survival. Examples of films include *Damnation Alley* (1974), *The Ravagers* (1979), *Stryker* (1983), *World Gone Wild* (1988), and *Badlands 2005* (1988)—and of course the original *Mad Max* (1979) and *The Road Warrior* (1981). The Mad Max quest is especially popular for low-budget films, since many minutes can be filled with motorcycle chases and long camera shots across desolate landscapes not too far from home base in Los Angeles. Some fictions combine both premises. In *Panic in the Year Zero* (1962) Ray Milland is a dad who helps his family through chaos after the bombing of Los Angeles. He changes from a typical suburbanite to a fierce survivalist and fights off such dangers as juvenile delinquents in a hot rod. *Hell Comes to Frogtown* (1987) sends one of the few remaining potent men to impregnate women in the wilderness, but he encounters dangerous mutants on the way. See Franklin, *War Stars*, 175–77.

For introductions to films about nuclear war and its aftermath, see Broderick, *Nuclear Movies*; Jack G. Shaheen, ed., *Nuclear War Films* (Carbondale: Southern Illinois University Press, 1978); and Wyn Wachhorst, "The Days After: Films on Nuclear Aftermath," in Carl B. Yoke, ed., *Phoenix from the Ashes: The Literature of the Remade World* (Westport, Conn.: Greenwood Press, 1987), 177–92.

14. The ravages of half-mad mobs of refugees from bombed cities is a subtheme in *Tomorrow* and another argument for better civil defense preparations. When writers bring survivors back to the city soon after the bomb, the depictions are vastly unrealistic. For example, the film *The World, the Flesh, and the Devil* (1959) uses the Adam and Eve plot to focus on three survivors of nuclear war who encounter each other in a New York where the dead and decaying bodies of eight million people seem to have evaporated without a trace. Vivian Sobchack, "Cities on the Edge of Time: The Urban Science Fiction Film," *East-West Film Journal* 1 (December 1988): 4–19, sees the unpeopled city as a major trope that expresses and repudiates the modern. We should also note the economics of production. It is cheaper to close off a few city streets on Sunday morning and set up a big fan to blow scraps of paper down the empty concrete canyons than to pay for elaborate sets and special effects depicting a ruined city.

15. Judith Merrill, *Shadow on the Hearth* (Garden City, N.Y.: Doubleday, 1950); Franklin, *War Stars*, 178.

16. Originally published separately, the story was included as one of the loosely linked stories that make up *The Martian Chronicles* (Garden City, N.Y.: Doubleday, 1950). The title comes from a poem by Sara Teasdale, written under the shadow of World War I.

17. Helen Clarkson, *The Last Day: A Novel of the Day after Tomorrow* (New York: Dodd, Mean, 1959). Helen Clarkson was a pseudonym for Helen McCloy, a successful writer of mystery and suspense fiction from the 1930s to the 1970s. Wagar, *Terminal Visions*, 186.

18. Pat Frank, *Alas, Babylon* (originally published 1959; New York: Harper Perennial Classics, 1999), 144. Pat Frank was the pseudonym of journalist Harry Hart, a successful journalist on foreign relations and military affairs who had written several previous novels. *Alas, Babylon*, appearing when Americans were worrying about a missile gap with the Soviet Union, was one of the best selling of the nuclear war novels. See C. W. Sullivan III, "*Alas Babylon* and *On the Beach*: Antiphons of the Apocalypse," in Yoke, *Phoenix*, 37–44.

19. Frank, *Alas, Babylon*, 162.

20. Paul Boyer's *When Time Shall be No More: Prophecy Belief in Modern American Culture* (Cambridge, Mass.: Harvard University Press, 1992) is an excellent introduction to this strand of American culture. Also see Edward James, "Rewriting the Christian Apocalypse as a Science-Fiction Event," in Seed, *Imagining Apocalypse*, 45–61.

21. *The Day After* is discussed in Charles E. Gannon, "Silo Psychosis: Diagnosing America's Nuclear Anxiety through Narrative Imagery," in Seed, *Imagining Apocalypse*, 104–107.

22. Sobchack, "Cities on the Edge of Time."

23. For a supplementary point of view, Eric Avila, in *Popular Culture in the Age of White Flight: Fear and Fantasy in Suburban Los Angeles* (Berkeley: University of California Press, 2004), argues that movies depicting the destruction of Los Angeles by mutant insects, Martians, and other such invaders were a means for expressing fear of racial difference.

24. Thomas Disch, in *The Dreams Our Stuff Is Made Of: How Science Fiction Conquered the World* (New York: Free Press, 1988), 83, points out that out of the first thirty novels cited by David Pringle, *Science Fiction: The 100 Best Novels*, seven are directly concerned with nuclear war and eight transpose the disaster to other forms via aliens, plagues, and the like. In the first category are Ray Bradbury, *The Martian Chronicles*, Bernard Wolfe, *Limbo*, Leigh Brackett, *The Long Tomorrow*, Alfred Bester, *The Stars My Destination*, Philip K. Dick, *Time out of Joint*, Pat Frank, *Alas, Babylon*, and Walter Miller, Jr., *A Canticle for Leibowitz*. In the second category are George Orwell, *1984*, George Stewart, *Earth Abides*, Robert Heinlein, *The Puppet Masters*, John Wyndham, *The Day of the Triffids*, Arthur C. Clarke, *Childhood's End*, Clifford Simak, *Ring around the Sun*, Edgar Pangborn, *Mirror for Observers*, and John Christopher, *The Death of Grass*.

25. Willy Ley, *The Conquest of Space* (New York: Viking Press, 1949).

26. Brace quoted in Charles Glaab, *The American City: A Documentary History* (Homewood, Ill.: Dorsey Press, 1963), 329; Ignatius Donnelly, *Caesar's Column: A Story of the Twentieth Century* (Chicago: F. O. Schulte, 1890); Nathaniel West, *The Day of the Locust* (New York: Random House, 1939). For more general fears of disorder, see Frederick C. Jaher, *Doubters and Dissenters: Cataclysmic Thought in America, 1885–1918* (Glencoe, Ill.: Free Press, 1964).

27. Larry Niven and Jerry Pournelle, *Lucifer's Hammer* (New York: Putnam, 1977); Chelsea Quinn Yarbro, *False Dawn* (Garden City, N.Y.: Doubleday, 1978).

28. Stephen King, *The Stand* (Garden City, N.Y.: Doubleday, 1978). References will be cited parenthetically in the text. The novel draws on King's short story "Night Surf," which also describes the survivors of a catastrophic virus. Set in New Hampshire, the story covers only one day. Its teenage protagonists share more with the children in William Golding's *Lord of the Flies* than with the more complexly realized and hopeful characters of *The Stand*. That story is found in King, *Night Shift* (Garden City, N.Y.: Doubleday, 1978).

29. *A Canticle for Leibowitz* consists of three novellas set roughly 600, 1,200, and 1,800 years after the first nuclear war. The rise of the Texarkanan Empire is found in the middle novella, "Fiat Lux." In 1939, Stanley Weinbaum's novella "Dawn of Flame" posited a similar sort of postcollapse America in which competing city-states battle to control the Mississippi Valley. There is a neo–New Orleans, the Ozarky, and Salui (Saint Louis), and a big battle at Starved Rock on the Illinois River. See Edgar L. Chapman, "Weinbaum's Fire from the Ashes: The Post-Disaster Civilization of *The Black Flame*," in Yoke, *Phoenix*, 85–96.

30. Leigh Bracket, *The Long Tomorrow* (Garden City, N.Y.: Doubleday, 1955), 14. Brackett was a successful screenwriter as well as novelist, working on such movies as *The Big Sleep*, *Rio Bravo*, and *The Empire Strikes Back*. Also see Diana Parkin-Sper, "Leigh Brackett's *The Long Tomorrow*: A Quest for the Future America," *Extrapolation* 26 (Summer 1985), and Donna M. DeBlasio, "Future Imperfect: Leigh Brackett's *The Long Tomorrow*," in Yoke, *Phoenix*, 97–103.

31. "The New Adam and Eve" was written in 1843 and included in *Mosses from an Old Manse* (1846). I retrieved the text from http://www.eldritchpress.org/nh/newae.html (accessed September 25, 2014).

32. The novel was republished as *Daybreak–2250 A.D.* and also paired with *No Night without Stars* as *Darkness and Dawn* (New York: Baen Books, 2003). Page references are to this latter edition. Alice Mary Norton, writing as Andre Norton, produced seventy-five

to eighty science fiction and fantasy novels, for both children and adults from the 1940s to the 1990s. She also wrote several World War II adventure books with teenaged heroes. *Star Man's Son* was written for the juvenile/teenage market, as is clear from the vocabulary, which sticks close to the word choices with the fewest syllables.

33. Norton, *Daybreak*, 6–7.

34. Ibid., 38.

35. Ibid., 132.

36. Kim Stanley Robinson, *The Wild Shore* (New York: Berkley, 1984).

37. The story was originally published in 1969. Page citations are to Terry Dowling, ed., *The Essential Ellison* (Omaha: Nemo Press, 1987), 927, 938.

38. In the decade or so after 1945, a number of city planners advocated planned decentralization of urban areas as a civil defense measure, in effect making suburbanization patriotic.

39. Susan Sontag, "The Imagination of Disaster," *Commentary* (October 1965): 42–48.

40. Martha Bartter, "Nuclear Holocaust as Urban Renewal," *Science Fiction Studies* 13 (July 1986): 148–58.

41. There is also a practical consideration. American postdisaster fiction can focus on the small town and countryside because North America is so big. Even a narrow peninsula such as Florida has room for new beginnings, not to mention the great central plains and western mountains. In contrast, Charles Gannon argues, nuclear war scenarios in physically constructed Britain tend to linger on the details of the devastated city because there is no practical place of refuge. Gannon, "Silo Psychosis," 107–109. Indeed, some classic British versions of the big catastrophe, such as John Wyndham's *The Day of the Triffids*, seem to focus on making do and muddling through.

PART III

Planetary Pioneering

A mélange of settlers from ten different human worlds in the Colonial Union have signed up to colonize a new earthlike planet on the dangerous edge of human-alien space in John Scalzi's *The Last Colony* (2007). Their transport delivers them across the vast interstellar void and lands them safely . . . on the wrong planet. They are pawns in a clandestine government conspiracy to steal the jump on the enemy by planting a colony whose location is secret even to the colonists. Left on their own, the settlers buckle down to build a fortified town that they name Croatan (they thought they were headed for a world named Roanoke). They lay out streets at right angles, throw up housing and workspaces, and build a wall by stacking empty shipping containers. It's a good thing that they have imitated a Roman legionary camp, for predatory werewolf things lurk outside—and that's just the start of trouble.

Scalzi has imaged planetary colonization that starts with a guarded camp that quickly grows into a fortified town with farm lands stretching outside the protected perimeter. Croatan looks a lot like Detroit in 1763—a frontier town with a few hundred people living on narrow right-angled streets inside a wall that was strong enough to resist attack by the forces of the Ottawa war leader Pontiac in 1763. Or maybe it resembles the fortified Russian colony of New Archangel (now Sitka) on the island coast of Alaska, where fierce Tlingit warriors drove the newcomers out once and kept the second effort to build a prosperous trading town pretty well pent up for several decades.

In a different fictional future depicted in Allen M. Steele, *Coyote: A Novel of Interstellar Exploration* (2002), refugees from a neo-fascist United States steal a starship meant for the first colonization beyond the solar system and divert it to their own secret destination. They name the massive moon that they take as their new home Coyote and their first settlement Liberty. They struggle to get crops in for survival, learn the weather, cope with food shortages, and deal with the nasty surprise of large, fast predators that look like a cross between an emu and a velociraptor. Twenty people at a time hold house-raising parties to construct one-room log cabins, followed by a grange hall, and a semilegal cantina that is operating on the edge of town within months. By the spring of the second long year, colonists have begun to learn the local ecology and are on the way to building a self-sufficient settlement.

The models here are frontier farm villages that once ringed the periphery of North America. Puritans in New England, French settlers along the Saint

Lawrence, and Spanish settlers on the northern frontier of Mexico laid out variations on the theme. Early New England grew when the colony granted a tract of new land to a group of settlers, who built a cluster of houses and divided the surrounding lands into farm plots and pastures—the whole constituting a "town." Maps and sketches of Los Angeles at the time of American takeover show a clearly defined center around an irregular plaza with church and some two-level buildings, but the rest of the settlement sprawled out to the south and east along irrigation canals and most residents made their living as farmers. Early San Antonio was the focus for a string of five missions along a twelve-mile stretch of the San Antonio River and residence for farmers who fed the missions and military garrison. In the 1740s, despite dangers from raiding Apaches, who forced farmers to venture out to their fields only in groups, the town continued to grow.

These examples suggest how easy it is for science fiction writers to reproduce the North American frontier on new planets. The stories through which we understand the western history are near at hand for framing visions of the future. Science fiction is filled with intrepid Lewis-and-Clarks, grizzled mountain men, hard rock miners fighting grasping corporations, and planetary engineers building the equivalent of future railroads. We view and read about the extraterrestrial equivalents of Boone's Station and Spanish-era Los Angeles, Texas piney woods and Kansas prairies, Butte and Virginia City.

In the short-lived television series *Firefly* and spinoff feature film *Serenity*, producer Joss Whedon mobilized the full panoply of clichés from film and paperback westerns in a science fiction setting. Some critics groaned at the resulting "six-gun sci fi," while others enjoyed the new take on old settings and tropes. Canceled after eleven episodes aired in 2002–2003, the show and film quickly developed a devoted fan following and, soon enough, an already impressive array of academic comment. Fun as it may be, however, the show also reveals some of the limits on what counts as what we might call the History Channel version of western history.

The following chapter looks in greater depth at homesteading on the high frontier. The experiences of homesteading, with its challenges of loneliness and landscape, have been one of the most fruitful sources of realistic western fiction for nearly a century and a half. Science fiction writers have responded to the actual homesteading experience and to these previous novelists and storytellers and to the national myth of covered wagons and madonnas of the prairie. They take it at face value, they explore the challenges of hostile planetscapes, they invert and question the homesteading myth, and they sometimes invent new stories to tell about taking up the land.

This excursion through imagined frontiers concludes with the work of Kim Stanley Robinson, one of the most creative figures in the world of science fiction. In framing one sequence of novels about the future of California and a second trilogy about the settlement of Mars, he has worked in explicitly historical terms. Both sets of books challenge traditional frontier narratives and incorporate themes and issues that characterized the new concerns of the "new western history" of the 1980s and 1990s. The Mars trilogy in particular explores the limits of individual heroism, the processes of community formation and "frontier democracy," the failure of frontiers as "safety valves," and the tension between advocates of environmental protection (Martian "reds") and advocates of resource development (Martian "greens"). New Martians repeatedly try to break free of the past on their new frontier and find each time that they are enmeshed ever more completely in the webs of history.

CHAPTER 9

Firefly, *Westerns, and the American West*

Zoe Washburne is first mate on the "Firefly" class starship *Serenity* as it hauls legitimate and illegitimate cargoes among the outer planets, crisscrossing a semi-independent border zone bounded by a powerful Alliance on one side and savage, cannibalistic Reavers on the other. A veteran of a failed war against the expansion of the Alliance, Zoe may be number two in command, but she's second in toughness to absolutely nobody on or off the ship. Strapped to her right thigh is a sawed off rifle that replicates the cut down Winchester 73 carried by Steve McQueen in the classic television series *Wanted: Dead or Alive* (1958–61).[1]

Zoe's weapon is one small detail among hundreds that gave the short-lived television series *Firefly* (2002) and the related theatrical movie *Serenity* (2006) the look and feel of an American western even though set at the start of the twenty-sixth century. The United States and China, as the dominant economies and cultures in the twenty-first century, have long since blended into a single society (characters toss Mandarin phrases into their English and eat with chopsticks as well as forks). After damaging and outgrowing Earth-That-Was, humankind has expanded outward and adapted new moons and planets for human use. There are now four sociopolitical rings around the original Earth. The Alliance coordinates and rules the older, richer worlds and has recently fought a bitter five-year War of Unification to win control and incorporate less developed worlds outside the Alliance core. Beyond the new political frontier are hardscrabble rim words that still maintain tenuous independence. Out in the wilds far from all civilization hover the Reavers, utterly depraved ship-bound pirates who are ten times worse than the bad guys in *Mad Max*.[2] Navigating the fringe in search of work and cargos, *Serenity* is a tramp freighter with four oddly assorted passengers and a crew of five.[3]

Creator, writer, and executive producer Joss Whedon made fourteen one-hour episodes of *Firefly*, with only eleven airing before the Fox network pulled the plug.[4] Fan anger and enthusiasm provided the impetus for pitching the feature film *Serenity*, which put the same characters and actors into a single movie that served as both a prequel and sequel to the TV episodes. In some circles, the "Firefly effect" now refers to the reluctance of viewers to get too involved with quirky or unusual television programs because they expect that anything innovative will get the quick hook. Enthusiastic fans continue to dress up as Browncoats, imitating the informal uniform of the rebels, flock to conventions and film revivals, and buy spinoff comics and graphic novels that fill narrative gaps between the television shows and movie.

Which Genre?

Whedon (fig. 9.1) has rather proudly described the film as consisting of "bits of genre mashed up" and as "a science fiction western noir action suspense drama."[5] It is the first two that dominate from the credits of both TV show and film. Long before we have seen Zoe's sidearm, the opening credits for *Firefly* set the tone. Bluesman Sonny Rhodes sings the "Ballad of Serenity" over twangy guitar, fiddle, and banjo as *Serenity* powers through space, as the actors are introduced, and, finally, as the ship sweeps low in the atmosphere over a herd of galloping horses. The title and the instrumentation take us back to Appalachian roots and country and western sounds. Each of five short stanzas with simple AABB rhyme scheme ends with the same assertive phrase: "You can't take the sky from me."

For an interstellar spaceship, "sky" represents the freedom of the vast galaxy, but given the music and the opening scene, it also evokes the vast, overarching skies of western North America—the Big Sky country of Montana, A. B. Guth-

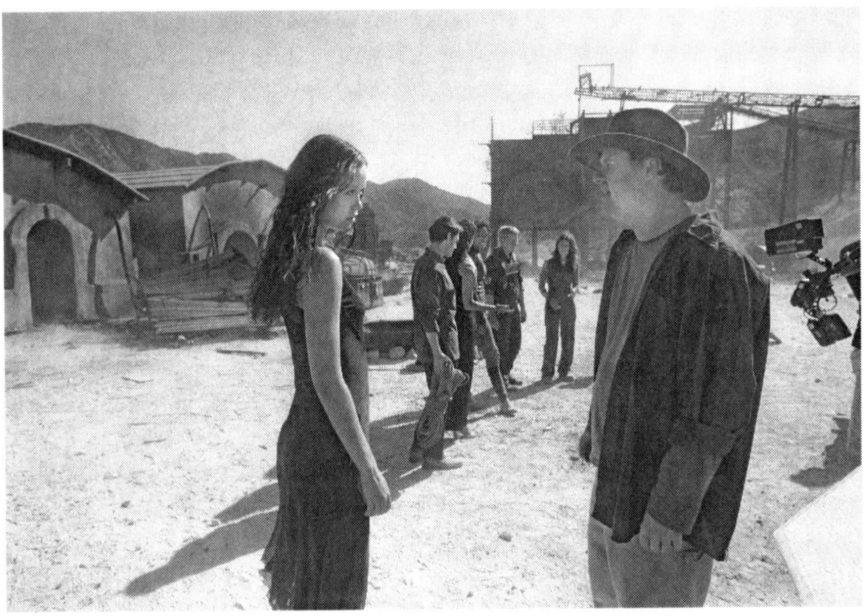

FIG. 9.1. Joss Whedon on location for *Serenity*. Director Joss Whedon and actress Summer Glau at a typical location in which different parts of southern California stood in for a wide range of worlds in both the film *Serenity* and television series *Firefly*. (Courtesy Universal/Photofest, Inc. © Universal Pictures)

rie, Jr.'s, novel *The Big Sky* (1947) about mountain men and fur trappers, the 1952 Kirk Douglas movie made from Guthrie's novel, and many more examples. Anyone who travels from the humid East to the arid West notices changes in the air—greater brightness, clarity, and resulting openness of vision. Texan Larry McMurtry has commented that he took for granted "space, a huge sky, and a sense of distance" until he moved east and that "the sky and the sun" are fundamental to the western experience.[6] Ross Calvin titled his meditation on the character of the Southwest *Sky Determines*. "The emotional and aesthetic effect of the sky is no less real than the practical one," he wrote in 1934. "Here one sees it all—180 glorious, colorful degrees of it. In any direction save downwards, it fills the larger part of the view and the eye cannot lift without being aware of its magnificence." Eight hundred miles farther west, Alison Lurie took sky and light as the symbol of the intrusive newness of Los Angeles, where the California sun shines with "impartial brilliance" on the transplanted New Englanders in *The Nowhere City*. The central character stands on his front walk and looks up at the "intense blue overhead, crossed by the trails of jet vapor, dimming to a white haze at the horizon."[7]

The sound palate from the opening continues to accompany *Serenity* in space like a leitmotif. Views of the ship in space are accompanied by the "recurrence of a solo fiddle player, sometimes accompanied by guitar, playing folk-like or bluesy figures." Inside, gun-for-hire Jayne Cobb sometimes takes out his guitar to pass the time. At episode's end, this ship does not whoosh away to martial march-time music like the starship *Enterprise* in *Star Trek*. Instead we get white letter credits on a black screen to the same instrumental mix as in the opening. The thin, nostalgic sound, says Whedon, was intended to highlight "the sparseness of their environment and the teeniness of them."[8]

Serenity's crew members dress the part of the recycled western (when they're not showing the East Asia influences that are also part of the series backstory). Costume designer Shawna Trpcic has summarized the influence periods for the show's look as "World War Two [for the Alliance] and the Old West, 1876 and the American Civil War, 1861, mixed in with 1861 samurai Japan." Simon Tam, the physician who books passage on *Serenity* for himself and his sister River as they try to escape the Alliance, dresses in white shirt and vest like Doc Adams in *Gunsmoke*. Captain Malcolm Reynolds, the central figure among the hodge-podge of *Serenity* crew and passengers, wears a long coat "steeped in the traditions of Western, Victorian and Civil War garments." Made from leather, it evokes buckskin jackets and the long dusters worn by characters in western films like *Once Upon a Time in the West* (1968).[9]

Props have the Old West look with a touch of steampunk. Mechanic Kaylee Frye, the hands-on genius who keeps *Serenity* going, toils in an engine room that might belong in a Joseph Conrad novel. Not for her are the sleek, shiny consoles with blinking lights by which Montgomery Scott and Geordi La Forge monitor mysterious dilithium crystals in *Star Trek* and *Star Trek: The Next Generation*.

Captain Mal Reynolds carries a functional slug-throwing firearm built around a small, modern revolver. Prop master Randy Erickson "did a lot of research on Civil War revolvers," adding modernistic touches but ending with a piece that resembled an old Colt single action that might have belonged to either H. G. Wells's time traveler or a western movie hero. Jayne Cobb carries a Bowie knife and an adaption of a Civil War Le Mat cavalry revolver.[10] The whole design scheme, says Erickson, "was very much influenced by the American Civil War, especially the hand guns and the rifle. It wasn't very 'spacey,' we made the choice between Buck Rogers and the Old West, and this is like the Old West, with some sort of technological twist in there."[11]

And there are the new worlds. Neither *Firefly* nor *Serenity* enjoyed the luxury of a high budget. Whedon decided to give the spaceship *Serenity* a complement of nine crew members and passengers in order to build in enough different personalities and conflicts among the regular cast to allow him to avoid the need to pay expensive guest stars for every television episode.[12] The film cost roughly $40 million rather than the more usual $100 million for a science fiction movie with high production values. Out of the necessity of shooting budgets, the several worlds on which *Serenity* lands for adventuresome episodes look just like the southern California version of Earth. The inhabitants are all humans, like the varied peoples of North America—no aliens and their expensive makeup requirements and special effects.[13]

In highlighting western settings, Whedon fixed his stories in a century-long science fiction tradition that began in the 1910s, when Edgar Rice Burroughs magically transported westerner John Carter from Arizona to Mars for a series of adventure stories beginning with *A Princess of Mars* in 1912. Because many new planets in addition to Mars are imagined as places of grand vistas and wide open spaces, the landscape of the West has continued to provide an easy model for writers and for readers who have come to expect new worlds to look a lot like Death Valley or Arizona or maybe the Dakotas.[14] When Chesley Bonestell painted vast, colorful, and detailed moonscapes and planetscapes for *Colliers* and other mass market magazines in the 1940s and 1950s, he worked in the tradition of western landscape painters like Thomas Moran and Albert Bierstadt, and many cover artists for science fiction magazines adapted the same imagery.[15] Bonestell turned to space art after a career as a Hollywood artist, and the classic movies *When Worlds Collide* (1951) and *Forbidden Planet* (1956) featured the same southwestern locations that so conveniently served western film producers. *Star Trek* beamed Captain Kirk, Mr. Spock, and Dr. McCoy down to dozens of planets that look exactly like Griffith Park in Los Angeles.

So *Firefly* sounds like a western, it sometimes looks like a western . . . and it also moves like a western, offering stories driven by many of the common tropes that pervade the genre.[16] The first episode to air—"The Train Job"—opens with a barroom brawl that starts inside the saloon, erupts through its doors onto a dusty small town street, and ends with the good guys rescued by their friends (who arrive in *Serenity*, instead of with some extra horses). The episode continues with a train robbery, a hardscrabble western-style mining town, and a crusty small town sheriff who carries a rifle in his final, thankfully peaceful encounter with Mal.

If "The Train Job" hits us over the head, the original pilot slides "westernness" in more slowly. Also titled "Serenity" and aired out of sequence, it starts with the backstory of Mal and Zoe in the War of Unification, forwards six years to introduce *Serenity* and its crew exploring a derelict ship in space, and then takes us to the dusty streets of a down-market spaceport where Mal picks up another cargo and passengers who round out the set of characters. Only in the closing minutes do Mal, Zoe, and Jayne land on the planet Whitefall, whose sagebrush hills look exactly like the fringes of Los Angeles County. He is there to make a deal with Patience, the weather-beaten matriarch and boss of the planet who appears at the rendezvous on horseback with a wide-brimmed slouch hat and shotgun on her saddle. She is like Barbara Stanwyck's character from *The Big Valley* (1965–69) with a nasty, cheating streak. The meeting ends in a shoot-out with Patience's henchmen toppled from their mounts and Patience herself pinned under her fallen horse. The effect is a few minutes of 1940s B-western that we have reached by spaceship and leave by the same, just in time for a chase scene with a vicious Reaver ship trailing *Serenity* through Whitehall's atmosphere.

The shoot-out between good guys and crooks is a venerable western trope (one of Patience's men even wears a black hat).[17] So is the cattle drive . . . which spans episodes "Shindig" and "Safe" (fig. 9.2). In the first episode, Mal makes a deal with a mildly shady businessman on the prosperous world Persephone to transport a herd of cattle off planet. Viewers are clued in on the nature of the "exciting new crime" only in "Shindig's" final seconds. The camera pulls back from a close-up of Mal Reynolds and his on-again, off-again love interest, Inara Serra, in tender conversation to show lowing cattle in the cargo hold under the walkway where they are sitting. As the follow-up episode opens the crew are unloading their cargo on the planet Jiangxi, with all the hassles of moving unhappy steers toward a makeshift corral and avoiding cow shit.

The cattle drive is one among many of the stock figures and situations that *Firefly* writers pulled from the western memory bank. The crew pull a bank robbery in "Trash" and have to fight off a nasty bounty hunter in "Objects in Space." Jiangxi proves to have a "General Supply" store featuring feed, branding irons, and horseshoes, along with disreputable cattle buyers who are wanted for murder. The payroll robbery in *Serenity* takes place in a general store that was designed to feel "western but not too western."[18]

"Our Mrs. Reynolds" opens with a team of horses pulling a "covered wagon" with a pioneer family (actually it is a barge on steel-barrel pontoons being towed up a shallow river). Bandits surround the wagon and demand its contents, only to be cut down when (surprise!) the family turn out to be Mal and his crack-shot crew. The second long action sequence in the film *Serenity* includes a long chase

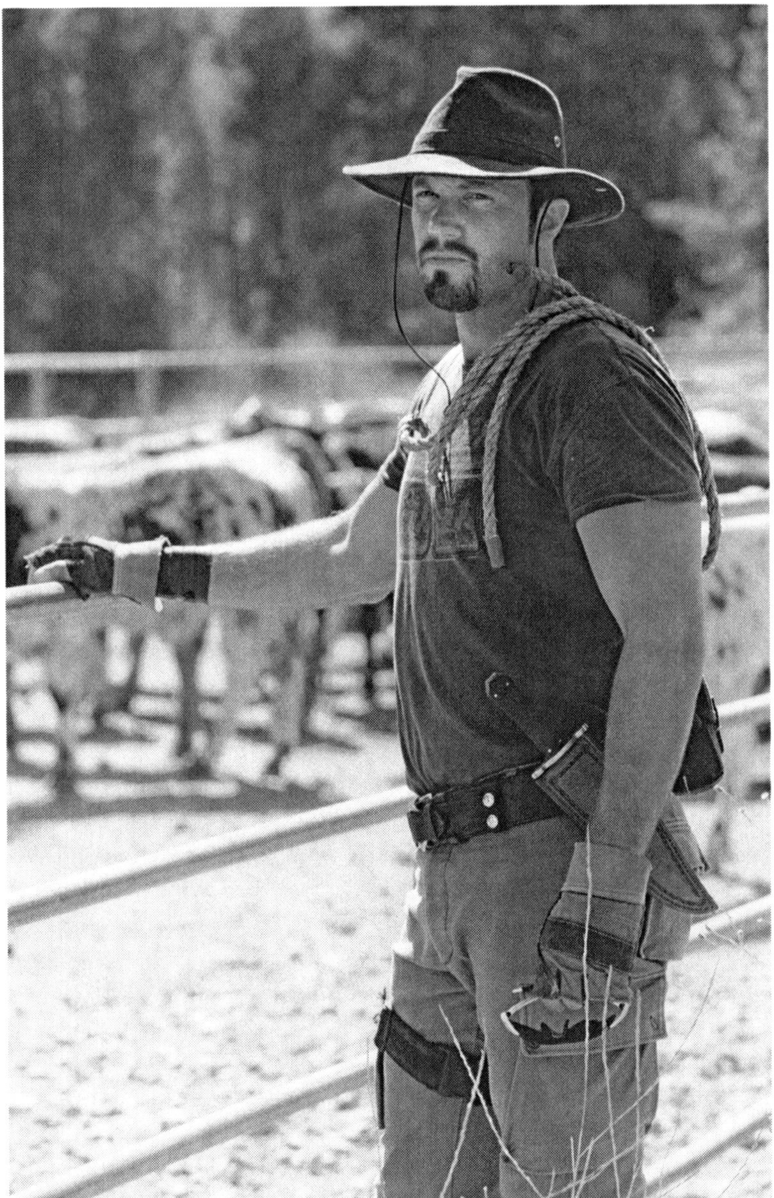

FIG. 9.2. Transplanetary cattle drive. *Serenity* crew member Jayne Cobb (Adam Baldwin) and a herd of cattle that the ship has just transported from one world to another as part of a semi-licit interplanetary deal. (Courtesy Fox/Photofest, Inc. © Fox)

screen with savage Reavers and fleeing good guys in hovercraft skimming and darting over a desert landscape. Later in the film, a Reaver fleet appears suddenly out of an "ion cloud" to surprise Alliance ships "like Indians riding over the hill to surprise the cavalry."[19]

Perhaps the most western of the television episodes is the never-aired "Heart of Gold." The *Serenity* crew detour to a dry, dusty world to defend a bordello run by one of Inara's friends against an aggrieved customer who is the boss of the nearby town. The brothel stands alone in the desert (although covered with silver space blankets to give it a futuristic look).[20] The bad guy, Ranse Burgess shows up to threaten the women on a hover scooter accompanied by horse-mounted henchmen (a bit like the mixture of horses and Jeep in the Roy Rogers television shows). He has enough money to build a real town, says Inara's friend, but he "wants to play cowboy." Burgess whips up a mob while standing on a balcony looking down at a classic western main street. The attackers arrive on horseback (and hovercraft) while the women and the crew fight back with nineteenth-century rifles from the barricaded whorehouse windows. A Joshua tree shows briefly against the skyline halfway through.

In the mid-1960s, Gene Roddenberry famously (and inaccurately) pitched *Star Trek* to network executives as *Wagon Train* to the stars. Joss Whedon goes one better, citing the classic film *Stagecoach* (1939) as an inspiration and model. Like the earlier film that made John Wayne a star, *Firefly* follows a set of mismatched individuals making their way in a single "vehicle" across empty but dangerous space with landings at worlds that function like the stagecoach's stops at isolated Dry Fork, Apache Wells, and Lee's Ferry (fig 9.3). Whedon is a third-generation screenwriter, whose grandfather (*The Donna Reed Show*) and father (*Captain Kangaroo, The Electric Company*) had successful careers writing for television, so it is no surprise that earlier movies and television frame his creative ideas. One key character, Inara Serra, was originally conceived as "something very *Deadwood*," referring to the 2004–2006 television series. "What it [Firefly] set out to be," he says, "was a mixture of genres, a *Stagecoach* kind of drama with a lot of people trying to figure out their lives in a bleak and pioneer environment. . . . [Fox] wanted gunplay aplenty and it was both a rhythmic and something of a moral adjustment to go, 'Okay, we're going to do a little more *Wild Bunch* than *Stagecoach*.'"[21]

Firefly and *Serenity* thus exist in an intertextual world. It is no surprise when others involved with the series, such as actor Adam Baldwin, who plays the mercenary Jayne Cobb [whose name may come from *J*ohn W*ayne*], draws on the same approach. "Well, *Firefly* is a Western," he has said, "and I grew up watching Westerns like *The Magnificent Seven, The Wild Bunch, Once Upon a Time in the West, The Good, the Bad, and the Ugly* . . . movies like that."[22] Critical commentary, most of it by people from the television/movie industry, media studies, and literature, highlights this closed world in which texts are validated by reference

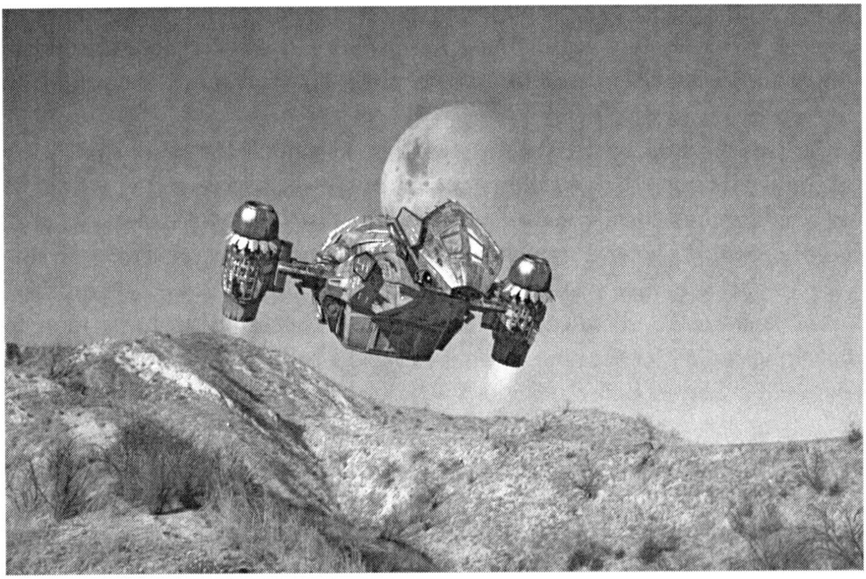

FIG. 9.3. *Serenity* over "western" landscape. Like the eponymous vehicle in *Stagecoach*, the space cargo ship *Serenity* carries a mixed set of passengers and crew across desert landscapes—on multiple planets. (Courtesy Universal/Photofest, Inc. © Universal Pictures)

to other texts. For example, novelist and literature professor Evelyn Vaughn puts her essay on the Civil War references in *Firefly* in dialogue with previous literature and not with actual history. She tries, but her heart is with Margaret Mitchell when she cites Rhett Butler as an authority on Confederate war industry, implicitly validating his historically inaccurate comment that the South had no cannon factory (Rhett, with his gun-running acumen, would have known about the very real Tredegar Iron Works in Richmond).[23]

In this intertextual universe, several *Stagecoach* characters transcribe straightforwardly onto the *Firefly* ensemble, although in ways that make them more powerful and appealing. The prostitute with a heart of gold from 1939 becomes Inara Serra, who has substantial wealth, self-possession, and high social status as a Companion. The alcoholic doctor in the stagecoach becomes Simon Tam, a very competent and morally upright physician who will sacrifice all to save his younger sister from the clutches of the Alliance. "Reverend" Doc Peacock, the whiskey salesman, transmogrifies into the genuine cleric Shepherd Book. Pilot Hoban Washburne, who can fly anything, is the most laid-back crew member, but he is no comic relief like stagecoach driver Andy Devine. Stoic captain Mal Reynolds (who turns out to have grown up on a ranch before he took up spacefaring!!) is the Ringo Kid (John Wayne) with more mature responsibilities. *Firefly* subtracts the gambler, the banker, and the pregnant cavalry wife and adds, much more interestingly, three strong women: Zoe the fighter, Kaylee the mechanical genius, and River Tam, a Buffy-like teenager with special powers who can kick ass.[24]

The creative team explicitly imagined "Heart of Gold" in relation to western movies. Writer Brett Matthews says that it was "the stock, Western-heavy episode we had always talked about doing—the crew of Serenity as *The Magnificent Seven/Seven Samurai*," as they come to the aid of a small, relatively defenseless community. Whedon's movie reference went back again to John Wayne: "Heart of Gold really was, let's do a Western, let's do Rio Bravo, let's do the siege . . . and get ouselves into a kind of classic Western scenario."[25]

Western clones have a bad reputation in science fiction, dating to the 1930s, 1940s, and 1950s, when magazine editors John W. Campbell and Horace Gold worked to define science fiction as distinct from other pulp magazine genres like true crime, detective, and cowboy stories.[26] And, indeed, Campbell and Gold were generally right, for that particular genre combination has usually been unsatisfactory. The *Firefly* narrative, to its great credit, is more complex than a number of science fiction novels that recycle single-narrative tropes from the western bookshelf. John Jakes, best known as the author of historical novels about the movement westward from the Appalachians, imagined a galactic bureaucrat forced to cope with a future super-Texas in *Six Gun Planet* (1970). In effect, the protagonist is a version of the tenderfoot or outsider, who comes west and learns to stand up to the local toughs and bad guys. In John Boyd's *The Andromeda Gun* (1974), an alien finds itself uneasily coinhabiting the brain of a nineteenth-century gunslinger. Another direct and satirical transplantation of the Old West is H. Beam Piper and John J. McGuire, *Lone Star Planet* (1959), in which the residents of New Texas herd mammoth cattle with helicopters and feel free to shoot meddling galactic bureaucrats.[27]

Star Bridge (1955), by James E. Gunn and Jack Williamson—each a very important figure in both science fiction writing and criticism—opens with scenery and action straight from the dustiest of western novels and movies. The hero is Alan Horn, a name that would fit any cowboy. A gun for hire, he is fleeing pursuers across the plains of North America on his way to Sunport, where the vastly powerful Tubes short-circuit Einsteinian relativity and connect Earth to the capital of the oppressive Eron empire. In the first two pages, the "tired buckskin pony" drinks at a spring behind a "looming mesa." A buzzard circles on the wind. There is a canteen on the saddle horn, dust stirred from the horse's hooves and caked on its lathered sides, a "heavy unitron pistol" slung under Horn's shoulder. His "hard, grey eyes" search "the hot, cloudless sky." "We've lost them, boy" he whispers as he pats the tired flank of his mount (the hope is too good to be true, of course). For another sixty-five pages, until Horn takes a wild Tube-ride to Eron and lands in the midst of a galactic revolution, the setting remains southwestern—reddened desert sun, canyons, cliffs, campfires, boot marks, and jackrabbit tracks in the red dust.[28]

To return to Whedon's comments about genre mixing, the 2006 movie supplements *Stagecoach* and *Outlaw Josey Wales* references with considerably more traditional science fiction film action and explicit allusions to other science fiction films. *Serenity* spends more of its time in space than in most of the TV episodes as a little ship fighting and dodging among bigger Reaver pirate ships and Alliance warships like the *Millennium Falcon* in *Star Wars*. The great science fiction film *Forbidden Planet* (1956), which translated *The Tempest* into space, provides specific referents: The name of the planet Miranda, where the Alliance carries out a fatal experiment with mind-modification, is a direct allusion. The repressed "monster from the Id" of the earlier film becomes River Tam's knowledge about events on Miranda, which the Alliance is trying to conceal. When the *Serenity* crew visit Miranda to discover that its entire population is dead, we see a wrecked ship with identification number C57D, the same as on the rescue ship in *Forbidden Planet*.[29]

Joss Whedon and Western History

Josh Randall, the gun-toting character played by Steve McQueen in *Wanted: Dead or Alive*, is a veteran of the Confederate army who has headed west to make a new beginning after southern defeat. Zoe Washburne and Mal Reynolds are both veterans of the War for Unification—also on the losing side. Reynolds has named his ship to remember the Battle of Serenity Valley, where the war was lost. And Joss Whedon has credited Michael Shaara's novel *The Killer Angels*, about the Battle of Gettysburg, as initial inspiration for *Firefly*.[30]

There were, to be sure, plenty of former Civil War soldiers who headed west, and Texas was itself part of the Confederacy, but that history has also colonized western fiction, where it has a mutated life of its own. The defeated and sometimes disillusioned Confederate who seeks freedom, redemption, and a new start in the wide open West (or wide open South Florida if you're E. J. Watson) is a standard western plot premise. Many of Hollywood's leading men played the part in the 1950s and 1960s: John Wayne (*The Searchers*, 1956), Alan Ladd (*Big Land*, 1957), Victor Mature (*Escort West*, 1958), Rock Hudson (*The Undefeated*, 1969), and Clint Eastwood (*The Outlaw Josey Wales*, 1976) . . . plus the less probable George Segal (*Invitation to a Gunfighter*, 1964) and Joseph Cotton (*Hellbenders*, 1967).

It was one thing to merge John Wayne heroism and the Lost Cause in the 1950s, when Americans still believed *Gone with the Wind* (well, maybe they still do, but not if they pay attention to their college textbooks). It is another to do so in the twenty-first century, hence Whedon's very explicit attempt to dissociate Reynolds from the taint of slaveholding. The TV series depicts slavery as a labor system that quietly functions on the fringes of the Alliance sphere rather than a basic element of economy of the outer planets. In "Shindig," some pool players tell Mal that, basically, they have been running slaves to "border planets." Mal later picks one of the guy's pocket, noting ironically that "they earned that with the sweat of their slave-trading brows." Left a bit vague is whether these "border planets" are now part of Alliance space, incorporated after the war. Are the conscripted workers being supervised by Alliance officials and corporations, or do they also find themselves toiling on still independent planets? It is clear, however, that upper-class society on the "Shindig" planet is complicit with slavery. When snobbish upper-class belles make fun of the hoop-skirted dress that the usually grease-streaked Kaylee acquires for a grand ball, one of the more gallant of the "southern gentlemen" rebukes the high-fashion ladies by referring to the number of slaves it must have taken to dress them so elegantly.[31]

Whedon thus distances the *Serenity* folks from slavery. Instead of defending the right of slavery to expand into new territories—the basic cause of the real Civil War—the Browncoats can be depicted as battling for something akin to states' rights (that is, planetary rights) and individual freedom, a purpose that matches the revised myth of the Lost Cause.[32] From a historian's point of view, however, what is interesting is not just that there were many antislavery southerners but that there were many sorts. So what sort of "antislavery southerner" is Mal Reynolds? Is he similar to the pro-Union yeoman farmers of East Tennessee? Does he resemble a pro-Union North Carolinian enmeshed in local economic and political battles? Is he like a Richmond or Nashville businessman who saw more profits from a free labor market than from one limited on one side by slavery? Is he, more likely, a Louisiana/Texas cattle drover caught between capitalist cotton plantations on one side and Kiowa and Comanche warriors on the other? In this case, we don't have enough backstory to know—also in keeping with the common presentation of the western hero as a man with no past.

In the new era that follows the War of Unification, the Alliance serves as the equivalent of the expanding national state of the later nineteenth and early twentieth centuries. Whedon says the Alliance is not to be taken as all bad (despite the unfortunate recycling of *Starship Troopers* uniforms for the film). "It's not really an evil empire," he has told an interviewer. "The trick was always to create something that was complex enough that you could bring some debate to it. . . . The messiest thing is that the government is basically benign."[33] Viewers will note that the very sympathetic character Shepherd Book has an ID card that gets him VIP treatment when he arrives seriously hurt at an Alliance base in "Safe." Inara states explicitly in "Out of Gas" that she supported unification and she continues to operate quite smoothly in the Alliance world. Jayne sat out the war. Simon and River are both products of the Alliance, although in flight after Alliance authorities have meddled with River's mind.

The intentions of the Alliance, like those of most national states, are peace and order. It formed as "a kind of utopia in which America and China . . . combined their technologies to get everyone off the depleted Earth." The Central Planets of the Alliance, Whedon wrote in a backstory memo, "worked in basic harmony with each other, and the Alliance Parliament ruled with fairness and intelligence."[34] The problem, as with all utopias, is that leaders fall prey to their sense of righteousness. The short-lived television series did not have enough time and narrative space to explore the upside of the Alliance. The movie required a structuring conflict and villain, a function that the Alliance fills. It has inadvertently committed genocide on the planet Miranda and is pursing River Tam because knowledge of the disaster is buried in her mind. *Serenity*, sheltering River, is caught between Reavers on one side and an implacable Alliance Operative who will stop at nothing to retrieve River. The Alliance, in other words, comes off a lot worse on screen than in Whedon's conception.

In reality, "refugee Confederates" in the late nineteenth-century United States more often than not were agents of the expanding state that they had earlier resisted. The postbellum cattle trade that looms so large in American mythology fed and supported railroad expansion that linked the western territories and states into the industrial economy of the Northeast. This was true for Edgar Watson in Florida and for the Texas cowboys who drove herds north to Kansas railheads. West Texas homesteaders, Colorado miners, and Sooners who rushed into Oklahoma did the same nation-building work.

In thinking about the potential of the Alliance, it is useful to recall some of the ways that the American national state transformed western North America in the half century after Appomattox. The federal government acquired and began to develop Alaska. It underwrote transcontinental railroads with vast grants of land. It sent scientific survey expeditions to inventory the resources of the continental interior. It set aside the first national parks and established national forests to protect watersheds and maintain a supply of timber. It encouraged mining and agriculture by repeatedly easing the terms for claiming public lands, funded irrigation works, dredged ports, and embarked on a dam-building career.

Here is where the *Firefly/Serenity* universe comes up against Whedon's romantic view of frontiers and pioneers, which is the second historical theme that he sees as ungirding the stories. Along with the Civil War, he was trying to recapture the "strength and toughness" of western settlers, "the experience of immigrants and pioneers moving west, the dangers and the desperation of the kind of person who'd go with their family and babies into unknown territory, where nobody wanted them, with nothing but what they could carry either on their backs or in their wagons."[35] In fact, few white people who went west after 1865 matched the Oregon Trail image. They depended on the national government to keep them safe, to offer them land, and subsidize their farms.

Rather than *Stagecoach* or *The Wild Bunch*, it is instructive to place *Firefly* alongside a relatively neglected western from 1958. *The Big Country* was a big budget production with big stars: Gregory Peck, Charlton Heston, Jean Simmons, Caroll Baker, Burl Ives. The vistas are grand, the scenery is stunning, and the soundtrack by Jerome Moross is among the best for any western. The director was the highly accomplished William Wyler, with two Academy Awards as best director already in hand for *Mrs. Miniver* and *The Best Years of Our Lives* and one to come for *Ben Hur*.

Most importantly, the complicated story has no heroic pioneers. The original scriptwriter hired to adapt a *Saturday Evening Post* serial by Donald Hamilton was Jessamyn West, a Quaker fiction writer best known for *The Friendly Persuasion* (1946), which Wyler had successfully adapted for the screen in 1956 with Gary Cooper as the lead and West collaborating on the screenplay.[36] In 1957, coproducer Gregory Peck engaged West to work on the screenplay for the big new western. According to her letters held at the Whittier College library, she received $5,000 for five weeks of work plus an additional week of touch-up, although she received official credit for adaption of the original story rather than for the screenplay. In an unpublished paper, Joseph Dmohowski has detailed the convoluted history of the film's script, which involved many more hirings and firings of writers, conflicts between Peck and Wyler, and changes up to the last minute.[37]

All that said, the resulting film subverts many common western movie clichés and previews some of the themes that younger historians of the American West would begin to explore in following decades. The plot revolves around the basic environmental issue of water scarcity and water rights that are claimed by competing Texas ranching clans, who run each other's cattle off the water source and battle six-gun to six-gun.[38] The water is owned by neither rancher, however, but by a Tejana school teacher, whose family has rightful claim in history and law. The intervening force is a former sea captain, who arrives with the intention of marrying the daughter of the more respectable rancher but who ends up with the school teacher. This outsider, played by Peck, brings the world to Texas: Asked if he's ever seen anything as big as Texas, he replies, "Two oceans," reminding historians if not viewers of the global context of western development.

Peck's character James McKay resembles Hoban Washburne more than Mal Reynolds or Jayne Cobb. He prefers to observe and look for possible compromise rather than fight at first opportunity, patience learned from life at sea. The first half of the film revolves around McKay's supposed cowardice, meaning his disinterest in fighting at the drop of a hat. Mal, in contrast, is quick to pick a fight and shoot on sight (only as necessary, of course). His thirst for individual freedom appears to have trumped political goals. He is, Whedon notes, a radical get-out-of-my-face libertarian whose choices in order to survive are not necessarily admirable.[39] As Inara tells him in "Shindig," "You never follow the rules, no matter what society you're in! You don't even get along with ordinary criminals either, which is why you are constantly getting into trouble." James McKay understands himself as embedded and constrained by social contract; Mal Reynolds is constrained only by intense personal loyalties.

The *Firefly/Serenity* universe is supposedly postracial. The ethnicity of strong Latino and African American characters is never remarked, and Asian influences are ubiquitous, although no important Asian characters appear. The Reavers are savages, but they originate from inside rather than outside the zone of Earth settlements. They are the unintended victims of Alliance experiments rather than alien "others." Although they ambush a wagon train in the manner of many westerns (the colony ship of settler families that Mal and his crew come upon in the "Serenity" television episode), they are definitely not the Apaches as depicted in *Stagecoach*. The Alliance, not savages, massacres every adult and child in the isolated desert mining camp where Shepherd Book has decided to live in the film *Serenity*.

In contrast, *The Big Country* does tackle ethnicity. The second half of the film revolves around McKay's growing romance with Julie Maragon, the local schoolteacher who has inherited the Big Muddy Ranch from her grandfather, whose ownership would presumably date from before the Treaty of Guadalupe Hidalgo. Although underplayed in the movie, her character is a true innovation in a western movie—a Latino character who is not a sombrero-wearing sidekick or caricature or a Latina who is not domestic help.[40] What's being violated by the ranchers is a long-established property right with community roots of the sort that is central to the history of the territories gained by the American conquest of northern Mexico. *Firefly*'s "take my land" lament is left unspecified, perhaps meant to reference actual confiscation, perhaps a metaphor for absorption within a larger economic system.

Degrees of Separation

From the first five minutes, viewers tuning into the first broadcast could not miss that *Firefly* was going to be a science fiction *western*. The first science fiction elements—a funky spaceship hovering over a planet and then passing a ringed planet—were unsurprising, but the western elements were a surprise. Were they the best thing about *Firefly*? They certainly helped many fans fall in love with the show. They made it distinct and far more interesting than, say, *Andromeda* (2000–2005), another science fiction television series about a ship and small crew roaming from planet to planet that is watchable but not memorable.

The western ambiance may also have been *Firefly*'s downfall. A number of critics suggest that linking interesting science fiction concepts to the outmoded and incompatible western genre set it up for failure.[41] Fox network executives did not know what to make of the show. They required Whedon to replace the planned first episode ("Serenity"), which was designed to set the story and characters in place, with "The Train Job." Written over a single weekend by Whedon and collaborator Tim Minnear, it highlighted the western look and western tropes. Over the next weeks, however, the network grew less happy with the western elements and pushed in the direction of science fiction action. Composer Greg Edmonson reports that the network increasingly disliked the western atmosphere, telling him, "Whatever you do, don't make this ["Our Mrs. Reynolds"] sound like *Little House on the Prairie*." Executive producer and writer Tim Minnear also says that "the network really, really hated the western elements," hence his decision to set the "Bushwhacked" episode about ambushed pioneer families on spaceships that had no sagebrush or tumbleweed.[42] As previously noted, the film *Serenity* has a more science fictionish look and very much a science fiction plot. The *Serenity* comic books that Dark Horse Comics has published with Whedon's input also downplay the western settings for spaceship interiors, generic planetscapes, and space battles.

Whedon recognizes the tension that this chapter has tried to explore, stating that the roots of *Firefly/Serenity* "are in the western film and in the history of the west (two remarkably different things)."[43] The parenthetical phrase is the crux. As he recognizes, western fiction and western history are two different things—not just theme (history) and variations (fiction and film) but act and shadow. *Firefly* and *Serenity* are remarkably creative in redeploying western imagery and tropes. Even the *Firefly* episode titles evoke western movie themes and action, such as "The Train Job," "Bushwhacked," "Shindig," and "Heart of Gold" (other titles are historically and genre neutral, such as "Safe" or "The Message").

At the same time, neither the producer nor the writers, including Whedon himself for four television episodes and the movie, had the time or freedom to explore the greater complexities of western history. A novelist like Kim Stanley Robinson, with the elbow room of a 1,600-page trilogy about the settlement of Mars, was able to engage the active concerns of western historians when he wrote in the 1990s (as discussed in the last chapter of this book). In contrast, network doubts, viewer expectations, genre conventions, and shooting location limitations pushed Whedon, Minnear, and others involved with *Firefly* to reengage westerns rather than western history. So did the background of the show's creators—in testing out his idea for the show, Whedon quite naturally checked in with his former film studies professor, not a history professor. The natural result is that *Firefly* and *Serenity* are stories about western stories, not about the West as a historical place.

Notes

1. This was McQueen's breakout role after starring as a teenager in *The Blob* (1958).

2. The didactic voiceover exposition at the start of the movie states: "The Central Planets were the first settled and are the most advanced, embodying civilization at its peak. Life on the outer planets is much more primitive and difficult. That's why the Central Planets formed the Alliance, so everyone can enjoy the comfort and enlightenment of true civilization. That's why we fought the War for Unification." In addition to future politics, terraforming moons and planets to create newly habitable worlds, and space travel, the science fiction elements include a variety of mostly failed efforts at mind control by the Alliance. The Reavers are the result of one such failed effort, as is the supercapable

teenager River Tam, who takes shelter on *Serenity* under the protection of her older brother Simon Tam.

3. The crew are Captain Malcolm Reynolds, veteran of a defeated rebel army; First Mate Zoe Washburne, who had served with Reynolds in the war; hotshot pilot Hoban "Wash" Washburne; mechanic and engineer Kaylee Frye; and mercenary Jayne Cobb. The passengers are Shepherd Derrial Book, a preacher and pastor between jobs; Inara Serra, a Companion, or highly trained courtesan; Dr. Simon Tam and his younger sister River Tam, both in flight from Alliance authorities who are after River.

4. For those who may have been boycotting television, Whedon is the creative force behind the innovative television series *Buffy the Vampire Slayer* and *Angel*, in addition to several movies and other television work.

5. "Taking Back the Sky: An Interview with Joss Whedon," *Serenity: The Official Visual Companion* (London: Titan Books, 2005), 24, 30.

6. Larry McMurtry, *Walter Benjamin at the Dairy Queen: Reflections at Sixty and Beyond* (Thorndike, Maine: Thorndike Press, 1999), 26, 97.

7. Ross Calvin, *Sky Determines: An Interpretation of the Southwest*, rev. ed. (Albuquerque: University of New Mexico Press, 1965), 28; Alison Lurie, *The Nowhere City* (New York: Coward-McCann, 1965), 4.

8. Christopher Neal, "Marching out of Step: Music and Otherness in the *Firefly/Serenity* Saga," in Rhonda Wilcox and Tanya Cochran, eds., *Investigating Firefly and Serenity: Science Fiction on the Frontier* (New York: I. B. Taurus, 2008), 195; Joss Whedon, "Into the Black: An Interview with Joss Whedon," in *Firefly: The Official Companion*, vol. 1 (London: Titan Books, 2006), 12.

9. Barbara Maio, "Between Past and Future: Hybrid Design Style in *Firefly* and *Serenity*," in Wilcox and Cochran, *Investigating Firefly and Serenity*, 206; *Firefly: Official Companion*, vol. 1, 84, 150.

10. *Firefly: The Official Companion*, vol. 2 (London: Titan Books, 2007), 106, 112.

11. *Firefly: Official Companion*, vol. 1, 78–81, 96.

12. "Taking Back the Sky: An Interview with Joss Whedon," in *Serenity: The Official Visual Companion* (London: Titan Books, 2005), 9–10.

13. This choice allowed Whedon to focus on character development, unlike *Cowboys and Aliens* (2011), in which action heroes Daniel Craig and Harrison Ford played action heroes in 1873 outfits.

14. Paul Carter, *The Invention of the Future: Fifty Years of Magazine Science Fiction* (New York: Columbia University Press, 1977), 60–72. The convention for depicting Venus was to copy Amazonian rain forests or perhaps Florida before air-conditioning.

15. Greg Metcalf, "American Images of Space and the Future as the Final Frontier," in Dorit Yaron, ed., *Possible Futures: Science Fiction Art from the Frank Collection* (College Park: University of Maryland Art Gallery, 2000), 42–51.

16. Several of the episodes do not have a western look but instead utilize the common science fiction choices of spaceship-only settings and bright modernistic architecture settings. *Serenity*'s Miranda sequence, in which the crew discover an entire world of desiccated corpses who died, basically, of boredom was shot at a futuristic Pomona high school that was finished only in 1999.

17. There is also a quick draw standoff at the climax of the movie—Mal being faster, of course.

18. Joss Whedon, commentary track for *Serenity*, directed by Joss Whedon, DVD (Los Angeles: Universal Studioes Home Entertainment, 2005).

19. Joss Whedon, commentary track for *Serenity* DVD.

20. *Firefly Official Companion* vol. 2, 169.

21. "Taking Back the Sky: An Interview with Joss Whedon," *Serenity: The Official Visual Companion* (London: Titan Books, 2005), 11; Whedon interview, *Firefly: Official Companion*, vol. 1, 6.

22. *Firefly Official Companion*, vol. 1, 94.

23. Evelyn Vaughn, "The Bonnie Brown Flag," in Jane Espenson, *Serenity Found: More Unauthorized Essays in Joss Whedon's Firefly Universe* (Dallas: Benbella Books, 2007), 189.

24. Fred Erisman, in "Stagecoach in Space: The Legacy of Firefly," *Extrapolation* 47: 2 (2006): 249–58, offers a detailed rehearsal of the parallels, similarities, and differences between the film and the series.

25. *Firefly: The Official Companion* vol. 2, 160, 174.

26. This point is compactly summarized in Bruce Bethke, "Cut 'Em Off at the Horsehead Nebula!" in Espenson, *Serenity Found*, 175–85.

27. John Jakes, *Six-Gun Planet* (New York: Warner Books, 1970), and John Boyd, *The Andromeda Gun* (New York: Berkley, 1974). See Robert Murray Davis, "The Frontiers of Genre: Science Fiction Westerns," *Science-Fiction Studies* 12 (1985): 33–41.

28. James E. Gunn and Jack Williamson, *Star Bridge* (New York: Collier Books, 1983), 1–2.

29. J. P. Telotte, "Serenity, Cinematisation and the Perils of Adaptation," *Science Fiction Film and Television* 1 (2008): 67–80.

30. "Taking Back the Sky," *Serenity: Official Visual Companion*, 8.

31. That society is also shown to have retrograde customs when Mal finds himself maneuvered into a duel with swords in defense of Inara's honor (although viewers are not presented with the same sort of moral judgment when Mal or Jayne shoots someone). See Vaughn, "The Bonnie Brown Flag," 187–201.

32. "Mal had fought for the South—not for slavery. I can't stress that enough." "Taking Back the Sky," *Serenity: Official Visual Companion*, 8.

33. Sharon Sutherland and Sarah Swan, "'The Alliance Isn't Some Evil Empire': Dystopia in Joss Whedon's *Firefly/Serenity*," in Wilcox and Cochran, *Investigating Firefly and Serenity*, 97. This is a point that Whedon repeatedly makes: "Taking Back the Sky," *Serenity: Official Visual Companion*, 9, 13, 18.

34. *Serenity: Official Visual Companion*, 10, 13.

35. "Taking Back the Sky," *Serenity: Official Visual Companion*, 8.

36. For the curious, she was a second cousin to Richard Nixon.

37. Dmohowski utilized Jessamyn West papers at Whittier College, Gregory Peck papers at the Herrick Library, Academy of Motion Picture Arts and Sciences, and Hollywood memoirs and biographies for his meticulous research.

38. Control of water on the Great Plains gave control of the surrounding land. Clever entrepreneurs who acquired title to land along streams and rivers had effective ownership of many square miles around. That strategy was effectively used, for example, by Colorado cattleman John Iliff, whose name survives on a Denver street and Methodist theological seminary.

39. "Taking Back the Sky," *Serenity: Official Visual Companion*, 11.

40. Julie is a highly assimilated character, friendly with the elite Anglo ranching family and occupying a professional role in the community. At the same time, Maragon clearly reads as a Hispanic name and her grandfather's land title would almost surely date from Mexican or Spanish authority. She is thus a representative of the Hispanic elite that was able to deal on somewhat equal terms with Anglo-Americans in the mid-nineteenth-century decades in places like New Mexico, southern Arizona, and southern California.

41. Ginjer Buchanan, "Who Killed *Firefly?*" in Jane Espenson, ed., *Finding Serenity* (Dallas: Benbella Books, 2005), 53; Nancy Holder, "I Want Your Sex: Gender and Power in Joss Whedon's Dystopian Future World," in Espenson, *Finding Serenity*, 144, 147; John C. Wright, John C, "Just Shove Him in the Engine, or The Role of Chivalry in *Firefly*," in Espenson, *Finding Serenity*, 157–61; Telotte, "*Serenity*," 70.

42. *Firefly Official Companion Volume One*, 84, 156. Also see Whedon's comments about "Heart of Gold" in *Firefly: The Official Companion Volume Two*, 174.

43. "Taking Back the Sky," 30.

CHAPTER 10

Homesteading on the Extraterrestrial Frontier

The colony was made up of homesteaders and townies. The townies worked for the government and lived in government-owned buildings. . . . But most of the colonials were homesteaders and that's what George had meant us to be. Like most everybody, we had come out there on the promise of free land and a chance to raise our own food.
—Robert Heinlein, *Farmer in the Sky*

Johnny Appleseeds

Ray Bradbury and Robert Heinlein define opposite poles in postwar science fiction. Bradbury made and sustained his reputation as a stylist who crafted small stories with big emotional wallops. He has published only one science fiction novel—*Fahrenheit 451*—but many collections of loosely connected stories that wander back and forth among science fiction, fantasy, and nostalgic realism. Heinlein started with space adventure stories for *Astounding* but soon learned how to sustain longer narratives in more than two dozen novels for adult and juvenile readers. He liked problems in physical and social engineering and protagonists with can-do values. In his literary heritage are bits of the Tom Swift books mixed with Jack London's politically charged romances. In contrast, Bradbury's models were the connected stories of Sherwood Anderson's *Winesburg, Ohio* and the miniature narrative poems of Edgar Lee Masters.

Beneath their stylistic choices, however, Heinlein and Bradbury had much in common. Both writers harkened back to middle western childhoods, but their ideas about the future drew as well on their firsthand experience of California during its great transformation during and after World War II.[1] In the later 1940s, each made crossover sales to mainstream magazines that were helping their readers understand the age of galloping technological change. In their very distinct voices, Heinlein's and Bradbury's mass market stories evangelized for the high frontier of space exploration and its power to redeem or rescue a troubled and threatened world.

In so doing, each writer at the same moment found room for a Johnny Appleseed figure in a story of extraterrestrial pioneering. Heinlein's *Farmer in the Sky* (1950) and Bradbury's *The Martian Chronicles* (1950) both feature characters who re-enact the story of John Chapman. It was certainly more than coincidence.

Americans had been working hard to recover or create regional folk heroes since the boom in folklore studies in the 1930s. The ability to identify American virtues with larger-than-life figures was a way to emphasize national distinctiveness and unity. Nazis might have had Thor and Odin in their attic, but Americans had Paul Bunyan, Pecos Bill, and Johnny Appleseed.[2] In 1948, Walt Disney studios released a nineteen-minute *Johnny Appleseed* animation with Dennis Day voicing the character and singing "The Sun, and Rain, and an Apple Seed."[3]

Bradbury's version is elegiac. "The Green Morning" is the ninth of the twenty-three loosely overlapping stories and vignettes that constitute *The Martian Chronicles*. Nearly all of the stories, set from 2030 to 2057, examine the effects of Mars landings and settlement on individual Earth people (and occasionally on the dying Martians themselves). In effect, they are thought experiments about the ways that middle-class Americans of the 1930s and 1940s might respond to an actual frontier.[4]

"The Green Morning" zooms in on Benjamin Driscoll, who has spent the previous month planting seeds across the landscape of Mars, digging holes, dropping in seeds, and bringing water from the canals: "The thing that he wanted was Mars grown green and tall with trees and foliage, producing air, more air." Fair enough. Bradbury postulates a red planet with atmosphere that is breathable but painfully thin, and Driscoll's self-appointed mission is to hurry its thickening as a sort of single-person terraforming team. His goal is practical, to provide the oxygen that feeds warm fires and eases straining lungs. "'That's what I'm here for,' he muses. 'In school they told a story about Johnny Appleseed walking across America planting apple trees. Well, I'm doing more. I'm planting oaks, elms, and maples, every kind of tree. . . . Instead of making just fruit for the stomach, I'm making air for the lungs.'" And on Bradbury's mythicized Mars, dedication brings success. Driscoll wakens to a green morning. His seeds are now great trees, grown "as tall as ten men . . . nourished by alien and magical soil and, even as he watched, throwing out new branches, popping open new buds."[5]

Heinlein offers a very different Johnny in the stony new fields of Ganymede. Johann Schultz, a farmer from Earth, is determined to transform Jupiter's third moon into a breadbasket for the solar system. To some settlers he seems like a crank: "Johnny Appleseed. That's what everybody calls him in town [says the lazy and scheming Mr. Saunders]. "He's nuts. You know what he did? He gave me a handful of apple seeds and acted like he had handed me the riches of Solomon."[6] Bill, the teenage narrator of *Farmer in the Sky*, knows better. Papa Schultz is a good and generous neighbor. Bill has seen Schultz's single apple tree, heard how he had persuaded it to grow, tasted its fruit—Winesaps this year, with Greenlings and Rome Beauties to come—and received a gift of seeds with suggestions about where and how to plant.

The Johnny Appleseed legend grew out of the early settlement of Ohio in the nineteenth century, where John Chapman was a successful orchardist, but the idea of tree planting as a civic cause originated west of the Missouri River, where natural tree cover was scarce. Arbor Day got its start in Nebraska in the 1870s as easterners reacted to the treeless prairie. The Nebraska legislature made it official in 1885 as the practice of tree planting as a good deed was spreading to other states. What is now Nebraska National Forest originated a century ago in efforts that planted twenty thousand acres of ponderosa pines on the barren Sand Hills. In the dust bowl years of the 1930s, westerners learned to plant shelter belts of trees to protect farmsteads and hold soil. Bradbury thus transported a *western* tree-planting impulse to Mars.[7]

Johnny Appleseed is the harbinger of agricultural settlement, and both writers place their stories directly in the tradition of the American farming frontier as it has been embodied in popular memory. The colony ships in *Farmer in the Sky* are the *Mayflower* and the *Covered Wagon*, and Bill carefully calculates that the trip from Earth to the Jovian moon will be three days shorter than the Pilgrims' original crossing of the Atlantic. "The Wilderness," toward the end of *The Martian Chronicles*, begins in Independence, Missouri, one of the jumping off points for the Oregon Trail. Women whose husbands are already on the red planet recall the American past as they wait to follow: "Is this how it was a century ago, she wondered, when the women, the night before, lay ready for sleep, or not ready, in the small towns of the East, and heard the sound of horses in the night and the creak of Conestoga wagons ready to go. . . . Is this then how it was so long ago? On the rim of the precipice, on the edge of the cliff of stars. In their time, the smell of buffalo, and in our time the smell of the Rocket. Is this then how it was?"[8]

The homespun image of Johnny Appleseed, and his western imitators, is a good entry into the homesteading theme in science fiction. Homesteading is a particular facet of the complex processes by which agriculturalists settle "empty" or underdeveloped territories, whether the prairies of North America or the imagined planets of science fiction, and it is a process with deep resonance in American history and national identity. Homesteading involves a settlement of new farms by individual families or small groups who hope first to be self-sufficient and then to raise crops and livestock for the market. As a topic of fiction, it has usually centered attention on individual character and family dynamics.

In the United States homesteading is both a general settlement pattern and a very specific practice that followed the passage of the Homestead Act in 1862. The Oregon Trail pioneers, whom Bradbury evoked in the preceding passage, found their Willamette Valley farms first and then figured out how to obtain title (eventually involving special congressional action). The 1862 law, however, offered 160 acres of the public domain to anyone who would cultivate and live on the land for five years. The timing coincided with the push of agriculture into the Great Plains (the Homestead National Monument is in Beatrice, Nebraska) and into fertile valleys tucked among the western mountains, making the Homestead

Act a key tool for developing the western half of the nation. Much of the West's economic history revolves around the inducements of the 1862 legislation and later modifications that adapted the terms to the region's dryer lands.

A focus on individual homesteading families, however, looks at the second installment of the settlement process. Settlers relied on their own pluck and luck, but they also depended on railroads, grain elevators, irrigation systems, and town merchants with stocks of seed and machinery—in short, on the infrastructure of regional development. In the same way, homesteading in science fiction stands in clear contrast to terraforming novels that retell the "modern" story of big science and state action on behalf of big goals. As Kim Stanley Robinson and Pamela Sargent highlight in their trilogies about the settlement of Mars and Venus, the big questions of terraforming have to do with public purpose and public action: What goals are worthy of the state? How can the costs and benefits of economic change be fairly allocated? How can large scale action be sustained over time?[9] But the unearthly landscape, whether previously terraformed or directly (luckily) habitable by human beings, can also be the setting for small-scale stories of individual and family settlement and adaptation. *These* are homesteading stories that draw on the rich experience and mythology of the American farm-making frontier. Terraforming narratives look from the top down, from the broad problems of technology and organization to the roles and conflicts of individuals within the big picture; in short, they are about power and politics. Homesteading narratives start literally from the ground up, considering the ways that individuals respond to deliberately chosen new places and how they do or do not work together among themselves and with their neighbors; in short, they're about families and neighborhoods.[10]

It is a truism that Americans often see the future, and especially the extraterrestrial future, as a frontier, writing the common stories of continental conquest and settlement forward for times and places yet unknown. There have been many types of frontier, of course, pioneered by miners, fur traders, timber workers, herders, dam builders, and, at times, expanding Indian peoples as well as European Americans. Science fiction has been an active, if indirect, contributor to a dialogue in which Americans have slowly been accepting a history that is more complex than a simple epic of "winning the West" through "undaunted courage." The newer understanding recognizes, as historian Elliott West wrote in 1990, that the American West has "a longer, grimmer, but more interesting story" that encompasses not only the full range of virtue and vice but also the voices of many disparate peoples—Navajo and Cheyenne, Chinese and Filipino, Hawaiian and French Canadian, Yankee and Mexican, European American, African American, and many others.[11] Of particular relevance to the concerns of science fiction, historians now view western North America in comparison with counterpart regions from Argentina to New Zealand, Kenya to Australia, Siberia to Brazil. In this framework, exploration of differences and similarities among historical settlement frontiers and the imagined frontiers of science fiction is an easy step.

This chapter examines homesteading as one of the many and often conflicted stories that Americans have developed behind the facade of "high frontier." The discussion starts with a simple and positive vision that reproduces and adapts ideas found in nineteenth- and twentieth-century fiction and civic discourse about the economic and political possibilities of the West. The following two sections look at more complex and often less hopeful understandings of homesteading futures, first with texts from the 1960s and 1970s, and then with texts from the 1990s. The treatment thus moves from straightforward and celebratory ways in which homesteading narratives are written onto the future to more ambiguous and questioning stories that reflect Americans' increasing ambivalence about aspects of their past.

O, Pioneers!

For the United States, homesteading history can be seen as starting with the spread of English-speaking settlers into and beyond the Appalachians in the later eighteenth and early nineteenth centuries, if not with the even earlier movement of Spanish-speaking farmers into the upper Rio Grande valley of New Mexico. However, homesteading is described and imagined most extensively and vividly for the central prairies, Great Plains, and western mountains roughly from the 1850s to the 1910s. We can note, in this regard, that although Laura Ingalls Wilder started her sequence of books with a little house in the big woods of the upper Great Lakes region, it was the little house on the prairie that made it to prime time television.

Out of this experience developed a common homesteading narrative with two prominent elements. The first is the challenge of learning to live off a strange land. The second is the problem of generational change as children prove better able than parents to learn and adapt to the new environment.

Most American homesteading stories start with the dangers and inhospitality of the physical setting. Think about some of the defining stories of the prairies and plains penned in the later nineteenth and early twentieth century. They are filled with drought, blizzards, grasshoppers, and sheer physical discomfort. Hamlin Garland's *Main-Traveled Roads* (1891) is filled with the crushing work of farm life and "the barn yard's daily grind." The immigrant Norwegian-Dakotans of Ole Rolvaag's *Giants in the Earth* (1927) deal with isolation and desolation, insect plagues, and endless winter. Jules Sandoz, as his daughter Mari Sandoz recounted in *Old Jules* (1935), brought his new wife to a dank sod hut where water and bugs dripped from the roof.

Recent writers who have revisited the homesteading narrative keep the same troubles in mind as physical challenges that must be controlled and overcome. The intrepid heroine of the movie *Heartland* (1980), crafted by screenwriter Annick Smith from the 1910 diaries of Elinor Stewart, finds Montana a place of blizzard and cold. The erudite Jane Smiley programs drought into the troubles facing the Newton family in 1850s Kansas in *The All-True Travels and Adventures of Lidie Newton: A Novel* (1998). Molly Gloss subjects her lonely woman homesteader in *The Jump-Off Creek* (1989) to bears, blizzards, and back-breaking hard work. Lydia Sanderson came to Oregon from Pennsylvania "seeking the boundless possibilities that are said to live on the frontier." The claim that she bought has nothing but a rat-infested cabin. The rain pours and cattle mire themselves in the boggy creek bottom. Windstorm and ice kill and scatter her livestock: "Crossing the field with the empty kettle, she fell on the ice and sat there crying dryly, tiredly. But she got up after a while and went on the rest of the way, because the goat was bawling, thirsty, waiting for her."[12]

But as Willa Cather reminds us, to homestead successfully is to learn to *understand* the land and natural processes that they face. *O, Pioneers!*, published in 1913, is Cather's first great novel and is the one book that more than any other that represents the homesteading story as understood in American culture. The book spans twenty years in the life of Alexandra Bergson and uses her story to dramatize the transformation of Nebraska from frontier to community. Alexandra grows up on the Nebraska prairie, turns the family homestead into a prosperous farm, and becomes a mainstay of a maturing agricultural region. The novel's first section is "The Wild Land." Here, in the early years of settlement, the place itself takes on active character as a "wild old beast" that resists human agency: "In eleven long years John Bergson [Alexandra's father] had made but little impression upon the wild land he had come to tame. It was still a wild thing that had its ugly moods. . . . Mischance hung over it. Its Genius was unfriendly to man."[13] This is the harsh landscape of failure and doubt: scorching sun, bitter winters, misadapted crops, and worn-out pioneers.

Alexandra sees it differently. She grows up with the country and comes to love it. The spirit of place speaks differently to her: "When the road began to climb the first long swells of the Divide, Alexandra hummed an old Swedish hymn. . . . For the first time, perhaps, since that land emerged from the waters of geologic ages, a human face was set toward it with love and yearning. . . . Her eyes drank in the breadth of it, until her tears blinded her. Then the Genius of the Divide, the great, free spirit which breathes across it must have bent lower than it ever bent to a human will before" (65). The new partnership of place and pioneer equates to progress; grinding isolation gives way to singing telephone wire, dilapidated shacks to neatly painted houses, hills of dry grass to rich fields.

Homesteading narratives are also family stories. Later in *O, Pioneers!* Cather has one of the characters muse: "And now the old story has begun to write itself over there. Isn't it queer: there are only two or three human stories, and they go on repeating themselves as fiercely as if they had never happened before, like the larks in this country, that have been singing the same five notes over for thousands of years" (119). Those same five notes are the tensions of fathers and sons, mothers and daughters, brothers and sisters. *O, Pioneers!* and *My Antonia* are both about daughters who guide and grow beyond their immediate families. Mari Sandoz had to escape from the fierce monomania of Old Jules before she could write about him. Even Mary O'Hara's *My Friend Flicka* (1941) is about father and son more than boy and horse.

Homesteading stories thus deal with folks whom writer Wallace Stegner calls "placed" people, the newcomers who "stuck" on their new lands to establish what historian Walter Nugent defines as "Type II" frontiers. These are frontiers of agricultural settlement by families, where there are close ties between farmers and the small towns that serve them, where newcomers work hard to establish schools, churches, fraternal organizations, and other social institutions and where levels of violence are low. They contrast with the "displaced" people of "Type I" frontiers—people who travel from one locale to another to harvest easily accessible natural resources. These are boom and bust frontiers that attract disproportionate numbers of young men who are rough, edgy, and often violent. Examples include California mining, Northwest logging, Alaska fisheries, and, in the imagination of the future, asteroid mining.[14]

Robert Heinlein—who imagined a Type I frontier in the asteroids in *The Rolling Stones*—neatly encapsulated the two homesteading themes in *Farmer in the Sky*. Heinlein is in many ways the quintessential American science fiction writer, and this relatively early novel for young people reaffirms the farming frontier as a source of positive values. First published in installments as "Satellite Scout" in *Boy's Life*, the national magazine for Boy Scouts, the book focuses on high school–aged Bill, whom we have already met. It starts in an overcrowded California, where sixty million people depend on a fragile system of nuclear powered desalination plants and "a million other gadgets."[15] Faced with constricting opportunities, Bill, his father, new stepmother, and stepsister emigrate to Ganymede in the company of six thousand other settlers.

The family's goal on Jupiter's third moon is to become homesteaders. The Colonial Commission has done the basic terraforming to provide a thin but breathable atmosphere, but it is up to newcomers to build a new society. Those who want to become farmers, like Bill and his father, can "prove" a homestead, transferring a nineteenth-century term to the twenty-first century. As with U.S. settlers after the Homestead Act of 1862, they can earn title to a future farm if they cultivate and live on it. The first steps are to crush the rocky surface into soil with special machinery—in effect, using "plow that broke the rocks." Hard work turns boulders successively into rocks, gravel, and powder, which can then be seeded with "good black soil from earth," carefully sterilized and then reseeded with "bacteria and fungi and microscopic worms."[16] Like much golden age science fiction, much of the fun comes from imagining technical details, as the problems of earthside soil conservation, a major issue of the middle decades of the twentieth century, are inverted into moonside soil creation.

Bill and his father do not work in isolation, for this is the frontier as Americans want to remember it—a place of sturdy yeoman farmers who happily cooperate through voluntary association. Dad earns money in town as an engineer, while Bill apprentices to neighbor Johann Schultz to learn the art of moon-farming. Schultz is generous with his experience and his resources, showing once again that "pioneers need good neighbors." There is a house raising scene straight from American frontier mythology, when Bill's Boy Scout troop and his father's coworkers pitch in to turn a pile of stone blocks into a dwelling, while the women cook wholesome food for the crew. This is what Ganymedians do; Bill has already participated in six house raisings himself because "you can't do it alone."[16] When a moonquake strikes soon after, the whole community pulls together in the rescue operations and rebuilding.

Pioneer grit has its rewards. Within two years, "you would never have known anything had happened. There wasn't a wrecked building in the community . . . and the town was booming." After the disaster, Bill is more determined than ever to stick it out rather than return to Earth for college. "I'm not going home, if I ever do, until I've licked this joint."[17] He sees his future in the new land, quite consciously on the model of the nineteenth-century frontier. While overcrowded Earth moves toward war over scarce resources, the colonists are increasingly self-sufficient. Looming wars on Earth will pass them by as Ganymede builds its own strength and looks outward to even newer frontiers—much as the United States watched nineteenth-century wars among European powers from across a wide ocean. The lesson is straightforward: America's westward movement worked once, and it can work again in new circumstances.

In the five-plus decades since Heinlein mapped the idealized homesteading frontier onto Ganymede, a number of science fiction writers have continued to utilize the standard homesteading themes at something like the same face value. Their work taps widely shared American values and assumptions, but it has not substantially advanced the genre beyond the 1940s and 1950s.

Given science fiction's adventure story roots, it is no surprise that stories about the settlement of new planets repeatedly revisit the problem of the harsh land as pioneers try to cope with ecologies that they do not completely understand and that fight back. The challenge can be simple inhospitality, with a Ganymede moonquake the equivalent of a "blue norther" blizzard on the Great Plains. More interestingly, crisis may arise from a mistaken intervention in the new ecology in ways reminiscent of American ecological disasters such as crowding the northern plains with far too many cattle to survive the severe droughts and snows of the 1880s or plowing beyond the line of adequate rainfall in the 1890s. The science fiction variations are endless, for readers and writers are well aware of the notorious examples of ecological disruption on Terran frontiers, as well as the scientific implications of the "Columbian exchange" between the ecologically isolated Eastern and Western hemispheres, with its massive trading of crops, animals, and deadly diseases.[18]

A good example is the first human colony on Avalon (Tau Ceti Four) as detailed by Larry Niven, Jerry Pournelle, and Steven Barnes in *The Legacy of Heorot*

(1987) and *Beowulf's Children* (1995). Two hundred carefully selected colonists have settled comfortably on a large, apparently safe island off the main continent. The ecology seems simple. Apart from equivalents of grass, trees, birds, rodents, and freshwater fish, the planet appears largely a blank slate that is open to earthly crops and animals. Indeed, it seems a paradise: "Golden fields. Silver rivers. . . . Year-round water supply and fertile croplands. . . . A beautiful place to start a new world, lovely enough to make him feel . . . almost at peace."[19]

We know that the picture is too perfect to be true, especially only seven pages into the book. The authors set up the first novel as an intellectual puzzle requiring scientific detective work, for readers can guess that an ecology with so few occupied niches is unstable. The colonists soon encounter implacable, carnivorous killing machines that they call "grendels" and learn how to kill them—only to discover the they have made their situation even more perilous.[20] By killing off the adult grendels on the island, they allow the thousands of harmless fish creatures ("samlon") to grow into grendels themselves. Only the presence of adult grendels, who devour each other's young, had prevented a grendel population explosion! It is as if slaughtering the buffalo has opened the way for saber-tooth tigers to spring up in their place.

The story is all quite exciting, for Niven, Pournelle, and Barnes are good action writers who follow the thriller model in which the colonists defend their settlement, are overwhelmed, save themselves at great cost, relax after defeating the monster, and then find that IT'S BACK! However, the authors' real interest is the hard science fiction challenge of building a scientific puzzle and laying down clues for the reader. They layer on interpersonal conflicts to keep the plot moving, and the climax is a classic defense-of-the-fort scene, but the novel is really about the process of learning a new land. The lesson for the reader, as well as the colonists, is to question assumptions. Their puzzle involves biology rather than physics or engineering, the mainstays of golden age science fiction, but the instructional spirit is the same.

In *Beowulf's Children*, the first generation born planetside are coming of age. Chafing at their parents' hard-learned caution, they establish their own beachheads on the mainland. They think that their parents are like Europeans in the New World, strangers in a new land, while they see themselves as native Avalonians: "They could not own the land, but they could be a part of it."[21] But the children too are confounded, because the mainland has new ecological tricks. They think they know all about grendels, but they encounter new types in new places and they suffer serious casualties from the planet's equivalent of killer bees, which swarm every fifty years or so. It is another "Avalon surprise" because the life cycle of the bees is tied to weather changes, which are tied to sun spot cycles. Again, there is plenty of intergenerational conflict to push the plot, but the heart of the book is setting and resolving a mystery.

In Marta Randall's *Journey* (1978), in contrast, the generational conflict *is* the story. Randall prefaces the novel with Cather's passage about "the same five notes."

Like many homesteading stories, *Journey* is about generations on the land. It pulls together many of the threads of the planetary settlement story, such as struggles for economic stability and the growth of communities, but its central concern is not the science of survival. The landscape reads easily, without mistakes and misunderstandings, for Aerie is a remarkably benign and fertile planet just waiting to produce a marketable crop. Instead, the "old story" that interests Randall is stress and adjustment within families, as telegraphed by the 1978 paperback cover, showing overlapping faces of parents and children, and the front-cover blurbs: "A human drama of passion and power" and "an epic novel of the last frontier."[22] Among western American fiction it has something in common with the Ivan Doig's novelization of his Montana family in *English Creek* (1984) and *Dancing at the Rascal Fair* (1987) or with Annie Dillard's fine historical novel *The Living* (1992) about generations on the shores of Puget Sound.

The plot is driven by father Jason Kennerin's love of the land, his ability to pass that love to his "dutiful" daughter Quilla, and the inability of his two sons to share the same commitment. Jason is a remittance man par excellence, whose family wealth allows him to buy the entire planet of Aerie sight unseen, but one who works at making it a new home. He experiments with crops, works with the sentient natives to develop a shared agricultural economy, and builds an estate and a family, two goals that are identical in his mind: "This—the land—that doesn't change. You put work and love into it, and it gives you food and fruit and flowers and beauty. . . . Making things grow—the importance of that doesn't change. I mean, things change, sure, but their importance—what they mean—that doesn't change much. Sunlight, the earth, water, children. Making life."[23]

As the Kennerins find a place for their planet in the larger economic and political system, a town grows at the foot of the hill below their house: dirty streets are paved, the one-room school becomes a four-story edifice, utility systems replace water hauled in buckets—all in roughly the same ten to twenty years timeframe that saw the transformation of raw settlements like Bismarck, North Dakota, or Cheyenne, Wyoming, into respectably pretentious towns. Meanwhile, Jason's children take on familiar family roles. The eldest daughter Quilla is a match for Alexandra Bergson. She's a bit plain looking, intense, and intelligent; she steadily takes on responsibility from her parents and becomes the colony's general manager and consensus queen at her father's death. One of her brothers parallels Alexandra Bergson's friend Carl Linstrum. Carl leaves Nebraska for Chicago, only to find that jobs in the city are all alike, while Quilla's brother is a restless romantic who gets into space as an apprentice on a cargo ship then officers a freighter. He may cut a romantic figure when he returns to visit, but he soon finds that space piloting is routine work and every space port much like every other. The younger brother cannot make his family match his ideal and therefore learns to manipulate his environment. Exiled from Aerie for abusing the natives through scientific experiments, he becomes a highly skilled physician and researcher. But in the end, he tires of his life and comes home to try to make the best of what he still thinks of as *his* planet and *his* family—the prodigal returned and the family trying to work out its future with economically successful homesteading as a backdrop.

Questioning a Myth

In the 1960s and 1970s, in counterpoint to standard retellings of the homesteading narrative, some writers began to question and undercut the popular story as a model for the future. Along with a number of other writers who were a couple decades younger than Heinlein and Bradbury, Ursula Le Guin and Philip K. Dick pushed the boundaries of the genre. Their generation explored substantive topics in science fiction—gender roles, drugs, and sometimes rock and roll—that had largely been kept under wraps in the hard science fiction of the 1940s and 1950s. They tested innovations in narrative form and style. And they wrote about homesteading in ways that questioned simple stories of success through perseverance.

In so doing, their fiction paralleled postwar historical writing that was probing beneath the surface of the western myth to find uncomfortable and incongruous realities that mismatch between dreams and realities. Novelist Wallace Stegner and historian Walter Prescott Webb documented the fundamental inhospitality of the arid West and the problems that arose when eastern expectations came westward. In Webb's memorable phrase, much of the American West was a "perpetual mirage" that defied eastern farming practices and technological solutions such as dry farming and irrigation. Literary scholar Henry Nash Smith, in one of the most influential works of post–World War II scholarship, analyzed the many ways in which the dream of a welcoming, garden-like continent had misdirected both political decisions and popular culture. Indeed, these scholars argued, expectations of individualism ignored the deep dependence of western settlers and communities on outside institutions.[24]

In Ursula Le Guin's 1974 story "The Eye Altering," to contrast with Randall or Niven, Pournelle, and Barnes, the process of learning a new planet has been abstracted into metaphor. The settlers on New Zion find the light and landscape ugly, brown, purplish, and dark red: "Dirty colors, the colors you got when you scrubbed your watercolors too hard."[25] In the new environment, they are aliens who depend on special enzymes to enable their bodies to metabolize the native foods. But one of the Zion born, sickly since his birth, decides to forgo the medication and take his chances with the local flora. His decision turns out to be correct, showing that many of the planet born have suffered not from Zion itself but from their loving parents' efforts to treat them as Earth born.

For Le Guin, with her family background in anthropology, the frontier story is ultimately about the cultural gap between pioneers and natives. To her very simple "technical" plot, metaphorical as it is (there is no attempt to suggest a physical mechanism) Le Guin added a second layer of adaptation. Genya, the young man who experiments with local diet, is also an artist, who has skillfully painted portraits and other pictures that the first generation can see and appreciate, but he now starts to paint Zion as it looks in its muddled ugliness; as he works, he comments that he is "just beginning to learn to see." But when one of his pictures of Zion is hung in the common room, where the older settlers are most at home, they see it as a beautiful countryside from Earth. It is still the same picture, but the Earth born realize that young people who have adopted and adapted to Zion see their surroundings as a beautiful landscape: "It's here. Zion. It's how Genya sees it. With the eyes and the heart. . . . . How do we know what a child of Zion sees? We can see the picture in this light that's like Home [Earth]. Take it outside, into the daylight, and you'll see what we always see, the ugly colors, the ugly planet where we're not at home. But he is at home! He is!"[26]

Where Le Guin was interested in cultural change, Philip Dick saw the frontier controlled by the inescapable power of capitalism and consumerism. Neither *Martian Time-Slip* (1964) nor *The Three Stigmata of Palmer Eldritch* (1965) is about homesteading *per se*. The former explores some curious propositions about the nature of consciousness and the latter uses its plot as an occasion for eccentric musing about the nature of God. Nevertheless, Dick set all of *Time-Slip* and a substantial chunk of *Stigmata* on the surface of a cynically conceived red planet whose social and economic life subverts the values of dedication, family, and neighborliness that lie at the heart of the homestead myth.

The Three Stigmata of Palmer Eldritch imagines a Mars of unrelieved bleakness. The planet is essentially a penal colony, peopled by homesteaders who have been drafted into their new lives. Their situation is like trying to set up farming in the very worst of the Dust Bowl. Newcomers may start off trying to farm, but their machinery quickly fails in the never-ending dust and Martian rodents eat the crops that have not shriveled. The only rational response is despair: "On all sides of him their abandoned, decaying gardens could be seen and he wondered if he would soon forget his. Maybe each new colonist had started out this way, in an agony of effort. And then the torpor, the hopelessness, claimed them." On this squalid frontier, the settlers learn to hate the land, not to love it. They huddle in tiny groups in subsurface hovels that they give names like Chicken Pox Prospects. There is no second generation to take over, only furtive, sordid sex and a super-LSD that lets members of a group share the experience of inhabiting a set of dolls and their miniature dollhouses—to be Barbie and Ken for a day. A Marsscape of dead fields, abandoned machinery, and rotting supplies is a stand-in for the universal failure of the frontier ideal: "He knew from edu-tapes that the frontier was always like that, even on Earth."[27]

Dick was correct that homesteading viewed realistically is a hard fit with American narratives of growth, for close examination of the historical experience shows as much disaster as triumph. Settlement from the eastern United States has repeatedly washed across the high plains into the Rocky Mountains, lingered for a decade or two, and then washed back. One generation of failure began with the Homestead Act of 1862, expanded with the first transcontinental railroads, and crashed in the drought and depression of the 1890s. More generous land laws and European hunger for American grain during World War I attracted another ambitious generation, who hit trouble in the 1920s and disaster in the 1930s. World War II, farm subsidies, and energy exploration subsidies fueled a third generation of ambition that crested and crashed in turn in the 1980s and 1990s.

Towns grew, perhaps even prospered, but they also failed. From the Texas Panhandle to the Dakotas is now a region of declining agriculture, aging population, and few in-migrants.[28] Just as the western American mountains are specked with the ghost town remnant of the mining frontier, the plains are slowly taking back small farm towns, while regional centers struggle to keep young people from the attractions of Denver, Seattle, or Minneapolis. Some areas actually peaked in population in the 1890s, others in the 1940s or 1950s. Jonathan Raban has chronicled the process of ambition and decline in eastern Montana in *Bad Land* and Larry McMurtry fictionalized the experience in *The Last Picture Show*. William Least Heat-Moon, has explored the thinning human imprint in central Kansas in *PrairyErth*. Geographers Frank and Deborah Popper aroused consternation and fascination when they noted that 388 western counties in 1980 supported fewer than six people per square mile, the shorthand for frontier conditions. Their proposal—really a metaphor—was to slowly return unneeded lands to a preagricultural ecology as a Buffalo Commons.[29] The made-up title *Pilgrims without Progress*, the banned book that supposedly encompasses the Martian settlement experience in *Stigmata*, would not be a bad summary for much of homesteading history.

Martian Time-Slip describes a superficially more successful Mars, but one in which the hopes of a family frontier have given way to the worst of 1960s suburbia, with many of the details taken directly from the popular suburban critique of the 1950s and 1960s.[30] The Martian homesteaders/householders that we see might as well be in San Bernardino County. They use water from the Martian canals for gardens rather than commercial agriculture. Husbands have second jobs, as machinery repairmen or black-market merchansiders, while wives carry on sexual affairs in the afternoons. There are ads for automatic farm tractors, but no picture of how they might be used. There is also agribusiness, represented by a "ranch" in an area purchased by a Texas oil tycoon and administered by Texas (but, joke on Texas, it is really a dairy farm).

Meanwhile, the way to make money is land speculation. The father of one of the homesteaders arrives unexpectedly from Earth with plans to buy land in the arid F.D.R. Mountains: "It was the last gasp of hope springing eternal in the old man; here there was land selling for next to nothing, with no takers, the authentic frontier which the habitable parts of Mars were patently not." In fact, the father is not a deluded romantic but a shrewd insider, attracted by an inside tip about a planned government facility that will cause the value to skyrocket. He does not need his son's warning: "Don't commit yourself, because it's a known fact that any Mars real estate away from the part of the canal network that works—and remember that only about one-tenth of it works—comes close to being outright fraud."[31]

Dick's 1960s Mars novels are satirical assaults on postwar American culture, with similarities to Kurt Vonnegut's *Player Piano* (1952) and Frederick Pohl and Cyril Kornbluth's *Space Merchants* (1953) and *Gladiator-at-Law* (1955), but they are also critiques of the nation's past. They are positioned both chronologically and conceptually between the historians and critics of the 1950s, who pointed out the misunderstandings inherent in the agrarian myth, and those historians of the 1980s and 1990s, who emphasize conquest, environmental devastation, and the corruptive effects of land monopoly. Dick's version of homesteading coincides with the ideas of several writers who have pointed out that the enterprising family of the homesteading West was caught from the start in a web of political and economic institutions beyond its control. If it existed at all, the agrarian family utopia of nineteenth-century American aspiration and twentieth-century nostalgia was, at most, a brief moment in a process dominated by big institutions and capital.[32]

Inventing New Stories

The writers whom I have examined so far worked with the assumption that high homesteading is possible, even when they highlight the human costs. In contrast, Kim Stanley Robinson, Jonathan Lethem, and Molly Gloss offer science fiction that addresses the same broad topic of agricultural settlement but steps outside the standard narrative. Writing in the 1990s, they anticipated and responded in different ways to William Kittredge's challenge to invent new stories that move beyond the simple pioneer imperative to claim and own new territory.[33] The three following examples render the settlement narrative more complex and more realistic. It is not that Robinson, Lethem, or Gloss are necessarily more negative or pessimistic than earlier writers (it is hard to beat P. K. Dick for a black view of the future) but that they are more willing to address both the ambiguities of homesteading and its larger contexts.

Kim Stanley Robinson in *Blue Mars* (1996) revisits the question of learning the land as a writer very aware of the contemporaneous wave of environmental activism and analysis. This third book in the Mars trilogy is set at a time when terraforming has made the red planet marginally habitable. It includes an extended episode in which one of the central characters takes several years off to cultivate a desolate piece of the Mars-scape, exploring the possibilities for the individual (that is, homesteading) that the vast scientific and bureaucratic project of terraforming has made possible. Where Niven, Pournelle, and Barnes made Cather's "wild beast" literal and Le Guin used it as a springboard to think about the conditions of cognition, Robinson understands it as natural system and metaphor both. The "genius of the divide" is what Nirgal seeks to understand : "Only the tiniest part of the basin would be his farm. . . . It wouldn't be self-sufficient, but it would be settling in. A project. . . . He would be an ecopoet."[34]

Introduced in the second volume, Nirgal is one of the first people born on the red planet. Given one of the many names for Mars in terrestrial languages, he encompasses the ways in which humans relate to their new planet. He grows up in a maverick community of idealists who are trying to create a natural alternative to the initial high-tech settlement. He wanders the planet as a young man, becomes political, and helps to negotiate Martian autonomy from Earth. He then drops out of public life to come to terms with his own maturity and mortality, looking more and more closely at the planet itself as the source of his identity before deciding on his homesteading experiment. The remainder of the episode traces years of detailed landscape modification *and* Nirgal's effort to inhabit the place fully—to think like a Mars-scape. By the time Mars reclaims the tract through a massive dust storm, Nirgal has become a true native of the new land. The detailed character grows in his understanding of his place in ways that match the "practice of the wild" as argued by western poet and essayist Gary Snyder (whom Robinson greatly admires). He has imagined a new story, even if one that cannot overcome the dust storm that eventually buries his homestead and brings the episode to a close.

Nirgal's years in the small, high basin acknowledge the social as well as ecological complexity of homesteading.[35] The episode begins and ends with community, not isolation. Below the ridge is a Tibetan-Martian settlement, whose residents are happy to have him as a distant neighbor and help him get started. Nirgal is a loner but not a hermit. He puts in stints of work with construction crews in a nearby city and manufactures blimpgliders as a cottage industry, making monthly trips to sell his latest work. He calls up other settlers for advice and entertains visitors.

The homesteading episode fails, but the overarching narrative of Mars is human success. Nirgal's work is part of an optimistic endeavor. His public role changes, as he deliberately becomes more marginal to the changing tides of Martian politics, but his personal drive is always to encompass the planet, to understand it in broad sweep and in detail. In his way, he is working out the family issue that has been with American settlers since the Massachusetts Puritans had to think up the Halfway Covenant: How does the second generation shape its own future while remaining true to the vision of original settlers? For Nirgal, it is necessary to understand the land before he can work out his own answer, which involves an eventual return to engage the changing Martian society.

Jonathan Lethem's *Girl in Landscape* (1998) moves in very close parallel to *Farmer in the Sky*. Written nearly fifty years later, and for a quite different audience, it shares episodes, scenes, and situations. Lethem takes the strangeness of high homesteading seriously and has an interest in the theme of generational transition—but with a vastly different tone and "take." Heinlein wrote from an era of technical and social optimism, Lethem with a voice of ironic doubt. The former repeated the modern story of progress and contained generational conflict *within* that story, while the latter explored the postmodern doubt that any social solution can suffice.

In the one-sentence capsule, *Girl in Landscape* has the same plot as *Farmer in the Sky*. A family migrates from a troubled and overcrowded Earth to a new planet, settles in the countryside, and experiences challenges that leave the teenaged protagonist chastened but ultimately determined to make it as a founder of the society. Lethem's characters understand the planet as a "frontier," themselves as "homesteaders," their tasks as "breaking new ground" and "tam[ing] the wilderness." But everything else is undermined or reversed from Heinlein. The protagonist is a thirteen-year-old girl, Pella Marsh, rather than a boy. Her mother dies and the remnants of her family are dysfunctional and apathetic, not cohesive and supportive. The new planet feels like exile: "The family was moving to a distant place, an impossible place. Distance itself haunted them, the distance they had yet to go."[36] It is not empty but inhabited by the sad remnants of a race that had once built huge arching structures. The challenges are social, sexual, and spiritual, not technological and economic. Disaster strikes from within rather than from without. The ending is resigned determination, not determined optimism.

The Marshes are the third family and the fourteenth to seventeenth humans in a valley settlement a day's journey from the port. One of the problems about homesteading here is that there is really nothing to do—no technical challenge. Familiar crops from Earth can be grown with difficulty, but there is no reason to bother. The ancestors of the native Archbuilders have left behind a ubiquitous plant whose tubers can produce the equivalents of potatoes, vegetables, cake, and meat. Mostly the women cook, the men sit around and talk, and the kids wander the valley and hills. If they had to leave Brooklyn, Pella wishes they had at least stayed in "Southport, the older, bigger town, where there were doctors, stores, a restaurant. . . . She already wished they lived there instead of here, in the new settlement without even a name, this place on the edge of nothing."[37]

The Archbuilders hover in the background. Those who interact with the settlement are feckless and childlike in curiosity. They join the children's lessons and hang around the general store until kicked out, like deracinated Indians at a trading post. They have lost the capacity or desire to construct the great arches that make the planetscape into a version of Monument Valley: "The settlement was at the farthest edge of a basin ringed by crumbled arches. Eroded spires that rose a thousand feet into the air. Fallen bridges, incomplete towers, demolished pillars. The valley was a monumental, roofless cathedral with only the buttresses intact, and the calm purple-pink sky of the Planet of the Archbuilders glowed like stained-glass windows between these vast ruined frames."[38]

The novel is driven by Pella's sexual awakening and her struggles to understand her sexuality in a social vacuum. This central tension comes directly from the classic western movie *The Searchers*, in which John Wayne searches compulsively for young Natalie Wood, who has been abducted by Indians. Lethem himself speaks of his "obsession" with that movie and its details of presentation. The book, with its bleak tone, also comes from Lethem's years in California and "that we've-reached-the-end-of-the-world" thing.[39] Pella is the Natalie Wood figure, abducted spiritually rather than physically. Her mind begins to resonate with the planet. She finds a hiding place in the hills where she dreams or goes into fugue states in which she takes on the point of view of ubiquitous small creatures like "quicksilver giraffes" that scurry around inside and out, allowing her secretly to observe the other people. She has become literally a girl *in* the landscape, not simply set against it but merging with it.

Both the novel's title and its development thus respond to the importance that Jane Tompkins places on landscape as a defining feature of the American western novel and movie. The desert (or the wide open spaces of the Planet of the Archbuilders) is the typical setting for the western, says Tompkins, because its openness places human beings directly in nature. Mary Lawlor similarly writes that: "The frontier was typically construed as a border zone that harbored mystery and danger, but that ultimately opened onto a plentiful, inviting space. . . . The wide, figuratively horizontal plane featured in such prospects gave material form to the ideals of democratic possibility so central to U.S. national culture from its beginnings." In turn, science fiction extends that openness to infinity, from cold desert surfaces of the Moon or Mars to the wide open spaces of entire galaxies. The western plains and desert are thus made boundless and their possibilities and dangers extended to the ends of the imagination.[40]

The self-sufficient, arrogant, and planet-wise rancher Efram Nugent is the stand-in for the movie's Ethan Edwards, the monomaniacal character played by John Wayne. It is easy to hear John Wayne's voice in Nugent's dialogue and mannerisms, to see Wayne's silhouette when Nugent is introduced standing against the skyline or described as physically imposing: "Possibly any space he inhabited was his, the way he moved his shoulders to carve the air."[41] Nugent's obsession is to maintain the separation between the two peoples. He's been on the planet for seven years, can talk one of their many languages, and can work with them. But he also holds these remnants of the race in contempt: "I think we ought to draw a line around this town we're starting here, Marsh. Make it a *human* settlement, a place where kids are safe. . . . I'm just talking about moving them out of our settlement. They don't care. They've got plenty of other places to wander around. A whole ruined planet for them to gawk at and wonder what the hell happened to their civilization."[42]

Nugent "searches" for Pella by keeping track of her movements and by playing on her growing sexuality to pull her back to human society. He seeks out her hiding place physically and spies on her dreaming body. His physical and moral presence upsets and attracts her. She wants his notice, angling for an invitation to his house, where she tries to come on to him (further confusing her and demonstrating his power over her). *His* sexuality, in the end, is his downfall. In the final crisis of sexually driven violence, Pella falsely but plausibly accuses him of rape in order to save one of the natives. One of the other teenagers then shoots Efram to death.

In the crisis, the ideas of town and family both collapse. The "might-be-town" shrinks rather than grows: "The spaces between things were growing instead. The silences." The only woman with domestic skills can scarcely hold her family together, let alone knead together a fragmented community. Individual pain and passion triumph. "There is no town, Pella thought. There never was one. There was only Efram and whatever he wanted. . . . Families that weren't in a town than wasn't."[43] The settlers return to Earth or flee into the outback, leaving Pella to rename it for her dead mother and start it over again. She is a survivor, who endures and carries on, but with the parental generation fled from the story. To adapt another phrase from Willa Cather, if there is to be a history of *this* country, it will surely be in Pella's heart and nowhere else.

Lethem thus situates himself in contrast to Kim Stanley Robinson as well as Robert Heinlein, for Robinson is a cautious utopian. Robinson embeds his characters in communities and civil societies, as the next chapter discusses in more detail. To be successful is to make the thoughtful compromises that are necessary when individuals work together to construct communities, something that Nirgal understands even in his years as a loner. Robinson takes the political process seriously and his most admirable characters are politically active, balancing their own desires against those of others. His preferred society in both trilogies manifests the "wise provincialism" that nineteenth-century philosopher Josiah Royce saw as the middle ground between radical individualism and corporate dominance.[44] Lethem's version of politics is Pella's failed and foolish father, defeated on Earth and unable to find an outlet for his "committee-chairing" skills in the intensely individualized and ego-driven community of his new home. The novel progressively strips away family members and community members as characters die, flee, or withdraw into catatonia. Only Pella is left, and only Pella's hard-won understanding and individual determination will be able to prevail on the homesteading frontier.

In contrast to Lethem but similar to Robinson, Molly Gloss offers a complex homesteading story in which the answer to individual doubts is community, not radical individualism. She also places the homestead narrative in a larger chronological frame by showing that the real drama may be in the decision to emigrate rather than the result. In *The Dazzle of Day* she takes on the steep challenge of injecting drama into Quaker decision-making practice—a far cry from the cardboard characters that Dick put through plots of corporate manipulation and individual greed. The bulk of the novel takes place on a "generation ship" toward the end of its long voyage from Earth to a new planet, but Gloss subverts the most common version of this setting by showing a society that has grown stronger and more cohesive over the generations rather than falling into anarchy, thus entering as plea for the power of social connections in a strongly individualistic genre.

Dazzle is a homesteading story in which life on the outward trail is more important than the arrival. The novel opens with a single chapter in which a member of a Quaker settlement in Central America struggles with the sadness of embarking on the great journey to the stars.[45] It ends centuries later with another short chapter in which one of the planet-born generation encounters the new planet's ferocity and danger and takes it all for granted as the conditions of life. In between, the body of the novel centers on the immigrant ship *Dusty Miller* as it nears the new planet and its passengers try to decide if it is habitable. In other words, the generations that interact directly in *Journey*, *Beowulf's Children*, *Girl in Landscape*, and "The Eye Altering" are drawn apart from each other in time and in place.

Because *Dazzle* is a novel about a community making up its mind, the plot line is about the struggle of the colonists to decide what to do about the new planet. They send probes and debate the findings that show a stormy, subarctic land that may barely be survivable. A manned reconnaissance ends with two of four explorers dead and the planet's inhospitality highlighted. The interstellar voyagers talk and set up committees, hear reports, and talk some more. Their ship may, just barely, have the capacity to seek out a new star system, but hopes and fears come to revolve around *this* one ball of rock and ice. Gloss takes the deliberations seriously—both the contrasting attitudes and ideas that the participants bring and the Quaker process through which insights are aired and a larger sense of the community emerges.[46]

Once the transfer has been made, the concluding chapter echoes Le Guin and Robinson, for new generations learn the planet in ways that the ship born cannot. "My mother has an old, religious reverence for books," muses one of the new generation. "My mother's understanding of this world, even after seventy years, is intimately linked to the fusty smell inside the covers of the books. . . . Mine is in the waxy panes of riverine ice, in the smell of a mouse's old bones and the spiny rustle of a ring-eye's nest. The landscape we inhabit as children, inhabits us."[47] It is a quasimystical sense of place, perhaps related to the altered seeing of Le Guin's short story and the deep landscape immersion of Nirgal, but it is also a fearsome understanding that takes stress and storm, disaster and death as parts of everyday experience. Indeed, the very wildness of the planet which so disturbed the star-born and pushed the first explorer into mental collapse ("'There was a wind!' he said wildly, as if that explained everything.") becomes an essential for the planet born ("The weather rode very slowly across the grass. . . . I suppose that was the first time I heard the earth speaking.").[48]

Uniquely among the writers considered in this chapter, Molly Gloss has written both historical fiction and science fiction about homesteading, and *The*

Dazzle of Day reflects that dual understanding. It is the most complex of the texts discussed in this essay because it critiques one historical moment—homesteading—by inserting it into larger processes of historical change. For Gloss, homesteading is a story of tensions between mobility and community. She writes within a long historical literature that sees the democratic experience rather than continental abundance as the determining national experience. In particular, a number of western historians emphasize the transfer of ideas and institutions from East to West, the continual reestablishment of values and institutions, and the hard-won formation of civil communities from individuals and families.[49] She wants readers to understand the story of homesteading not as the achievement of an end state but as one part of a larger process, directing our attention to the longer histories of prelude and consequence of which the crafting of family farms is only a brief stage.

Science fiction writers, historical novelists, and historians are tilling the same ground as critics of the American past. They have been moving toward similar understandings of the national experience—as embodied in the history of the West—whether by re-evaluating historical sources or reflecting on standard narratives in fictions of the future. As this analysis has tried to show, science fiction homesteading stories are most challenging when they step beyond the frames of adventure tale and family saga to place homesteading within larger narratives of economic development and cultural transfer. Academic historians who have taken on this task are often grouped as practitioners of a "new western history." There is no similarly convenient term for writers as disparate in specific interests and sensibility as Philip Dick and later Kim Stanley Robinson, Jonathan Lethem, and Molly Gloss, but they are participants in the same debate about the underpinings of one the prominent American creation stories.

Notes

Epigraph: Robert Heinlein, *Farmer in the Sky* (New York: Ballantine, 1975), 105.

1. Heinlein was born in Butler, Missouri, in 1907. He attended the U.S. Naval Academy and then lived in California and Colorado after illness in the 1930s cut short his navy career. Bradbury was born in Waukegan, Illinois, in 1920 and moved with his family to Los Angeles in the mid-1930s, where he lived until his death. Heinlein tended to see the Pacific West as an exuberant realization of the American get-up-and-go that had conquered continental frontiers (e.g., engineer Dan Davis in *The Door into Summer*). Bradbury's response has been a pained flinch from the cacophony of information-rich cities in favor of a nostalgic re-creation of small town scenery and society.

2. For example, see Daniel Hoffman, *Paul Bunyan: Last of the Frontier Demigods* (Philadelphia: University of Pennsylvania Press, 1952); Robert Price, *Johnny Appleseed: Man and Myth* (Bloomington: Indiana University Press, 1954).

3. In both animated films and live action television, Disney in the 1950s rummaged through American history for a variety of 100 percent American heroes—Davy Crockett,

Mike Fink, Pecos Bill. Neil Gaiman's prize-winning fantasy *American Gods* (2001), which imagines the fate of Old World gods struggling to survive in North America, briefly introduces John Chapman as a mythologized culture hero who complains that upstart Paul Bunyan now gets all the attention.

4. Gary K. Wolfe, "The Frontier Myth in Ray Bradbury," in Martin Harry Greenberg and Joseph D. Olander, eds., *Ray Bradbury* (Edinburgh, UK: Paul Harris Publisher, 1980), 33–54.

5. Ray Bradbury, *The Martian Chronicles* (New York: William Morrow, 1997), 101, 102, 106.

6. In the American Northeast, in contrast, growing conditions are such that much of the once-cultivated landscape has reverted to woods with no special human intervention.

7. Bradbury, *Martian Chronicles*, 158–59.

8. For theoretical framework, see James C. Scott, *Seeing Like a State: How Certain Schemes to Improve the Human Condition Have Failed* (New Haven: Conn.: Yale University Press, 1998). For an application to western U.S. history, see Donald Worster, *Rivers of Empire: Water, Aridity, and the Growth of the American West* (New York: Pantheon, 1985).

9. Historians have usually approached homesteading via family and community microhistory, as in Merle Curti, *The Making of an American Community* (Stanford, Calif.: Stanford University Press, 1959), John Mack Faragher, *Sugar Creek: Life on the Illinois Prairie* (New Haven, Conn.: Yale University Press, 1986), and Dean May, *Three Frontiers: Family, Land, and Society in the American West, 1850–1900* (New York: Cambridge University Press, 1994).

10. Elliott West, "A Longer, Grimmer, but More Interesting Story," *Montana: The Magazine of Western History* 40 (Summer 1990): 72–76.

11. Molly Gloss, *The Jump-Off Creek* (Boston: Houghton Mifflin, 1989), 168, 185.

12. Willa Cather, *O, Pioneers!* (Boston: Houghton Mifflin, 1913), 20.

13. Walter Nugent, "Frontier and Empire in the Late Nineteenth Century," *Western Historical Quarterly* 20 (Autumn 1990): 393–408; Wallace Stegner, *Where the Bluebird Sings to the Lemonade Springs: Living and Writing in the West* (New York: Random House, 1992), 199.

14. Heinlein, *Farmer in the Sky*, 22.

15. Heinlein, *Farmer in the Sky*, 146. The allusion is to the Pare Lorentz documentary film *The Plow That Broke the Plains*, which deals with settlement, the dust bowl of the 1930s, and conservation efforts.

16. Heinlein, *Farmer in the Sky*, 147, 150.

17. Heinlein, *Farmer in the Sky*, 186, 183.

18. Alfred Crosby, *The Columbian Exchange: Biological and Cultural Consequences of 1492* (Westport, Conn.: Greenwood, 1972), and *Ecological Imperialism: The Biological Expansion of Europe, 900–1900* (New York: Cambridge University Press, 1986).

19. Larry Niven, Jerry Pournelle, and Steven Barnes, *The Legacy of Heorot* (New York: Simon and Schuster, 1987), 7. "Him" in the passage is Cadman Wayland, the lone military man among the settlers, who has a justified sense of ill ease.

20. The grendels have evolved the capacity to boost their rate of oxidation for short periods, allowing them to move at frightening speed. However, they need to remain close to water so that they can quickly cool themselves after these bursts of energy conversion. On this principle of biophysics turns the defense of the colony.

21. Larry Niven, Jerry Pournelle, and Steven Barnes, *Beowulf's Children* (New York: Tor, 1995), 132.

22. Marta Randall, *Journey* (New York: Pocket Books, 1978).

23. Ibid., 125.

24. Wallace Stegner, *Beyond the 100th Meridian: John Wesley Powell and the Second Opening of the West* (Boston: Houghton Mifflin, 1954); Walter Prescott Webb, "The American West: Perpetual Mirage," *Harper's* 24 (May 1957); Henry Nash Smith, *Virgin Land: The American West as Symbol and Myth* (Cambridge, Mass.: Harvard University Press, 1950): 25–31. The troubled application of one aspect of the myth is the subject of David Emmons, *Garden in the Grasslands: Boomer Literature of the Central Great Plains* (Lincoln: University of Nebraska Press, 1971).

25. Ursula Le Guin, "The Eye Altering," originally published in 1974 and reprinted in *The Compass Rose* (New York: Harper and Row, 1982), 157.

26. Ibid., 166, 169.

27. Philip K. Dick, *The Three Stigmata of Palmer Eldritch* (1965; reprint, New York: Vintage Books, 1991), 142, 159

28. William Frey, "Three Americas: The Rising Significance of Regions," *Journal of the American Planning Association* 68 (Autumn 2002): 349–55.

29. Jonathan Raban, *Bad Land: An American Romance* (New York: Pantheon, 1996); William Least Heat-Moon, *PrairyErth* (Boston: Houghton Mifflin, 1991); Larry McMurtry, *The Last Picture Show* (New York: Dial Press, 1966); Deborah Popper and Frank Popper, "The Buffalo Commons: Metaphor as Method," *Geographical Review* 89, no. 4 (October 1999): 491–510. They point out that the extensive tracts of National Grasslands are the result of a similar process following the 1930s.

30. Scott Donaldson, *The Suburban Myth* (New York: Columbia University Press, 1969).

31. Philip K. Dick, *Martian Time-Slip* (New York: Ballantine, 1964), 13, 10.

32. William Robbins, *Colony and Empire: The Capitalist Transformation of the American West* (Lawrence: University Press of Kansas, 1994); Melvyn Dubofsky, *We Shall Be All: A History of the Industrial Workers of the World* (Chicago: Quadrangle, 1969); Mike Davis, *City of Quartz: Excavating the Future in Los Angeles* (New York: Verso, 1990); Donald Worster, *Rivers of Empire: Water, Aridity and the Growth of the American West* (New York: Pantheon, 1985); J. Anthony Lukas, *Big Trouble: A Murder in a Small Western Town Sets Off a Struggle for the Soul of America* (New York: Simon and Schuster, 1997).

33. William Kittredge, *Who Owns the West?* (San Francisco: Mercury House, 1996).

34. Kim Stanley Robinson, *Blue Mars* (New York: Bantam Spectra, 1997), 385–87.

35. As Heinlein does for Ganymede, Robinson offers fascinating details of ecological change. Nirgal builds small dams to trap water and thin soil. Lichen has already colonized the basin, so he sows other seeds and spores and observes which ones thrive. Other modified plants that have been seeded on Mars begin to spread into the basin on the wind. He buys loads of topsoil and earthworms. After worms will come moles, mice, marmots, rabbits. Plants bloom with the new spring. Where Avalonians have to fight to learn, Nirgal simply has to inhabit a place, to experiment and experience. Nevertheless, the planet still fools him, first with a viroid infection that withers the grass, junipers, and potatoes, then with a dust storm that buries the cirque a meter deep. "In time, other winds would blow some of this dust away. Snow would fall on the rest of it. . . . Water would carry the dust

and fines away, down the massif and into the world. But by the time that happened, every plant and animal in the basin would be dead." Robinson, *Blue Mars*, 402–404.

36. Jonathan Lethem, *Girl in Landscape* (New York: Doubleday, 1998), 1.

37. Ibid., 62–63.

38. Ibid., 48. "They turned a corner and the view opened before them. A spread of enormous ruins, shapes Pella hadn't seen before, including another intact arch, huge, that framed a lop-sided heart-shaped chunk of sky" (ibid., 97). Note the emphasis on the big sky, both as a trope of the American western and because you could no longer go out under the sky unprotected on Earth.

39. Interview with Jonathan Lethem, at www.randomhouse.com/boldtype/0598/lethem/interview.html (accessed September 22, 2014).

40. Jane Tompkins, *West of Everything: The Inner Life of Westerns* (New York: Oxford University Press, 1992); Mary Lawlor, *Recalling the Wild: Naturalism and the Closing of the American West* (New Brunswick, N.J.: Rutgers University Press, 2000), 2.

41. Lethem, *Girl in Landscape*, 112.

42. Ibid., 114–15. The Archbuilders have similarities to the Bleekmen in *Martian Time-Slip*, although Dick's race seem most closely modeled on native Australians.

43. Lethem, *Girl in Landscape*, 229, 257–58.

44. Tom Moylan, "Utopia Is When Our Lives Matter: Reading Kim Stanley Robinson's *Pacific Edge*," *Utopian Studies* 6 (1995); Carol Franko, "Working the In-Between: Kim Stanley Robinson's Utopian Fiction," *Science-Fiction Studies* 21 (1994).

45. There is a significant Quaker presence in Costa Rica drawing on both U.S. transplants and native Costa Ricans.

46. See Michael J. Sheeran, *Beyond Majority Rule: Voteless Decision Making in the Religious Society of Friends* (Philadelphia: Philadelphia Yearly Meeting, 1983). There are close parallels between the depiction of Quaker decision practices and the town meeting politics in Robinson's *Pacific Edge*.

47. Molly Gloss, *The Dazzle of Day* (New York: Tor, 1997), 252.

48. Gloss, *Dazzle*, 187, 253

49. Richard White, *It's Your Misfortune and None of My Own: A New History of the American West* (Norman: University of Oklahoma Press, 1991); Robert V. Hine, *Community on the American Frontier: Separate but Not Alone* (Norman: University of Oklahoma Press, 1980).

CHAPTER 11

Falling into History

The Imagined Wests of Kim Stanley Robinson

Red Mars is Kim Stanley Robinson's highly praised science fiction novel published in 1993.[1] Its pivotal section carries the title "Falling into History." More than two decades have passed since permanent human settlers arrived on the red planet in 2027, and the growing Martian communities have become too complex to be guided by simple earth-made plans or single individuals. The section centers on John Boone, an explorer-hero ("the first man on Mars") and charismatic co-leader of the first one hundred settlers. As he spends three years wandering and visiting scattered settlements, he finds that Martian society is outgrowing his capacity to comprehend and direct.

> He had been on the road for years now . . . cutting ribbons at the opening of one thing or another—a town, a well, a weather station, a mine, a mohole—and always talking, talking in public speeches or private conversations, talking to strangers, old friends, new acquaintances . . . and all in an attempt to inspire the people to figure out a way to forget history, to build a functioning society. To create a scientific system designed for Mars, designed to their specifications, fair and just and rational and all those good things. To point the way to a new Mars! And yet after every year that passed, it seemed less likely. . . . Events were out of control, and more than that, out of anyone's control. (*Red Mars*, 283)

Robinson is a novelist who takes history seriously. The fall into history is the transition from the carefully controlled circumstances of a single contingent of first-comers to the intractability of multiple groups, peoples, values, and agendas. It is the collapse of the open-ended possibilities of a new place into the constrained situations of historicity—the concatenation of habits, hopes, and vested interests that characterize any society. In the words of critic Robert Markley, Robinson imagines a situation in which utopian schemes are inevitably "undone by the distance between the idealized operations of a frictionless system and the wear and tear of embodied, historical experience."[2]

Robinson himself is a Californian, raised in Orange County in the later 1950s and 1960s and now living in Davis. One of the most popular and honored science fiction writers of the last three decades, his reputation is based on two trilogies that hold mirrors to multiple historical experiences, prominently including that of the American West. The books that describe "Three Californias"—*The Wild Shore* (1984), *The Gold Coast* (1988), *Pacific Edge* (1990)—are explicitly regional, imagining alternative futures for Orange County over the twenty-first century.

Red Mars (1993), *Green Mars* (1994), and *Blue Mars* (1996) constitute a single densely written novel of the settlement of the red planet over two centuries ("a triple decker in the old style," says the author[3]) that transposes many of the problems of the American West to a new setting. Robinson is thus a distinctively western writer whose books are imagined discussions of the very stuff of western history, the inhabitation of "empty" places and their transformation into unexpected sorts of communities. He has himself commented: "I think of myself as a Californian writer more than I do a science fiction writer, and would be happy to be grouped with the California writers. To be grounded in that way, even regionalized, would be a very good way of giving some physicality or heft to the inclination of science fiction to be otherworldly by being set in the future."[4]

It is not surprising that a California/western writer may also be a science fiction writer. Americans have long projected political and cultural hopes on the West in forms that range from geopolitical boosterism to communitarian experiments. And we have been particularly eager to burden California with often contradictory roles as arcadia, utopia, and featured player in the collapse of civilization.[5] Science fiction is a natural extension of such western discourse, reinscribing the hopes and fears that shaped stories of the nineteenth- and twentieth-century West onto settings that stretch even more broadly across space and more deeply into time. Indeed, for many writers of speculative fiction, the western experience of the United States has served as a template for fictional futures. The result, at times, is a seamless connection of centuries—a common set of stories that link the historical past to the imagined future.[6]

Americans have long found it easy to apply the capacious frontier metaphor to realms beyond the stratosphere. Most television viewers know of the Starship *Enterprise*, which boldly voyages through "space: the final frontier" in endlessly recycled episodes of *Star Trek*. Closer to home, Disneyland juxtaposed the rocketships of Tomorrowland and the coonskin caps of Frontierland.[7] "Space operas" as western horse operas with ray guns were a staple of pulp magazine fiction in the 1930s and 1940s. The Buck Rogers and Flash Gordon movies of the same era even inspired a Gene Autry serial called *The Phantom Empire*, in which Gene alternates between singing cowboy duties and captivity by ray-gun wielding Thunder Riders from the one-hundred-thousand-year-old subterranean "scientific city" of Murania.

More recently, the idea of a High Frontier for American ingenuity and enterprise has been a political project. The rhetoric of John F. Kennedy connected the New Frontier to the goal of a manned mission to the moon and former astronaut John Glenn later invoked the image of space as "the modern frontier for national adventure."[8] In the 1970s, Gerard K. O'Neill gave the metaphor an engineering twist with his detailed proposal for a "high frontier" of inhabited artificial satellites. The U.S. National Commission on Space in 1986 described the settlement of North America as a prologue to the space frontier. Lobbying organizations and publishers continue to keep alive the idea that the necessary next frontier will be space exploration, translating an old maxim as "upward the course of empire takes its way."[9]

Robinson himself challenges these well-worn conventions by emphasizing community rather than heroism, civic life rather than adventure, and environmental management rather than economic opportunity. His trilogies address both the scientific-industrial politics of the high frontier and the literary formulas that underlie this political project. By taking seriously the possibilities of a cooperative commonwealth, both in *Pacific Edge* and in the Mars books, he questions the inevitability of capitalist economies. His attention to the dynamics and problems of social inclusion and exclusion undercut the easy nationalism of the earthly and unearthly frontiers. His attention to settlement and society contravene the dynamic of perpetual change that is embedded in the frontier myth.

My specific goals in this final chapter are, first, to explore the ways in which Robinson as a western American author understands history and pivots his narratives on issues of historical interpretation, and, second, to examine how he incorporates into his fictions some of the familiar tropes and interpretations of the American western experience. The larger, implicit subject is the incorporation of western American history into popular culture, viewed through the ways that Robinson uses and transforms issues central to historical understanding and interpretation of the American West and other European settlement frontiers. In particular, we can gain new insights into the meaning of the West in American minds by examining how Robinson has dealt with such issues as the future of urbanization, the possibilities of intentional communities and of economic cooperation, governance on a settlement frontier, the responsibilities of leadership in a democracy, the clash between raw nature and human use of the landscape, and the political tensions between colony and imperium. There is, I believe, much in Robinson's projections of future historical change that incorporates or echoes the critical thinking about environment, conquest, inequality, and community associated with the "new western history" with its emphasis on the multiplicity and complexity of events and the contingency of narratives.[10] Reading his work may make us more sensitive participants in this historical conversation and give us greater understanding of how increasingly complex ideas about the American West are entering the world of popular culture.

Robinson and History

Kim Stanley Robinson explicitly defines science fiction as historical in character—as articulated narratives that can be seen as anchored at their origins in "real" times and circumstances. "In every science fiction narrative," he writes, "there is an explicit or implicit fictional *history* that connects the period depicted to our present moment." That is to say, science fiction is narrative that starts with or assumes the historical present and writes it forward. In a different interview, he makes a parallel point in calling science fiction "the history that we cannot know."[11] Readers can assume that a plausible sequence of events might lead from their present to the events in the story and can observe how the writer varies the assumptions behind those events. Science fiction is thus a set of thought experiments, as Martian society is itself characterized during one of the political debates in *Green Mars* (376).

Robinson's definition differentiates true science fiction from many of the books and videos that sit on the "science fiction" shelves in libraries, bookstores, and Red Box video outlets. Science fiction is not cheerful Harry Potter fantasies nor dark vampire melodramas; it is not extraterrestrial monster-slaying tales, sword-and-castle-in-a-different-universe romances, nor space operas set in some other galaxy a long time ago. Instead, Robinson aligns himself with "hard" science fiction writers who have crafted explicit "future histories" such as Robert Heinlein, David Brin, and Ken MacLeod and with so-called cyberpunk writers like William Gibson and Neal Stephenson who project the near future of an electronically linked and mediated society.[12]

Robinson argues the virtues of historical fiction as a counterpart of science fiction. In comments on the work of historical novelist Cecelia Holland, he states that historical fiction and science fiction share the challenge of making intelligible the inner workings of alien cultures, and thereby illuminating our own cultural and social values. He also shares Holland's interest in politics—in the ways that people wield power and the ways that the powerless can resist the powerful. It is therefore possible "to write historical fiction for the same reason one writes science fiction: to take advantage of the psychological power of the estrangement effect, which in pulling readers momentarily out of their ordinary world views, gives them the chance to see things anew."[13]

In comments on his own work, Robinson places himself on a map of literary influences anchored by Joseph Conrad's socially embedded adventures and Thomas Pynchon's ability to ground surreal narratives on the foundations of existing times and places. Several of Pynchon's purportedly mainstream novels—particularly *The Crying of Lot 49* (1966) and *Vineland* (1990)—deal with oddly off-kilter Californias that start out as places that we can recognize but drift inexorably into places of the imagination. The oppressor state that lurks beneath the sunny California surface in *Vineland* looks like the dark future that has been explicitly avoided in *Pacific Edge*. In the Martian narrative, the center of gravity slowly shifts from the challenges faced by individuals to the complexities of bringing change to living societies. This is the same progression that we see in Conrad from the isolated protagonists of *Almayer's Folly* (1895) and *Lord Jim* (1900) to the complex colonial society described in *Nostromo* (1904) and the ambiguities of revolution as analyzed in *The Secret Agent* (1907).

Robinson is a theoretically sophisticated writer. He earned an M.A. in English from Boston University and a Ph.D. from the University of California–San Diego, where he worked with the influential literary scholar Fredric Jameson, perhaps best known as the critic who deconstructed the Westin Bonaventure Hotel in Los Angeles in "Postmodernism: The Cultural Logic of Late Capitalism."[14] Robinson's dissertation examined science fiction writer Philip K. Dick, whose work anticipated the shifting viewpoints of postmodernism and includes the story that Ridley Scott turned into the movie *Blade Runner*.[15] As a licensed but nonpracticing academic, Robinson is fully aware of the traps in seeing history as sets of analogies, which mislead us as often as they help, . . . although the unpacking or deconstruction of historical analogies is central to his Mars fiction.[16] In *Red Mars*, for example, John Boone tries to warn unhappy settlers that they are not the exact equivalent of the "hardy pioneer colonists" of 1775 and that changed circumstances make it impossible to re-enact the American Revolution (348). In *Blue Mars*, the crafters of a new Martian constitution pick carefully among the numerous analogies from the political travail of twentieth-century Earth.[17]

Robinson also turns history writing and the politics of memory into one of the motifs of his novels. A central character in *The Wild Shore* is the village storyteller, who manufactures a useable past for the survivors who eke out a livelihood from farming and fishing along the southern California coast. Still a teenager when the bombs fell, he creates an imaginary career, adds three decades to his life, and spins tall tales into a half-accurate history to inspire the postdisaster generations. *Pacific Edge* alternates a communitarian present in the year 2065 with excerpts from a diary that touches on the political struggles that led to that particular set of social and economic institutions. The author of the diary is the same individual as the storyteller in the other book, living through a different future.

In the Mars trilogy, Robinson uses the science fiction gimmick of longevity treatments to maintain the members of the "first hundred" settlers through two centuries of Martian history. Their understanding of the present in light of their (and others') reinterpretations of the past changes and becomes one of the themes and driving factors for the second and third volumes. Robinson models the problems and selectivity of historical memory and history writing in the memories of these characters. They habitually search the past for historical comparisons to understand the new Martian politics and society—usually with little success. They worry that they are forgetting the meaning of their own lived past (*Green Mars*, 359). They repeatedly contemplate the character of historical understanding (*Blue Mars*, 678, 713) and stand bemused or infuriated when they find themselves reinterpreted as characters in history books or even in opera (*Green Mars*, 540–42). The stories they tell about their own pasts become factors in the shaping of their present and future.[18]

California Futures

The first trilogy, written in the 1980s, imagines three very different futures for Orange County, California. *The Wild Shore* (1984) describes a village climbing back to tribalism after the neutron bombing of the United States. The historical record is truncated, and the survivors are too busy toiling for food and shelter to sift historical fact from fiction. The southern California of *The Gold Coast* (1988) is a straight-line projection of an overcrowded "condomundo" where alienated young people do designer drugs with eyedroppers, drive automobiles with electronic guidance systems, and toy with terrorism against the transnational corporations that twist their coils around every activity. *Pacific Edge* (1990) offers the alternative of a federation of ecologically sensitive communities, organized around the "small is beautiful" precepts of Ernest Schumacher and the principles of social ecology and mutual aid articulated by political philosopher Murray Bookchin.[19] Americans have used the political process to gradually rein in corporate America and focus self-government at the local level, although each community remains part of a larger world economy.

Social scientists and planners have developed increasing sophistication about the differences between forecasts and scenarios. Forecasts are quantified analogies that may use sophisticated mathematics but that still succeed or fail on the accuracy of their assumptions; the most important question about forecasts is why and how much change is likely to *change*—that is, what is likely to alter present short-term trends, rates, and structures.[20] In contrast, scenario building attempts to consider possible interrelationships of technical, economic, social, cultural, and political factors. Scenario building in one sense is history on fast forward. Focused on the future, it utilizes disparate pieces of information within a broad context to create an understandable narrative. It may produce surprises, stimulating imaginative construction of alternative possibilities. And it welcomes the techniques of narrative to give "body" and presence to future possibilities; planners increasingly think of their task as "persuasive storytelling" that links the present to a future.[21]

Robinson demonstrates that his Orange County fictions are precisely these sorts of alternative scenarios by building in specific continuities across the books, a characteristic that he reinforces with a reference in *Pacific Edge* to Lawrence Durrell's "Alexandria Quartet" of novels, which retell the same story from four points of view. Like much historical writing, the stories are grounded on the importance of place—a particular stretch of coast from Point Dana to San Onofre, the ridges and canyons that trail off the Santa Ana Mountains. The protagonist in each is a young man who matures, in part, by attracting and then failing to hold a strong woman. Each book makes it clear from the roster of characters that Orange County in the twenty-first century will be as much Latino as Anglo. The character Tom Barnard appears in each book at the end of a very different but logically derived life. The storyteller of *The Wild Shore* and the diary keeper of *Pacific Edge*, he ends his life in *The Gold Coast* in a nursing home, reminiscing to occasional visitors. And the books share an explicitly historical motif of digging up the past. Each opens with a group of friends wielding shovels—

trekking to abandoned San Clemente to loot a grave for imagined treasure in *The Wild Shore*, digging beneath the street for the fun of discovering relics of the twentieth century in *The Gold Coast*, cheerfully sharing required community work on a street project in *Pacific Edge*.

The trilogy is a set of variations on the common trope of "seeing the future in California." An imposing scholarly literature, it examines the ways in which greater Los Angeles served through the twentieth century as the summary or shorthand for the American future, the place to get a preview of things to come. More than half a century ago, Carey McWilliams argued that California was twenty years ahead of the rest of the nation. Los Angeles, claimed Neil Morgan in 1960, was "the center of gravity in the westward tilt" that was creating the America of tomorrow in the West of today. Postwar critics called Los Angeles "the ultimate city," the "prototype of the supercity," the "leading city." Richard Elman was a bewildered New Yorker who traveled to Compton, California, in 1967 "with the thought in mind that this was the future."[22]

More recently, another scholarly generation has declared greater Los Angeles as the prototype for the twenty-first-century city. A "Los Angeles School" of urban studies now argues, essentially, that we have in the SoCal metropolis a new urban form and dynamic that is postmodern. Its cityscape and spatiality, its economy and social ecology—all are fragmented, flexible, fluid . . . not so much formless as constantly in reformation. As expressed by Allen J. Scott, Michael Dear, Edward Soja, and others, this is a metropolis that exemplifies not its past but a coming future. And it is a metropolis where Orange County may seem to manifest the newest of the new as a postsuburban exopolis that can only be understood through fragmentary snapshots.[23]

Place—the Orange County setting—thus matters as the key to the trilogy's impact as well as serving as a factor in each narrative. It seems unlikely that a Fort Wayne trilogy or a Preble County, Ohio, trilogy, no matter how carefully done, would attract the same readership. As Robinson has agreed, Orange County's role as an "awful paradigm for the future . . . could not be replaced by just any American city or suburb."[24] All three of Robinson's futures gain resonance as subtle departures and challenges to the standard dystopian Los Angeles of *Blade Runner* and the fictional variations on a Los Angeles apocalypse that Mike Davis recently summarized in *The Ecology of Fear*.[25] Davis roots his dark vision in *City of Quartz* in the collapse of hope in his southern California hometown of Fontana. In contrast, Tom Barnard in *Pacific Edge* (300) explicitly identifies the California of *his* childhood in the 1980s as a "pocket utopia."

> California when I was a child was a child's paradise, I was healthy, well fed, well clothed, well housed, I went to school and there were libraries with all the world in them and after school I played in orange groves and in Little League and in the band and down at the beach and every day was an adventure, and when I came home my mother and father created a home as sold as rock, the world seemed solid! And it comes to this, do you understand me—I grew up in utopia.

> But I didn't. Not really. Because while I was growing up in my sunny seaside home much of the world was in misery, hungry, sick. . . . I had been on an island. . . .
>
> And if-if! if someday the whole world reaches utopia, then that dream California will become a precursor, and sign of things to come, and my childhood is redeemed.

To get to that dream is to engage in politics, for the challenges and processes of democratic self-government set another theme that cuts across the three books and leads toward the second trilogy. *The Wild Shore* contrasts local town meeting democracy and the strong-man government that emerges from the ruins of San Diego. The second and third books contrast unsuccessful and successful ways to undercut the military-industrial complex. Slapdash terrorism in *The Gold Coast* turns out to be not only ineffective but corrupted by corporate power. *Pacific Edge* foregrounds the process of representative democracy—lobbying, bargaining, and the use and abuse of bureaucratic rules to advance local interests. In the background narrative, improvements have been achieved incrementally, with political mobilization and organizing over multiple decades. In the intense local debate over developing a portion of the town's remaining open space, change again comes by increments through lobbying and votes in the town council.[26] Taken together, the books are an examination of how history happens as well as what history might mean.

Mars As the New West

The Mars trilogy is panoramic in scope and written from multiple points of view. The books follow the development of Martian society from the first settlement by a team of fifty Russians and fifty Americans, through debates over environment change, immigration, the development of multiple cultures, efforts at political independence, two rounds of constitution making, "international" negotiations, generational conflicts, and changing social values. The structure is a series of long sections that take the viewpoints of key figures from the first hundred or their descendants. Taken together, the three volumes array the points of view of ten characters across thirty-two sections that average about sixty pages each.[27] The approach is reminiscent of John Dos Passos's *The 42nd Parallel* (1930), *1919* (1932), and *Big Money* (1936). Another comparison is a contemporary writer whom Robinson cites as an influence: Peter Matthiessen, whose Florida frontier trilogy *Killing Mister Watson* (1990), *Lost Man's River* (1997), and *Bone by Bone* (1999) is discussed is chapter 5.

Robinson's vision of this future clearly draws on the history of North America. The narrative is premised on the technological capacity to terraform Mars (in effect making pastures of plenty from dry desert lands). In the tasks set for the original one hundred settlers are echoes of Jamestown and Philadelphia, Astoria and New Archangel; in their careful selection for skills and temperaments are parallels to the schemes of nineteenth-century utopian socialists. Evolving experiments in political independence and self-government drive the story. Complicating the political history are conflicts between "reds" and "greens," the factions in this case ironically reversed from our current usage—the reds representing those who desire to leave Mars unaltered "wilderness" and the greens those who wish to adapt it to human use.

The titles—*Red Mars, Green Mars, Blue Mars*—trace the success of terraforming through massive engineering interventions to raise the ambient temperature and atmospheric pressure, to bring water to the surface, and to introduce plants and animals bioengineered from Earth originals. There is careful and fascinating detail about the terraforming process—options, choices, setbacks, side effects, accomplishments. The technical dimension is reminiscent of the cetology and whaling lore in *Moby Dick*, and Robinson himself argues that "there is no intrinsic reason why scientific detail cannot be as interesting as the stage business of a chase scene."[28]

By imagining a "first hundred" settlers equally divided among Russians and Americans, Robinson can draw on two structuring metaphors drawn from nineteenth- and twentieth-century history. One is the promise and problems of socialist revolution against the power of capital. The second is the possibilities and processes of community building in new lands. The first is the big, dramatic framework. The second underlies Robinson's projections of the evolution of everyday life on the high frontier. Both metaphors tie the hypothesized history of Mars to repeated falls into history—the failures of Russian socialism and French revolutionary utopianism; the transformation of New England between the 1630s and the 1680s, of Utah from the nineteenth to the twentieth century, or of any new place that wriggles free from the expectations of its founders.[29]

Red Mars, the first volume, pivots on the possibilities and failures of revolution, and it is full of the intertextuality that literary critics enjoy. A key character among the first hundred is Arkady Bogdanov, a charismatic revolutionary who preaches independence from Earth and helps to trigger a failed revolution in 2061 (the Martian equivalent of Russia's 1905 revolution). Martians regroup and try again successfully in 2127 with much better organization—think October 1917—when the oppressive regime is under external stress from eco-catastrophe on Earth. Bogdanov the character bears the name of a real Bolshevik leader, Alexandre Bogdanov, author of his own science fiction novel *Red Star* (1907) about the establishment of socialism on Mars.[30] Referenced as well is Nikolai Cherneshevsky's feminist utopia of the 1860s, *What Is to Be Done?* The phrase is modified for the section on failure of the first revolution in *Red Mars* (as "what have we done" in Japanese translation as *senzeni na*) and for the first section on constitution making in *Green Mars*; the heroine of the constitutional convention is Nadia Chernyshevsky, another of the first hundred.

History in the Mars narrative is always conditional and mutable. It is made through the articulation of ideas, public debates, power plays, and assassination.

It is balanced between structure and agency, culture, politics, and economics. It is "whole, nonrepeatable, and contingent" (*Green Mars*, 220). It escapes the power of Bogdanov, Boone, his rival Frank Chalmers, or Earth-based corporations to direct and shape. It shows the messiness of human life—there is always "more trouble, more history, between us and any decent society," Robinson commented in a 1996 interview.[31]

By *Green Mars* and *Blue Mars*, the increased complexity and density of cultures and institutions and "history" make action more problematic and complex. The heroes are now the constitution makers and by implication the scientists who help to create an inhabitable Mars. No single narrative can now contain the multifarious history. The model of the Russian revolutions drops away, for no simplifying theory works, in favor of Madisonian political compromises. The meat of the process of community formation is engaged conversation, engaged politics. The key events are now the forging of a revolutionary compact after the first failure ("What Is to Be Done" in *Green Mars*) and the establishment of formal government after a successful breakaway from Earth's control ("A New Constitution" in *Blue Mars*). Nadia the builder of engineering works and constitutions emerges as the story's new hero.[32]

Robinson's Mars books are written explicitly against two alternative uses of Mars as frontier. One is the reinscription of the North American conquest narrative onto Mars in fantastic fictions that pay no attention to the science of transportation or settlement. Edgar Rice Burroughs kicked of the genre with "Under the Moons of Mars" (1912), in which western American John Carter takes refuge in an Arizona cave to escape Apache warriors, only to find himself on "Barsoom," facing much the same situation in a landscape that looks quite southwestern. Carter, whom Burroughs seems to have modeled on the protagonist of *The Virginian*, continued his Martian adventures in a dozen books over several decades. The John Carter books were the implicit foil for Ray Bradbury's blithely unscientific but very self-conscious inversion of the same story in *The Martian Chronicles* (1958) with episodes of genocide, labor exploitation, wasted landscapes, and ghost towns.[33]

From the opposite side of the science/humanities divide is a technologically specific literature that bundles hard science and entrepreneurial values to proclaim Mars as the most practical high frontier. Aerospace engineer Robert Zubrin zeroed in on the next planet in *The Case for Mars: The Plan to Settle the Red Planet and Why We Must* (1996), invoking the spirit of Frederick Jackson Turner to proclaim that a new Martian frontier will help us recapture the soul of America and spark the formation of the Mars Society.[34] Recent science fiction novels that focus exclusively on dramatizing the technology of Mars exploration include planetary scientist Geoffrey A. Landis's *Mars Crossing* (2000) and Zubrin's own *First Landing* (2001). Both use that simplest of plots: the stranded explorers who must strike out across country with undaunted courage and work as a team to save themselves. Zubrin also puts his understanding of the

American past into the mouth of Kevin McGee, the historian who accompanies the mission:

> I'm a historian, and I know that a society cannot have progress, or growth, or hope, unless there is an open frontier. That's what made America in its frontier days such a powerful engine of progress for all humanity. . . . We became the most creative nation in history, because we could see the infinite potential of the human mind. . . . We don't build new cities any more, and so we've begun to think of ourselves not as builders of our country, but as mere inhabitants. Our frontier has been gone too long, and now our nation is losing its spark.[35]

Robinson, too, is a historian, and one who is more subtle than Zubrin's fictional Kevin McGee. His fiction is suffused with an awareness of the American West as a historically shaped place. Where the Orange County books present possible extensions of western history, the Mars books adapt and utilize the themes and tropes through which Americans have come to understand that history. These themes illustrate and drive the action, and they are themselves challenged or interrogated by the dynamics of the fictions. And, most intriguingly, they are framed in ways that show familiarity with the themes and criticisms that the so-called new western historians were elaborating in the same years that Robinson was writing. These concerns have been summed up by Patricia Limerick with a series of "C" words: conquest, continuity, convergence, and complexity, to which we might add capitalism and community (with nods to William Robbins and Robert Hine).[36]

As the American West has been, the Martian frontier is projected as a place of often rapacious resource development. The theme of conquest, which is central to the new western history, takes the form of the conquest of nature. The first hundred begin with exploration and road building. Subsequent settlers construct high-speed transit lines, build dams, and dig mines. They tap geothermal heat, pump out aquifers, and seed bioengineered plants to add weight, heat, and oxygen to the Martian atmosphere. With no building codes and environmental regulations in place, large corporations dig and run, build company towns on the cheap, and play workers of different nationalities against each other (*Green Mars*, 228). Like the mountain West, Mars is an urban frontier of gateway cities and production cities from which miners and eventually agriculturalists spread outward: Sheffield stands in for a port city like San Francisco, Burroughs for an industrial city like Denver, Serenzi Na for a mining town like Butte, Bradbury for small agricultural cities like Grand Junction.

The history of the American West is testimony to the momentum of engineering technology, the easy step from can do to should do. So too is Martian history. The power and nearly inexorable appeal of terraforming technologies is similar to the American impulse to apply more and more technology to capture and deliver western water. In fact (the twentieth century) and in fiction (the twenty-second century), we see the ramp up from smaller to larger projects, the aesthetic attraction of the technical intervention, the promise of better life, the opening of land to settlement and use (*Green Mars*, 459–61, 475). Technical papers at a terraforming conference morph easily into grant applications from ambitious scientists (*Green Mars*, 213).

The terraforming project brings out contrasting environmentalisms of preservation and utilization. The ideas of western irrigation utopians like William Smythe echo in the American advocates of use. They find allies among the Russians, who are also development advocates, reflecting their own national history; the experience they bring is that of intensive exploitation of Siberia and central Asia. We also hear the voices of preservationists who try to think like a Mars-scape. In a landscape that has never before supported human beings, there is no way to deny that wilderness and other concepts through which we understand the physical settings of human life are socially constructed.[37] At one point in the recurring debate over the future of the planet, scientist Sax Russell argues that "the beauty of Mars exists in the human mind. Without the human presence it is just a collection of atoms. . . . It is we who understand it and we who give it meaning." American ecologist Ann Clayborne, who longs for an unchanged Mars, counters that to truly see Mars requires "fitting into it as it is, and worshiping it with our attention" (*Red Mars*, 177–79). Another character "humanizes" Mars by devising the aerophany, a "landscape religion, a consciousness of Mars as a physical space suffused with kami, which was the spiritual energy or power that rested in the land itself" (*Red Mars*, 229). More concretely, the protagonists later come to understand the irony of protecting the natural setting from resource development by selling its attractions for tourism.[38]

As in the American West, the place itself takes on the role of actor and influence. We hear echoes of western visionaries such as Gary Snyder, whom Robinson lists as a favorite poet.[39] The Mars-scape looks like the California desert (*Red Mars*, 40), Monument Valley (*Red Mars*, 183), and the Painted Desert (*Red Mars*, 261). It is also "a Utah of the imagination" (*Blue Mars*, 275). Characters look like "a weatherbeaten sodbuster" (*Green Mars*, 364) and a scientific outpost like "a desiccated café in the Mojave" (*Red Mars*, 245). Settlers reproduce the flora and fauna of a southwestern canyon in a Martian valley that is tented over to hold in atmosphere (*Green Mars*, 425).

The idea that a frontier is social safety valve acts as an exogenous force driving the story. Mars functions as a symbolic (even if not practical) release valve for an Earth collapsing from environmental stress. Crowded countries put in their claims for Martian land and resources, and illicit immigrants arrive despite official quotas and limits. Everyone knows that another planet cannot really relieve pressure at home, but home governments are unwilling to give up the fiction. The planet is linked inextricably to the history of Earth, becoming a cauldron where multinational immigration reproduces old ethnic identities and cultures in desperately pure forms.

Robinson thus incorporates the idea of high frontier as safety valve into the narrative but shows it as a belief that is no more accurate for Mars than it was for western North America. The willingness of national governments on Earth to peddle the myth of a safety valve complicates the politics of environment and independence. Demands from back home constrain decisions on Mars about the pace of terraforming, for "millions on Earth wanted to come to Mars, to the 'new frontier,' where life was an adventure again" (*Red Mars*, 170). As the settlers later move toward a first revolution, Frank Chalmers notes one of their problems: "Did you see that program aired on Eurovid about all the open land on Mars? . . . It was like a real estate ad" (*Red Mars*, 389). John Boone uses the imagery of "frontier outpost" to inspire settlers to common purpose (*Red Mars*, 380) and Arkady Bogdanov uses the rhetoric of a free and open frontier to recruit settlers from the United States to his revolution (*Red Mars*, 425)—both efforts that end in failure.

The result is that the safety valve fails on both demographic realities (the mismatch between tens of thousands of immigrants and billions on the home planet) and on cultural conflict. Arkady Bogdanov's vision of inventing a new Martian culture from scratch crashes against the persistence of cultural differences among immigrants from Switzerland and India, the United States, Arab nations, and many other cultures. So does John Boone's alternative hope of easily blending the best ideas of Earth into a new society. Here is the theme of convergence from the new western history, an exploration of the ways in which a "white" frontier (pioneered in this case by Americans and Russians) is complicated by the arrival of immigrants from very different cultures, just as the presence of native peoples and the arrival of Latinos, Chinese, Japanese, Filipinos, and many others has complicated the development of an Anglo-American West. The constitution makers struggle to reconcile respect for cultural peculiarities with universal rights, hoping at best for "a lot of different cultures coexisting" (*Green Mars*, 337).

Questions of resource use and community come together in the relations between Earth and Mars, metropolis and colony. Central to the action is the clash between local autonomy and the domination of outside capital and corporations, another of the central issues of the new western history.[40] Beyond the direct tensions of capitalists and workers, Robinson argues that the global and local are interdependent because local opportunities are always embedded within larger structures. Mars cannot exist without a viable Earth.[41] The societies are linked through cultural heritage and information exchange. The web of economic and cultural connections remains too strong to allow isolated purity. As Americans discovered after 1783 and again after 1815, the web of connections that tie new settlements to their places of origins are not easily severed or ignored (*Blue Mars*, 23).

To be sure, one temptation in the face of pressure from Earth is to light out for the country in a repetition of a romantic version of western America. Nirgal, the epitome of the first Mars-born generation, reaches for the outback when things get too crowded and for a time becomes an isolated homesteader, re-enacting another model of the western American experience. The narrative's wildcard, a stowaway on the original voyage, also heads for the hills. He takes on the identity and role of the North American trickster Coyote ("Coyote is out there in the back of the hills, breathing the air already and doing what he wants, the bastard" [*Green Mars*, 48]). He travels the backlands organizing for economic separateness and political separation, and he argues passionately against connection to the past, but his influence gradually wanes.[42]

As in the American West, such individualism contrasts and clashes with very specific sectarian versions of community.[43] The empty Mars-scape invites secular and religious utopian colonies. In the demimonde beyond corporate control, and between revolutions, are colonies and communities of Sufis, Baptists, Quakers, and Rastafarians. There are followers of Rousseau, adherents of Fourier, and, in another academic joke, acolytes of Foucault (*Green Mars*, 230, 326). There are also Mars's radical first ecoterrorists and mystical Mars worshipers in the self-contained community of Zygote, concealed under the south polar ice. Hiroko Ai, the prophet of aerophany, explains the intention to John Boone: "We have a vision of what life on Mars can be. We could see it wasn't going to go that way. We have been proved right by what has happened since. So we thought we would establish our own life. . . . We want to try it, to show by experiment how we can live here. Someone has to show what you mean when you talk about a different life, John Boone. Someone has to live the life" (*Red Mars*, 374).

In fact, heroic individualism is replaced not by utopian experiments but by the merits of civic life. Robinson's alternative for Mars is also the great alternative for understanding western America: frontier as community building. The course of the Mars books problematizes end-state utopias (this is also why the Russian model drops away). The future must be found in the unruly and morally complex processes of community making, not in intellectualized schemes. We have, I think, a fictionalized version of Stanley Elkins and Eric McKitrick's meaning for Frederick Jackson Turner's frontier in the challenges of working together and Robert Hine's search for western community in the bonding of people with place.[44]

The pivotal figures of the trilogy remain John and Nadia, the people who talk. The true solution is to build civil society through conversation. Mars at its best, says critic Carol Franko, is "an argumentative and interdependent confederation of diverse communities."[45] Boone seeks utopia through dialogue, and the speech in which he sums up his ideas about forging a new Martian society pulls together and packs together thoughts and suggestions that he has picked up in years of conversation (*Red Mars*, 378–81). Nadia and her supporters seek stability through negotiation. They work the hallways during political meetings and do the hard work of community organizing. Franko references literary theorist Mikhail Bakhtin and the literary-linguistic idea of "dialogism" in which meaning emerges from the continual interaction among people, their words, their actions, and their unspoken ideals.[46] In Bakhtin's view, novels establish their worlds by setting multiple voices in interaction, allowing their characters to form new meanings from the play within and between persons and words.

Frontier and Utopia

These theoretical statements return us as well to the ideas of *Pacific Edge*, where utopia is also a "the process of making a better world, the name for one path history can take, a dynamic, tumultuous, agonizing process, with no end" (*Pacific Edge*, 95).[47] This preferred Orange County is a utopia achieved through legislation. Political participation matters, the process is more important than the end state, and victories can be real even if small and sometimes morally ambiguous. In Robinson's view, "Utopia has to be rescued as a word, to mean 'working towards a more egalitarian society, a global society.'" Utopia is "a road of history, something we are working within."[48]

Like many contemporary writers in the social sciences and cultural studies, Robinson wants to explore the challenges that face conscious community building and the deliberate construction of civil society. As do many historians, he structures his narratives around the discords between utopian expectations and the practical compromises of an ethnically and culturally mixed society. These are the same concerns that animate Mikhail Bakhtin's criticism and make his ideas relevant, for that work is an effort to reinvigorate the political functions of fiction and to explore the ways in which literary texts must be understood in the context of their culture. In response to critics who suggested this connection, Robinson introduced an explicit reference to Bakhtin in *Blue Mars* as a way to argue that no one voice can be authoritative in a complex society.

A number of readings of Robinson's work are possible within this framework of social meaning. Science fiction critics, for example, tend to see both trilogies as reviving the critical utopias that flourished in the ferment of the 1970s, especially among writers with sympathy for that decade's feminist analysis. Ursula Le Guin, Marge Piercy, Joanna Russ, and Samuel Delany are examples of such "new wave" science fiction writers whom Robinson acknowledges as influences.[49] Socialist critics focus on the exposition of the "gift economy" in the Mars narrative as an alternative to capitalism. And, to be sure, the books devote substantial attention to the possibilities and problems of an economy based on the principle of sustainability, or seeking to make one's impact on natural systems neutral in the long run.[50]

I remain intrigued by the western history reading. The Orange County volumes are explicit efforts to think through possible contingencies of western American development. We can contrast their "postmodern" orientation to incremental change with Ernest Callenbach's earlier and "modern" vision of a comprehensive and enlightened acceptance of Ecotopia.[51] The echoes of North America on the Martian frontier are also so pervasive that they need to be acknowledged and understood as critical commentaries on the American experience. At the same time, much of the new western history has itself been a political project, concerned to surface and legitimate alternative voices and understandings, expanding the public sphere, and criticizing the effects of unequal power.

Robinson and many new western historians have been probing the same questions—the power of capital, the imperatives of technology, the roots of community in shared action, the tensions between planetary and parochial values, the moral complexity of social choices, the power of past choices to constrain and direct the present.[52] Martians repeatedly try to build new societies innocent of history and fail each time. The books are thick with people. The protagonists are surrounded with a dense supporting cast, who have their own goals and points of view, thereby mirroring the constraints on real historical actors.[53] As a foundation for all of these topics, the theme of continuity is everywhere in the trilogies as each generation deals with an ever more complicated and historicized present, just as it is present in the minds of newer western historians. To swipe a turn of phrase, they come out of something in the same intellectual soil, out of the same American effort to probe the past in order to maintain a critical hope for the civic future.

Notes

1. *Red Mars* won the annual Nebula award of the professional organization of science fiction writers. *Green Mars* won the Hugo award from science fiction fans. Page numbers in the Mars trilogy refer to the Bantam Spectra paperback edition. The books are *Red Mars* (1993), *Green Mars* (1995), and *Blue Mars* (1997). The books in the "Three Californias" trilogy, in sequential order, are *The Wild Shore, The Gold Coast*, and *Pacific Edge*. References to *The Wild Shore* (1984) and *Pacific Edge* (1990) are to the Orb paperback editions issued in 1990. References to *The Gold Coast* (1988) are to the St. Martin's Press version. References will be cited parenthetically in the text.

2. Robert Markley, "Falling into Theory: Simulation, Terraformation, and Eco-Economics in Kim Stanley Robinson's Martian Trilogy," *MFS Modern Fiction Studies* 43 (Fall 1997): 775.

3. David Seed, "The Mars Trilogy: An Interview," *Foundation: The Review of Science Fiction* 68 (Autumn 1996): 76.

4. Kim Stanley Robinson to author, August 14, 2001.

5. William Alexander McClung, *Landscapes of Desire: Anglo Mythologies of Los Angeles* (Berkeley: University of California Press, 2000); Mike Davis, *City of Quartz: Excavating the Future in Los Angeles* (New York: Verso, 1991).

6. Insightful studies of the connections between science fiction and the American uses of standard literary genres and sensibilities, such as the romance and the gothic novel,

include David Ketterer, *New Worlds for Old: The Apocalyptic Imagination, Science Fiction, and American Literature* (Bloomington, Ind.: Indiana University Press, 1974); David Mogen, Scott P. Sanders, and Joanne B. Karpinski, eds., *Frontier Gothic: Terror and Wonder at the Frontier in American Literature* (Rutherford, N.J.: Farleigh Dickinson University Press, 1992); Gary Westfahl, *Space and Beyond: The Frontier Theme in Science Fiction* (Westport, Conn.: Greenwood, 2000); David Mogen, *Wilderness Visions: The Western Theme in Science Fiction Literature*, 2nd ed. (San Bernadino, Calif.: Borgo Press, 1993); Gary K. Wolfe, "Frontiers in Space," in David Mogen, Mark Busby, and Paul Bryant, eds., *The Frontier Experience and the American Dream* (College Station, Tex.: Texas A&M University Press, 1989), 248–63; Beverly J. Stoeltje, "Making the Frontier Myth: Folklore Process in a Modern Nation," *Western Folklore* 46 (October 1987): 235–53.

7. Michael Steiner, "Frontierland as Tomorrowland: Walt Disney and the Architectural Packaging of the Mythic West," *Montana: The Magazine of Western History* 48 (Spring 1998): 2–17.

8. John Glenn quoted in Ray A. Williamson, "Outer Space as Frontier: Lessons for Today," *Western Folklore* 46 (October 1987): 259.

9. Gerard K. O'Neill, *The High Frontier: Human Colonies in Space* (New York: Morrow, 1976); *Pioneering the Space Frontier: The Report of the National Commission on Space* (New York: Bantam, 1986); Harry Shipman, *Humans in Space: 21st Century Frontiers* (New York: Plenum, 1989).

10. The "new western history" is a catchall term for a disparate set of scholars whose work emphasizes the costs as well as benefits of the European occupation of western North America and the continuities between the nineteenth and twentieth centuries in the American West. It also involves concern for multiple ideas about the meaning of the western experience and careful attention to voices that were under represented in early versions of regional history, such as women, wage workers, immigrants, and people of color. Representative publications include Patricia Nelson Limerick, *Legacy of Conquest: The Unbroken Past of the American West* (New York: Norton, 1988); Richard White, *It's Your Misfortune and None of My Own: A New History of the American West* (Norman: University of Oklahoma Press, 1991); Patricia Nelson Limerick, Charles E. Rankin, and Clyde A. Milner II, *Trails: Toward a New Western History* (Lawrence: University Press of Kansas, 1991); Clyde A. Milner II, Carol O'Connor, and Martha Sandweiss, eds., *The Oxford History of the American West* (New York: Oxford University Press, 1994).

11. Kim Stanley Robinson, "Notes for an Essay on Cecelia Holland," *Foundation: The Review of Science Fiction* 40 (Summer 1987): 54; Bud Foote, "A Conversation with Kim Stanley Robinson," *Science-Fiction Studies* 21 (1994): 52.

12. This is not to say that Robinson shares Heinlein's Ayn Rand–ish political philosophy or the viewpoints of the cyberpunks, whom he characterizes as an expression of the 1980s mentality of "caving to capitalism and concentrating on how to get one's own without worrying about the larger picture . . . going with the flow of the world supermarket." Thomas E. Jackson, "Interview with Kim Stanley Robinson," *New York Review of Science Fiction* 117 (May 1998): 15. Ken MacLeod states that "history is the trade secret of science fiction, and theories of history are its invisible engine" in his introduction to the U.S. edition of *The Star Fraction* (New York: Tor, 2001), 11.

13. Robinson, "Cecelia Holland," 60.

14. Fredric Jameson, "Postmodernism, or the Cultural Logic of Late Capitalism," *New Left Review* 146 (July–August 1984).

15. *Blade Runner*, directed by Ridley Scott (1982). Other of Dick's fictions were the seeds for the films *Total Recall*, directed by Paul Verhoeven (1990), based on the story "We Can Dream It for You Wholesale," originally published in *Magazine of Fantasy & Science Fiction* (April 1966), and reprinted in *The Collected Stories of Philip K. Dick*, vol. 2 (New York: Citadel, 1990); and *The Truman Show*, directed by Peter Weir (1998), based on *Time Out of Joint* (Philadelphia: Lippincott, 1959).

16. See Ernest May, *Lessons of the Past: The Use and Misuse of History in American Foreign Policy* (New York: Oxford University Press, 1973); Richard Neustadt and Ernest May, *Thinking in Time: The Uses of History for Decision Makers* (New York: Macmillan, 1986); Peter Stearns and Joel Tarr, "Forecasting the Future: Historical Analysis and Technological Determinism," *Public Historian* 9 (1987): 31–54; Otis Graham, "The Uses and Misuses of History: Roles in Policymaking," *Public Historian* 5 (1983): 5–19.

17. Seed, "Mars Trilogy," 79.

18. Carol Franko, "The Density of Utopian Destiny in Robinson's *Red Mars*," *Extrapolation: A Journal of Science Fiction* 38 (Spring 1997): 56–65; Markley, "Falling into Theory," 788. Robinson's understanding of history is far different from Isaac Asimov's adolescent image of a mathematical calculus of historical forces in the Foundation novels. The scientific genius behind terraforming, searches for a "science of history" to explain the rise of social conflict but gives up in the face of historical contingency (see *Green Mars*, 205–206). Robinson's use is also different from that of science fiction writers who frequently adopt metahistorical cycle-of-civilization models—from Gibbon, Spengler, Ibn Khaldun, and other macrohistorians—as mechanical devices to structure grand narratives of far futures. Indeed, Robinson has his own fun with such models by introducing the Martian historian Charlotte Dorsa Brevia who in the 2170s publishes a "dense multivolumed analytical metahistory" that explains Martian society as the logical result of millennia of contests between existing and emergent social and economic systems that eventuate, conveniently in the 2170s, in a new democratic age (*Blue Mars*, 482–84). Her work sounds like nothing if not Hegel and Marx writ large.

19. Shaun Huston, "Murray Bookchin on Mars! The Production of Nature in Kim Stanley Robinson's Mars Trilogy," in Rob Kitchin and James Kneale, eds., *Lost in Space: Geographies of Science Fiction* (London, 2002), 167–79.

20. Andrew Isserman, "Projection, Forecast, and Plan: On the Future of Population Forecasting," *Journal of the American Planning Association* 50 (Spring 1984): 208–21.

21. Larry Hirschhorn, "Scenario Writing: A Developmental Approach," *Journal of the American Planning Association* 46 (Spring 1980): 172–83; Peter Hall, *Great Planning Disasters* (Berkeley: University of California Press, 1980); James Throgmorton, *Passion, Reason and Power: Electric Power Planning in Chicago from 1973 to 1993* (Chicago: University of Chicago Press, 1996).

22. Carey McWilliams, *California: The Great Exception* (reprint; Westport, Conn.: Greenwood, 1971); Neil Morgan, *Westward Tilt: The American West Today* (New York: Random House, 1963), 3–12; Christopher Rand, *Los Angeles: The Ultimate City* (New York: Oxford University Press, 1967); Arthur L. Grey, Jr., "Los Angeles; Urban Prototype," *Land Economics* 35 (August 1959): 232–42; Werner Hirsch, "Los Angeles: A Leading City,"

in Werner Z. Hirsch, ed., *Los Angeles: Viability and Prospects for Metropolitan Leadership* (New York: Praeger, 1971), 237–41; Richard Elman, *Ill-at-Ease in Compton* (New York: Pantheon, 1967), 4.

23. Allen J. Scott and Edward Soja, eds., *The City: Los Angeles and Urban Theory at the End of the Twentieth Century* (Berkeley: University of California Press, 1996); Michael J. Dear, Greg Hise, and E. Eric Schockman, eds., *Rethinking Los Angeles* (Thousand Oaks, Calif.: Sage, 1996); Rob Kling, Spencer Olin, and Mark Poster, eds., *Postsuburban California: The Transformation of Orange County* (Berkeley: University of California Press, 1991).

24. Kim Stanley Robinson to author, August 14, 2001.

25. Mike Davis, *The Ecology of Fear: Los Angeles and the Imagination of Disaster* (New York: Metropolitan Books, 1998).

26. Tom Moylan, "'Utopia Is When Our Lives Matter': Reading Kim Stanley Robinson's *Pacific Edge*," *Utopian Studies* 6 (1995): 9.

27. There are five sections for Nadia Chernyshevsky, the engineer and political leader; five for Ann Clayborne, the ecologist and advocate of red Mars; five for Sax Russell, the scientist; five for Nirgal, the second-generation leader; four for Maya Toitovna, the charismatic and manipulative leader of the Russian contingent; two for Frank Chalmers, the political pragmatist; two for Michael Duval, the psychiatrist; two for Art Randolph, the political facilitator; one for John Boone; and one for Zo Boone of the third generation.

28. Jackson, "Interview with Kim Stanley Robinson," 18.

29. We can also read "falling into history" as reference to the biblical fall from innocence in Genesis 3–4. *Red Mars* is structured around the rivalry of American leaders John Boone and Frank Chalmers, in effect the senior and junior brothers. In the flash forward that opens the book, Chalmers arranges Boone's assassination and thereby recommits the sin of Cain.

30. John Newsinger, "The Martian Trilogy," *Monthly Review: An Independent Socialist Magazine* 49 (December 1997): 53–55; Alexander Bogdanov, *Red Star: The First Bolshevik Utopia*, ed. Loren R. Graham and Richard Stites, trans. Charles Rougle (Bloomington: Indiana University Press, 1984); Nikolai Cherneshevsky, *What Is to Be Done?*, trans. Michael R. Katz (Ithaca, N.Y.: Cornell University Press, 1989).

31. Seed, "Mars Trilogy," 77.

32. It is interesting to note that Greg Bear's *Moving Mars* (New York: Tor, 1993) also pivots on the politics and politicking of anticolonial revolution, although it gives greater importance to a technological means for accomplishing the aim of independence.

33. Edgar Rice Burroughs, "Under the Moons of Mars," originally published in *All-Story Magazine* (1912) and republished as *A Princess of Mars* (Chicago: A. C. McClurg, 1917); Ray Bradbury, *The Martian Chronicles* (Garden City, N.Y.: Doubleday, 1958); Gregory M. Pfitzer, "The Only Good Alien Is a Dead Alien: Science Fiction and the Metaphysics of Indian-Hating on the High Frontier," *Journal of American Culture* 18 (Spring 1995): 51–67; Richard Slotkin, *Gunfighter Nation: The Myth of the Frontier in Twentieth-Century America* (New York: Atheneum, 1992); Paul Carter, *The Creation of Tomorrow: Fifty Years of Magazine Science Fiction* (New York: Columbia University Press, 1977), 60–69.

34. Robert Zubrin and Richard Wagner, *The Case for Mars: The Plan to Settle the Red Planet and Why We Must* (New York: Free Press, 1996); Markley, "Falling into Theory," 779.

35. Robert Zubrin, *First Landing* (New York: Ace Books, 2001), 240–41.

36. Patricia Nelson Limerick, *Something in the Soil: Legacies and Reckonings in the New West* (New York: Norton, 2000), 18–21; William Robbins, *Colony and Empire: The Capitalist Transformation of the American West* (Lawrence: University Press of Kansas, 1994); Robert V. Hine, *Community on the American Frontier* (Norman: University of Oklahoma Press, 1985).

37. William Cronon, ed., *Uncommon Ground: Toward Reinventing Nature* (New York: Norton, 1995).

38. Hal Rothman, *Devil's Bargains: Tourism in the Twentieth Century American West* (Lawrence: University Press of Kansas, 1998).

39. Jackson, "Interview with Kim Stanley Robinson," 15–18.

40. Robbins, *Colony and Empire*.

41. Moylan, "Utopia," 8, 19; Seed, "Mars Trilogy," 77.

42. Western American mythology is also reproduced in the afterlife of John Boone. His reputation, after his death, becomes legend and conflates with tales of Paul Bunyan on Mars . . . who in turn encounters a Martian Big Man a hundred times larger yet than Paul and Babe (*Red Mars*, 386).

43. Markley, "Falling into Theory," 782.

44. Hine, *Community on the American Frontier*; Stanley Elkins and Eric McKitrick, "A Meaning for Turner's Frontier: Part I: Democracy in the Old Northwest," *Political Science Quarterly* 69 (September 1954): 321–53.

45. Franko, "Utopian Destiny," 60.

46. Franko, "Utopian Destiny," 61. Mikhail Mikhailovich Bakhtin was a Russian literary critic and philosopher (1895–1975) who worked during the Soviet era. His work first came to the attention of American scholars at the end of the 1960s. There is a very substantial enterprise devoted to translating Bakhtin's fragmentary works from Russian and interpreting them in terms of literary theory and epistemology. Bakhtin wrote sympathetically about the historical imagination (e.g., the work of Marc Bloch) and opposed metahistorians like Spengler who treated societies as fixed units rather than open and constantly changing constructs. There are interesting parallels between the ideas of Bakhtin and those of political philosopher Jürgen Habermas, who has emphasized open dialogue within a public sphere as the foundation of democratic society.

47. Carol Franko, "Working the 'In-Between': Kim Stanley Robinson's Utopian Fiction," *Science-Fiction Studies* 21 (1994): 192; Moylan, "Utopia," 4, 11.

48. Foote, "Conversation," 56; Seed, "Mars Trilogy," 77.

49. Ursula K. Le Guin, *The Dispossessed* (New York: Harper and Row, 1974); Joanna Russ, *The Female Man* (New York: Bantam, 1975); Marge Piercy, *Woman on the Edge of Time* (New York: Knopf, 1976); Samuel R. Delany, *Triton* (New York: Bantam, 1976). See Jackson, "Kim Stanley Robinson," 17.

50. Another use of the western experience is the settlers' concern to develop cultural strictures against potlatching, or the use of excessive gifts to obtain moral leverage over and above the needs for everyday life. See *Green Mars*, 291–93.

51. Ernest Callenbach, *Ecotopia* (Berkeley, Calif.: Banyan Tree Books, 1975).

52. The index of Patricia Limerick's *Something in the Soil* has twenty-one subtopics listed under American West; seventeen of them, from "accumulated memories and stories of" to "tourism in," are also applicable to "Three Californias" and the Mars books.

53. My thanks to Amy Bridges for this insight.

Index

Illustrations are indicated with italicized page numbers.

CPSIA information can be obtained
at www.ICGtesting.com
Printed in the USA
FSOW01n0541020915
10450FS

9 780806 148366